ERY — meats

FIS

FRUITS ❖ VEGETABLES

BEANS
21¢

CORN
2 2¢

35¢

1949

FRESH

SPICE
THYME
HOUSE

Mix together
ith cornstarch
stir until thick
remove f

t fresh ripe
pberries
ash and force
or fine sieve. Add
mixture to a boil o
er until it forms a hea
VARIATION
Canned or Frozen
y be used instead of fresh
Crème de Cassis: Comb
up with 2 ounces (¼ cup
sis before serving.
Kirsch: Flavor syrup
le Berries: If
d. let them

All for the good life

James Beard

THE FIRESIDE
COOK BOOK

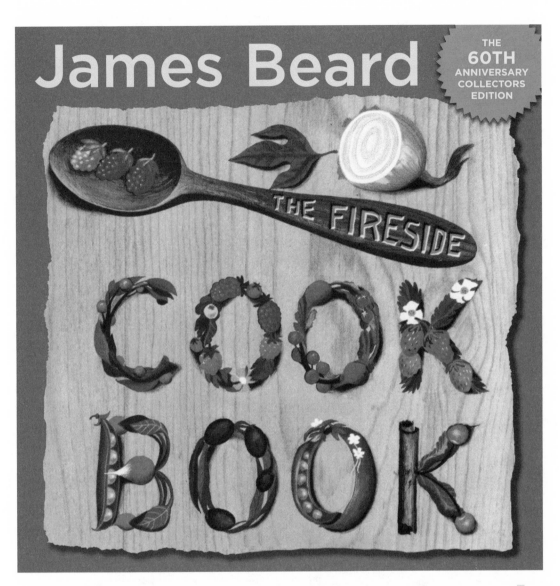

James Beard

THE 60TH ANNIVERSARY COLLECTORS EDITION

THE FIRESIDE COOK BOOK

THE CLASSIC GUIDE TO FINE COOKING FOR BEGINNER AND EXPERT

PICTURES BY
Alice AND Martin Provensen

FOREWORD BY
Mark Bittman

SIMON & SCHUSTER
New York London Toronto Sydney

Simon & Schuster
1230 Avenue of the Americas
New York, NY 10020

This Simon & Schuster hardcover edition October 2008

SIMON & SCHUSTER and colophon are registered trademarks of Simon & Schuster, Inc.

For information about special discounts for bulk purchases, please contact Simon & Schuster Special Sales at 1-800-456-6798 or business@simonandschuster.com.

Manufactured in the United States of America

10 9 8 7 6 5 4 3 2 1

Library of Congress Cataloging-in-Publication Data
Beard, James.
  The fireside cook book: a complete guide to fine cooking for beginner and expert, containing 1217 recipes and over 400 color pictures. With illus. by Alice and Martin Provensen.
    p.   cm.
1. Cookery, American. I. Title.
TX715 .B37
641.5   49-11569

ISBN-13: 978-1-4165-8967-9
ISBN-10:   1-4165-8967-8

FOREWORD

Most of James Beard's books teach cooking, and well. So I wonder what the great man thought of this one when it appeared. Published the year before I was born—and therefore about twenty years before I started cooking and first saw it—it's filled with lovely, Frenchified, now overcute (cooking mice? were they kidding?) and so-retro-they're-hip illustrations. Did he like these, which add to the book's aesthetic pleasures (in fact, this is one of the sweetest-looking cookbooks ever) but barely, if at all, to its practicality?

I would think it mattered little to him. I think what mattered is that he had put together the book he wanted; and I get the feeling that this—of all of Mr. Beard's many books—was the one in which he most directly addressed what we used to call "the housewife," the person responsible for getting dinner on the table daily. It's among the least fussy, the least technical, even the least literary, but it may be the most useful. It teaches wonderfully.

It remains a book that any home cook could pick up and learn a thing or two from. If some of the references are more than a little esoteric, well, you never know when you might need to know how to dress a partridge. How was he to forsee that partridge would become scarce while prosciutto (which he kindly translates for us as "Italian ham") would become commonplace?

If the book is dated—and it is—it also brilliantly demonstrates that good home cooking hasn't changed much in almost sixty years. In succinct fashion—the book is barely 300 pages!—he teaches us how to make pasta from scratch and sauce it with garlic and oil, a sauce few Americans knew even at the time of his death in 1985. He shows how to cook cut-up chicken in so many ways that no other book on the subject would be necessary. The seafood section is short but comprehensive; the appetizers—a specialty not only of his but of the era—nothing short of brilliant.

In short, this is a comprehensive cookbook that has been admired for over a half century (perhaps most by me and others who've tried our hands at similar works). But it's not just the depth of knowledge—completely belied by the charming illustrations—that makes *The Fireside Cook Book* so valuable: It is Mr. Beard's style. This was a man who warded off the onslaught of convenience foods, that most horrible food trend of the postwar years, firmly holding his ground in saying, as he does in "A Word of Advice" (page 13), "Good food cannot be made of inferior ingredients. . . ."

This was man who preached moderation, thrift, and improvisation over extravagance, waste, and rigidity. These are the best qualities a cooking teacher can bestow on us; all the rest follows from here. He understood that times were changing ("Take time both to cherish the old and to investigate the new"). He understood that international cuisine was the wave of the future, though he didn't fuss much about that (or anything else, for that matter). He would undoubtedly be equally heartened and dismayed by some of the trends that have come to the fore since his death: so-called convenience foods and a lack of cooking on the one hand; a widespread abundance of fine ingredients and a newfound appreciation for them on the other.

None of which would have changed his mission at all: The man was born to teach cooking, and he did it as well as any American before or since. And you can see this in the pages that follow.

—Mark Bittman

THE FIRESIDE
COOK BOOK

*A Complete Guide to Fine Cooking
for Beginner and Expert
Containing 1217 Recipes
and Over 400 Color Pictures*

by

JAMES A. BEARD

with Illustrations by

ALICE AND MARTIN PROVENSEN

SIMON AND SCHUSTER • NEW YORK

1949

ACKNOWLEDGMENT

The author expresses his thanks to the following persons for their advice and co-operation in the preparation of this book:

Jeanne Owen, of the Wine and Food Society; Jack and Sam Aaron, of Sherry Wine and Spirits; Marjorie Dean, of General Foods Corporation; and Earle MacAusland, of Gourmet Magazine.

J. B.

CONTENTS

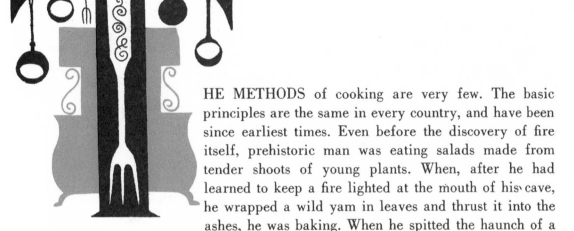

HE METHODS of cooking are very few. The basic principles are the same in every country, and have been since earliest times. Even before the discovery of fire itself, prehistoric man was eating salads made from tender shoots of young plants. When, after he had learned to keep a fire lighted at the mouth of his cave, he wrapped a wild yam in leaves and thrust it into the ashes, he was baking. When he spitted the haunch of a fresh-killed saber-tooth tiger over the flame, he was engaged in a process that is repeated by a thousand modern housewives each week as they prepare the Sunday roast. His descendants of the twentieth century, in fact, have lately been at some pains to imitate not only his procedures but even his equipment—the only difference being that they spend considerable sums for elaborate duplicates, in stainless steel, of the green sapling on which their prehistoric ancestor spitted his meat, and that they call their purchase an "outdoor barbecue" and are apt to make a good deal of fuss over its installation.

Although, if pressed, we are ready to acknowledge our debt to this far-off ancestor, we are apt to do it grudgingly. After all, we say to ourselves complacently, early man ate merely to exist; we eat to savor and enjoy, as well. In short, we are cooks; and of cookery, which may be broadly defined as a more or less passionate concern with what happens to food between its acquisition and its consumption, our primitive forebears knew nothing.

I am not so sure. The first of our prehistoric ancestors who gave his judicial attention to mastodon steak and concluded that it tasted better and was less tough when cooked to a rosy pink, rather than casually seared, became, in my opinion, a cook. By the same token, the man or woman of today who adopts an attitude of indifference to the preparation of a porridge or a pudding loses all claim to the title.

It is not the invention of famous dishes by particular chefs, however celebrated, but the search for food itself—the discoveries of processes by which plants and animals of this planet could be made to yield their edible properties, of ways by which such foods might be brought into cultivation and preserved for future use, and of still other foodstuffs native to far parts of the world—these are the real milestones in the story of food. When or how it became known that grain could be milled and baked into bread, that an infusion of the ground bean of the coffee tree would yield a comforting and bracing beverage, that spices made cooked meats more savory (indispensable knowledge in the days of tainted meats before refrigeration) we do not know. That such developments and discoveries were as important to civilization as the invention of the wheel or the discovery of atomic energy there is not the slightest doubt.

It is to the highly developed civilization of the Chinese that we owe our greatest cookery debt. The golden road to Samarkand was traveled by many hardy ancients of western Europe who returned, after crossing half the world by caravan in search of jewels and the spices that were very nearly as valuable, with tales of the wondrous foods they had eaten in far Cathay. It was Marco Polo who introduced paste to the Italians and started macaroni, spaghetti, and noodles on the road to their place among the basic staples of the western world.

When one investigates the cookery of the ancient world up to the time of Rome, the conclusion is inescapable that, despite the tales of Near Eastern and Mediterranean splendor, there was little piquancy or variety in the diet of those days. The spitted meats, goat cheeses, honied pastries, and the use of olive oil that characterize Near Eastern cookery today have come down to us in very nearly the same forms in which they appeared in ancient times. As might be expected, it was in Athens, where cultural development reached its highest peak, that the greatest culinary refinements were achieved. The importance, in the Golden Age ideal, of a wise regard for things of the flesh as part of the life of the "whole man" is nowhere better exemplified than by the ancient Athenian practice of raising from slavery to the place of honored citizen any cook who achieved perfect mastery of his art.

Roman civilization, which borrowed so extensively from the previous cultures of the Mediterranean world and frequently vulgarized them, was not slow in learning the joys of good eating. The Romans took what was best from the diverse cooking and eating habits that existed within the boundaries of their Empire and presented it in a most exaggerated style. Probably nothing in the gastronomic world has ever been known to equal the scope and vulgarity of a Roman banquet. A rich Roman might spend weeks planning a meal that would be more lavish and include more curiosities than the banquet previously given by a friend—or an enemy.

In cookery, however, as in so much else, the Romans played the invaluable role of disseminators, carrying their skills to every corner of the Empire. Some of their introductions are still local or regional specialties in Europe. *Escargot Bourguignonne,* a snail dish that is a specialty of Dijon in the south of France, was probably Roman in origin, for the wealthy Roman household had great cages or nets where hundreds of snails were cultivated and fed on wheat, honey, and wine, eventually to be eaten with a sauce which resembles the French dish of our own time.

The first printed cookbook appeared in 1480. Compiled by Baptista Platina, it was called *De Honesta Voluptate et Valetudine* and contained over three hundred recipes, together with—as remained the custom up to the end of the last century— a good deal of medical advice, prescriptions for various remedies, and suggestions on how to keep fit through exercise. From the sixteenth century on the printed word became, in cookery as in every other phase of culture, of incalculable value in preserving cooking skills and eating habits from one generation to the next and in providing a means whereby the food habits of widely separated countries might be exchanged.

In the great days of the French court, famous chefs were honored as highly as the distinguished musicians, and their patrons spared no expense to procure the finest and most exotic ingredients and to maintain vast numbers of servants to assist in the preparation of repasts in which the courses often resembled a procession of elaborate sculptures or miniature stage-settings more closely than they did the foods from which these marvels had been fashioned. The tradition of elaborately decorated foods persisted in the great houses of nobility and men of wealth from the Middle Ages down to the time of the great chef Carême, at the turn of the eighteenth century.

It was at the end of the fifteenth century that the art of cooking underwent its most significant revolution—a sort of cookery renaissance coming in the wake of the Renaissance of art that had already spread northward from Italy. But, where the Renaissance in the arts reflected a rediscovery of the civilization of the ancient world, it was the discovery of a new world that had such a profound effect on the everyday living habits of Europe. In a certain respect, the voyage of Columbus was, quite simply, a search for food. His object was to discover a short water route to the Orient, and it was primarily spices and other foodstuffs that made trade with the Orient so important to the merchants of Europe. What Columbus found, of course, was a world of untapped natural riches in comparison with which the wealth of the Far East appeared insignificant.

Corn, turkeys, tomatoes, peppers, chocolate, pineapples, yams, strawberries, a variety of new kinds of seafood—all these were the gifts of the new world to the old. At the same time, the discovery of the Americas, by increasing European prosperity, accelerated the development of a style of living far superior in its luxury and refinement to the rude life of medieval days. In such a cultural climate, of course, cookery and the domestic arts thrive and flourish.

Those who crossed the ocean to cast their lot with the new world at first hand naturally had a considerably rougher time of it. Our North American ancestors had much to learn—how to domesticate the wild fruits and vegetables, which included the Indian's great gift, maize; how to adapt the crops they were familiar with in the old world to the climate of the new; and how to keep alive while thus engaged. Out of their trials and errors the regional cooking of this country evolved. As is the case in all countries, it bears traces of the food habits native to its earliest settlers: the influence of the French is strong in the cuisine of New Orleans, of the Spanish in the food of the Southwest, and of European cookery in general, sometimes for good, often for bad, in the cooking of the country at large.

More than other countries with longer histories or narrower traditions in food, however, America has the opportunity, as well as the resources, to create for herself a truly national cuisine that will incorporate all that is best in the traditions of the many peoples who have crossed the seas to form our new, still-young nation. At its best, American cookery is as straightforward, honest, and delicious as the fish that swim off its shores or the cornmeal dishes that were the mainstays of its earliest settlers. At its worst, it is a careless imitation, not merely of what is least good in the tradition of other countries, but, what is still worse, of its own tradition. Witness the sins that are daily committed in scores of public dining rooms—and private ones, for that matter—in the name of Southern fried chicken.

The fact that today's cook, especially in our country, commands such a vast variety of ingredients makes her potential achievement in the kitchen so much the more inspiring, and her failures, when made through carelessness or indifference, so much the less excusable. It is in the devout hope that indifference, the only cardinal sin of cookery, may be forever banished from his readers' kitchens that the author has compiled this book.

A WORD OF ADVICE

There is absolutely no substitute for the best. Good food cannot be made of inferior ingredients masked with high flavor. It is true thrift to use the best ingredients available and to waste nothing. If you use the best butter, eggs, cream, meat, and other ingredients, and use them carefully and wisely, you will have less waste than if you search for bargains and end up with a full garbage pail.

Plan ahead. Plan carefully and shop in advance for what you need. Planning saves money, as well as time and steps.

Stagger your preparations so that they fit in with your other duties. If you prepare vegetables and other ingredients in advance, the last-minute rush is greatly eased and you will have a few minutes to relax and enjoy the paper or a chat before dinner. Plan so that you do not have three or four things which need attention at the same time.

Avoid having too many courses. If the food is good, that is all the more reason to limit the number of dishes, so that each may be fully savored.

Divide your meal into separate entities. As we shall try to show in the vegetable chapter, many vegetables are important enough to have single billing on your menu and should be served as a separate course.

Give as much care to simple dishes and the humbler foods as you do to elaborate dishes and ambitious menus. At the same time, do not neglect to take advantage of new developments in the growing, shipping, preserving, and cooking of food. Take time both to cherish the old and to investigate the new.

CULINARY TERMS

Acidulated water: Water mixed with an acidifying agent: 1 teaspoon lemon juice or vinegar to 1½ quarts water.

Bake: To cook in an oven by dry heat. Term formerly applied to meats as well as breads, cakes, pastries. Meats so cooked are *roasted*.

Barbecue: Originally, to cook an entire carcass at an open fire or over a pit. Term now denotes any type of outdoor cookery of meat, and even dishes cooked indoors when served with the type of pungent sauce customary in the outdoor barbecue.

Baste: To pour fat or liquid over food while cooking to moisten, glaze, or flavor it.

Beat: To mix, by hand or by rotary or electric beater, until smooth and light, with a brisk rotary motion which scoops under part of a mixture and lifts it up and over.

Blanch: To dip into boiling water for a few minutes to loosen skins or to whiten. Applies to fruits and nuts and to preparation of fruits and vegetables for canning, freezing, and preserving.

Blaze: To pour liquor over a dish or around it and ignite it.

Boil: To cook in any liquid brought to the boiling point and kept there during entire process.

Boiling point: Temperature at which entire surface of liquid is agitated and bubbling.

Bone: To remove the bones, as from a fish.

Braise: To brown meat, poultry, or vegetables in a little hot fat; then add a little liquid, cover closely, and cook over low heat.

Bread: To roll in or coat with crumbs before cooking.

Broil: To cook by direct heat. Food to be broiled is placed over, under, or in front of flame or heating unit. The broiler may be perpendicular or horizontal. Some broilers apply heat to two surfaces at once, in which case half the usual time is required for cooking.

Caramelize: To melt sugar in heavy pan over very low heat, stirring constantly, until it is a deep brown.

Chop: To cut in small pieces.

Clarify: To clear a liquid, such as soup, by adding slightly beaten egg white and the egg shells. These coagulate the particles in the liquid, which is then strained.

Cream: To rub until soft, smooth, and creamy with a heavy spoon or firm spatula.

Cube: To cut into even-sided pieces—generally, small pieces.

Cut in: In pastry making, to distribute the shortening evenly through the dry ingredients. It is literally cut in with two knives or a pastry blender.

Devil: To serve with a hot sauce and, sometimes, with crumbs.

Disjoint: To cut a fowl into cooking or serving pieces by dividing at the joints.

Dot: To place small bits of a substance on a surface.

Dredge: To coat by sprinkling with, or rolling in, a dry, fine-particled substance, such as flour, meal, or sugar.

Dust: To sprinkle lightly with a dry substance, such as flour, sugar, or spices.

Fillet: To remove flesh of fish, poultry, or meat from the bone prior to cooking. A fillet is thus a piece of fish, poultry, or meat without a bone. The term also refers to the tenderloin of beef. A filet mignon is a steak cut from the smaller end of a fillet of beef, usually cut rather thick.

Flambé: A French term meaning *blazed*.

Fold: To add to a mixture a delicate ingredient without allowing the air already beaten in to escape. Mixing spoon cuts vertically through the mixture, continues across the bottom of the bowl, and turns upward, folding under part over the surface.

Fricassee: To brown in fat, poach in broth with flavorings, and serve with a sauce.

Fry: Strictly, to cook in hot fat or oil deep enough to cover. In this country the term, sometimes expanded to *pan-fry*, has come to mean the same as *sauté*. Anything cooked in hot fat on the stove in a skillet is said to be "fried"—not strictly the case. The terms are differentiated in this book.

Grate: To reduce to small particles by rubbing against a grater.

Grill: See *broil*.

Grind: To reduce to small particles or powder with rotary cutters or a pestle.

Julienne: Cut in fine strips the size and shape of matches.

Lard: To insert small pieces of fat in lean meat for flavor and juiciness. Fat may be put in gashes in the meat, or run through with a larding needle. Thin slices of fat salt pork, bacon, etc., placed over meat or wrapped around it, may be substituted for larding.

Liaison: Thickening element in a sauce, such as flour (most common), egg yolk, arrowroot, cornstarch, crumbs, potato, or rice flour.

Marinade: The spiced, acid liquid in which foods marinate.

Marinate: To let stand in a marinade—usually a mixture of oil, vinegar or wine, spice, and herbs—to flavor or tenderize.

Mince: To chop or cut very fine.

Pan-broil: To grill on the stove in a skillet with no fat. Pan is intermittently rubbed with fat to prevent sticking, and fat drawn out by heat is poured off. A thin layer of salt in the pan may be substituted for the rubbing with fat.

Pan-fry: To sauté.

Parboil: To pre-cook or partly cook in liquid.

Pare: To remove outside skin or covering.

Plank: To broil or roast and serve on a plank.

Poach: To cook gently in liquid kept below the boiling point, so that its surface barely trembles. Fish, fruit, and eggs are all poached, not boiled, to maintain texture and shape and to retain color.

Purée: Vegetables, fruits, etc., forced through a sieve or ricer to produce a smooth, soft food.

Roast: To cook, uncovered, in the oven or in front of a fire on a spit.

Roux: Mixture of fat and flour blended over low heat—the first step in all sauces in which flour is the thickening agent.

Sauté: To fry lightly in a small amount of hot fat, turning frequently.

Scald: To heat to just below the boiling point. (To scald milk or cream, heat it in a double boiler until just below the boiling point. This prevents scorching and sticking.)

Sear: To apply heat (usually to meat) quickly so as to harden the outside and prevent juices from escaping.

Sift: To put through a fine sieve.

Simmer: To cook in a liquid at a temperature slightly below boiling. Small bubbles of steam rise to the surface, which, however, remains almost motionless.

Skewer: Metal or wooden pin used to hold meat in shape or to close openings in it. A long metal skewer is used for grilling small pieces of meat and vegetables or fish—called cooking *en brochette*.

Stir: To mix with spoon or fork, using a rotary motion. Stirring does not aërate as beating does.

Try out: To heat meat fat (including bacon), cut in small pieces, until fatty part melts away from membranes. Heat should be very low; or a double boiler may be used.

THE SEASONING SHELF

Seasonings and other augmentations can lift a dish from the commonplace to the distinguished. But seasoning should be done with a light touch. There is nothing more unpleasant to the palate than too much thyme or cinnamon or an overwhelming taste of cognac or wine. Nor should flavorings be mixed with too free a hand just because you have them on your shelf. One herb is enough for most dishes. Certain herbs and seasonings have a special affinity for certain foods. Others are allied to particular foods by long tradition.

Herbs have become increasingly popular in this country, and there are many commercial herb products on the market. Learn the main facts about herbs before you stock up with every attractive package you see in the shops.

The following list is a guide to herbs, spices, and augmentative seasonings you may want to use from time to time. Do not, if you are a novice, get them all at one time. Keep only fresh packages, so that the herbs do not dry out and lose their pungency.

HERBS

Basil: A perfect flavoring for tomato dishes and sauces; much used in Italian cookery. Excellent with veal and vegetables, salads, and some fish. It is easy to grow; in large cities pots of this herb are often kept in the window.

Bay: Not really an herb, but the leaf of the laurel tree. Useful in many meat dishes, with lentils and beans and in sauces and ragouts. Use with care—the flavor is pronounced. One leaf supplies a tremendous amount of flavor.

Chervil: A delicate herb with lacy foliage. Perfect in a salad with another flavor to support it. Useful in summer soups. Complements fish. Excellent in piquant cold sauces.

Chive: Except for parsley, this member of

the onion family is the most useful of flavoring agents. Easy to grow, either in a window-sill pot or in gardens. Welcome in practically any dish; enhances other flavorings.

Dill: A lacy, pungent herb for fish dishes, salads, eggs, sauces, and some meats. With cucumbers, makes a delightful blend of flavors.

Fennel: Used mainly for flavoring fish. As a vegetable, sometimes called Italian celery or finocchio, it is a magnificent appetizer and may be served cooked. Has a refreshing anise flavor.

Horseradish: The root of the plant is used for this fiery flavoring. Magnificent as a sauce for meats or fish, or when served, plain or mixed with sour cream, with roast beef or steak.

Marjoram: Sweet marjoram is one of the most popular herbs. People who like it use it with vegetables, in salads, and with many meat dishes.

Mint: To me, useful only in mint juleps. If you like mint sauce with lamb—please, let it be optional with your guests.

Oregano: Wild marjoram; indispensable for all Latin cookery. Has charm and pungency lacking in sweet marjoram.

Parsley: Adds distinction to countless dishes. Too often used merely as a garnish. The delicate moss-curled parsley and the coarser, more roundly flavored Italian parsley are available all year. Fried parsley is perfect with fish or with steak.

Poultry seasoning: A mixture of herbs, time-saving but not really satisfactory. Apt to contain an overpowering amount of sage.

Saffron: Made from a flower stigma and imported from Spain. Colors as it flavors. For flavoring rice dishes and many Spanish and Latin dishes. Use with care.

Sage: Used extensively in stuffings and with meats, especially pork, in America and England. Use with care. (For my taste, there should be a society for the prevention of sage!)

Sorrel: A delicately acidulous herb little known in this country. Most refreshing in summer. For salads, soups, and seasonings, and as a vegetable.

Tarragon: Indispensable for salads and sauces. Excellent with chicken, veal, and in stuffings.

Thyme: Pungent yet delicate, useful in a thousand ways—in stews, soups, salads, stuffings, and with meats.

SPICES AND SEASONINGS

Allspice: The berry of the pimiento tree. An amalgam of flavors, useful in certain cookery and in baking.

Capers: Pickled buds of a shrub of Spanish origin. Very pleasant in sauces, salad dressings, and with meat.

Celery seed: Useful for seasoning sauces and stews. Much used in making pickles.

Chili powder: Pulp of various types of chilies, dried and bottled. Comes in sweet and hot varieties. Used for Mexican dishes and as a basis for chili sauce.

Cinnamon: Ground Saigon cinnamon, the finest kind, is useful in baking and with fruits, and with certain combinations of herbs and spices for some meat dishes and pickles.

Cloves: Of these buds the Amboyna are the best. Use in many ways—with discretion. In cooking many meat dishes, an onion is

stuck with a clove for added pungency. Used in desserts and, in ground form, in baking.

Curry powder: A mixture of many herbs and spices, prepared in several ways. For Indian dishes and for flavoring dressings and certain sauces.

Garlic: A faithful friend for almost any type of seasoning. Use with discretion.

Ginger: A root, or rhizome, useful whole and ground. Used in baking, in certain meat dishes, and in Oriental cookery.

Mace: A spice made from the outer coating of nutmeg, faintly like nutmeg in flavor. Used in baking and in some soups and stews.

Mustard: Dried and ground seeds of the mustard plant make a powder called "English mustard" that is hot and pungent. Used widely for sauces, salad dressings, flavoring.

Mixed with water, it is served with meats. Blended with wine or vinegar and other herbs, it becomes "French mustard." Mustard seed is used extensively in pickles, some salad sauces, and Oriental dishes.

Paprika: A spice prepared from the dried fruit of Turkish peppers. Has, like parsley, been used extensively merely as a prettifier. The delicate sweet-pepper flavor adds much to veal, chicken, beef, etc. The Hungarian is preferable to the Spanish, for it is the more pungent. Use with care.

Pepper: The two most common varieties of black pepper are Java and Tellichery.* Java is much more pungent, more delicate. Grind your own pepper as you use it. Ready-ground pepper has more bite but lacks quality.

Salt: The indispensable source of flavor. In most dishes, without salt you have nothing. Many people use coarse salt (the best comes from England) and grind it in a mill at table.

Shallot: In this country, probably the least known of the onion family. It is russet-skinned and grows in bunches. Used extensively by European cooks because it flavors delicately and fragrantly without smothering. Available in shops in most large cities, especially where there is a foreign population. In England, used a great deal for pickles.

Vinegar: Originally, sour wine. We are prone to use vinegar which is too highly acid, and too much of it. For salads and general cooking, use a fine red or white wine vinegar. For me, cider vinegar is too highly acid and dominating. Malt vinegars are used for pickling.

OTHER FLAVORING AND ENHANCING AGENTS

Bottled sauces: An immense variety are available. Try them and decide which you like. Some of the most renowned are the Escoffier sauces from England. Sauce Diable is excellent; Sauce Robert very good. Both are useful to have on the shelf for punctuation of certain dishes or sauces. Dijon mustard comes in characteristic crocks. An excellent tarragon-flavored mustard from France is available.

Cepes: Members of the mushroom family, apparently native to France. Sometimes grow exceedingly large, and have a most unusual texture and flavor. Come in tins, packed in brine. May be used for an hors d'oeuvre, entrée, or vegetable course.

Chutney: Of many types, mango chutney is most familiar. Used with meats or curry dishes.

Glacé de viande: A concentrated meat essence for flavoring and enriching sauces, gravies, etc. Available in specialty shops.

Mushrooms: Make innumerable dishes more delicious. A delicacy alone, they also serve as a meat-stretcher and lend importance to a simple sauce, egg dish, or casserole. Hence, though not inexpensive, they are a good investment. Besides the cultivated mushrooms, there are excellent tinned ones (those broiled in butter are best) and fine dried ones. The dried are mostly imported and can be found in shops handling imported foods.

Olive oil: Spanish, Italian, and French oils are most common; Greek and American oils are available too. Olive oil is a necessity. It has flavor, texture, excellent food value; it is the one all-around oil that always brings best results. If you do not care for it, try peanut oil, which is bland and excellent for frying, and good for salad dressings.

Truffles: These "black diamonds of gastronomy," members of the fungus family, grow underground near a certain type of oak tree. Black, somewhat crisp, they have a most luxurious aroma. A white truffle from Italy has a distinct garlic odor. Truffles from Perigord, traditionally associated with classic cookery, add distinction to many dishes. They come in cans holding 1 to 12 or more. Some are peeled, others brushed, still others *au naturel.*

Wines and Spirits: Some persons ask, "What is a good cooking sherry?" I am not aware that there is any such thing. A wine used in cooking should be as good as for drinking. If you are preparing a dish with white wine or red wine, use part of the bottle for cooking and drink the rest with the meal. This book, incidentally, will show you how many wines and spirits other than sherry may enhance your meals.

* The Spice Islands firm in California produces a cracked Java with a fine, long-lasting flavor. Bellows has a cracked Tellichery which is available in some specialty shops.

THE CALORIE QUESTION

ALONG WITH the pleasures of eating comes, for many of us, the problem of the calorie count—of keeping our weight within reasonable limits, and of keeping well nourished. Some persons can eat what they please, weigh what they should, and maintain robust health. To them I say, "Congratulations!" For others, here are a few words of advice on diet generally.

The food needs of people vary according to their constitutions, health, and activities. A large-framed matron cannot make herself into a wispy lass by dietary self-torture. An athlete normally needs more food than a chair-borne executive or a beach-borne beauty. Most emphatically, anyone with an illness that involves diet has food requirements that are best prescribed by a physician. And the same is true of any person who is considerably—say, more than 10 pounds—overweight or underweight.

For most people, the avoirdupois problem is simply to readjust minor bulges or flat places for a more esthetic effect. They should obtain and get acquainted with a small nutrition chart showing the amounts of calories, proteins, and vitamins provided by the main foods. By increasing or decreasing their calorie intake, and otherwise keeping their diet balanced, they can ordinarily gain or lose weight safely and without undue privation. This book will suggest many dishes that will both tempt your appetite and help you downward or upward, as you desire, toward the golden mean.

Generally, the calorie-packed foods are the candies and other sugared things, breads and pastries, fats and meats, cream and cheeses, plus incidentals such as dried beans, nuts, and thick sauces and soups. An innocent little piece of fudge (which your system should not notice at all!) represents 100 calories, the cream in your coffee 69, a doughnut (despite the hole) 200, and a modest fruit sundae 800 calories. Yet the average daily intake of a 150-pound adult is only around 2700 calories! Obviously, even a moderate eater may achieve a grand-piano figure by habitually reaching for the wrong items.

Always maintain balance in diet. The wispy lass who, yearning for a more buxom silhouette, gorges daily on roast goose, creamed potatoes, and éclairs, to the exclusion of vegetables and fruits, may well acquire not only extra pounds but a case of vitamin deficiency, digestive disorders, and assorted dental cavities as well. The lady who, desiring outlines less suggestive of an office safe, bans everything from her table but watercress and tea, may suffer a like fate. Dairy products, cereal foods, vegetables (rich in minerals and vitamins), fruits, meats and eggs (rich in protein)—all have a place in the normal diet. Eat enough, not too much, of all of them. That way lies health and normal weight.

TO GAIN WEIGHT

increase calorie intake 500
to 1000 calories per day.

½ avocado = 300 calories

1 cup strawberries =
90 calories

1 slice chocolate cake =
350 calories

1 cup fruit sundae =
800 calories

1 muffin = 125 calories

1 piece of pie = 350 calories

1 plain cookie = 75 calories

TO LOSE WEIGHT

decrease calorie intake 500
to 1000 calories per day.

Hors d'oeuvres can make your reputation as a cook, for in many instances they are the first thing people eat in your home. In some cases they are the only opportunity people have to know your cooking. Therefore, be certain they are indicative of your best efforts.

In its true meaning, an hors d'oeuvre is a first course at luncheon or occasionally at dinner which is, as the literal translation of the words implies, completely removed from the other things served. It is a collection of bits and pieces, well flavored and pungent, which are served in sufficient quantity to sharpen the appetite but not deaden it. Often a complete luncheon or supper of hors d'oeuvres is a delight and then, of course, your imagination can run riot in selecting the variety.

A single dish, such as a fine paté de foie gras or crabmeat rémoulade or oysters, may also be served as the hors d'oeuvres course. As a matter of fact, if you serve foie gras you should do so at the beginning of the meal, for if, as is very often done, you serve it with the salad and after you have consumed other courses, it is too heavy and the enthusiasm for this magnificently flavored and textured luxury has been lost.

If you are preparing cocktail snacks for a number of guests, plan things which are in reality finger food. If you must have rich and runny bits, provide people with plates and napkins and places to sit.

Gold Music Wine Tobacco and Good Cheer

COCKTAIL SNACKS

DUNKING BOWLS

Bowls for dipping are one of the most popular drink accompaniments. If it is an informal group you are entertaining, you will find one or two of these to be good help-yourself ideas.

Cheese Bowl

½ pound cream cheese	2 tablespoons chopped
Cream	onion
Two 2-ounce tins anchovies	2 tablespoons chopped
2 tablespoons chopped	parsley
chives	1 teaspoon salt

Moisten cream cheese with cream, mixing with a fork until well softened. Add anchovies which have been chopped and mixed with the oil in the tins, then onion, parsley, chives, and other seasonings. Taste for seasoning before adding salt, for some anchovies are saltier than others and require less salt in the mixture. Sprinkle with chopped parsley. Serve with knives for spreading.

VARIATIONS

Vegetable Bowl: Blend well the following and add salt to taste: 1 pound cottage cheese, ½ cup finely cut green onion, ¼ cup grated raw carrot, ¼ cup heavy cream, 4 radishes, sliced, and ¼ cup chopped green pepper.

Scandinavian Bowl: A most satisfactory spread or dip is made as follows: Soften ½ pound cream cheese with lemon juice until it spreads easily. Add 2 tins mashed boneless and skinless sardines, ¼ cup chopped parsley, 1 teaspoon paprika, ¼ cup chopped chives, and pimientos. Arrange in a mound on a large plate for serving and decorate the plate with strips of pimiento.

Thirst Inviter

1 large clove garlic	2 chopped hard-cooked eggs
1 pint sour cream	
1 teaspoon dry mustard	1 green pepper, chopped
1 tablespoon grated horseradish	1 tablespoon chopped parsley
	2 tablespoons chili sauce

Grate garlic and blend with sour cream. Beat in with a wooden spoon dry mustard, horseradish, and eggs. Blend in parsley, green pepper, and chili sauce. Allow to stand for 2 hours before serving so that the flavors become blended with the cream.

Fines Herbes Bowl

¼ cup chopped parsley	1 teaspoon salt
2 tablespoons chopped fresh dill	¼ cup chopped chives
1 pint sour cream	1 chopped green pepper

Blend the above and allow to stand for an hour or two. Correct seasoning before serving.

STUFFED EGGS

Stuffed eggs are the most popular of all the millions of snacks to serve with cocktails.

Hard-cook eggs by placing them in boiling water or cold water and cooking them just below the boiling point for 10 to 15 minutes.

Eggs kept in the refrigerator will crack if introduced directly into boiling water. If eggs are cold, place in lukewarm water.

Cool eggs rapidly with cold water. This prevents darkening of the yolk and enables you to shell them more easily.

Cut eggs in half either horizontally or vertically and remove the yolk. If you cut them vertically, you may have to trim a bit of the white so that the eggs will stand on a plate. Blend mashed yolk with seasonings and replace in the halves of the white. Decorate with chopped parsley, paprika, a slice of stuffed olive, or a tiny pickled onion. Chill.

Fillings for Stuffed Eggs: The following recipes are for 6 eggs:

Pungent Eggs

6 hard-cooked eggs	1 teaspoon chopped onion
2 tablespoons mayonnaise	1 teaspoon dry mustard
½ teaspoon or more of salt	1 tablespoon chopped parsley

Mash the yolks of eggs well with a fork. Add mayonnaise, salt, onion, and mustard, and blend thoroughly to a smooth paste. Fill the egg halves and decorate with parsley. Chill well before serving.

Ham-flavored Eggs

6 hard-cooked eggs	1 teaspoon dry mustard
¼ cup ground cold ham	1 teaspoon salt
Mayonnaise	

Mash yolks of eggs and blend in ham and mustard. Add enough mayonnaise to make a smooth paste. Taste for seasoning before adding salt.

Anchovy Eggs

6 hard-cooked eggs	2 tablespoons anchovy paste
1 tablespoon chopped chives	1 teaspoon lemon juice

Blend yolks of eggs with chives, anchovy paste, and lemon juice. You will probably not require salt for this recipe, as the anchovy paste usually makes it salty enough.

Mushroom Eggs

6 hard-cooked eggs	1 tablespoon chopped parsley
¼ cup ground chicken	
2 tablespoons ground raw mushrooms	Mayonnaise
1 teaspoon salt	Pimiento

Blend the yolks of eggs with chicken and mushrooms. Add parsley, salt, and enough mayonnaise to make a smooth paste. Fill the egg halves and decorate with thin strips of pimiento.

MEAT HORS D'OEUVRES

Tongue Rolls

1 teaspoon chopped onion	Salt
2 teaspoons horseradish	Parsley, chopped
½ teaspoon dry mustard	12 thin cold tongue slices
1 package cream cheese	

Blend onion, horseradish, and mustard with cheese and salt to taste (about ½ teaspoon). Trim edges of tongue slices and spread slices with cream cheese mixture. Roll very tightly, being careful not to break the meat slices. Secure with toothpick and dip ends into finely chopped parsley.

Beef Rolls

½ teaspoon dry mustard	12 anchovy fillets
Water	Onion, chopped
12 thin strips of rare roast beef	Parsley, chopped

Mix mustard with enough water to make a smooth paste. Spread strips of roast beef, about 1 by 4 inches, with a little of the mustard, lay a fillet of anchovy on each meat strip, and sprinkle with chopped onion and parsley. Roll, secure with a toothpick, and dip edges into parsley. Chill before serving.

Salami Wedges

1 package cream cheese	1 tablespoon chopped chives
½ teaspoon dry mustard	36 slices fine-grained salami
½ teaspoon salt	2 tablespoons chopped parsley
1 clove garlic, grated	

Blend cream cheese with the following seasonings until they form a smooth paste: dry mustard, salt, garlic, and chives. Spread 12 slices salami with the mixture, top each with another slice of salami, spread again with the mixture, and top with a third slice of salami. With a sharp knife cut the salami sandwiches into quarters, dip the edges into parsley, and arrange on a serving plate.

Salami Cornucopias

Fine-grained salami, sliced thin	1 clove garlic
1 package cream cheese	3 tablespoons chopped parsley
½ teaspoon salt	½ teaspoon dry mustard
1 teaspoon horseradish	

Remove the outside skin of the salami. Cut the slices in half and wind them around the little finger to form cornucopias. Press the edges together firmly with the fingers and place them in a large meshed rack or cake cooler. Chill in the refrigerator for an hour.

Prepare a filling (for 24 cornucopias) by blending into a smooth paste cream cheese, salt, horseradish, garlic, parsley, and dry mustard. Fill a pastry tube (either the metal or the canvas type) and fill the cornucopias. Chill for an hour or so before serving; or, the cornucopias may be made in the morning and kept in the refrigerator till serving time.

CANAPES

Except for pastry cooking, there is no more imaginative field in cookery than the preparation of canapés. Great variety in flavor and form and in attractive arrangement and amusing decoration is possible. Flavor and texture are most important. A wonderful assortment of materials can be used. Plan them carefully and season with imagination.

Bases for Canapés: Never use just plain bread. The only types of untoasted bread that have any place in making snacks are the heavy Russian rye bread, salty rye, or pumpernickel. Cut it into squares or circles, butter it well, and use it for the base for your canapés. Don't let it stand too long, or it will lose its quality.

Toast, unless it is fried toast, is apt to get very flabby and uninteresting. Fried toast is made by cutting shapes from a fine-textured bread, toasting one side, and then cooking the pieces, untoasted side down, in a skillet with plenty of butter. Keep the heat very low and fry the pieces of bread until they are golden brown. Drain on absorbent paper and keep warm until used.

Melba toast may be bought in packages at most grocery shops and is excellent for a base. It comes in long fingers and in neat squares especially designed for canapés.

Certain types of biscuits and crackers are useful for canapé mixtures. Choose those which do not lose their crispness quickly.

Cucumber slices and thin slices of crisp zucchini may also be used for canapé bases, but these must be kept very crisp until time to serve them.

(1) Fillets of anchovies neatly arranged on fried toast fingers. Add a squeeze of lemon juice and crumbled, hard-cooked egg yolk.

(3) Thin slices of smoked salmon on buttered toast with a squeeze of lemon juice and a little freshly ground pepper.

(4) A thin slice of smoked salmon with a thin slice of cold baked ham, a little freshly ground pepper, and a touch of chopped parsley.

TOPPINGS

TOASTS

AND

(2) Thin slices of hard-cooked egg sprinkled with chopped parsley and topped with a curled anchovy fillet.

(5) Remove the meat from a small cooked lobster. Cut into small bits and mix with 1 tablespoon chopped onion, 1 tablespoon chopped parsley, 1 tablespoon chopped seeded tomato, ½ teaspoon salt, and enough well-flavored mayonnaise to bind. Heap on small pieces of fried toast and top with finely chopped parsley.

(8) Chop 4 raw mushroom caps very fine and mix with 1 tablespoon chopped parsley, 1 tablespoon chopped chives, and ¼ cup ground cooked ham. Bind with mayonnaise until it is of a good consistency for spreading.

FOR

BISCUITS

(6) Mix ½ pound finely ground lean raw beef with 1½ teaspoons dry mustard, 1 clove garlic (grated), 2 tablespoons chopped parsley, and 1 tablespoon Escoffier Sauce Diable. Blend well and spread on toast or dark bread fingers. Sprinkle with finely chopped hard-cooked egg.

(7) Mix ½ cup finely ground cold white meat of chicken, 1 tablespoon finely chopped onion, 1 tablespoon chopped parsley, and 2 tablespoons ground blanched almonds. Add enough well-seasoned mayonnaise to bind. Rectify the seasoning and spread on rounds of fried toast. Top with a toasted or salted almond.

(9) Drain and flake 1 can crabmeat. Mix with 1 tablespoon grated onion, 2 tablespoons chopped parsley, 1 hard-cooked egg, finely chopped, and enough mayonnaise—which you have flavored well with curry powder and just a touch of cayenne—to make a firm mixture. Spread with chopped parsley and chopped hard-cooked egg.

Cream Cheese Spreads

The basic foundation for each of these spreads is ¼ pound cream cheese. Combine ingredients and blend together thoroughly with a fork and spoon until smooth and of a good spreading consistency. Spread on pieces of fried toast, biscuits, or crackers. Decorate with:

Chopped parsley
Paprika
Chopped hard-cooked egg

Chopped pecans
Chopped toasted almonds
Chopped pimiento

Combine the cheese with any of these:

1 tablespoon chopped onion
2 tablespoons chopped parsley
2 tablespoons chopped chives
½ teaspoon salt
2 tablespoons chopped fresh dill

1 tablespoon anchovy paste
1 tablespoon chopped pickled onion
2 tablespoons chopped parsley
Lemon juice and salt to taste

¼ cup finely cut smoked salmon
½ teaspoon freshly ground black pepper
Lemon juice to moisten

¼ cup finely cut India chutney

¼ pound mashed Roquefort cheese
1 teaspoon Worcestershire sauce
2 tablespoons finely chopped raw mushrooms

Meat Spreads

Use these pastes for spreads. Or you may arrange them in a dish, garnish it well, and serve one or two or more pastes surrounded by a selection of bases. In this way each guest may serve himself and there is no danger of toasts or crackers drying out.

(1) Grind together:
    ½ pound cold baked ham
    4 sweet gherkins
    1 small white onion, peeled

  Mix with:
    1 teaspoon dry mustard
    Enough sour cream to bind into smooth paste

(2) Grind together:
    ¼ pound cold boiled tongue
    1 small onion, peeled

  Mix with:
    2 teaspoons horseradish
    1 teaspoon Hungarian paprika
    Enough sour cream to make a heavy paste
    Salt to taste

(3) Grind together:
    1 cup cold turkey or chicken
    ½ large green pepper, seeded and cleaned

  Mix with:
    1 hard-cooked egg, chopped
    1 tablespoon chopped parsley
    2 teaspoons salt, or more
    Mayonnaise to make a stiff paste

HOT HORS D'OEUVRES

Stuffed Mushrooms

1 cup crabmeat
1 tablespoon dry bread crumbs
1 tablespoon chopped onion
1 teaspoon salt

2 tablespoons chopped parsley
1 egg, lightly beaten
12 mushroom caps
Buttered crumbs
Parmesan cheese

Mix crabmeat with dry bread crumbs, onion, salt, and parsley. Add egg and mix well. Fill mushroom caps with the mixture and sprinkle with buttered crumbs and cheese. Place in moderate oven (350°) until lightly browned or under preheated broiler, with the broiler rack 3 inches from the flame. Allow to brown lightly before serving.

VARIATIONS

With Shrimp: Finely cut shrimp may be substituted for the crabmeat.

With Swiss Cheese: Top with a thin slice of Swiss cheese before running under the broiler.

Chopped Meat Snacks

1 pound ground round steak (lean)
1 tablespoon Heinz steak sauce
1 clove garlic, grated
1 teaspoon salt
3 tablespoons butter

¼ pound grated cheddar cheese
½ teaspoon dry mustard
1 tablespoon chopped parsley
1 teaspoon black pepper

Mix the ingredients until they are thoroughly blended. Form into tiny balls about the size of large marbles. Cook very quickly in the butter in a skillet, being careful to brown the balls nicely on all sides. Drain on absorbent paper and serve hot with toothpicks or cocktail picks.

Cheese Croquettes *

2 eggs
½ teaspoon salt
½ teaspoon dry mustard
1 tablespoon Escoffier
  Sauce Diable

½ cup dry bread crumbs
1 cup grated Swiss cheese
1 cup grated American
  cheese

Separate eggs and beat the whites very stiff. Mix the yolks with salt, dry mustard, and Escoffier Sauce Diable, and combine with dry bread crumbs. Mix all well with Swiss cheese and American cheese, and fold in the whites of the eggs. Form into balls or sticks, dip in beaten egg yolks and crumbs, and fry in deep fat heated to about 380°, or hot enough to brown a 1-inch bread cube in 45 seconds.

Cheese Tartlets

Pastry dough
4 eggs
¾ cup grated Swiss cheese
1 teaspoon flour

⅔ cup milk
¼ teaspoon pepper
¼ teaspoon nutmeg
½ teaspoon salt

Roll flaky pastry dough quite thin and fill tartlet shells or tiny muffin tins with the paste. Flute the edges with a pastry cutter and prick the bottom of each shell with a fork. Beat eggs slightly and add Swiss cheese, flour, milk, pepper and nutmeg, and salt. Stir till well mixed and fill tartlet shells ⅔ full. Bake 12 to 15 minutes in a hot oven (425°).

Hot Turnovers

You may use a great variety of fillings for turnovers, which you will find easy to serve and good to eat. If they are made small enough, there need be no fear of the filling escaping on to your furnishings or your guests. They may be made of puff paste or flaky pastry, whichever is your specialty.

Cut the rolled-out dough of either type of pastry into small rounds, place a small amount of the filling on one half, double it over, and pinch the edges together. Brush with beaten egg and bake in a hot oven (425°) for about 15 minutes or until cooked through.

Suggestions for Fillings:

(1) Anchovy fillets.

(2) Tiny squares of smoked salmon with ground pepper and a little lemon juice.

(3) Whole boneless and skinless sardines with just a sprinkle of lemon juice and a dash of chopped onion and chopped parsley.

(4) Tiny sausages which have been pre-cooked to free them of all fat.

(5) Ground cold chicken mixed with crumbled crisp bacon and a little sour cream. Salt, pepper, and chopped parsley to taste.

(6) Ground cold chicken mixed with a little chutney and a teaspoon of curry powder.

(7) ½ cup cold ham ground, then mixed with 1 teaspoon dry mustard and a tablespoon of Madeira. Salt to taste.

(8) Chopped raw beef mixed with onion, chili sauce, Worcestershire, and salt and pepper to taste.

(9) Grated Swiss cheese mixed with a little French mustard.

(10) 6 chicken livers chopped, then mixed with 1 egg, 2 tablespoons chopped parsley, 1 tablespoon chopped onion, and 1 teaspoon Worcestershire sauce.

You may also use any of the fish or meat pastes given earlier in this section for canapés or fillings.

HORS D'OEUVRES FOR LUNCHEON

These may be served as a first course with a light entrée and a fruit dessert to follow; or a luncheon may be made up entirely of various hors d'oeuvre dishes. In the latter case you would want to serve some vegetable dishes, fish hors d'oeuvres, a selection of cold meats, and certain accompaniments.

There is nothing more delightful than a complete luncheon of hors d'oeuvres, especially on a hot day in summer. The color and variety of the various dishes, particularly when accompanied by a well-chilled bottle of, say, a fine tavel or a Moulin à Vent, rewakens the most heat-dulled appetite.

---

* Reprinted from *Hors d'Oeuvres and Canapés* by James Beard, by permission of M. Barrows & Co., publishers.

FISH FOR THE HORS D'OEUVRE TRAY

Most of these are ready-prepared and may be found at your fish dealer's or at a delicatessen which specializes in such things. In practically every city in the country there is one shop which makes a specialty of imported and domestic delicacies, and in many of the larger cities you will find several to choose from. Other fish preparations, which will be noted as we go along, come in tins, ready for the table. Read the labels well to be certain that you are getting what you ask for, for some tinned fish are prepared in olive oil, others in peanut oil, and some in cottonseed oil. I feel it is always preferable, if possible, to select those put up in olive oil.

Smoked Salmon: Have it sliced paper-thin, and purchase the best quality obtainable. Serve with lemon or lime juice and freshly ground pepper.

Smoked Sturgeon: One of the most delicate of fish and a fine addition to any tray. Have it sliced very thin.

Smoked Whitefish: A most delicate fish with a most unusual flavor. Divide into neat sections.

Smoked Eel: Cut small fillets from the bone and serve this richly flavored fish with lemon.

Smoked Cod: This product differs in type and flavor in different parts of the country, but it is a most welcome addition. Slice thin.

Smoked Trout: A most delicately flavored and tinted fish which is a great treat. Skin the trout and cut into long fillets with a very sharp knife. Serve with lemon.

Herring: You will find a variety of different types of herring: herring in sour cream with onions; herring in a wine sauce; rollmops—rolled fillets of herring, sometimes with a piquant stuffing; herring salad, which is flaked herring combined with other flavorful ingredients and a delightful change from the accepted way of serving it.

Smoked Oysters: A delicious luxury; quite rich.

Tinned Fish

Anchovies: Fillets of anchovies are put up in olive oil, either plain or rolled. Serve as they are or with sliced hard-cooked egg or in Anchovy Salad Niçoise.

Anchovy Salad Niçoise

Garlic	Chopped parsley
2 tins anchovy fillets	2 green peppers
¼ cup olive oil	3 tomatoes
1½ tablespoons wine	6 shallots
vinegar	20 ripe olives

Rub a salad bowl with garlic. Open tins of anchovy fillets and drain the oil into the salad bowl. Combine with olive oil, parsley, and wine vinegar. Add the anchovy fillets, green peppers cut in fine strips, and tomatoes which have been peeled and seeded. (Peel, cut the tomatoes in fifths, and remove the small seed sections with a sharp, small knife.) Add shallots, which you have peeled and cut into small pieces, and ripe olives. Toss the ingredients and allow to stand for an hour or two before serving.

Another way to serve anchovies for hors d'oeuvres is to arrange the fillets in a small crystal or china serving dish and garnish with chopped parsley, chopped egg yolk, chopped egg white, and capers, with a little additional olive oil.

Tuna Fish: Excellent tuna may be bought in tins with olive oil added. This may be served *au naturel* or with the addition of chopped parsley and chopped green pepper or pimiento.

Sardines: There are many varieties of sardines—French, Portuguese, Norwegian, with or without skin, in olive oil and in other oils. Many sardine fanciers feel that the French or Portuguese in olive oil with the skin still on are the most delicious, but the smaller Norwegian type are also tasty and a good buy. The boneless and skinless type are flavorful enough to serve for hors d'oeuvres and are more pleasant to mix with other ingredients.

MEATS FOR THE HORS D'OEUVRE TRAY

The well-stocked delicatessen that sells prepared and cured meats of all types is not widely found in this country. Nevertheless, in urban centers and communities where a large part of the population is of foreign extraction, one may find a wide assortment of these meats.

In certain sections of the country one finds delicious sausages and meat products peculiar to the region. Certain French, Dutch, German, Czech, and Polish farmers make small amounts of really unusual and appetizing meat products. Use these wherever possible, for they add an additional note of variety to your service.

Ham

There are many types of ham from which to choose, including:

Virginia Ham: To be served in thin slices or in cornucopias.

Boiled Ham: Cut in thin slices and serve with a little mustard, English or French.

Prosciutto and Westphalian Hams: Imported from Europe or copied in this country. They are both eaten without cooking. They should be sliced on a machine to a paper thinness and served with coarsely ground black pepper.

Smoked Tongue

Thin slices of smoked tongue are an acceptable addition to the cold meat tray.

Capicola

An Italian-style smoked loin or butt of pork. It is highly seasoned with coarse red peppers and herbs, and is a thoroughly delicious prepared meat. Slice very thin.

Sausages

We have a fairly wide variety of sausages available in our markets. There is little, if any, of the imported meat of this type coming over, but there are many good domestic varieties from which to choose. Occasionally one finds a French, Italian, or Middle European butcher who makes his own, and very good they often are. These are some of the most satisfactory types for hors d'oeuvres:

Salami: The Italian style and the kosher salamis, some highly flavored with garlic, some coarse-grained and some fine-grained.

Mortadella: An Italian sausage of fine flavor and coarse texture.

Cervelat: A rather dry, well-seasoned sausage which is available everywhere.

Summer Sausage: A much more bland type of sausage than the others, but always a favorite.

Liver Sausage: One finds goose-liver sausage in most good shops, regular and smoked liverwurst, liver loaves, and what are known in France as *pâté maison*, or the pâté of the house.

Blood Sausage: Several different types of this sausage are available.

Bologna: There are as many varieties of bologna as there are soaps on the market. Some are excellent and some not even worth carrying home. This is a problem for you to investigate for yourself.

APPETIZERS

COCKTAIL **SNACKS**

HORS D'OEUVRES

CANAPÉS

Canapés can be good and tasty if you will take the trouble to prepare them carefully and season them with imagination.

SMOKED POULTRY AND GAME

Smoked Turkey: America has developed the smoked turkey through the last fifteen or twenty years to perfection. It is one of the most delightfully unusual foods available. Thin slices of smoked turkey make a most acceptable hors d'oeuvre, either for a cocktail party or for the hors d'oeuvre course. It will keep quite a long time and may be used for many hot dishes as well as cold. You may also buy it by the pound in some delicatessens.

Smoked Capon: This may also be found on the market and is quite as good as the turkey. Being a smaller bird, it is a more practical buy for many homes. Serve the bird whole and slice it at the table as it is needed. It is a luxury item, and there is no need to waste the meat by having it pre-cut, which encourages it to dry out.

Smoked Goose and Smoked Goose Breast: These also are available. Both are excellent for a service if one wants variety.

Smoked Pheasant: In some parts of the country smoked pheasant may be purchased. I find it the least interesting of the smoked fowl, but it is there if you choose to try it.

Cold, Highly Seasoned Meat Loaf: This is often served in thin slices as part of the hors d'oeuvre collection.

VEGETABLE HORS D'OEUVRES

Vegetables à la Grecque

¼ cup olive oil
1 lemon or 1½ tablespoons wine vinegar
½ teaspoon salt

Herb bouquet (peppercorns, parsley, chervil, tarragon, perhaps a sprig of thyme, bay leaf)
1 clove garlic

Vegetables à la grecque are vegetables cooked in a bouillon as follows: Make a sauce with the olive oil, juice of lemon or wine vinegar, salt, herb bouquet, and garlic, and enough boiling water to cover the vegetables. Poach the vegetables very slowly in the sauce. When they are just tender, but not mushy, remove them, strain the sauce, and cook it down to half the quantity. Pour over the vegetables and chill.

You may prepare in this manner any of the following vegetables:

Tiny artichokes which have been trimmed and cleaned, and soaked in acidulated water for an hour before cooking
Celery hearts, halved and cleaned
Cauliflower
Tiny white onions
Fingers of eggplant
Fennel, finnochio, or Italian celery, whichever it is called in your locality
Zucchini, or Italian squash, cut either in slices or in quarters
Mushroom caps

Vegetables Vinaigrette

Poach your vegetables in a sauce à la grecque, in a highly seasoned water, or in chicken broth. Allow them to cool and serve in a vinaigrette sauce.

Serve in this fashion any of the following vegetables:

Asparagus	Celery
Cauliflower	Leeks
Broccoli	Zucchini
Fennel	Shredded or whole green beans
Tiny whole beets	
Cooked lentils	Sliced beets
Cooked dried white beans	Mushrooms, raw and sliced thin
Cucumber (raw)	

Be sure not to overcook vegetables cooked and served in this manner. They should still retain a certain "bity" quality. Furthermore they should never boil, but merely poach or simmer.

Vegetables in Sour Cream

Cucumbers in Sour Cream: Slice cucumbers very thin. Salt them and add chopped fresh dill, and cover with sour cream. Chill for an hour before serving.

Cabbage with Sour Cream Dressing: Shred red or white cabbage very thin. Allow it to soak in ice water for an hour. Drain well. Combine with sour cream dressing.

Sour Cream Dressing

Combine 1 cup sour cream, 1 tablespoon grated horseradish, 2 tablespoons grated Swiss cheese, ½ teaspoon salt, ½ teaspoon black pepper, and 1 teaspoon dry mustard, and beat well with a wooden spoon. Pour over shredded cabbage and mix thoroughly.

Beets in Sour Cream: Peel and slice cold cooked beets. Cut each slice into uniform strips. Marinate the strips of beet in a French dressing for several hours or overnight. One hour before serving, drain off the French dressing and mix the beets with sour cream.

Vegetable Salads for Hors d'Oeuvres
Potato salad
Russian salad
Celery salad
Celery root rémoulade
String bean and artichoke salad

Raw Vegetables
Several plates of raw vegetables or a plate of various mixed raw vegetables is acceptable in the mélange of things served for hors d'oeuvres. They should be the choicest the market affords and should be carefully cleaned and crisped in ice water before serving.
Radishes: The tiny rosy ones, as fresh and crisp as you can find them. If the tops are fresh and green, leave them on for eye appeal.
Onions: Tiny green onions, carefully cleaned and freshened in water. Always a pleasant addition.

Celery: Celery hearts, strips of celery, or stuffed celery (using any of the canapé spreads) are good additions.

Fennel: The anise-flavored Italian root is a change.

Pepper: Strips or rings of green pepper.

Carrot: Strips of tender raw carrot.

Watercress: Watercress is a decorative addition as well as a delicious tidbit.

Tomatoes: Sliced tomatoes, plain or with French dressing.

Stuffed Eggs: Any of the recipes for stuffed eggs are acceptable for this type of service. Or you may serve:

Eggs à la Russe: Cut 6 peeled hard-cooked eggs in half. Place them in a serving dish, yolk side down, and cover with Russian dressing. Decorate with capers.

ACCESSORIES

There are numerous things one may find in jars or tins which may be offered as accompaniments to the hors d'oeuvre service. Among them:

Olives: Green, green ripe, ripe, or stuffed.
Pimiento: Strips or halves of pimiento.
Artichoke Hearts: You will find these preserved in olive oil.

SEAFOOD APPETIZERS

Oysters

At least for those of us who live in centers near the sea, oysters have a most important place in the list of appetizers. They are served, freshly opened, on the half shell. Six oysters are usually considered a serving, and the shells are arranged on chopped ice in a deep plate. You may serve a cocktail sauce with them, but the addition of lemon, salt and pepper, horseradish, and Tabasco is usually ample. A dry white wine—a riesling or chablis—is a perfect accompaniment to oysters, as are thin slices of buttered dark bread. Some people may prefer oyster crackers or toast, but a good dark rye or pumpernickel bread and sweet butter make a perfect choice.

Clams

Little necks or cherrystone clams may be served in the same way and are considered quite as much of a delicacy. They, too, may be served with a cocktail sauce or merely with lemon and horseradish, salt, and pepper.

Smoked Salmon for a First Course

Thin slices of the very finest Nova Scotia or Columbia River smoked salmon make an ideal first course. Serve it on a plate garnished with a few greens, with a half lemon for each person. Pass the pepper grinder and a cruet of olive oil. Melba toast or dark bread cut in thin slices and spread with sweet butter are necessary accompaniments.

Cocktail Sauce for Seafood

½ cup chili sauce	½ teaspoon salt
1 tablespoon Worcestershire sauce	1 tablespoon horseradish
½ cup tomato catsup	1 teaspoon fresh-ground black pepper
½ teaspoon dry mustard	

Blend well the chili sauce, Worcestershire sauce, tomato catsup, salt, horseradish, black pepper, and dry mustard. Serve in a sauceboat or in individual glasses with each serving.

Smoked Trout for a First Course

This delicate and magnificently flavored fish makes a fine appetizer. Remove the skin carefully with a small, sharp-pointed knife so that the flesh is not marred or flaked. Serve a half or whole trout per person and garnish the plates with a little parsley and two quarters of lemon.

Seafood Rémoulade

For a first course you may serve crabmeat, shrimp, or lobster with a rémoulade sauce (see below). Arrange seafood, except lobster, on watercress, endive spears, or chicory. Top with rémoulade sauce and sprinkle with chopped parsley. Lobster looks more attractive if served in the shell, allowing ½ lobster per person.

In the East one finds both the lump and the leg crabmeat. You may use either one for this service. In the West the legs of the Dungeness crabs are usually considered the choice part. Arrange crab-leg meat on greens and serve with the sauce.

Shrimp may be found in various sizes from the tiniest of sweet shrimp from Alaskan waters to the giant prawns from the Eastern and Gulf seaboard. Arrange on a bed of greens and serve with rémoulade sauce.

Rémoulade Sauce for Seafood

1 cup mayonnaise	2 hard-cooked eggs, chopped
1 clove finely chopped garlic	1 teaspoon dry mustard
1 tablespoon chopped parsley	½ teaspoon chives
1 tablespoon capers	1 teaspoon anchovy paste
½ lemon	1 teaspoon chopped fresh dill

Mix ingredients and allow to stand for 2 hours before serving, so that the flavors become well blended. Serve with seafoods or eggs.

FRUIT APPETIZERS

Grapefruit

A half grapefruit is a refreshing and thoroughly light appetizer which may be served plain or with a maraschino cherry for added color.

If you heat the grapefruit slightly in the oven, you will have added flavor and juiciness.

For broiled grapefruit halves, sprinkle with brown sugar or coat the top with honey and dot with butter. Add a tablespoon of Madeira and place under the broiler, preheated to 350°, to brown pleasantly before serving.

Melon

Ripe melon makes one of the most refreshing first courses, especially on a hot day. Serve a quarter, a half, or slices of any type of melon, well chilled. A quarter of lime or lemon brings out the flavor and adds to the refreshing quality of the fruit.

Melon with Ham: The Italian-style ham called prosciutto or Parma ham is served very often with slices or wedges of melon, for a pleasing combination of flavors. It should be accompanied by the pepper grinder when served.

Melon Balls: With a ball-shaped cutter scoop out balls of various kinds of melon and blend them together for a fruit cup. The addition of a little kirsch or port is pleasant. You might use canteloupe, honeydew, watermelon, and casaba, depending upon what the market affords.

Avocado

The avocado, or alligator pear, is often used by itself and in combination with seafoods for a first course.

Half Avocado: Serve half an avocado on a bed of greens with a vinaigrette sauce, which may be put in the well from which the seed has been removed or passed separately.

Avocado with Seafood: Stuff avocado halves with shrimp, crabmeat, or lobster, and serve with a rémoulade sauce or with Russian dressing. This can also be a main dish for a spring or summer luncheon.

Friends are like melons....
to find one good one you must a hundred try.

Fruit Cup

This is a popular appetizer and one frequently ordered—or, at all events, offered—in restaurants, but I feel that it is extravagantly overrated. You may combine practically any fruits you desire, but hold to fresh fruits for a first course! Canned and sweetened fruits at the end of a meal occupy a most important place, but as a first course they are entirely too sweet. Citrus fruits and fresh fruits which have a slight tartness are the ones to use for a fruit cup.

In these days of small kitchens there is seldom the space for the soup or stock pot which was a permanent fixture in the kitchens of other days. Now, too, one may purchase tins of consommé or chicken broth, or prepare a quick substitute for stock with powders or cubes. For much of the cooking where stock is required this is the ideal arrangement for most housekeepers. Dehydrated broth will also serve the purpose, and the value of the pressure cooker is ideally demonstrated when stock is required, for it cuts the time required for cooking and gives a concentrated essence which is ideal for most requirements.

Basic Beef Stock

4 pounds beef shin (including 1½ pounds marrow bone)	Celery
	Parsley
	Bay leaf
3 tablespoons butter or oil	2 leeks
3 quarts cold water	Thyme
1 tablespoon salt	2 egg whites (optional)
2 onions	Crushed egg shells (optional)
2 cloves	
3 or 4 carrots	

Shin is excellent for this, together with the marrow bone, which should be sawed into small pieces. Purchase about 2½ pounds of meat and 1½ pounds of bone.

Cut the beef into small pieces so that you will get all the good from it. Brown the meat very quickly in butter or oil and place in a deep kettle (an 8-quart one will do). Add the marrow bone and cold water. Bring this to a boil and allow it to boil briskly for 5 minutes; then skim the top of the liquid. Reduce the heat to simmering and allow the meat to cook slowly for at least 3 hours. The scum which will form should be skimmed from time to time during the cooking process. Keep the kettle covered except when you are skimming the surface.

After 1 hour of cooking, add salt (coarse salt is far more flavorful for this type of cookery). After salting the stock, add onions stuck with cloves, the carrots, a few branches of celery with their leaves, a few sprigs of parsley, a bay leaf, the leeks, and a few sprigs of thyme.

Strain the soup through cheesecloth and allow it to cool very quickly without cover. Skim off the fat from the top. Use absorbent paper to collect the small particles of fat that float on the surface after you have skimmed it.

If you wish to clarify the broth, add 2 egg whites, lightly beaten, and the crushed shells of the eggs. Allow this to come to a boil and boil briskly for 2 minutes. Strain through two thicknesses of cheesecloth.

Remove the marrow from the bones and add it to the broth, or serve it on toast with the broth.

VARIATIONS

With Cooked Bird: You may add the carcass of a cooked bird (chicken, turkey, duck, goose, or game) to the beef and proceed as above. Bones from a roast or steak may be used, or from any cooked meat except mutton or lamb scraps with a great deal of fat or corned or smoked meat.

With Vegetables (I): For a vegetable soup, proceed as above, but cut the meat in very fine dice and brown well. Make a small bag of cheesecloth for the herbs and seasonings, and add it after 1 hour's cooking. An hour before serving time, add 1 cup each of finely diced carrots, finely cut onions, sliced leeks, finely diced turnip, finely cut celery, and finely shredded snap beans. Allow to cook until vegetables are just tender.

Now remove the seasoning bag and then the marrow bones; extract the marrow and add it to the soup. Skim off the fat, but do not strain. Pour into large soup plates and add well-dried stale bread which has been warmed in the oven, or croutons if you wish. Sprinkle generously with chopped parsley.

With Vegetables (II): Prepare soup; strain, cool, and clarify as directed. Bring 1 quart of the stock to the boiling point and add ½ cup each of finely shredded carrots, finely diced onions, finely shredded snap beans, and finely cut celery. Simmer until vegetables are just tender and add ½ cup tender green peas or ½ package frozen peas which have been thawed (page 261). Taste for seasoning, add a generous quantity of chopped parsley, and serve at once.

Pressure Cooker Beef Stock

1½ pounds lean beef	2 or 3 small carrots
3 or 4 tablespoons butter	1 onion
or oil	2 cloves
Knuckle bone	Parsley
1 tablespoon salt	Thyme
Bay leaf	6 cups water

Brown the lean beef (from the shank or the round) in butter or oil. This may be done in the pressure cooker. Add a knuckle bone, salt, a bay leaf, carrots, onion stuck with cloves, 1 or 2 sprigs parsley, a sprig of thyme, and the water. Cover and secure the cooker, and cook at 15 pounds for 15 to 20 minutes.

Allow to cool in the cooker before removing cover. Strain through a double cheesecloth and skim off all fat. Use as you do other stock.

Soup of the Evening, Beautiful Soup

Veal or White Stock

3 pounds veal knuckle	Bay leaf
1 pound veal neck or lean veal	1 or 2 stalks celery
	Parsley
2 or 3 carrots	3 quarts cold water
1 onion	1½ tablespoons salt
2 cloves	

Cut veal in small pieces. Place in an 8-quart kettle with carrots, an onion stuck with cloves, a small bay leaf, celery, and a few sprigs of parsley. Pour over this the cold water and bring slowly to a boil. Skim the scum from the top as it forms, cover, and simmer very slowly 3 or 4 hours or longer.

After the broth has cooked 1 hour, add salt and cover again.

Strain this broth through a triple thickness of cheesecloth.

Pot au Feu

2 pounds lean beef	2 or 3 turnips
Whole fowl or 2 pounds wings and backs	4 or 5 leeks
	4 quarts water
1½ pounds shin bone with marrow	Parsley
	Thyme
2 onions	1 clove garlic
Cloves	1½ tablespoons salt
5 or 6 carrots	

This is a classic dish of the French countryside and is prepared in many ways in different regions of the country. Basically it is a combination of beef, chicken, and vegetables. The broth is usually served first, and after that the boiled beef and the chicken with the vegetables from the pot. Horseradish sauce is sometimes served with it, or mustard.

The beef may be brisket, round, or rump. Use either a whole fowl or 2 pounds of wings and backs from the shops which specialize in selling chicken in parts. You will also need 1½ pounds of shin bone with marrow. Place these things in an 8-quart kettle with onions

stuck with cloves, carrots, turnips, and leeks with the green cut away.

Cover with water and bring to a boil very slowly. Boil for 5 minutes and skim off the scum from the top. Add 1 or 2 sprigs parsley, a sprig of thyme, and a clove of garlic. Reduce the heat, cover the kettle, and allow to simmer 4 hours. After 1 hour's cooking add salt.

Remove the meat and the chicken from the kettle and keep warm. Strain the broth, remove some of the vegetables from the strainer, and add them to the dish with the meat. Skim off the fat from the broth.

Serve bowls of the broth with pieces of well-dried French bread. Serve the meat and —if you have used a whole bird—the chicken with the vegetables, and pass either mustard or horseradish sauce. A good green salad with this, and perhaps some excellent cheese, make a hearty meal.

Consommé

1½ pounds lean beef, diced	4 carrots, sliced
1 pound lean beef, whole	3 stalks celery with leaves
1½ pounds marrow bone	3 or 4 leeks, cleaned and thinly sliced
1½ pounds veal knuckle	1½ tablespoons salt
Butter	3 sprigs parsley
3½ quarts water	2 sprigs thyme
1 pound chicken wings and backs	*1 clove garlic
Chicken carcass	1 bay leaf
2 onions	6 peppercorns
Cloves	3 beaten egg whites with crushed shells

Cut 1½ pounds lean beef in 1-inch dice and brown very quickly in either beef fat or butter. Place in an 8-quart kettle with whole piece of lean beef, marrow bone, and veal knuckle, and cover with the water. Bring to a boil and allow to boil 5 minutes. Skim off any scum that forms.

Cover and simmer for an hour. Add chicken wings and backs, chicken carcass, onions stuck with cloves, sliced carrots, celery with the leaves, leeks, and salt. Season with parsley, thyme, garlic, bay leaf, and peppercorns. Cover and allow to simmer very slowly for 4 hours.

Strain the consommé through a double thickness of cheesecloth, skim off the fat, and remove with absorbent paper towels any particles that remain. Clarify with egg whites and the crushed shells, and strain again through three thicknesses of cheesecloth.

Serve either hot or cold.

VARIATIONS

With Rice: Cook 3 or 4 tablespoons well-washed rice in either broth or water until about ¾ cooked. Add rice to a quart of consommé, heat to the boiling point, and simmer about 5 minutes. Rectify the seasoning and serve.

With Pastes: Cook macaroni, spaghetti, vermicelli, or other pastes, such as the seashell or butterfly pastes, in boiling salted water until just barely tender. For 4 cups consommé, you will need approximately 2 or 3 ounces paste. Add to consommé and heat to boiling point. Rectify the seasoning and serve at once. You may serve with this a sprinkling of grated Parmesan cheese.

Julienne: Cut 2 small carrots, 1 small white turnip, and 2 leek tops into fine, matchlike sticks. Cook these in 2 tablespoons butter in a covered saucepan over a low flame for 5 minutes. Add ½ cup consommé and continue cooking until just tender. After this you may add, if you wish, a few green peas and a few beans cut in very fine shreds, and cook a few minutes longer. Combine the vegetables with 4 cups consommé, taste for seasoning, and sprinkle generously with chopped parsley. Serve very hot.

With Avocado: Just before removing consommé from the heat, add thin slices of ripe avocado.

With Mushroom: Add thinly sliced raw mushroom caps to hot consommé just before serving. Taste for seasoning and add a small amount of sherry to each cup.

With Pimiento: Add finely shredded or cut pimiento to consommé and garnish with paprika and chopped chervil or parsley.

Madrilene: Combine 3 cups consommé with 1 cup tomato purée and a sprig of basil. Add 1 teaspoon salt, 1 tablespoon finely chopped onion, 6 peppercorns, a bay leaf, and a clove of garlic. Allow this to simmer 15 to 20 minutes, remove from fire, and strain through cheesecloth. Serve either hot or cold.

Or, combine consommé with 1 cup peeled, seeded, and chopped tomatoes. Add the other seasonings with the addition of 1 clove and cook 20 minutes. Strain through double cheesecloth.

With Parmesan Cheese: Serve clear consommé with small rounds of fried toast heaped with grated Parmesan cheese and browned lightly under the broiler.

Vegetable Broth

You may use the vegetable juices from cooking vegetables for the table in combination as a vegetable broth, if you wish, or you may make a broth as follows:

2 large Spanish onions	4 or 5 ripe tomatoes
4 carrots	2 quarts water
1 medium-sized head celery	1½ tablespoons salt
Small bunch parsley	1 egg white with crushed shells
4 or 5 leeks	

Peel and slice onions, scrape and slice carrots, and cut celery head in small pieces, using tops as well. Wash a small bunch of parsley. Clean leeks and cut into thin slices. Peel and seed the tomatoes.

Combine these vegetables with the water and salt, and simmer 1½ hours.

Strain through a double cheesecloth and clarify with 1 egg white, slightly beaten, and the crushed shells. Strain again and cool.

This is a light delicate broth which may be used hot or cold or combined with other ingredients.

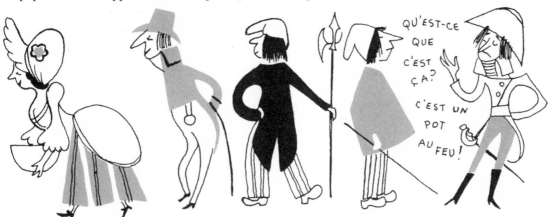

QU'EST-CE QUE C'EST ÇA? C'EST UN POT AU FEU!

Chicken Broth

4-pound dressed fowl, or 3 pounds backs and wings	Several chicken feet (optional) Parsley

Use either a 4-pound dressed fowl or 3 pounds backs and wings. If you wish, you may add several chicken feet, which should be carefully cleaned and split.

Cover the chicken with cold water in a large kettle and bring to a boil very slowly. After it has boiled 5 minutes, skim off any scum that has risen to the top. Cover, and reduce the heat to simmering. Add a sprig of parsley and simmer 2 to 3 hours.

If you are using a fowl for the broth, remove it when the breast is tender, cut the entire breast off the carcass, and return the carcass to the broth pot. The breast meat may then be used for hash, salad, or cold chicken.

Remove the carcass and strain the broth through a cheesecloth. When the fat rises to the top, skim it off very carefully and pick up the stray bits of fat from the surface with an absorbent paper.

Serve chicken broth clear or in any of the following ways:

(1) Add noodles, preferably the fine ones, cooked in boiling salted water until just tender.

(2) Add julienne strips of the white meat of chicken.

(3) Cook a small amount of rice in the chicken broth and serve it in the cups with the broth.

(4) Combine equal quantities of chicken broth and tomato juice. Add a clove, a slice of lemon, and a small onion. Heat together for 15 minutes. Strain and serve.

(5) Cook julienne strips of carrot in chicken broth until tender and add a few green peas.

(6) Use as a base for most cream soups.

(7) Use for cooking certain vegetables.

If you have the space for it in your refrigerator, you will do well to keep a jar of choice broth on hand—for many uses.

Cream of Chicken Soup

4-pound hen	1½ cups cream
2 or 3 leeks	2 egg yolks
Onion	2 tablespoons sherry
2 or 3 cloves	Paprika
Several celery tops	Blanched almonds, thinly
1 tablespoon peppercorns	shaved (optional)

Choose a good plump hen that is not too fat through the body. Place it in a pot with leeks, onion stuck with cloves, celery tops, and peppercorns. Cover with cold water and simmer till the chicken is tender.

Remove the bird and simmer the soup for another half hour. Season to taste, skim the fat, and strain through a cheesecloth.

Cut the meat from the bones of the chicken and put the meat through a fine grinder or chop very fine. Place in the strained broth and heat thoroughly, after which add cream and egg yolks. Stir constantly till soup is slightly thickened. Add sherry and serve with a sprinkling of paprika and tiny shreds of white meat on top. Thinly shaved blanched almonds may be used as a garnish as well.

Crème Vichyssoise

8 or 10 large leeks	Salt and pepper
3 tablespoons butter, margarine, or chicken fat	½ teaspoon nutmeg
	3 or 4 cups sweet or sour cream
2 or 3 cups chicken broth	Chopped chives
4 medium-sized mealy potatoes	

The following is my recipe for this soup, which in plain English is a cold leek-and-potato soup. I like it because it tastes the way I think it should.

Cut the green tops from the leeks and cut the white parts into 1-inch lengths. Sauté the white parts gently—being careful not to brown them—in butter, margarine, or chicken fat. When they are wilted, add 1 cup chicken broth and simmer gently. While you are doing this, have the potatoes boiling on the stove.

When the potatoes are tender and the leeks cooked, combine them, add another cup of chicken broth, and let them simmer together 10 minutes. Crush the potatoes with a fork so that they become saturated with the leek flavor. Salt and pepper to taste, and add ½ teaspoon nutmeg.

Force the vegetables through a fine sieve with the broth. Add another cup of broth, or more if the vegetable purée seems too thick. When cool, place in the refrigerator and chill for 18 to 24 hours.

The last step is to add cream, sweet or sour, or a mixture of the two, to the purée. You will need about 1½ cups cream to each quart of purée. For this, suit your own taste.

Be sure that the soup is ice cold when it is served. Chopped chives are added to each cup as it is served, or passed separately.

VARIATION

Many people relish one teaspoon or more, according to taste, of curry powder added to the purée when it is hot.

Turkey Soup

Turkey carcass	Celery
3 carrots	Parsley
1 onion	Salt

Cover a turkey carcass and trimmings (and any bits and pieces which lurk on the platter on which the bird was served) with cold water in a large kettle. Cut or break the carcass into several pieces.

Add carrots, onion, celery tops and outside stalks, parsley, and additional salt. Cover and simmer 2 hours.

Strain through a cheesecloth and serve, or use as a base for other soups and sauces.

VARIATION

You may use the carcass of any bird—or any wild game—for the same type of soup.

FISH SOUPS

For fish soups and chowders, see FISH AND SHELLFISH in this book.

CREAM SOUPS

The greatest fault of most cream soups is that they are heavy with flour or cream sauce which has been used for thickening. The most delicate cream soups are those thickened lightly with cream and egg yolks. These give a more positive flavor and a far better texture, without the floury quality which is often so objectionable. Quick-cooking tapioca may also be used for a thickener in many cream soups.

Cream Soups—Basic Procedure

Cook peeled and cut vegetables in chicken broth or consommé until tender. Season with lightly sautéed onion, herbs, parsley, etc., while cooking. Purée vegetables and return to heat over hot water. Thicken with cream and egg yolks or with cream and tapioca or with arrowroot. Rectify the seasoning, add wine if desired, and serve with garnishes such as chopped parsley, paprika, chopped chervil, or tarragon, pimiento strips, etc. 1 cup puréed vegetable or vegetables and 2 cups broth will combine with 1 cup cream and 2 egg yolks to make 6 servings of soup.

VARIATIONS

Cream of Asparagus: Cook asparagus in chicken broth until the asparagus is just tender. Season with salt, pepper, parsley, and a little onion while cooking. When cooked, put through the sieve or purée strainer, or mix in an electric blender if you have one. Heat broth and puréed asparagus in double boiler, and add cream which has been well mixed with the egg yolks. Stir constantly until the soup is lightly thickened—until a wooden spoon is lightly coated. Do not allow it to boil. Taste for seasoning. Sprinkle with chopped parsley.

Cream of Corn: Heat 1 cup cooked corn kernels in 2 cups chicken broth. Season with salt, pepper, and a little grated onion or finely chopped green pepper. When boiling, pour over 1 cup cream mixed with 2 egg yolks, a little at a time, stirring constantly. Blend well together and rectify the seasoning.

Cream of Carrot: Cook 1 cup scraped and sliced carrots with a sprig of parsley, 1 small white onion, and salt and pepper to taste in 1½ cups chicken broth or consommé until soft. Purée the carrots and return to chicken broth over hot water. When hot, add 1 cup heavy cream mixed with 2 egg yolks, and stir constantly until mixture is blended and lightly thickened. Serve with a garnish of chopped parsley.

Cream of Celery: Cook 1 cup finely cut celery and tops in 2 cups chicken broth, adding salt, pepper, and parsley for flavoring. You may add 1 tablespoon finely chopped onion as well, if you wish. When tender, purée the celery, return it to broth, and place over hot water. When just at the boiling point, add 1 cup cream mixed with 2 egg yolks. Stir constantly until the soup is lightly thickened. Garnish with chopped parsley and finely chopped celery tops.

The same procedure may be used for other vegetable soups, such as those with broccoli, cauliflower, leeks, onion, peas, spinach, watercress, etc.

Cream of Potato and Leek Soup (Potage Parmentier)

2 large Idaho potatoes	1 teaspoon salt
3 cups stock or chicken broth	Pepper
	1 tablespoon butter
2 leeks (white parts only), finely chopped	1 cup cream
	Parsley

Peel the potatoes and cut into small pieces. Cook them in stock or chicken broth with leeks, salt, and a few grains of pepper. When the potatoes are tender, put them through a fine sieve and return the purée to the broth with a good tablespoon of butter. Reheat and add the cream gradually. Serve very hot with chopped parsley.

Clam Purée

3 medium-sized onions	1 quart raw clams
3 large potatoes	½ cup scalded cream
2 cups milk	Butter

Chop onions very fine and slice potatoes very thin. Place them in a saucepan, cover, and cook for 45 minutes in as little water as possible. Bring milk to a boil and pour it on the onions and potatoes. Lower the flame, and mash the potatoes and onions with the milk. Chop clams very fine. Add them to the mixture and simmer this for just 10 minutes.

Put through a sieve, return smooth purée to pan, and add cream and several pats butter. Serve very hot with a piece of butter melting on surface of each service.

Cream of Tomato Soup

1 small carrot, peeled	1½ teaspoons salt
1 small onion, peeled	1 teaspoon fresh-ground black pepper
2 stalks celery	
3 tablespoons butter	1 teaspoon sugar
2 cups tomato purée or 2 cups fresh tomatoes	1 clove garlic
	⅛ teaspoon soda
2 cups chicken broth	2 tablespoons butter
Basil	1 cup heavy cream
1 clove	2 egg yolks

Chop the carrot, onion, and celery very fine. Cook these quickly in the butter for 5 minutes. Combine with: tomato purée or tomatoes, peeled and seeded and chopped fine; chicken broth; ½ teaspoon basil or 4 or 5 leaves fresh basil which have been cut in fine strips; clove; salt; pepper; and sugar. Add garlic and cook over low heat 1 hour. Strain, and add soda and butter. Reheat and add heavy cream mixed with egg yolks, stirring constantly until mixture thickens.

VARIATIONS

With Tapioca: Reheat strained tomato mixture with 2 tablespoons quick-cooking tapioca and add 1 cup cream just before serving. Serve with finely chopped parsley and chives.

Other Variations: This soup may also be served without the addition of cream. You may thicken it with 2 tablespoons quick-cooking tapioca if you wish. Or add ⅔ cup cooked rice just before serving.

Cream of Pumpkin or Squash Soup

1 cup cooked pumpkin or squash	1 teaspoon fresh-ground pepper
2 cups chicken broth	1 tablespoon finely chopped parsley
1 tablespoon finely grated onion	
	1 cup heavy cream
Nutmeg	2 egg yolks
1 teaspoon salt	Paprika

Purée pumpkin or squash. Add chicken broth, grated onion, a few grains nutmeg, salt, pepper, and parsley. Heat in upper part of double boiler over hot water. When liquid has reached the boiling point, add heavy cream mixed with egg yolks. Stir till lightly thickened. Serve with paprika and chopped parsley.

VARIATION

The addition of a glass of Madeira just before serving is a great help to this soup.

Borsch

1 cup finely chopped cabbage	1½ cups canned tomatoes
1 cup diced potatoes	½ cup beet juice
½ cup diced carrots	1 cup diced cooked or canned beets
1 stick minced celery	1 small teaspoon vinegar
1 small onion chopped	Salt and pepper
2 quarts good beef stock	1 spoonful sour cream
3 tablespoons butter or beef fat	Finely chopped parsley or dill leaves

Prepare vegetables. Heat stock to boiling. In a heavy pan that can be closely covered melt butter or beef fat. Put prepared vegetables into fat, turn fire low, and shake covered pan over heat about 5 minutes. Add hot stock.

Put tomatoes through fine sieve and add to soup. Add beet juice. Simmer gently. When vegetables are tender, add beets and vinegar. Season to taste with salt and pepper. Remove from fire before beets lose color. Serve with sour cream and parsley or dill leaves on top of each portion.

Cream of Mushroom Soup

½ pound mushroom caps, finely sliced	1 teaspoon fresh-ground black pepper
Mushroom caps (2 per person)	2 cups chicken broth
3 tablespoons butter	1 cup heavy cream
1 teaspoon salt	2 egg yolks
	2 tablespoons chopped parsley

Sauté sliced mushroom caps in butter until lightly browned. Add salt, pepper, and broth.

While the soup is simmering, sauté 2 mushroom caps for each person to be served in the butter (try to pick caps of a uniform size).

When the soup has simmered 15 minutes, add heavy cream mixed with egg yolks and cook, stirring constantly, until slightly thickened. Add parsley and serve at once, garnished with the sautéed mushroom caps.

Duchess Soup

2 tablespoons minced onion	⅛ teaspoon pepper
2 tablespoons butter	4 cups milk
2 tablespoons quick-cooking tapioca	½ cup grated American cheese
1¼ teaspoons salt	2 tablespoons chopped parsley

Sauté onion in butter in saucepan until tender. Add tapioca, salt, pepper, and milk. Place over low or medium heat and cook until mixture comes to a boil, stirring constantly. Remove from heat, add cheese and parsley, and stir until cheese is melted.

(Makes 4 to 6 servings.)

Green Split Pea Soup (I)

1 pound quick-cooking green split peas	Salt
4 cups chicken broth	1 teaspoon black pepper
2 tablespoons grated onion	1 cup heavy cream
	Croutons
	Chopped parsley

Quick-cooking split peas, both green and yellow, are available in all markets nowadays. They save the nuisance of soaking overnight and long cooking.

Cook peas with chicken broth until peas are tender. Simmer gently; do not boil. Put peas through a fine sieve and add grated onion, 1 teaspoon or more salt, and pepper. Reheat until peas and broth are well mixed and almost at the boiling point. Add heavy cream and stir well. Serve with small croutons.

This soup may also be chilled and served cold. Sprinkle with chopped parsley.

Green Split Pea Soup (II)

Ham bone or end of ham	Salt
2 quarts cold water	Croutons, cream, or ½ cup tomato purée
1 onion	Sliced frankfurters or chopped ham (optional)
Cloves	
Bay leaf	
1 pound quick-cooking green peas	

Place the ham bone or end of a ham in the cold water and cook for 1½ hours. Add onion stuck with cloves, a bay leaf, and peas. Taste the broth before adding salt, for the salt content of various types of ham differs. Simmer until the peas are cooked through.

Purée the peas and taste for seasoning. Reheat and serve plain with croutons, or add cream or tomato purée. You may garnish this soup with sliced frankfurters or with small bits of chopped ham from the ham bone.

VARIATIONS

With White Pea Beans: Purée the beans or leave them whole and serve with crisp bacon bits.

With Lentils: You may purée the lentils or leave them whole. Sliced frankfurters or hot Italian or Spanish sausage, and chopped parsley and chives, are a good addition to lentil soup.

With Red Kidney Beans: These may either be puréed or served whole in the soup. The addition of cubes of ham and a little Madeira is excellent.

Onion Soup au Gratin

4 or 5 Spanish onions, peeled and sliced or diced	4 or 5 chicken or beef bouillon cubes dissolved in 1 quart water
4 tablespoons butter	Salt and pepper
1 quart stock or chicken broth, or	Toasted French bread
	Grated Parmesan cheese

Sauté onions in butter until lightly browned. Add stock, broth, or bouillon either to the skillet in which you have browned the onions or to a large casserole to which you transfer the onions. Salt and pepper to taste, allow the soup to come to a boil, and simmer 15 minutes. Serve with slices of well-toasted French bread heaped with grated Parmesan cheese and lightly browned under the broiler. Serve with additional grated cheese.

VARIATIONS

Clear Soup: Strain soup. Serve with toasted French bread and grated Parmesan cheese.

With Wine: Add ½ cup dry white wine to the broth after adding broth to the onions.

In Casserole: Transfer soup to individual casseroles. Top each one with a slice of toast and heap with grated cheese. Place in a moderate oven (375°) for 10 minutes.

Sorrel Soup

1 large Idaho potato, peeled and diced	1½ cups fresh sorrel leaves
2 cups chicken broth	2 tablespoons butter
1 teaspoon salt	1 cup heavy cream
	2 egg yolks

Cook potato in broth till tender. Add salt. Wash 1½ cups sorrel leaves and break or cut in small pieces. In butter, in a skillet, wilt sorrel quickly and cook 3 or 4 minutes. Add to potato-broth mixture. Cook 10 minutes together. Add heavy cream mixed with egg yolks and stir till slightly thickened. Serve hot or chilled.

VARIATION

Proceed as above. Just before serving, add 4 tablespoons Madeira. Blend well with soup.

Beet and Sorrel Soup

3 or 4 young beets	Sour cream
2 cups chicken broth	Scallions, thinly sliced
1 teaspoon salt	Slices of cucumber
2 cups sorrel	Hard-cooked eggs, finely chopped
2 tablespoons butter	
½ cup chicken broth	

Peel and slice, or dice, beets. Cook in broth with salt. Wash and chop sorrel, wilt it in butter in a skillet, add broth, and cook until tender. Combine sorrel and beets and purée them. Chill thoroughly in refrigerator. Serve cold with sour cream, scallions, cucumber, and hard-cooked eggs.

CANNED SOUPS

The consommés and chicken broths are, of course, invaluable for making many soups. Turtle consommé and turtle soup may be used as a base for various soups. The vegetable soups (the condensed ones) may serve as bases for many creamed soups and bisques. Herbs, cream, and perhaps Madeira or sherry added to the soups will make them interesting. A discriminating selection of seasonings such as curry, various bottled sauces—Tabasco, Worcestershire, and steak sauce—will give new zest to the soups.

The addition of finely chopped onion, chives, parsley, basil (for tomato soups), tarragon, etc., will improve the quality of canned soups. Combinations of soups, enhanced by herbs and seasonings, are frequently good, also—for instance, tomato soup combined with pea soup and flavored with curry and a sprinkling of chives. Chicken broth combined with tomato soup makes a pleasant change when flavored with basil or with curry powder. Some soups on the market, such as a shrimp soup brought out by a specialty house, are excellent when strained and chilled and served with sour cream.

Boula

1 can pea soup	Whipped cream
1 can turtle soup	Grated Parmesan cheese
3 tablespoons Madeira	

Boula (origin unknown) is a soup that combines pea soup and turtle soup. Use 1 can pea soup to 1 can turtle soup. Heat them together and add the Madeira.

There are two ways of serving. One is to serve in cups with whipped cream. The other is to serve in individual ovenproof casseroles. Top with whipped cream and sprinkle with grated Parmesan cheese. Place the casseroles under the broiler for a few minutes to brown the cheese.

FISH AND SHELLFISH

FISH

Fish deserve a far greater popularity than they now enjoy. There are fish of a great variety of textures, flavors, and forms to be found in almost any fish market, and prices often run considerably under those for meat. It may be that lack of imagination in cooking and serving, seconded by the almost invariable overcooking of one of the most delicate of foods, have contributed to a regrettable lack of appreciation of fish. Fish should be cooked only long enough to coagulate the flesh—just long enough to erase the rather translucent appearance of raw fish. Overcooking hardens the fibers. The delicate-meated fish called "white fish" in the Pacific area is often "cooked" by immersion in lime juice for a few hours and makes a most delicious cold luncheon or supper dish.

SELECTING FISH

Fish may be grouped under two headings: "fat" fish and "lean" fish. Fat fish have oil running through all the flesh, and lean fish have a drier flesh with the oil centralized in the liver. The fat fish are best for broiling, poaching, or baking, although some of the lean fish will broil very well. The lean fish are good for sautéing, deep-fat frying, and fish chowders.

You may buy fish whole, with bone, boned and whole, filleted, or in steaks. Steaks are slices cut across the fish. Fillets are the fleshy sides of the fish removed from the bone. The skin may be left on one side or entirely removed before cooking.

In shopping for fish, look for a smooth, moist skin, firm flesh, a fresh odor, bright eyes and gills, and firm fins and tail. Allow 1 pound of solid fish for three persons (for two if purchased with bones and skin).

DRESSING FISH FOR COOKING

Large scales should be removed. Hold the fish by the tail and with a blunt, firm knife scrape the scales thoroughly, holding the knife at about a 20-degree angle and working from the tail to the head. Do not scrape too briskly or you will have the scales flying.

"Run" the fins, or ask your dealer to do this for you. If you do it for yourself, you may want to wait until after the fish is cooked, when the bones may be removed more easily. In this case, do not cut the fins too close to the body. Leave the fin bones in sight so that when the fish is cooked you can remove them more efficiently. Or you may cut down into the flesh on either side of the fins to remove them and scoop out the entrails.

To clean a fish, slit the body on the stomach side and scoop out the entrails very quickly. Remove the clotted blood and wipe the fish out well with a damp cloth. If you are serving the fish whole, leave the head and tail on; otherwise cut them off with a sharp knife or scissors.

If it is necessary to skin the fish, cut off the back fins and cut a thin strip of skin along the entire length of the back. Cut skin away from the bony part of the gills. Then take a firm hold on the skin and strip it off from the head to the tail. Turn the fish over and repeat the process on the other side.

To bone a fish, clean it and cut off the head. Insert a very sharp knife with a pointed blade between the backbone and the flesh and cut down from the head to the tail, close to the bone. Turn the fish over and repeat the process on the other side. Then lift out the entire backbone of the fish and pick out any small bones that remain.

SUGGESTED FISH FOR BROILING

BROILED FISH

Broiling is a most satisfactory method of cooking fish and one of the simplest. Fish, unlike meat, is broiled most successfully on only one side, since the turning that one gives meat tends to break a fish in pieces. So do not broil fish on the broiling rack. Use a flat, square, or oval pan.

Heat the broiler to about 450° and heat the pan at the same time. Oil the pan well with olive oil and place the fish on the pan, skin side down. Brush well with butter, using more butter if the fish is of the lean variety. Broil the fish about 4 inches from the flame until nicely browned and until the flesh is just set and flaky.

Broiled fish is best served simply, with either melted butter mixed with lemon juice, or butter softened and mixed with plenty of chopped parsley. Elaborate sauces are too pretentious for broiled fish, and broiling, correctly done, brings out the special goodness of fresh fish as nothing else can. Fish cooks most quickly in fillet form. Fillets should be well brushed with butter and basted with butter during the cooking process, for fillets have a tendency to dry out.

Fish steaks about 1 to 1½ inches thick may be broiled. Baste with melted fat or a mixture of melted fat and white wine during cooking.

When broiling steaks of fish, you may turn them and broil and brown on both sides, though this is not necessary when you have heated the pan well before placing the fish in the oven. If you do turn the fish, do so with two large spatulas, being very careful not to break it.

Large whole fish should be boned and split and broiled open, well brushed and basted with butter.

Some people prefer dredging fish with flour before broiling, but this is not necessary. Your fish will develop a crustier surface if floured, but plenty of butter also will give it a delicious coating.

Transfer cooked fish to a hot platter with the aid of spatulas, or broil fish in an ovenware dish on which you can serve it. Serve with lemon wedges in addition to the lemon you may have used for lemon or parsley butter.

Broiling Time: *Fillets* need 5 to 8 minutes of broiling, depending upon thickness and texture.

Whole fish, dressed, such as mackerel, sea bass, weakfish, whitefish, and flounder, will require 10 to 15 minutes, depending on thickness and size. Testing for flakiness with a toothpick or a small skewer will determine quickly whether the fish is done.

Fish steaks averaging 1 inch in thickness will take 8 to 10 minutes of broiling.

Whole fish, split, should take 8 to 14 minutes, depending upon size and texture. They should be basted plentifully with butter during the process.

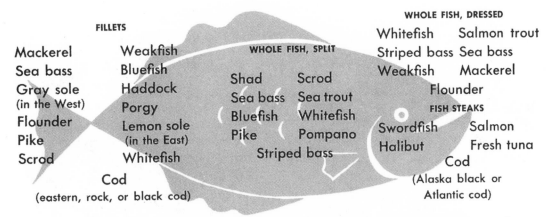

FILLETS

Mackerel
Sea bass
Gray sole (in the West)
Flounder
Pike
Scrod

Weakfish
Bluefish
Haddock
Porgy
Lemon sole (in the East)
Whitefish

Cod (eastern, rock, or black cod)

WHOLE FISH, SPLIT

Shad
Sea bass
Bluefish
Pike

Scrod
Sea trout
Whitefish
Pompano
Striped bass

WHOLE FISH, DRESSED

Whitefish
Striped bass
Weakfish

Salmon trout
Sea bass
Mackerel
Flounder

FISH STEAKS

Swordfish
Halibut

Salmon
Fresh tuna
Cod (Alaska black or Atlantic cod)

Do not try to broil frozen fillets until thoroughly thawed, unless otherwise stated.

BAKED FISH

Many of the larger fish are much better baked in a very hot oven (450°) than broiled. There is less drying out in baking than there sometimes is in broiling and the entire process is much easier.

Prepare fish for baking just the way you prepare fish for broiling. Oil your pan and butter the fish well. Heat the oven and bake the fish, basting occasionally, until it is just cooked through. It will brown during the baking process, not as crustily perhaps as under the broiler, but more delicately. Allow 1 or 2 minutes more cooking time. Test with a toothpick or small skewer for doneness.

Another method of baking small fish or fillets is to preheat the oven to very hot (450°-500°), dip the fish into milk and bread crumbs which have been salted, and then brush with olive oil or melted butter. Place in the hot oven and bake just 10 minutes.

Baked Stuffed Fish

Fish of 3 to 7 pounds are excellent when stuffed and baked. Use any type of stuffing you wish, though to my mind a stuffing of thinly sliced onions, sliced tomatoes, and parsley in sprigs, with green pepper or green onions added, if desired, is as good as one can find. It gives flavor to the fish and is fresh on the palate in a way that a bread or herb stuffing is not. Add plenty of butter to the vegetable stuffing and season with salt and pepper.

Have the head and backbone removed before stuffing, if desired. When baking the fish with the head on, split the flesh between the rib bones and cut through the fish from the head to the tail. Fill loosely with the stuffing and either secure the fish with toothpicks or skewers or sew it together. (The latter is less desirable, for the fish may burst as it cooks.)

Arrange the fish in an oiled baking pan, or lay the fish on a buttered piece of cooking parchment and place it in the oiled pan. This will enable you to slip it off onto a serving platter more easily.

If you wish to make a circle with the fish's head and tail meeting, arrange the fish and secure it with skewers. Slash the flesh at the back in one or two places and brush well with butter or place small pieces of bacon in the slashes. Dot the fish generously with butter or strip with salt pork or bacon. Preheat the oven to very hot (500°).

Allow approximately 10 minutes per pound in baking fish. Reduce the oven temperature to 350° after the first 10 minutes and baste frequently. Or bake in a hot oven (400°), allowing approximately 12 minutes per pound.

Serve baked stuffed fish with parsley butter or lemon butter or with a sauce, such as cucumber hollandaise or an egg sauce.

You may add red or white wine to the baking pan—1 cup will be ample—and use the wine for basting. The blend of wine and butter will make a delicious sauce for the fish when it is cooked.

SUGGESTED FISH FOR BAKED STUFFED FISH

Bluefish	Sea trout
Scrod	Swordfish steak
Small whole salmon	Striped bass
Large halibut steak	Salmon trout
Shad	Cod

Salmon, center cut from larger fish

SUGGESTED FISH FOR SAUTE

Trout	Pompano
Smelts	Halibut
Brook trout	Porgies
Haddock	English sole
Salmon	Butterfish
Pike	Red snapper
Flounder	Ling cod

Fillets of lemon and gray sole

SAUTEED FISH

This is one of the most simple and satisfactory methods of preparing small fish or fillets.

Sautéed fish needs butter and plenty of it. Fillets, especially, seem to absorb a great deal of butter. Brisk heat is needed but not so brisk as to burn the butter. Fish should be sautéed just long enough to brown lightly and to be cooked through. Serve immediately. Do not overcook, because fish does not tenderize as it continues to cook; often it toughens and gets oily.

For variety, dip fish in milk or beaten egg yolk and roll in flour or bread crumbs.

For the dish Sauté Meunière, sauté fish in butter and sprinkle with lemon juice and plenty of chopped parsley just before removing from the pan. A little additional butter added at the last minute is an improvement.

POACHED FISH

Poaching is the correct procedure for fish loosely described—and, all too often, carelessly cooked—as boiled fish. The fish is brought just to the boil in either salt water or a court-bouillon (see below), then simmered very gently until cooked. This type of cookery is ideal for certain fish, notably salmon, which may then be served either hot or cold. If you use a court-bouillon, it may be strained and used as the base of a sauce or an aspic.

Wrap fish to be poached in cheesecloth and tie the ends or loop them so that it will be easier to lift the cooked fish out of the pan and unroll it onto a plate or platter.

Allow approximately 6 to 10 minutes per pound, and be certain you know the weight of the fish before cooking; overcooking can ruin good fish. The flesh should be flaky and firm, never mushy.

In poaching fillets or small pieces of fish, allow about 1 minute per ounce. Test with a toothpick.

Court-Bouillon (I)

Trimmings of fish (head, fins, bones, etc.)
1 cup red or white wine
2 quarts water
1 medium onion stuck with 2 cloves
6 peppercorns
½ bay leaf
1¼ tablespoons salt
2 sprigs parsley
Pinch of thyme

Obtain extra trimmings, if needed, at the fish dealer's. Cover fish pieces with water and add wine, onion, peppercorns, bay leaf, salt, parsley, and thyme. Simmer 20 minutes. Strain and set aside until ready to use for the fish.

Court-Bouillon (II)

Trimmings of fish
1 cup red or white wine
2 quarts water
2 or 3 sprigs parsley
6 peppercorns
1 carrot cut in thin strips
1 onion stuck with 2 cloves
½ bay leaf
1¼ tablespoons salt

Mix the above ingredients. Bring to a boil and cook 5 minutes before adding fish.

SUGGESTED FISH FOR POACHING

Salmon
Eel
Halibut
Trout
Whitefish

Turbot
Salmon trout
Red snapper
Skate
Haddock

There are as many good fish

CHANDLER

There are "fat" fish and "lean" fish. Fat fish have oil running through all the flesh, but lean fish have a drier flesh, with the oil centralized in the liver. Fat fish are best for broiling, poaching, or baking; lean fish, for sautéing, deep-fat frying, and chowders.

Fish should be cooked only long enough to make the rather translucent raw flesh opaque.

in the Sea as Ever came out of it

VARIATION

¼ cup wine vinegar may be substituted for the wine in a court-bouillon.

Small fish or fillets are often poached in white wine with or without the addition of water. A small amount of white wine will suffice if you baste often during cooking.

Hot poached fish may be served with Hollandaise sauce, a Sauce Mousseline, a Velouté made with the fish stock, a Sauce Mornay made with fish stock, or an egg sauce made with fish stock.

Cold poached fish may be made into an aspic, using the fish stock for the jelly. It may be served with a mayonnaise, a green mayonnaise, tartar sauce, or a rémoulade.

Salmon, the most popular cold fish, may be cooked whole or in large pieces. Or you may poach individual steaks and either chill them in stock or put them in aspic in individual molds. A whole salmon, poached and then covered with an olive oil mayonnaise and served with cucumber salad and eggs in jelly, makes one of the finest of summer meals.

FRIED FISH

Fried fish is most popular in America and England, but I cannot write of it with much enthusiasm. To cook a delicate fish in deep hot fat tends to rob it of its texture and flavor.

If you do fry fish, use a deep-fat fryer. Heat the oil or fat to 380°, or to a temperature at which a 1-inch cube of bread will brown in 20 seconds. Dip the fillets or small fish in flour, then in beaten eggs, and roll in bread crumbs or corn meal. Fry a few at a time in the deep fat. Fillets will require 4 to 6 minutes, and a small fish 3 to 5 minutes. When browned, drain on absorbent paper in

a warm place. Be careful that you allow the fat to reheat before adding additional fish.

VARIATION

Marinated: Fish may be marinated in French dressing for additional flavor and dipped in crumbs before cooking.

Fish and Chips

The popular English dish of "fish and chips" may be made for a large party if you have two French fryers and can manage to fry potatoes and fish at the same time. This is a good idea for a beer party.

RECIPES FOR FILLETS

In the following group of recipes for dishes prepared with fillets, the particular kind of fish is not specified. Use fish which is available and at its best in your locality, and take advantage of the season for new, fresh catches wherever possible. A fresh-caught flatfish is to be preferred to a cold-storage pompano, deli-

cacy though pompano is. Where fresh fish is not to be had, use frozen fillets of the variety you like best.

The following recipes serve 4 persons, allowing 1 fillet per person. If you wish to plan for more, increase the recipe by one-fourth for each fillet used.

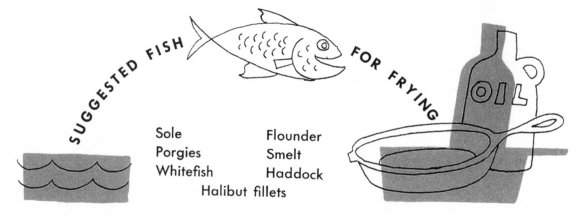

SUGGESTED FISH FOR FRYING

Sole   Flounder
Porgies   Smelt
Whitefish   Haddock
Halibut fillets

Fillets with Anchovies

1 small tin anchovy fillets	1 tablespoon lemon juice
4 fish fillets	3 tablespoons chopped
Flour	parsley
7 tablespoons butter	Watercress
Salt and pepper	Lemon wedges

Open and drain tin of anchovy fillets, reserving the oil in which they are packed. Dredge fish fillets (sole, flounder, perch, etc.) in flour. Melt 4 tablespoons butter in a skillet and sauté the fish, cooking it 3 to 5 minutes or until nicely browned. Season to taste with salt and pepper, remove to a hot platter, and top each fillet with 2 anchovy fillets. Add 3 tablespoons butter to the pan along with the anchovy oil, lemon juice, and parsley. Blend all ingredients well with the butter and pour over the fish. Garnish the platter with watercress and lemon wedges. Serve at once.

(Serves 4.)

Fillets Florentine

2 pounds spinach	Sprig of parsley
Salt	4 fish fillets
4 tablespoons butter	2 tablespoons flour
½ cup water	¼ cup heavy cream
½ cup white wine	Few grains nutmeg
3 peppercorns	Few drops lemon juice
1 small onion stuck with 1 clove	Grated Parmesan cheese

Cook the spinach, drain, and chop very fine. Season to taste with salt and add 2 tablespoons butter. Arrange the spinach on a well-buttered oval baking dish and keep warm.

Combine water with white wine, peppercorns, onion, and parsley. Bring to a boil and let cook 5 minutes. Add fish fillets (1 to a person) and simmer for 5 minutes or until fish is just cooked through.

Remove to a hot plate, let the liquor simmer 2 or 3 minutes longer and strain.

Melt 2 tablespoons butter in a saucepan or in upper part of double boiler and blend it well with flour. Stirring constantly, gradually add the strained broth from the fish; continue stirring until thickened. Add cream, correct seasoning, and add nutmeg and lemon juice.

Place cooked fillets on the bed of spinach, cover with the sauce, and sprinkle liberally with grated Parmesan cheese. Place the dish in a very hot oven (475°) for 5 minutes or until the cheese is delicately browned.

(Serves 4.)

Fillets Amandine

⅔ cup almonds	Salt
4 fish fillets	Lemon juice
7 tablespoons butter	Flour

Blanch almonds in boiling water, slip off skins, and shred them. Dredge fish fillets with flour. Melt 4 tablespoons butter in a skillet, add fillets, and cook quickly (6 to 8 minutes).

Then add 2 tablespoons butter and ½ cup shredded almonds and stir so that the almonds brown lightly. Season to taste with salt, and sprinkle with a little lemon juice. Remove fillets to a hot platter, add another tablespoon butter, and let almonds cook another minute or so. Pour almonds and butter over fish and serve at once. *(Serve 4.)*

VARIATION

Cook almonds separately for a few minutes in 5 tablespoons butter, shaking pan occasionally and allowing butter and nuts to brown lightly. Pour over fish just before removing from pan. Sprinkle with a little lemon juice.

Stuffed Fillets

9 tablespoons butter	¾ cup white wine
1 teaspoon scraped onion	½ cup water
6 finely chopped mushrooms	3 peppercorns
12 mushroom caps	3 or 4 sprigs parsley
1 tablespoon chopped parsley	Thyme
½ cup crabmeat	2 tablespoons flour
Salt	¼ cup heavy cream
4 fish fillets	2 egg yolks
	Buttered crumbs
	Grated Parmesan cheese

Select thin and broad fillets. Lemon sole and gray sole (flounder) are the best.

Melt 3 tablespoons butter in a small skillet. Sauté for 3 minutes the onion, mushrooms, and parsley, and combine with crabmeat. Salt to taste and blend well. Reserving the mushroom caps, spread this mixture on fish fillets, and roll and secure with toothpick or tie with light string.

Combine white wine with water, ¼ teaspoon salt, peppercorns, parsley, and a little thyme, and bring to the boiling point. Simmer rolled fillets in bouillon 6 to 8 minutes, basting frequently. When fish is cooked, remove carefully to a shallow baking dish. Strain the broth and reserve it.

In the upper part of the double boiler combine 2 tablespoons butter and the flour, and blend well. Add, stirring constantly, 1 cup strained broth and continue stirring until nicely thickened. Blend in heavy cream mixed with egg yolks and stir until well blended;

do not let it boil. Pour the sauce over the fillets, from which you have removed the toothpicks or string. Sprinkle with buttered crumbs and grated Parmesan cheese and place under the broiler for just a minute to brown lightly. Garnish with sautéed mushroom caps and serve at once. *(Serves 4.)*

Baked Fillets, Pioneer Style

2 medium onions	Pepper
4 tablespoons butter	½ cup buttered crumbs
Salt	Chopped parsley
4 fish fillets	Crumbled crisp bacon
Olive oil	

Slice onions very thin. Sauté in butter until just transparent. Salt to taste.

Oil a shallow baking dish with olive oil. Arrange fillets on baking dish and sprinkle with salt and pepper. Cover with the sautéed onions and sprinkle with buttered crumbs. Bake in a hot oven (400°) 12 to 15 minutes or until fish is cooked. Sprinkle with parsley and bacon. Serve at once. *(Serves 4.)*

Baked Fillets, Polish Style

4 large fish fillets	3 tablespoons chopped
Olive oil or butter	fresh dill
Bread crumbs	½ cup sour cream
Salt	Chopped parsley
3 medium-sized onions	

Oil a loaf tin well with olive oil or butter. Sprinkle heavily with bread crumbs. Place in it, in alternate layers, fish fillets, onions (sliced paper-thin and sprinkled with salt), chopped fresh dill, and a spreading of sour cream. Top with a layer of sour cream and mask the sides thickly with sour cream. Bake in a moderately hot oven (375°) approximately 25 minutes or until sour cream is a golden color.

Unmold the loaf, sprinkle with chopped parsley and dill, and serve at once. The onions will not be cooked through but will flavor the fish and be of an interesting texture. This should be cut in slices rather than by lifting off the layers of fillets. *(Serves 4.)*

OTHER FISH RECIPES

Baked Salmon with Seafood Stuffing

6- or 7-pound salmon	1 cup buttered crumbs
1 small onion, finely	1 cup crabmeat or small
chopped	cooked shrimp
Butter	2 egg yolks
5 mushrooms, sliced thin	6 or 7 strips bacon
Salt and pepper	1 cup red wine
Few sprigs of thyme	Flour
Parsley	

Have the head of the salmon removed, and clean the fish well. Sauté onion in 4 tablespoons butter until just transparent. Add mushrooms, 1 teaspoon salt, thyme, and 3 tablespoons chopped parsley. Combine mixture with buttered crumbs and crabmeat or shrimp, and bind with egg yolks. Stuff the salmon and secure with toothpicks or skewers. Place the fish in a well-oiled baking pan. Slash the sides in 2 or 3 places, strip with bacon or dot with butter, and sprinkle with salt and pepper. Add red wine to the pan and place in a preheated, very hot (475°) oven.

After 10 minutes reduce heat to 350° and continue baking until cooked, allowing 10 minutes per pound for the first 4 pounds and 5 minutes for each additional pound. Baste with the wine and drippings in the pan, adding more wine if needed. Thicken the liquor with balls of butter and flour. Or pour sauce from the pan over the fish. Surround the platter with plenty of parsley which has been

fried in deep fat for 1 to 2 minutes.

(Serves 6 to 8.)

Baked Striped Bass

3- to 5-pound striped bass	Salt and pepper
Spanish onion	Butter
Ripe tomatoes	1 cup red wine
Chopped parsley	Flour

Have the backbone of the bass removed. Oil the inside surface well and stuff with thin slices of Spanish onion, slices of ripe peeled tomatoes, and plenty of chopped parsley. Sprinkle with salt and pepper to taste. Place the fish in a flat baking pan and dot liberally with butter. Bake in a hot oven (400°) for 5 minutes.

Add wine to the pan and baste the fish. Continue baking, allowing approximately 6 to 7 minutes per pound of fish. Baste 2 or 3 times during cooking process. Remove the fish to a hot platter and pour the sauce from the pan over the fish, or thicken with small balls of flour and butter, mixed. *(Serves 4.)*

Baked Boned Shad

Have the shad boned by the fish dealer. A good shad boner is born, or, at the very least, highly trained; not developed at home. If you have no one to bone your shad, have it dressed whole, but be prepared for countless fine bones in the delicious meat.

Arrange the shad, skin side down, in a well-oiled baking dish. Sprinkle with salt and dot liberally with butter. Bake in a preheated hot oven (400°), basting occasionally until shad is lightly browned and tender when tested with a toothpick. Allow about 6-7 minutes per pound. Cover liberally with parsley butter and sprinkle with lemon juice. This is most delicious stuffed and baked with the roe.

Shad Roe

Many people think shad roe should be parboiled or broiled, but such is not the case. This makes it hard and dry, whereas shad roe should be tender and juicy. For 1 pair of roe, melt 6 tablespoons butter in a skillet but do not let it get hot and smoking. Dip the roe lightly in flour and place in the pan, dipping both sides in the melted butter. Cover and let simmer in the butter, turning once during the cooking process. Season with salt and lemon juice, and serve with crisp bacon or with baked shad.

Planked Baked Fish

Use whitefish, shad, bluefish, sea trout, or striped bass for planking. Choose an oak, hickory or ash plank. Oil the plank well, place it in a cold oven, and heat the oven to very hot (450°). Clean the fish. You may bake the fish whole or split. If it is whole, bake it skin side down and baste it often. Salt and pepper the fish and rub it well with olive oil or dot with butter. Remove the hot plank from the oven and place the fish in the middle of the plank, reserving room for the decorations, and brush the exposed part of the plank with more oil. Place the plank in the oven and bake for 15 minutes, basting twice. If you use split fish the cooking time will be less. Test the fish with a toothpick and baste frequently.

Reduce the heat to hot (400°) and continue baking for 10 minutes. Remove from the oven and surround with mashed potatoes which have been whipped with plenty of butter and cream. You may also arrange vegetables around the fish if you wish. Brush the potatoes with a little beaten egg yolk and return to the oven for 4 minutes or run under the broiler for a few minutes to brown. Spread the fish with parsley butter and surround with lemon wedges and some parsley which has been fried in deep fat for 1 or 2 minutes. Serve at once on the plank.

VARIATIONS

With Vegetables: If you wish to make an elaborate dish, force the mashed potatoes through a pastry tube in any form you desire and arrange an array of vegetables, such as small whole tomatoes, frenched string beans, and asparagus tips, around the fish. Decorate the fish with lemon slices and rings of green pepper and chopped parsley.

With Cucumber Hollandaise: Proceed as above. Decorate fish with sautéed mushroom caps, sautéed fresh shrimp, and lemon slices. Serve with a cucumber Hollandaise sauce.

Maryland Fish Stew

1 pound salt pork	Salt and pepper
3 pounds filleted fish	4 tablespoons chopped
6 raw potatoes, sliced thin	parsley
4 medium-sized raw	4 cups tomato juice
onions, sliced thin	6 eggs

Traditionally, this is made in an iron kettle, but an iron Dutch oven or any heavy pot will do. Try out salt pork, cut in small dice, until crisp. Remove the crisped pork, drain on absorbent paper, and reserve in a hot place.

Using the pork fat for a base, place a layer of filleted fish (sea trout, rock cod, flounder, haddock, or other fish), cut into 4-inch strips, in the kettle. Arrange alternate layers of fish, thinly sliced raw potatoes, and thinly sliced raw onion until the kettle is ¾ full. Sprinkle each layer with salt, pepper, and chopped parsley. Pour over this enough tomato juice to cover the top layer. Simmer slowly until potatoes are tender. Add additional liquid if it cooks down too quickly. Just before serving, drop eggs on top to poach in the broth. Sprinkle crisp salt pork pieces over top. Serve with hot cornbread. *(Serves 6.)*

Chiopino

½ cup olive oil	1 cup tomatoe purée
1 tablespoon chopped garlic	Salt and pepper
	Paprika
1 tablespoon chopped parsley	1 cup red wine
	Few leaves of sweet basil
1 tablespoon chopped celery	2 dozen clams
1 tablespoon chopped green pepper	3 pounds filleted fish (bass, haddock, cod)
	1 pound raw shrimp
2 cups solid-pack tomatoes	1 small lobster or crab

Chiopino is a fish stew that seems to be native to northern California. It is served to many a tourist on Fisherman's Wharf in San Francisco, though originally it was an outdoor dish along the coast.

Heat olive oil in a Dutch oven or a large kettle. Sauté garlic, parsley, celery, and green pepper until lightly browned. Add solid-pack tomatoes and tomato purée. Season to taste with salt, pepper, and paprika, and add red wine and sweet basil. Simmer 1 hour.

During this time wash clams well and steam in very little water just until the shells open. Strain the liquid from the clams and add to the sauce. Cut fish into small pieces. Shell raw shrimp and cut up lobster with shell or clean and break up a crab. After the sauce is cooked, add the prepared fish, shrimp, and lobster or crab, and cook until done. Add clams at the very last. Serve the stew in bowls accompanied by red wine and plenty of toasted French bread. *(Serves 6.)*

Whitebait

Whitebait are tiny fish, about the size of baby sardines, which are most delicious. Merely wash them well, for they are eaten heads and all. Roll them in corn meal and sauté quickly in olive oil, turning carefully with a wooden spoon. They will brown lightly and become quite crisp on the outside. Serve with wedges of lemon.

Whitebait Pancakes

1 pound whitebait	¼ cup grated Parmesan
3 eggs	cheese
3 tablespoons chopped	Salt and pepper
parsley	Chopped sweet basil
1 finely chopped clove of	Flour
garlic	Olive oil

Wash and drain whitebait. Place in a large mixing bowl with eggs, parsley, garlic, Par-mesan cheese, salt and pepper, and a little basil. Mix with enough flour to hold the fish together—approximately 1 cup. Form into small cakes, sprinkle lightly with flour, and fry the cakes in olive oil until well browned and cooked through. Serve with a tartar sauce. *(Serves 4.)*

Sautéed Eels

3 pounds eels	2 or 3 cloves garlic
Flour	Salt and pepper
¼ cup olive oil	Chopped parsley

Have the fish dealer skin and clean the eels. Cut in 3-inch lengths and dredge with flour. Heat olive oil in a skillet and sauté garlic in the oil. Sauté the eels quickly until nicely browned on all sides, salt and pepper to taste, and sprinkle liberally with chopped parsley. *(Serves 4.)*

SHELLFISH

LOBSTER

Lobsters should be purchased alive, although they may be bought cooked. Frozen lobster meat may be bought in 1-pound cans. Quick-frozen lobster tails from South Africa are available in most shops. There is a great difference between the North Atlantic Coast lobster and the so-called lobster or Langouste of the Gulf and the Pacific Coasts, the most obvious difference being in the claws. An Eastern lobster has large, meaty claws, while the Langouste's are small.

Small lobsters under 2 pounds are the most delicate and desirable. Larger ones tend to be tough. The tail carries the great part of the good meat. The white flesh of the claws and the body, the roe, and the liver of the lobster are all edible. The shell of a live lobster is a mottled green and red, which turns to a bright red when cooked.

To Split a Lobster: Lay the lobster on its back. Using a large French knife or a kitchen cleaver, make a deep incision down the center of the lobster from head to the end of the tail. Give the knife or the cleaver one quick blow with a hammer so that the shell and the meat are severed at one time. The splitting may also be performed with a pair of heavy kitchen scissors, cutting through the shell and the meat. Remove the dark vein that runs through the body at the center, using a very sharp knife. Also remove the stomach or "lady." The green liver and the "coral" or roe are considered a delicacy. The spongy material at the side of the body is the lungs, which are not edible.

Boiled Lobster

Bring a large pot of salted water or a court-bouillon (page 53) to a rolling boil. Grasp the live lobster by the middle of the back and push it into the boiling water headfirst. Cover the pot and simmer 15 minutes. Then cool the lobster in the liquor.

To serve boiled lobster, which may be eaten hot or cold, arrange lobster halves on serving plates or a platter, removing the claws and cracking them lightly with a nutcracker. Hot boiled lobster may be served with melted butter, parsley butter, Hollandaise sauce, or a Sauce Mousseline.

If you have young chicken lobsters, serve one to a person; otherwise a half lobster will usually suffice. Cold lobster may be arranged attractively in the shell on a bed of watercress or other greens and served with mayonnaise, rémoulade, Ravigote, or vinaigrette sauce.

VARIATIONS

With Almonds: Cold lobster meat may be removed from the shell and the claws and blended with almonds which have been blanched and shredded, and with any of the above sauces.

With Shrimp: Blend small shrimp with mayonnaise or rémoulade sauce and the meat from the body of the lobster. Reserve the meat which you have taken from the lobster claws. Return the shrimp mixture to the lobster shells, top with additional mayonnaise, arrange on a bed of greens or watercress, and garnish with quarters of hard-cooked egg and the claw meat from the lobster.

With Crabmeat: Proceed as above, substituting crabmeat for the shrimp.

Broiled Live Lobster

Split the live lobster (page 61). Brush the meat lavishly with melted butter, sprinkle with salt and pepper, spread the lobster out flat on a broiler rack, shell side down, and broil 4 inches from flame 12 to 14 minutes for small lobsters; 16 to 18 minutes for larger lobsters.

Remove the lobster to hot platter and serve with melted butter, parsley butter, or lemon butter. Garnish with lemon slices and parsley which has been fried in deep fat for a minute or two.

VARIATIONS

Fines Herbes: Sprinkle lobster with chopped chives and chopped parsley before brushing with butter or add mixed chives and parsley when broiled.

Maryland Style: Remove stomach and lungs from shell of the lobster. Stuff with crab meat, butter well, and broil as above.

With Crumbs: Sprinkle broiled lobster liberally with well-buttered crumbs before serving.

Lobster Fra Diavolo

1 lobster	½ small clove garlic
Pure olive oil	Salt and pepper
1 small bay leaf	Dash of cloves
4 sprigs fresh parsley	Dash of mace
1 sprig thyme	2½ cups fresh tomatoes
2 teaspoons finely chopped shallots	2 tablespoons brandy

Remove meat from a split live lobster, allowing 1½ pounds live weight per person. Fry meat in olive oil over a hot flame for 8 to 10 minutes, stirring constantly. Add a bouquet garni composed of bay leaf tied together with parsley, thyme, shallots, and garlic, mashed to a paste. Season to taste with salt and pepper. Add cloves and mace. Add tomatoes, stewed separately. Cover pan and cook over gentle heat about 20 minutes, stirring frequently. Discard the bouquet garni. Pour brandy over the lobster, and set the spirits aflame. Serve around a mound of plain boiled rice.

Baked Lobster

Prepare lobsters as for broiling. Sprinkle liberally with buttered crumbs, chopped parsley, and finely chopped shallots, and dot with butter. Bake in a moderately hot oven (375°) 25 to 30 minutes and serve as you would broiled lobster.

Baked Stuffed Lobster

Meat from 2 cooked lobsters	1 cup Béchamel sauce
½ cup toasted bread crumbs	2 tablespoons sherry
	Grated Parmesan cheese
	Buttered crumbs

Cut meat in good-sized serving pieces—do not chop or shred. Mix with crumbs and Béchamel sauce, flavored with the sherry. Stuff the lobster shells. Sprinkle with grated Parmesan cheese and buttered crumbs, and brown under the broiler 4 inches from flame.

(Serves 4.)

Lobster Newburg

2 cups lobster meat	1 cup heavy cream
4 tablespoons butter	3 egg yolks
¼ cup brandy	Salt and pepper

Sauté lobster meat, cut in large cubes, in butter for 5 minutes. Add brandy and blaze. In upper part of a double boiler heat cream which has been blended with egg yolks, stirring constantly until mixture coats the spoon. Combine this sauce with the lobster. Taste for seasoning. Blend well, and do not let the sauce cook after the lobster is added, or you will have a curdled sauce. Serve on crisp toast or in croustades. *(Serves 4.)*

SHRIMP

Shrimp abound in all United States coastal waters. They vary a great deal in size. The Alaskan shrimp are exceedingly small and sweet. Others range in length from those of 2 inches to the mammoth prawns, which often measure 7 inches. Shrimp are usually bought with the heads removed and the bodies packed in ice for shipment to the various markets. They are purchased either green (uncooked) or cooked and shelled and ready to eat. Green shrimp are bought in the shell and are better if shelled before cooking. When shelling shrimp, remove the intestinal vein which runs the length of the body and which is visible as a small black line just under the surface.

Boiled Shrimp

Shell shrimp and cover with court-bouillon (page 53). Cook the shrimp in the court-bouillon 5 to 8 minutes. Either drain or allow them to cool in their liquor.

Shrimp Cocktail

Arrange boiled shrimp on a bed of water-cress or other greens. Or arrange them in a cocktail glass surrounded by crushed ice. Serve with a sauce—cocktail rémoulade, Ravigote—or with mayonnaise.

French Fried Shrimp

Shell 2 pounds of green shrimp. Remove the black veins but leave the tails on. Then dip the shrimp into fritter batter or in beaten egg and roll in crumbs or cornmeal. Fry in deep, hot fat (380°) 4 to 7 minutes or until shrimp are brown. Serve with lemon butter, tartar sauce, or green mayonnaise. If shrimp are to be served as a main course, surround platter with French fried parsley. Shrimp prepared in this way may be served very successfully as a hot hors d'oeuvre.

(Serves 4.)

Sautéed Shrimp

6 tablespoons butter	2 tablespoons chopped
2 tablespoons finely	parsley
chopped shallots	½ cup heavy cream
2 to 3 cups cooked shrimp	Salt
1 teaspoon curry	

Melt butter in a skillet and cook shallots until just transparent. Add cooked shrimp to the pan, tossing to brown them lightly. Add parsley, curry, and heavy cream. Salt to taste and allow to simmer 3 to 4 minutes. Serve on rice, crisp toast or toasted English muffins.

(Serves 4.)

Shrimp and Corn Sauté

1½ cups corn kernels	1½ cups cooked shelled
1 green pepper, seeded	shrimp
and finely chopped	Salt and pepper
4 tablespoons butter	Paprika
½ cup heavy cream	

Sauté corn kernels (fresh, canned, or quick-frozen) with green pepper in butter. Add shrimp and heavy cream. Cover and let the mixture simmer 3 or 4 minutes or until shrimp are heated through. Add salt and pepper to taste. Sprinkle with paprika and serve as a main course for luncheon. Crisp French bread and green celery complement this dish.

(Serves 4.)

CRABS

Mature crabs are hard-shelled. As a young crab grows, the shell is shed. The new shell hardens in 2 or 3 days. A crab caught during this period is called soft-shelled. Such crabs are in season from May to October. They should be cleaned by the fish dealer.

Crabs may be bought alive or cooked. Crabmeat is available by the pound.

To clean a Dungeness crab, break off claws and legs and crack the shells. Remove back and intestine, then slice the body with a sharp knife. With care, pick out the meat from claws and body with a nut pick or a long-tined fork, removing the bits of shell.

Crabmeat or cracked crab may be served with any of the salad or seafood sauces, such as rémoulade, Ravigote, mayonnaise, or Russian dressing, mentioned in the chapter on Sauces. Crabs are often served cracked, a half to a whole crab per person. Each person must extricate the meat from the shells and dip it into sauce.

Deviled Crab

1 pound lump crabmeat	2 tablespoons finely
1½ cups toasted bread	chopped celery
crumbs	3 eggs
6 mushroom caps, thinly	½ cup cream
sliced	1 teaspoon salt
2 tablespoons finely	½ teaspoon pepper
chopped onion	Few leaves dried tarragon
2 tablespoons finely	Butter
chopped parsley	

Add to crabmeat bread crumbs, mushroom caps, onion, parsley, celery, eggs, cream, salt, pepper, and dried tarragon. Mix thoroughly and pile into individual ramekins or shells. Top with bread crumbs and dot with butter. Bake 15 minutes in a hot oven (400°) or brown under the broiler. Serve very hot.

(Serves 4.)

Creamed Crab

1½ cups Béchamel sauce	½ teaspoon black pepper
4 tablespoons butter	2 tablespoons parsley
1 pound lump crab meat	½ cup blanched, shredded
1 tablespoon grated onion	almonds
1 teaspoon salt	3 tablespoons dry sherry

Prepare Béchamel sauce first. Then sauté crabmeat in butter with grated onion, salt, black pepper, parsley, and almonds. Combine crabmeat and sauce, and add sherry. Serve on rice or toast, or serve in croustades. Sprinkle liberally with chopped parsley and a few shredded almonds. This mixture may also be folded into an omelet. *(Serves 4.)*

Soft-Shelled Crabs Sauté

Have 12 small soft-shelled crabs cleaned by the fish dealer. Melt ½ cup butter in a large skillet. Place the crabs, back side down, in the hot butter and sauté 5 minutes. Season with salt and pepper. Turn and cook 3 minutes more. Serve very hot with tartar sauce or parsley butter. *(Serves 4)*

VARIATIONS

Amandine: ¼ cup blanched, shelled almonds may be sautéed with the crabs.

Fines Herbes: Add 2 tablespoons chopped parsley, 2 tablespoons chopped chives, and 1 tablespoon chopped tarragon to the pan when sautéing crabs.

CLAMS

Clams come in soft-shelled and hard-shelled forms. Quahogs are round, hard-shelled clams from the Atlantic Coast. The small clams such as small young quahogs, or little necks, and the cherrystones are excellent served raw on the half shell or in seafood cocktails. Soft-shelled clams have a light shell and long neck and are found both in the Atlantic and the Pacific. They are excellent for steaming and are also used for frying, for broth, and for roasting at clambakes. Razor clams are native to the Pacific Coast and resemble an old-fashioned razor in shape. The tender part is excellent in a cocktail or sautéed in butter. The whole clam is sometimes cleaned and fried. It is excellent when ground for use in sauces, chowders, and omelets.

Clams on the Half Shell

If you wish to serve raw clams, have the fish dealer open the clams for you. Serve on the half shell on a bed of ice with lemon, salt, and pepper, or with any desired cocktail sauce.

Steamed Clams

Soft-shelled clams or little necks are best for steaming. Allow about 18 clams per person.

Place the clams in a shallow pan with enough water barely to cover. Sprinkle a small amount of cornmeal over them and let them stand a few hours. The cornmeal will be absorbed in their systems, help to clean out the sand, and give a good flavor.

Scrub the clams thoroughly and rinse. Place an inch of water in a large kettle, cover, and steam over a gentle flame until the shells partially open. Serve very hot, with individual dishes of melted butter and the broth.

Clam Broth

Use 4 dozen hard-shelled or little neck clams, 1 onion, and a stalk of celery. Simmer 1 hour and strain through cheesecloth. Discard clams. *(Serves 4.)*

Clam Chowder

2 dozen small little neck clams	1 large potato, peeled and cut in small pieces
¼ cup diced salt pork or bacon	1 cup water
	Salt and pepper
3 small onions, finely diced	1 cup heavy cream
	Pinch of thyme

Steam little neck clams until they open. Remove from the shells and reserve the broth.

Render salt pork or bacon until crisp. Remove the crisp bacon or salt pork to absorbent paper. Sauté onions in the pork fat.

Cook potato in water until tender. Season with salt and pepper.

Combine the onions, potato and clam broth and cook in the upper part of a double boiler until it reaches the boiling point. Add heavy cream and stir until the mixture is well blended and heated through. Add clams and allow them just to heat. Season to taste. Add a pinch of thyme and lastly add the diced crisp bacon or salt pork. Serve immediately with toasted crackers. *(Serves 4.)*

Mussels Mariniéres

48 mussels	1½ teaspoons flour
6 shallots, finely chopped	1 tablespoon chopped parsley
4 tablespoons butter	
1 cup dry white wine	

Clean and brush mussels thoroughly. Place them in a saucepan with the shallots and white wine. Cook for several minutes until they open. Remove the mussels to a serving dish and reduce the liquid in the pan to about half its quantity. To thicken, stir in flour and butter kneaded together. Perfect the seasoning and add parsley. Pour over the mussels. Serve at once.

Clam Soup

2 cans minced clams	2 egg yolks
2 tablespoons butter	Dash of paprika
1 cup heavy cream	

Put minced clams and their liquid in upper part of a double boiler. Add butter and heavy cream which has been blended with egg yolks. Stir until slightly thickened but do not allow to boil. Serve in cups with a dash of paprika. *(Serves 4.)*

The choicest scallops to be had are the small bay scallops, about ½ inch thick and a pinkish white. They are in season from early fall until late spring. The larger, or deep-sea, scallops are in season the year around.

Scallops may be either sautéed in butter, dipped in fritter batter and fried in deep hot fat (380°), or dipped in melted butter and broiled very quickly. They are often served with crisp bacon or in combination with other seafood dishes. Tiny bay scallops, served raw with a cocktail sauce (page 36), will be found very palatable.

Baked Seafood in Shells

½ cup small shrimp or large shrimp cut in small pieces	4 tablespoons butter
	Salt and pepper
	1½ cups sauce Velouté
½ cup crabmeat	Buttered crumbs
½ cup bay scallops	Grated Parmesan cheese

Combine small shrimp or large shrimp cut in small pieces, crabmeat, and bay scallops. Sauté in butter 4 or 5 minutes. Season with salt and pepper to taste. Combine with sauce Velouté and pile in individual shells or small ramekins. Top with additional sauce Velouté. Sprinkle with buttered crumbs and grated Parmesan cheese and brown quickly under the broiler. Serve very hot. *(Serves 4.)*

POULTRY

CHICKENS

Chickens, like other poultry, are divided into certain grades for the market. These are the categories into which they fall:

Birds may be listed as near-by or fresh-killed poultry, meaning that they have been killed and chilled not long before being sent to market. Cold-packed or chilled poultry is that which has been kept in cold storage. These birds if kept too long lose a good deal of their flavor. Quick-frozen birds, which are disjointed or frozen dressed ready for the table, are excellent and may be cooked either thawed or frozen. One thing to remember is never to refreeze a frozen bird after it has thawed.

BASIC PROCEDURES

Broilers are 7 to 12 weeks old. They range from 1 to 2½ pounds. The 1-pound broilers are sometimes called "squab broilers" and are often served whole—one to a person. The larger ones are usually split or quartered, and broiled or sautéed. They may also be roasted very quickly. Half a broiler is usually considered a portion, except for the very large ones. Naturally, if they are to be sautéed, the birds are disjointed.

Fryers may be birds of either sex from 14 to 20 weeks old and ranging from 1 to 3½ pounds. The best ones have a full, plump breast, compact structure, and some fat. They may be split, cut, or disjointed for cooking, and are used for frying, sautés, and roasting.

These are chickens of either sex from 5 to 10 months old. A roasting chicken should have a soft, pliable breastbone in addition to the structural qualities governing selection of broilers and fryers. Do not pick one with long hairs on it, for this denotes age and lack of care. Roasting chickens are used not only for roasting but for casserole dishes and may be used for fricassees and for boiling, although the flavor is not as good as that of a fowl for the latter methods of preparation.

A mature hen is called a fowl. It is probably the most flavorful of all chickens, although it requires long, slow cooking—either braising, fricasseeing, or boiling, which is more correctly called poaching. They range from 3 to 8 pounds and are usually quite fat. The excess fat may be used for cooking; it will be found ideal for certain dishes. A fowl is either prepared whole or cut into convenient-sized serving pieces.

Unsexed male birds. They are at their best from 6 months to a year old. Because of the more or less inactive life they lead, they develop into large and delicately fleshed birds. Often weighing as much as 8 or 9 pounds, a capon is an excellent buy for roasting, braising, or serving cold.

Drawing: It is seldom that one buys a bird without having it drawn, but if you do, this is the way to attack it.

Singe the bird first over a flame to remove the fuzz and, if there are additional pinfeathers, extract them with a pair of tweezers. Cut a small hole in the vent with a pair of sharp kitchen shears or a sharp knife. Make the incision as small as possible, especially if you are going to stuff the bird. Insert your fingers and loosen and remove the intestines carefully, making sure to remove the gall sac, which is attached to the liver, without breaking it. Separate the liver, heart, and gizzard from the other intestines.

To clean the gizzard, cut through the thickest part and remove the lining and the inner sac. With a very sharp knife cut the flesh away from the gristly lining of the gizzard.

Cut through the skin at the back of the neck and remove the neck, the windpipe, and the crop. Cut out the oil sac above the tail and discard it. Wash the interior of the bird and wipe the exterior with a damp cloth.

To Disjoint a Chicken: With a very sharp knife, cut through the skin around the thigh. Cut through the joint which joins the thigh to the body and remove the leg and thigh. You may separate leg and thigh at the knee joint also, if you wish. Cut through the joint at the base of the wing, and either remove the wing entirely by cutting it away from the breast at the joint or tear off the long strip of white meat from the breastbone with the aid of your knife. The latter is the proper procedure if you are to sauté a young chicken.

Remove the other leg and thigh and the other wing. Split the chicken in two with a sharp knife or small cleaver, separating the breast from the back and rib cage. The breast may then be cut into two pieces, the back separated from the rib cage, and the back disjointed into two pieces as well.

Remember *not* to use a fine stainless steel knife when cutting the joints and bones. Have a heavy-duty knife in your kitchen which you use for that purpose and take it to your butcher to have it sharpened from time to time.

BROILED CHICKEN

Broiling is the simplest method of preparing chicken. A broiled chicken can be exceedingly delicious or very uninteresting. The secret of good broiling is a constant and even heat and plenty of lubrication. High-heat broiling with a quick searing tends to dry and toughen the flesh and make the resulting dish totally unpalatable.

If you are cooking more than one bird, see that you purchase those of uniform size so that the cooking time will be the same for all.
Preparation: Broilers (except for squab broilers, which are left whole) are split down the back. Ask your butcher to remove the spinal column and the neck; or if you are splitting the broiler yourself, use a very sharp, small knife and cut along both sides of the spinal column and remove the entire piece with the neck. Next remove some of the breastbone so that the chicken will lie flat in the pan or on the rack.

Clean your birds, singe and clean the skin, and allow to stand at room temperature for an hour before cooking. Quick-frozen birds will need no preparation other than thawing.
Broiling: Preheat the broiler. Or if you are using charcoal, build a bed of coals and place the bird 3 to 4 inches from it.

Rub the outside of the chicken well with oil or butter, and sprinkle with salt and pepper. Place the chicken on the broiling rack, skin side down, so that the bony side is about 3 inches from the flame. Allow the chicken to cook 12 to 20 minutes, according to size, before turning.

Turn the skin side up, brush well with butter or oil, sprinkle with salt and pepper and a little paprika, and allow the broilers to cook until done.

To test for doneness, cut into the flesh of the thigh; if there is still red juice running, the chicken needs additional cooking. White meat cooks more quickly than dark meat, and as a consequence one should always test the dark. I prefer the dark meat to have just a blush of pink and therefore never allow the chicken to cook until it is thoroughly well done, for then the flesh tends to be dry.

Serve the chicken at once on a hot plate with the juices from the pan or additional butter. Sprinkle with chopped parsley just before serving, if desired.

Serve with tiny new potatoes browned in butter or with crisp shoestring potatoes. Peas cooked with tiny white onions in plenty of butter are an excellent accompaniment, though I prefer them served after the chicken course. Some crusty French bread or a roll is a necessity so that one may sop up all the goodness on the plate.

VARIATIONS

Parsleyed Broilers: Proceed as in basic recipe. After removing chickens from broiler, roll the skin side in finely chopped parsley before serving. Pour juices from pan over the chickens and serve at once.

Deviled Broilers: Proceed as in basic recipe. When broilers are cooked, roll in buttered crisp crumbs. Press firmly into crumbs, holding hot broilers with paper napkins or a cloth, so that your hands will not be burned. Return to the broiler for a few minutes to brown crumbs lightly. Serve with devil sauce.

Marinated Broilers: Mix together 1 cup olive oil, 3 shallots, finely chopped, 3 tablespoons chopped parsley, 1/2 teaspoon coarse-ground black pepper, 1 tablespoon wine vinegar, 1 tablespoon dried tarragon, and 1 teaspoon salt. Pour into shallow pan or deep platter.

Place 2 broilers (4 halves) skin side down in the mixture and allow to stand for 1 hour. Turn the broilers bone side down and allow to stand for another hour.

Before placing on broiling rack, turn each piece once again, so that each side of the halves will be well covered with the oil mixture. Use the herbed marinée for basting and oiling your chickens while they are cooking. *(Serves 4.)*

Herb-stuffed Broilers: Obtain two broilers. Chop very finely 1 cup parsley (Italian parsley if you can get it, for it has a much more delightful flavor and blends well with other herbs), 1 small bunch chives (enough to make about ¼ cup), and 3 or 4 sprigs fresh tarragon or 1 tablespoon dried tarragon. Mix thoroughly with 6 tablespoons softened butter and 1 teaspoon salt.

Loosen the skin covering the breast of the chicken by running a sharp-pointed knife between the skin and the flesh. Do this very carefully so that you do not pierce the skin. With the fingers and a spoon, stuff each broiler half with the herb mixture so that it completely covers the flesh of the breast and so that the breast surface is even. Oil the broilers well with butter or oil and proceed as for broiled chicken (page 68), being careful that the skin side of the broilers does not brown too quickly after you turn them over.

Serve with pan juices poured over the broilers. *(Serves 4.)*

Glazed Broilers: These are especially good cooked on the outdoor grill, although they are equally delicious as a supper or dinner dish indoors. They are prepared with a pungent barbecue sauce in which they should marinate for an hour. They should be brushed frequently during the cooking process with the same sauce.

Allow the broilers to marinate in 2 cups of the sauce for an hour. Place them on the broiling rack, brushing both sides with the barbecue sauce several times during the cooking.

Serve with cottage fried potatoes, green noodles, crisp French bread, and a good red wine, and pass additional barbecue sauce. For an outdoor meal a good Chianti is a very good choice. Complete the meal with a green salad and some excellent cheese.

CHICKEN SAUTE

Many people confuse frying and sautéing. Frying really means to fry in deep fat or enough fat to cover the particular article being fried. Sautéing means to cook in a small amount of fat and to cook over a low flame for most of the process.

For chicken sauté, halves, quarters, or convenient-sized serving pieces of chicken may be used.

Melt the fat in the pan or heat it until hot but not burning. Butter or olive oil, or occasionally bacon fat, is used for sautés. Sometimes one combines butter and olive oil. Place the chicken in the pan and brown quickly on both sides. Reduce the heat when the chicken is nicely browned, cover, continue cooking. The pan is covered for the latter part of the process so that the chicken becomes tenderized more quickly and the cooking is thus accelerated. Test the chicken with a fork or toothpick to determine its state of doneness.

Midway in the cooking of a sauté, which takes from 25 to 35 minutes, the principal flavoring agents are introduced. These may be shallots, mushrooms, peppers, tomato sauce, herbs, or any of a variety of things.

It is sometimes wise to remove the white meat to a hot platter or dish when it is cooked and continue cooking the dark meat, for it is the white meat which cooks first. If you are making a sauce for the chicken, remove the chicken to a hot dish, make your sauce, and return the chicken to the pan for a few moments or pour the hot sauce over it before serving.

Chicken sauté is one of the simplest of dishes to prepare and perfect when entertaining a small number of people, for it does not need a great deal of preparation.

Plain Chicken Sauté

2- to 2½-pound broiler or young frying chicken	¼ cup dry white wine
Salt and pepper	1 tablespoon chopped parsley
6 tablespoons butter	

Disjoint the broiler or young frying chicken. Salt and pepper it. Melt butter in a large skillet. Allow the butter to become hot but not brown; it is right when it reaches the bubbly stage. Brown the chicken quickly on both sides. When nicely browned, reduce the flame and continue cooking, covering the pan for 10 minutes of the cooking time and allowing the chicken to cook very slowly. A 2- or 2½-pound chicken should take about 25 to 35 minutes to cook thoroughly without drying out.

When the chicken is cooked, remove to a hot platter. Add dry white wine to the pan and a generous tablespoon of chopped parsley. Rinse the pan well with the wine so that it blends with the juices of the pan, and pour over the chicken.

Serve at once with crisp toasted French bread. Chill the rest of the bottle of wine and drink it with your chicken. *(Serves 2 or 3.)*

VARIATIONS

With Mushrooms: Proceed as in basic recipe. When chicken is half cooked (after browning and cooking 12 minutes), add 4 shallots, finely chopped (if shallots are not available, use small white onions); 1 green pepper cut in small dice; and ½ cup sliced mushroom caps. If the additions to the pan absorb all the butter, you may find it necessary to add more butter. Remove the cooked chicken to a hot platter, add 2 tablespoons finely chopped parsley to the pan, and mix well with the other ingredients. Pour over the chicken before serving.

Herbed: Proceed as in basic recipe, and after 15 minutes' cooking add ¼ cup finely chopped mixed herbs—I suggest chives, parsley, tarragon, thyme, chervil. Turn the pieces of chicken well in this mixture and add ½ cup dry white wine. Allow the chicken to continue cooking until done. Remove the pieces to a hot platter, add ¼ cup more of the white wine to the pan, and blend with the other ingredients. Pour over the hot chicken and serve.

Amandine: Disjoint and prepare two 2-pound broilers as in basic recipe. Dredge with flour, salt, and pepper. (You may put the flour, salt, and pepper in a paper bag, add the chicken pieces, and shake it well. This gives a thorough coating which is more efficient than pressing each piece in flour.) Melt ½ cup butter in a large skillet. Brown the chicken well in the melted fat and, when nicely browned, reduce the flame and continue cooking. When the chicken has cooked for 10 to 12 minutes, add ½ cup blanched, thinly sliced almonds. Continue cooking till chicken is tender and almonds slightly browned. *(Serves 4.)*

Paprika: Prepare two 2-pound chickens for sauté (page 69). Disjoint and dredge with flour, pepper, and salt. Melt ½ cup butter in a large skillet, brown the chicken well on both sides, and reduce the flame. Add ¼

cup dry white wine and continue cooking. When the chicken is about half cooked, after about 12 to 15 minutes, add 2 small white onions, finely chopped, and 2 teaspoons Hungarian paprika. Turn the chicken well so that all the pieces are mixed with the paprika. Cover, and continue cooking for 5 minutes. Remove the cover and turn the chicken once more. When it is cooked, remove it to a hot platter and add to the pan 1 cup heavy cream. Blend well with the sauce in the pan, rectify the seasoning, and pour the hot sauce over the chicken.   *(Serves 4.)*

Italian: Prepare two 2-pound broilers for sauté (page 69). Salt and pepper the pieces. Heat 1/3 cup olive oil in a large skillet and brown the pieces of chicken on both sides in the hot oil. Reduce the flame and continue cooking. After 10 minutes add 1 clove garlic, finely minced; 3 small onions, finely chopped; 3 tablespoons chopped parsley, and 1/2 cup finely shredded Prosciutto (Italian-style ham). Mix well with the chicken pieces, add 1/2 cup red wine, and continue cooking for 5 minutes. Add 1 cup tomato purée (the Italian type) which has been simmered for 5 minutes

with 1 teaspoon dried basil or a few leaves of fresh basil. Turn the pieces of chicken so that they are thoroughly coated with the sauce mixture, and continue cooking until tender. Remove the chicken to a hot platter. If the sauce has cooked down and is too thick, add another 1/4 cup red wine. Pour the sauce over the chicken and sprinkle with chopped parsley.

With Bacon: Prepare two 2-pound chickens for sauté (page 69). Dredge with flour, salt, and pepper. Cook 6 or 8 rashers bacon in a large skillet until crisp. Remove the bacon to absorbent paper and brown the pieces of chicken on both sides in the hot bacon fat. Reduce the heat and continue cooking.

Midway in the cooking process—after about 12 minutes—add 4 finely chopped shallots and 2 tablespoons chopped parsley, and mix well with the chicken pieces. Cover and continue cooking until chicken is tender. Remove the chicken to a hot platter. Add 1/2 cup heavy cream to the sauce in the pan and mix well. Pour this over the chicken and sprinkle the crumbled bacon rashers over the top.   *(Serves 4.)*

Provençale: Prepare two 2-pound broilers for sauté (page 69). Heat 1/3 cup olive oil in a large skillet. Salt and pepper chicken and brown it well in the hot oil. Reduce the heat, add 1/4 cup dry white wine, and continue cooking.

After about 12 minutes add 1 clove finely chopped garlic and 2 medium onions, chopped, and allow to cook with the chicken for about 5 minutes. Add 6 or 8 medium-sized mushroom caps, thinly sliced, and the pulp of 3 tomatoes which have been peeled, seeded, and chopped in small dice. Turn the pieces of chicken so that the added seasonings become thoroughly distributed, and continue cooking until the chicken is tender.

Remove the chicken to a hot platter, add another 1/4 cup white wine, and blend well with the sauce in the pan. Taste for seasoning, add another tablespoon of chopped parsley, and pour the sauce over the chicken.

If glacé de viande is available in your community, a piece the size of a walnut added to the pan when the chicken is removed improves this dish.   *(Serves 4.)*

Poulet Vallé d'Auge

This delightful chicken dish, native to Normandy, is a true and delicious example of honest regional cookery. Poulet Vallé d'Auge commemorates the countryside of a land which is famed not only for its apple orchards but for its cream, butter, and dairy products and the general excellence of its food. Jeanne Owen has faithfully reproduced it for us in *A Wine Lover's Cook Book* * as follows:

"For four people:

"Two small chickens, each cut in 4 pieces. Sauté the pieces in ½ cup fresh butter, and when they are about half cooked pour over them ¼ or a scant ⅓ cup of Calvados (apple brandy) and blaze; then add 6 shallots, chopped, 1 tablespoonful of parsley, 1 sprig of fresh small-leafed thyme (it can be removed before serving), and salt and pepper. Blend well and add 6 tablespoons cider; cover and finish cooking. Just before serving add, slowly, 6 tablespoons thick cream, stirring it into the juices in the pan. Rectify the seasoning and serve."

Quick Curry of Chicken

2 small chickens	3 medium-sized white onions,
6 tablespoons butter	ground or chopped
Salt and pepper	1 tablespoon curry powder
⅓ cup dry white wine	½ cup coconut milk
	½ cup heavy cream

Prepare chickens for sauté (page 69). Heat butter in a large skillet until bubbly and add cut-up, salted, and peppered chicken. Brown well on both sides. When nicely browned, add ¼ cup dry white wine, reduce the heat, and continue cooking.

After 10 minutes add the white onions, put through the grinder or chopped very fine. To this add a tablespoon—or more, if you like a strong flavor of curry—of good curry powder mixed with 2 tablespoons white wine. Cover and cook for 10 to 12 minutes.

Remove the cover and test for tenderness, turning the chicken again so that all sides of the pieces are bathed in the curry sauce.

When the chicken is tender, remove the pieces to a hot platter and keep hot. Taste the sauce for seasoning and, if you feel that you need additional curry, add another tablespoon, or less. If fresh coconuts are available, add coconut milk. Failing this, add another ¼ cup white wine and blend with the sauce. Finally, add slowly heavy cream, stirring constantly.

Serve the chicken with fluffy rice and small dishes of chutney, grated fresh coconut, crumbled bacon, and slivered blanched almonds, and pass the sauce separately. *(Serves 4 to 6.)*

* Published by M. Barrows and Co., Inc., New York.

Chicken Sauté Marengo

For years there has been a gastronomical battle over this dish, which had its origin in necessity of the most exacting type. It was the night of June 14, 1800, after the battle of Marengo. It had been a victory marred only by the death of Desaix, and Napoleon had called his generals together and ordered food. The generals were far away from the source of provisions, and Dunan, the chef of Napoleon, was faced with providing a dinner from absolute scratch.

A resourceful man, Dunan inquired at a neighboring farm and found that he could acquire chickens. A garden close by offered only tomatoes and garlic. Dunan himself had a flask of oil and some cognac. He cleaned the chickens, sautéed them in the oil, added the tomatoes and the garlic, and swilled the pan with cognac.

Napoleon and the generals must have enjoyed it, for the dish has come down to our time, bearing the name of the battle site. Other chefs have added many things to the dish—crawfish, fried eggs, mushrooms, and practically everything else—and claimed it is the original. But to be truly a disciple of Dunan you will sauté your chickens in oil, add chopped tomatoes and crushed garlic, and rinse the pan well with cognac.

2 small broilers	½ cup tomatoes, peeled,
¼ cup olive oil	seeded, and cut fine
Salt and pepper	12 mushroom caps
1 clove garlic, crushed	2 tablespoons butter
1 jigger cognac	

Prepare broilers for sauté. Heat olive oil in a skillet and brown the pieces of chicken on both sides. Salt and pepper well, reduce the flame, and continue cooking. When the chicken is half cooked, after about 10 minutes, add garlic. When the chicken is tender, remove it to a hot platter and keep warm.

Add to the pan the tomatoes and 1 jigger cognac. Allow the tomatoes to cook down in the oil and cognac for 4 or 5 minutes or until the sauce is well blended. Serve with a garnish of sautéed mushroom caps, prepared by sautéing the caps in 2 tablespoons butter for 10 minutes, or until tender. Salt and pepper to taste, and serve with the chicken.

(Serves 4 to 6.)

FRIED CHICKEN

This is a subject that one hesitates to attack because of the constant bickering about method—the type of fat and the kind of cooking process that should be used. There are the batter school and the crumb school, the cream-gravy addicts and the deep-fat adherents, etc. One comes to feel that the greatest difference of opinion between the North and the South centers in the correct preparation of fried chicken.

Basically there are three or four generally accepted methods:

(1) The chicken, rolled in flour, is cooked in 1 inch of fat until well browned. Then it is either covered for continued cooking or placed in the oven to cook.

(2) The chicken is dipped in crumbs or batter and cooked in deep fat for 10 or 12 minutes, and then transferred to the oven.

(3) The chicken is dipped either in egg and crumbs or in batter, and cooked entirely on top of the stove in about 1 inch of fat.

Fats used for frying chicken include butter, which is by far the best; olive oil or vegetable oil, the former being preferable; lard; bacon fat; and vegetable shortening.

Batter fried chicken, widely known as fried chicken, Southern style, has a crisp, brown crust that is pleasant to look at on a plate, but I have found it disappointing to eat, for the chicken tends to dry out completely or to be rather slimy under its coating of batter.

Shenandoah Fried Chicken

2 3-pound fryers	Oil or leaf lard
3 eggs	Salt and pepper
½ cup milk	3 tablespoons flour
3 cups cracker crumbs	1 cup cream
½ cup flour	1 cup rich milk
Butter	

Cut fryers into convenient serving pieces. Beat eggs slightly and add milk. Pour into shallow bowl. Roll crackers rather coarsely until you have 3 cups. Spread on oiled paper. Sift ½ cup flour onto the paper. Preheat oven to moderate heat (350°). Have a 2-quart oven-proof casserole, or two smaller ones, ready at the stove.

Heat enough butter in a large skillet to give you 1 inch of melted fat. You may use oil; or, if you live in the country and have your own leaf lard, use that. The fat should be very hot; if it is butter you are using, be careful it does not burn or darken.

Dip pieces of chicken in flour and in the egg mixture and roll well in crumbs. Place in hot fat, being careful not to crowd the pan. Brown well on both sides, turning with a spoon and fork or with kitchen tongs. Salt and pepper well and, when golden brown, transfer pieces of chicken to casserole and place in preheated oven. Proceed until all chicken is browned, adding more fat if necessary. Allow chicken about 18 to 22 minutes in the oven.

Remove all the fat from the skillet except 3 tablespoons, leaving the bits of chicken and crumbs which have browned in the pan. Blend 3 tablespoons flour with the fat and slowly add cream and milk. Stir until thickened, and salt and pepper to taste.

Mashed potatoes or boiled new potatoes are traditional with this dish. So are corn on the cob or corn fritters. During the last century, surprisingly, fried parsley was considered a perfect accompaniment, and it is.

(Serves 6.)

Creole Fried Chicken

2 2½-pound fryers	¾ cup flour
2 eggs	Salt and pepper
½ cup milk	Fat
1½ cups dry bread crumbs	

Cut frying chickens into serving pieces. Beat eggs slightly and mix with milk. Place the chicken pieces in a shallow bowl and pour the egg-and-milk mixture over the pieces. Allow to stand for 2 hours.

Mix crumbs and flour together and season well with salt and pepper.

Heat enough fat in a large skillet to make a depth of 1½ inches. When the fat is hot, remove pieces of chicken from the egg mixture, dip into the crumb-and-flour mixture, and place in the hot fat. Brown quickly on both sides, then cook, covered, for 10 minutes. Then uncover and cook until tender.

When the chicken is tender, remove to absorbent paper for a minute or two and arrange on platter. Serve with cream gravy, as above, boiled rice, sautéed corn, and hot biscuits. *(Serves 6.)*

VARIATIONS

With Corn Meal: Proceed as above, omitting the flour and crumbs and substituting corn meal.

With Flour: Omit egg mixture and crumbs and merely dredge chicken pieces well with flour.

CHICKEN FRICASSEE

Different parts of the world have different ideas as to what a fricassee really is. In this country the accepted form is to poach a chicken until tender, add a roux of butter and flour to the broth, and serve the chicken with dumplings or noodles or rice. In some countries a fricassee is browned and cooked with stock until tender and served with various vegetables. A sauce thickened with egg yolk and cream is very often served with this. Other cooks use white wine as the cooking liquid for both fowl and vegetables, and the sauce has, in addition to the cream and egg yolk, a squeeze of lemon juice.

The best type of bird to use for a fricassee is a fowl, which takes slow simmering to tenderize it. The extra labor of preparing this most flavorful of chicken dishes is well repaid.

Chicken Fricassee, American Style

4- or 5-pound fowl	2 tablespoons butter
1 onion	2 tablespoons flour
2 cloves	1 cup cream
1 bay leaf	2 egg yolks
Parsley	Lemon juice
About 2 teaspoons salt	

Singe, clean, and disjoint the fowl. Place the fowl in a large kettle with the onion stuck with cloves, a bay leaf, and a large sprig of parsley. Cover with cold water and place over a medium heat until it barely reaches the boiling point. Turn the heat down low, cover, and simmer for an hour.

Test for tenderness with a fork at the end of an hour and add ½ teaspoon salt per pound of chicken. Continue simmering until the chicken is tender but not mushy. (Chicken that literally "falls off the bones" is never flavorful or pleasant in texture.) The cooking time depends entirely upon the age and tenderness of your fowl.

Remove the pieces of chicken from the broth and place them in a bowl or casserole, and keep them warm. Skim the fat which has risen to the top of the broth and strain the broth through a fine sieve lined with two thicknesses of cheesecloth.

Melt butter in a skillet and add to it flour. Blend well over a low flame until you have a thick paste. Gradually add 2 cups of the chicken broth, stirring constantly, and allow it to thicken slightly. Add, stirring constantly, cream mixed with egg yolks. Stir until it is thoroughly blended but do not allow to boil. Rectify the seasoning; add a generous sprinkling of chopped parsley and just a squeeze of lemon juice.

Arrange chicken on platter, surround with mounds of boiled rice or buttered noodles, and cover with the sauce. Sprinkle a little additional parsley on top.

In addition to the noodles or rice, a green vegetable such as peas or Frenched green beans is excellent with this dish. A good salad of greens with a French dressing or a fruit dessert of some sort is a fitting end to this meal, for it is hearty fare. *(Serves 4 to 6.)*

VARIATIONS

Chicken Paprika: Add 2 or more teaspoons Hungarian paprika to the butter-and-flour mixture when making your sauce. Proceed as above, but omit the chopped parsley. Sprinkle paprika on top when serving.

With Corn Bread: When chicken is removed from the broth, cut meat from the bones in large sections for serving. Prepare sauce and add to it the chicken pieces and 12 mushroom caps which have been sautéed in butter. Blend well and serve over thin squares of hot corn bread, or serve with spoon bread.

Chicken Pie: Place pieces of chicken (prepared as in basic recipe) in a 2-quart casserole with 12 sautéed mushroom caps and top with a rich biscuit dough rolled out to a thickness of ⅜ inch. Be certain you have something in the center of the casserole to hold up the crust—there are several types of holders for crust on the market—which may be placed in any sort of deep pan when baking.

Biscuit Topping

Sift 2 cups self-rising flour and measure it into a bowl. Add 5 tablespoons butter and cut it into the flour. When well blended add enough milk, mixing it in with a wooden spoon, to make a very soft dough. Roll out on a floured board, knead dough slightly, and roll to about ½ inch thick. Wrap dough around a rolling pin or a large bottle and transfer it to top of casserole and unroll, taking care to cover the edge. Bake in a hot oven (450°) 15 minutes. You may add 2 tablespoons finely chopped parsley to biscuit dough when mixing.

A BIRD
IN THE HAND...

CHICKEN TODAY

FEATHERS TOMORROW

Brown Fricassee of Chicken

3- to 4-pound fryer	½ cup parsley, chopped
12 to 14 small carrots	1 cup flour
7 tablespoons butter	Salt and pepper
18 to 20 very small white onions	Chicken or veal stock or 2 chicken bouillon cubes
15 small mushrooms	¾ cup heavy cream

Singe, clean, and disjoint the frying chicken. Scrape and clean carrots and brown in 3 tablespoons butter over a medium flame. Peel onions. Clean and cap the mushrooms. Chop enough parsley to make ½ cup. Sift the flour and spread it on a piece of oiled paper. Dredge the chicken pieces in the flour, and salt and pepper each piece.

Melt 4 tablespoons butter in a deep, covered skillet. Brown the pieces of chicken on each side until a golden brown. Reduce the heat and add enough hot chicken or veal stock to cover the chicken. If you do not have stock, use 2 chicken bouillon cubes dissolved in boiling water. Cover the pan and allow to simmer about 15 minutes.

Add the carrots and onions and continue cooking, adding the mushrooms about 5 minutes before the chicken is cooked. This should take from 30 to 50 minutes, according to the size of the chicken.

Remove the pieces of chicken and vegetables to a hot platter or casserole, add chopped parsley to the pan, and allow it to cook for 3 or 4 minutes. Add, slowly, the heavy cream and blend well with the sauce. Rectify the seasoning and pour the sauce over the chicken.

Serve with boiled rice or buttered noodles.

(Serves 4 to 6.)

VARIATION

Chicken à l'Angevine: The same fricassee may be prepared by substituting a white wine (in the traditional French preparation it is made with an Anjou wine) for the stock. Add the cream at the end and blend in the same way, then add a bit of lemon juice.

POACHED (BOILED) CHICKEN

Boiled chicken is not a very tempting term. *Poule au pot* and *pollo bollito*, the French and Italian versions of the same name, sound much more glamorous and interesting. But the flavor, if the dish is carefully prepared with the proper seasonings and attention, is just the same. However, by boiled chicken I do not mean the tired meat which remains after the making of a chicken broth, but the succulent dish which is the result of careful seasoning and close attention to the cooking.

A large fowl is the most satisfactory bird to serve in this fashion, although a roasting chicken or a large fryer is delightful prepared in the same manner. A favorite Jewish dish is boiled chicken with vegetables and matzoth balls, served with a large quantity of the broth. The French stuff the bird, sew it up tightly, and cook it very slowly along with a bit of veal and some bacon or salt pork. The broth is served first as a soup, with bits of the veal, then the meat and the stuffing as a main course. In this country boiled chicken is usually accompanied by very light dumplings.

Preparation: Choose a fowl of 5 or 6 pounds and singe, clean, and prepare it for cooking. If you are using a stuffing, sew up the vent very securely after stuffing so that the liquid will not seep into your stuffing during the cooking process. If you are not stuffing the bird, place 2 or 3 sprigs of parsley and a bay leaf inside the bird. Truss and tie the bird securely so that it will hold its shape during the cooking process. Place the fowl in a deep kettle with tightly fitting cover. In addition to salt (½ teaspoon per pound of chicken after 1 hour's cooking), you may add any or all of these things for seasoning:

Onions	Bay leaf
An onion stuck with 2 cloves	Thyme
Celery	Parsley
Carrot	Peppercorns

Cooking: Cover with boiling water. (Cold water draws the juices from the meat and boiling water seals them in.) Cover the pan and allow the chicken to simmer—not boil—until tender. The length of time depends entirely upon the weight and age of your bird. The only sure test to puncture the meat with a fork or a toothpick. Be certain that it is the dark meat that you test, for it is slower to tenderize than the white meat.

Remove the chicken, when cooked, to a hot platter or casserole. Strain the broth through a fine sieve lined with cheesecloth and return to the kettle. You may reduce the broth, if it seems too thin, by cooking it uncovered over high heat.

Serve the chicken as it comes from the pot, or serve some of the broth first and then the chicken, with any of the following:

(1) Steamed rice.

(2) Buttered noodles with small croutons.

(3) Dumplings. (Mix 2 cups flour, sifted with 4 teaspoons baking powder, with ½ teaspoon salt and about 1 cup milk. Toss together lightly with a fork until you have a very soft dough. Drop by spoonfuls into simmering chicken broth. Cover pan and allow to cook for 13 minutes without removing cover.)

(4) Macaroni or spaghetti.

(5) Potatoes mashed with plenty of butter and cream and whipped to a frothy lightness.

(6) Hot corn bread.

(7) Spoon bread.

(8) Hot baking-powder biscuits.

(9) Popovers.

Use the broth from cooking for a sauce or make a thicker sauce, as follows: To 2 cups of hot broth add 1 cup heavy cream mixed with 3 egg yolks. Stir constantly until the liquid has the texture of thick cream. Season with salt and pepper, and add a liberal quantity of chopped parsley.

VARIATIONS

With Vegetables: Add, during the last hour of cooking, 6 or 8 medium-sized onions, peeled, and 6 or 8 carrots, scraped and cleaned. Serve with the chicken.

Italian Style: Remove meat from bones after cooking and cut into large dice. Sauté, in 3 tablespoons olive oil, 1 large onion, finely chopped, and a clove of garlic. When the onion is just transparent, add 1 cup chicken broth and 1 cup Italian tomato paste. Season with 1 teaspoon salt, a few leaves of fresh basil (finely chopped) or a teaspoon of dried basil, 1 teaspoon ground black pepper, and 2 tablespoons chopped parsley. Allow this to simmer for 10 minutes and add to the chicken meat. Place over a very low flame to keep warm.

Cook 1 pound spaghetti or green noodles in boiling salted water until tender but not too soft—about 9 minutes. Arrange spaghetti or noodles on a platter and top with the chicken mixture. Serve with grated Parmesan cheese.

Stuffed: Stuff with your favorite stuffing, or try this one:

Sauté ½ pound sausage meat slowly until it is free of most of its fat. Cook 2 medium-sized onions, finely chopped, in 2 tablespoons butter until just transparent and add cleaned and finely chopped giblets. Add 1 tablespoon chopped parsley, 1 teaspoon salt, and ¼ teaspoon thyme. Cook gently for 5 minutes and add to 3 cups dry bread crumbs and mix well. Beat 6 egg yolks slightly, add to the mixture, and blend thoroughly with the other ingredients.

Stuff the chicken, taking care that the stuffing is not forced too tightly, or you will not have room enough for expansion. Cover the stuffing with a stale bread crust and sew up the vent securely to prevent seepage during cooking.

Place the chicken in a deep kettle with an onion stuck with 2 cloves, a bay leaf, 1 or 2 carrots, a sprig of parsley, and several peppercorns. Add 1 quart water and simmer until the chicken is tender, keeping the kettle tightly covered. After an hour's cooking add ½ teaspoon salt per pound of chicken. Turn the chicken.

Country Style: Prepare the chicken as described just above, with the following additions: Place in a deep cooking kettle 2 pounds brisket of beef, or the equivalent from the shank, and a small piece of salt pork. Cover with water, add an onion stuck with 2 cloves, a bay leaf, a generous sprig of parsley, 3 or 4 peppercorns, and 3 teaspoons salt. Allow to boil rapidly for 5 minutes.

Remove the scum from the top, reduce the heat, and allow to simmer for 1 hour before adding the chicken. Allow the chicken to simmer until tender.

Serve bowls of the broth first and the chicken and beef and pork second, if you wish, or serve bowls of broth with the chicken and beef. Creamy mashed potatoes or rice is an ideal accompaniment for such a dinner, together with a green salad of large proportions and heated French bread.

COLD CHICKEN DISHES

There are endless ways of using cold chicken, either by deliberately planning to have it available or by using cold chicken leftovers. The common creamed chicken on snippets of toast is not what I have in mind. One may serve soufflés, hash, sandwiches, chicken mayonnaise, chicken salad, or just cold chicken in a variety of fashions.

Whole chicken served cold is a delightful dish for a buffet supper or late supper in the evening. It may or may not be stuffed, and should be of a golden hue and juicy and well flavored. It should not be iced in the refrigerator. A chicken roasted far enough ahead to cool but not chill, so that the skin retains its crispness and the meat its juices, is fresh and inviting. Ham or tongue are natural complements to cold chicken and may be served with it.

A cold boiled chicken is delicious, but rather a pale and uninteresting morsel when placed on the table. There are a number of more interesting ways of preparing a boiled chicken for cold service.

Mayonnaise of Chicken

2 cups cold chicken	¼ cup chopped parsley
1 egg yolk	Tarragon, dry or fresh
1 cup olive oil	Endive, chicory, or romaine
1 tablespoon wine vinegar	greens
1 teaspoon salt	2 hard-boiled eggs
1 teaspoon dry mustard	Pimiento strips

A mayonnaise of chicken is a far more delicious and distinguished dish than the inevitable chicken-and-celery salad.

Cut chicken in large dice—not too small. For guests, use only the white meat. Otherwise use the dark as well.

Make a mayonnaise of the egg yolk and olive oil. (Despite the convenience of electric mixers, I find that nothing is as good for mayonnaise as the fork and the hand.) Flavor the mayonnaise with wine vinegar, salt, and dry mustard. Add chopped parsley. A few leaves of fresh tarragon, finely cut, or a teaspoon of the dry tarragon is a great help to this sauce.

Arrange the chicken pieces on some interesting greens, such as endive, chicory, or romaine. It is always pleasant to get away from what is called "a nest of crisp lettuce." Practically any other salad green is more flavorful and looks more inviting.

Cover the chicken with mayonnaise and garnish with slices of quartered hard-boiled eggs, capers, strips of pimiento, and a sprinkle of chopped parsley. *(Serves 4.)*

VARIATIONS

Amandine: Use sliced blanched almonds for this dish.

Argenteuil: Surround the chicken mayonnaise with cold asparagus tips which have marinated in a French dressing for an hour.

Garden Style: Garnish with thin slices of cucumber and thin strips of green pepper.

Tomato Surprise: Fill large tomatoes, which have been peeled and cleaned of all seeds and pulp, with the chicken.

For a summer luncheon, serve any of these chicken dishes with a clear soup, either hot or jellied, popovers with butter, and a bowl of fresh strawberries with kirsch.

For a supper, serve with a clear soup, thin slices of cold Virginia ham, and heated French bread. Frozen pineapple cubes which have been thawed and anointed with a little kirsch make a satisfactory final course.

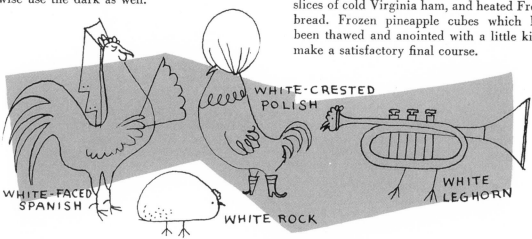

WHITE-CRESTED POLISH

WHITE-FACED SPANISH

WHITE ROCK

WHITE LEGHORN

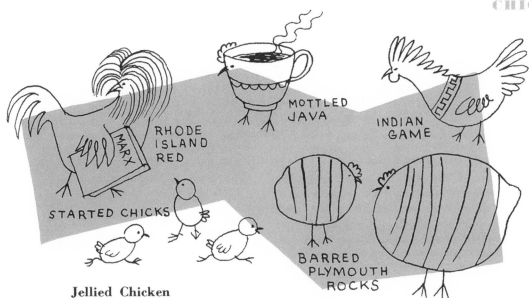

RHODE ISLAND RED

MARX

STARTED CHICKS

MOTTLED JAVA

INDIAN GAME

BARRED PLYMOUTH ROCKS

Jellied Chicken

There are several ways to serve a cold chicken in jelly:

(1) Cut the chicken in small pieces, mix with the jelly, and chill in molds. You may add ham, blanched almonds, herbs, hard-cooked eggs, or olives to the mixture. This is usually served with a mayonnaise or a sour cream sauce.

(2) Leave the chicken whole and, when the jelly is thickened but not set, apply a coat of jelly to the entire surface of the chicken. Chill quickly and add another coating. You may decorate the chicken with fresh tarragon leaves (in which case, flavor the gelatin mixture with tarragon), sliced stuffed olives, truffles cut into thin slices, thin shreds of pimiento, etc. Serve on a large platter garnished with greens and sliced hard-cooked egg, cucumber, tiny tomatoes, etc.

(3) Place the chicken in a mold, breast down, arrange garnishes around it, and set it with a gelatin mixture.

(4) Arrange slices of cold chicken and ham on a platter with appropriate garnishes: slices of truffle, hard-cooked eggs, olives, capers, etc. Cover with a thin coating of jelly and chill thoroughly.

Basic Chicken Jelly

Use unflavored gelatin for all jellied meat dishes. One envelope of the unflavored gelatin combines with 2 cups of liquid. Add any desired flavoring to this mixture and allow it to cool to the consistency of unbeaten egg white before you add other ingredients or use it to glaze.

For a chicken jelly, use the broth remaining from cooking your chicken, after you have removed the fat and strained the broth. Reduce it to about one half. Taste for seasoning. Dissolve 1 envelope gelatin in ½ cup cold broth and add 1½ cups hot broth. If you are adding another liquid, subtract the amount from the broth you use for mixing. Thus, in making chicken jelly, if you wish to add ½ cup white wine, merely add 1 cup hot broth and add the wine after you have made the jelly mixture.

Chaud-froid of Chicken

1 package (1 tablespoon) unflavored gelatin	1 cup sauce Velouté
½ cup chicken, ham, or mushroom broth	⅓ cup heavy cream
	Truffles, olives, etc., to decorate

Chaud-froid is a thickened sauce of butter, flour, broth, and cream which may be mixed with gelatin and is used to cover poultry or game for elaborate or simple dishes for a cold buffet or supper. This method of treating cold poultry may be used with great success for entertaining in the garden or at a large buffet dinner.

Dissolve gelatin in ¼ cup cold broth. Mix with ¼ cup hot broth. Blend the mixture with 1 cup heated sauce Velouté, add ⅓ cup heavy cream, and mix thoroughly. Strain and cool.

Use this sauce to coat the bird, or dip sections or slices of the bird in the sauce. Decorate with truffles, tarragon, blanched almonds, mushroom caps, sliced olives, or vegetables. Chill until serving time.

Creamed Chicken

Creamed chicken can be a most appetizing and versatile dish. It can be prepared with several different sauces served on a variety of bases and combined with any number of meats, fish, or vegetables. It can be a delicious company dish or a satisfying family left-over meal.

Combine 1 cup diced cold chicken with 1 cup Béchamel sauce and heat through. Rectify the seasoning and serve:

In patty shells	In noodle ring
On squares of corn bread	With hot rice
	With wild rice
On hot biscuit	With waffles
On toast	On English muffins
On croustades	Rolled in French pancakes

VARIATIONS

With Mushrooms: Substitute sautéed mushroom caps for half the amount of the chicken. Flavor with Madeira.

Virginia: Substitute diced ham for half the amount of chicken. Flavor with Madeira.

Au Gratin: Place slices of chicken in a casserole. Cover with sauce flavored with Madeira. Sprinkle with buttered crumbs and grated Parmesan cheese. Brown in hot oven or under broiler. Serve with fresh asparagus or broccoli.

With Clams: Substitute minced clams for half the chicken. Flavor with dry white wine. Use clam broth in equal parts with chicken broth in the sauce.

With Oysters: Combine half oysters and half chicken. Use half oyster liquor with chicken broth in the sauce.

Chicken à la King: Add 1 cup sliced mushrooms and 1 finely cut green pepper to 3 tablespoons chopped pimiento and add to the sauce with the diced chicken. Flavor with Madeira or sherry.

ROAST CHICKEN

A roast chicken, hot or cold, is a most delicious meal. Stuff it or not, and serve it with tiny roast potatoes and broccoli with drawn butter. In summer, when green corn is plentiful, a cold roast chicken and corn on the cob make a delightful meal. This, with a good green salad and some chilled fruit, is a dinner that will serve both family and guests. When roasting chickens, allow about 1 pound per person.

Trussing a Chicken: Trussing means tying and skewering the bird into shape before cooking. First fold the wings back so that their tips are under the back. Press the legs and thighs close together tightly against the body of the bird, securing them with two skewers run through the joint into the body. Tie white string around the tips of the legs and around the tail, and leave two long pieces of string which are crossed in the middle of the back and tied, after securing the wings

to the piece of excess skin which remains after removing the neck.

Sometimes a piece of salt pork is tied around the breast of the bird for lubrication during cooking. This, as well as all string, is removed before serving.

Preparation: Use a broiler, a fryer, or a roasting chicken of from 2 to 6 pounds for roasting (or a capon up to 9 pounds). Singe, clean, and dress the chicken, removing all pinfeathers. Rub the interior with half a lemon. Use any of the stuffings given on page 192 if you wish to stuff the chicken; or if not, stuff a little parsley and a sprig of tarragon or thyme in the cavity. Butter the bird well and place in a preheated oven.

Cooking: Small chickens fare better if they are roasted quickly in a moderately hot oven (400°). A moderate oven (350°) is better for larger birds. Allow about 18 to 20 minutes to the pound. If a chicken is cooked too long, it is apt to become dry and uninteresting. You can tell when a chicken is done by testing the dark meat. If there is still pink liquid running from the leg or thigh when you test it with a fork, the chicken needs additional cooking.

Baste the chicken with butter from the pan or additional butter every 10 minutes. When the chicken is done, remove it to a hot platter and pour the juices from the pan over it.

Tiny squab chickens may be roasted very quickly in a hot oven (450°) and served whole—one to a person. They may be stuffed or not. Be careful when roasting the tiny chickens not to overcook them.

If you are to serve cold chicken, cook your birds in the morning or early afternoon and let them cool rather than chill. A bird cooled without refrigeration is much more crisp on the outside, and the meat is juicier and more flavorful. A faint touch of the oven heat should remain.

The word "gravy" too often stands for a thick flour mixture that smothers anything good. If you try serving your chicken with only the juices from the pan, you will never go back to a thickened gravy again. If, however, your life is not complete without "gravy" and you feel that chicken without it is not chicken, this is the way to prepare it:

Chicken Gravy

Pour all but 4 tablespoons of the fat from the roasting pan over the roasted chicken. Scrape the pan well to loosen all the bits of crisped skin and chicken which may lurk there, add 3 tablespoons of flour to the fat in the pan, and blend well. Stirring constantly, add 2 cups chicken broth or rich milk and continue stirring until thickened. Season with salt and pepper, and pour into a sauceboat.

Roasting Chickens Outdoors

Prepare chickens as above.

Place pieces of bacon or salt pork over the breasts or have a bowl of melted butter, chicken broth and white wine, mixed, or a barbecue sauce for basting.

Arrange the chickens after they have been trussed and tied on a spit, and place them in front of or over the coals. Turn frequently and brush often with your basting liquid.

CHICKEN CASSEROLE DISHES

Chicken in casserole may be a braised chicken served whole, a disjointed bird cooked with various seasonings, or dishes made of leftover chicken mixed with other flavorings and, usually, with some starchy vegetable—rice, noodles, spaghetti, etc.

Braised Chicken in Casserole

Singe, clean, and truss the chicken. Brown it very quickly in a large skillet in which you have melted ½ cup butter or ¼ cup olive oil.

Turn the chicken on all sides and see that it is well browned.

Place the chicken in a large casserole and add the fat from the skillet. You may then add any seasonings you desire and a small amount of liquid—water, broth, or wine—and cover the casserole. Place it in a moderate oven (350°) and cook until the chicken is tender. Tenderness can be tested with a fork. Serve in the casserole surrounded by the vegetables and the other flavorings.

Chicken Casserole with Lentils

2 cups lentils
½ bay leaf
1 onion stuck with 2 cloves
1 teaspoon salt
Boiling water
1 4-pound roaster cut up for fricassee

Flour, salt, pepper
6 tablespoons butter
5 rashers bacon
Chicken broth (or hot water with 2 bouillon cubes dissolved)

Soak lentils, or use quick-cooking ones. Place in a deep kettle with onion, salt, and bay leaf. Cover with boiling water to 1 inch over top of lentils and simmer gently until lentils are tender. Dredge the chicken pieces in flour, salt, and pepper. Brown quickly in the butter, which you have melted in a large skillet. Place pieces of browned chicken in casserole and cover with cooked lentils and liquid. If there is not enough liquid, add chicken broth or hot water in which you have dissolved 2 bouillon cubes. Cover casserole and bake in a slow (350°) oven for 1 to 1½ hours, or until chicken is tender. Add additional liquid if the casserole cooks dry. Top with bacon for the last 15 minutes of cooking.
(Serves 6.)

VARIATIONS

With White Wine: Substitute white wine for broth when cooking the casserole.

Italian Style: Add 8 to 10 slices imported salami to casserole before placing in oven.

Old-fashioned Chicken Casserole

1 4- or 5-pound roasting chicken
6 tablespoons butter
2 cups broth
3 tablespoons chopped parsley

4 tablespoons flour
12 small carrots, scraped
12 small onions, peeled
Sprig of thyme
3 cups milk
Salt, pepper, nutmeg

Singe, clean, and cut up the chicken for fricassee. Dredge with salt, pepper, and flour. Melt the butter in a skillet and brown the pieces of chicken quickly on all sides, placing only a few pieces at a time in the pan. Place the browned pieces of chicken in a large casserole and reserve the fat.

Add the peeled onions, the carrots, and the seasonings to the casserole. Cover with 2 cups broth. Cover casserole and place in a medium (350°) oven for 45 minutes.

While chicken is cooking, add 4 tablespoons flour to the fat in the pan and blend well. Add milk slowly, stirring constantly, and cook over low heat until the mixture thickens. Salt and pepper to taste, and add a sprinkle of nutmeg to the sauce. Pour the sauce over the chicken in the casserole and continue cooking for 25 to 30 minutes or until chicken is tender and the sauce has mixed well with the juices in the pan.
(Serves 6.)

Tiny boiled new potatoes and quick frozen peas are a pleasant accompaniment.

DUCK

Many people, when they think of duck, think only of roast duck. In reality there are so many interesting ways to prepare duck that, with the real connoisseurs, roast duck often takes a back seat. For instance, steamed or boiled duck may be attractively combined with vegetables in Chinese-style recipes. Or duck may be braised and served with any one of a number of delicious sauces.

Preparation: Remove giblets from duck and wash. Push back skin around neck of duck and cut the neck off. Cut off wing tips and remove pinfeathers with tweezers. Wash duck thoroughly, inside and out, with cold water. Dry carefully.

To Skin Duckling: With a sharp-pointed knife, cut the skin from the neck to the vent, first along the breast of the duck, then along the backbone. Loosen the skin by running the knife underneath, close to the flesh. Peel the skin back as it is loosened, cutting the skin where necessary but keeping the flesh intact.

It is really easy and simple to remove the skin, since there is a solid layer of fat between skin and flesh. If you prefer, ask your meat dealer to skin the duck for you.

To Roast: Fill with favorite stuffing, or roast unstuffed.

To Braise: Cut in quarters or smaller servings. If desired, remove skin from duck before cutting it in pieces.

To Steam, Boil or Pressure-cook: Cut duck in quarters or smaller servings.

Duck Giblets

Place giblets, neck, wing tips, and any pieces of fat from around vent opening in small saucepan with 2 cups water and ½ teaspoon salt. Cook, covered, over moderate heat until tender, about 40 minutes. Skim broth and pour it off.

If skin and fat have been removed from duck before cooking, cook this with the giblets, using 3 cups water and 1 teaspoon salt. Use in cooking as desired.

Serve giblets with duck, or use both giblets and broth in soup or in special sauces to be served with the duck.

When duck is cut into pieces and cooked with a sauce, you may want to use the giblets with the meat. But when serving roast duck you may prefer to use the giblets, cooked as directed, for some other purpose.

Giblets may be diced and used with the duck broth for a wide variety of soups such as spinach, watercress egg drop, and vegetable soups. They may be put through a meat grinder and used in soufflés, or added to duck broth containing dissolved unflavored gelatin for a molded paté. Or try them diced and used with leftover duck meats in salads, omelets, and duck à la king.

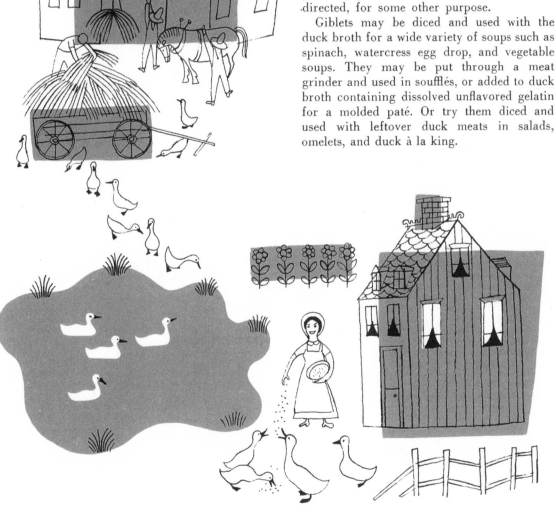

ROAST DUCKLING

Prepare duck for cooking as directed above (page 84). Place duck, breast side up, on a rack in a shallow baking pan about 10 by 14 inches and not more than 2 inches deep. Do not prick the skin, since this allows some of the meat juices to run out during roasting and does not increase the amount of fat which cooks out. Do not cover, add water, or baste.

Roast stuffed or unstuffed duck in a moderately slow oven (325°) about 1½ hours, or until a meat thermometer placed in the stuffing registers 180°F. At the end of 1 hour turn the duck back side up to finish roasting.

The length of time needed to cook duck of average weight is not in exact ratio to its weight. A 5- or 7-pound duckling, New York dressed, requires approximately the same roasting time as a 6-pound duckling.

3½ to 5 pounds, drawn weight—Cook about 25 minutes per pound

5 to 7 pounds, New York dressed weight —Cook about 18 minutes per pound

To save delicious duck fat for other cookery, some people pour it off during the roasting. This difficult feat is unnecessary, since little fat is expressed until the last half hour and this will not discolor in a slow oven.

Roast Duck—Stuffed

Lightly fill body cavity of duck with about 4 cups of desired stuffing. Do not pack too full. Insert several small poultry pins from one side of vent to other. Lace opening with light twine. It is not necessary to truss a duck, since the legs are short and the wings lie close to the body.

Roast Duck—Unstuffed

Place a few celery leaves and a few slices of onion inside the duck for flavor. Discard the vegetables after roasting.

Roast Duck with Orange Sauce

For the famous duck à l'orange, before roasting insert ½ peeled orange in cavity (later removed), sew opening, and truss. When roasted, serve duck surrounded with skinned orange sections, lemon slices, and watercress, with a bowl of orange sauce. For sauce: Remove fat from roasting pan (about 1 cup), sprinkle with ½ teaspoon arrowroot or flour, and stir over low flame. To 2 teaspoons sugar caramelized over a low fire, add 1 tablespoon wine vinegar, mix with gravy, and add juice of ½ orange. When ready to serve, add 1 teaspoon each of grated orange and lemon rind.

BOILED, STEAMED, AND BAKED DUCKLING

Boiled Duckling

When duck meat is to be used for salad, chop suey, duck à la king, duck pie, or casserole of duck, you may prefer to boil the duck rather than roast it. Have the butcher cut duck in quarters.

Prepare duck for cooking as directed. Place duck, together with giblets, neck, 3 cups water, and 2 teaspoons salt, in Dutch oven or large frying pan. Cook, tightly covered, over low heat until duck is tender—about 45 minutes.

Set pan in a cool place, remove cover, and let duck cool in broth 30 minutes. Pour broth into a bowl and allow fat to rise. Pour fat into a jar with tight-fitting cover, broth into a suitable covered container. Place duck in covered container. Store fat, broth, and duck in refrigerator until needed.

Steamed Duckling

Prepare duck for cooking as directed (page 84). In small roaster with tight-fitting cover place 2 cups boiling water. Place duck, breast side down, on rack in pan. Cover and steam over moderate heat until duck is tender— about 45 minutes. After 30 minutes, remove cover and turn duck. Replace cover and finish cooking. Serve hot with duck giblet gravy (page 85) or cool and use like boiled duck.

Duck in Wine Sauce

5- to 6-pound duck	1 small bay leaf
½ clove garlic, minced	⅛ teaspoon thyme
2 tablespoons flour	1 teaspoon salt
2 cups red wine	8 small white onions,
8 mushrooms, sliced	peeled
2 sprigs parsley	8 small carrots, trimmed

Remove skin and fat from the duck. Cut duck into serving-sized pieces. Cook skin and fat with giblets and neck according to directions for cooking giblets (page 85). Allow fat to rise to top of liquid and pour off.

Melt 2 tablespoons duck fat in large frying pan. Brown the pieces of duck in fat over moderate heat. Remove to 9-inch casserole.

Add garlic to fat and cook 1 minute. Stir in flour. Add red wine, mushrooms, parsley,

bay leaf, thyme, and salt. Bring to a boil, stirring constantly, until sauce thickens. Place 8 small white onions, peeled, 8 small trimmed carrots, and duck giblets in casserole with duck. Top with sauce. Cover tightly. Bake in moderate oven (350°) until duck and vegetables are tender, about 1¼ hours. *(Serves 4.)*

BRAISED DUCKLING

Have your meat dealer cut the duck in quarters or smaller servings. Prepare the duck for cooking as directed (page 84). Place skin side down in Dutch oven or large frying pan. Cook, uncovered, over moderate heat for 45 minutes, pouring off accumulated fat. Continue to cook, covered, for another 30 minutes, or until duck is tender and nicely browned, turning occasionally. Serve with giblet gravy (page 85) or a special sauce.

To finish cooking the duck in a sauce, braise uncovered for 45 minutes as directed. Drain off the accumulated fat. Then add your sauce and continue to cook, covered, for 30 minutes over low heat or in a 325° oven.

Braised Duck in Black Cherry Sauce

5- to 6-pound duck	½ teaspoon salt
1 tablespoon duck fat	1 bay leaf
1 tablespoon onion, minced	⅛ teaspoon marjoram
	1 No. 2 can black cherries
1½ cups duck broth or ½ cup red wine	2 tablespoons cornstarch

Have the butcher cut the duck into quarters. Braise the duck, as above. Meanwhile, cook giblets (page 85). Drain off liquid. Allow fat to rise to top and pour it off. Place 1 tablespoon fat in saucepan, add minced onion, and cook over low heat about 3 minutes. Add duck broth or wine, salt, bay leaf, and marjoram.

Open 1 No. 2 can black cherries and drain cherries. Combine ½ cup cherry juice and the cornstarch. Stir into hot broth. Cook, stirring constantly, until sauce thickens and boils. Remove bay leaf. Add cherries and heat

thoroughly. Serve hot over braised duck quarters. *(Serves 4.)*

Pineapple Duck

5- to 6-pound duck	1 medium-sized green pepper, cut into 1-inch squares
Water	
Salt	
3 tablespoons duck fat	2 tablespoons cornstarch
½ clove garlic	1 tablespoon lemon juice or vinegar
1 cup duck broth	
1 cup canned pineapple, drained and diced	1 teaspoon Kitchen Bouquet or soy sauce

Have the butcher cut the duck into quarters. Place the duck in a 6-quart saucepan or Dutch oven with neck, giblets, 4 cups water, and 2 teaspoons salt. Cook, covered, over moderate heat until tender, about 45 minutes to 1 hour. (Or cook in pressure saucepan according to directions.)

Remove duck. Drain off liquid. Allow fat to rise to the top and pour it off. Remove skin and cut duck meat in pieces about 2 inches long and ½ inch square.

Place duck fat in large frying pan or Dutch oven and add garlic. Cook over low heat 2 minutes; remove garlic. Add duck meat and cook over moderate heat 5 minutes, tossing lightly.

Add 1 cup duck broth, the pineapple, and the green pepper squares. Blend together and stir in cornstarch, ¼ cup water, 1 teaspoon salt, the lemon juice or vinegar, and the Kitchen Bouquet or soy sauce. Add to broth. Cook, stirring lightly, until juice thickens.

Serve with hot cooked rice. *(Serves 4.)*

OTHER DUCK DISHES

Broiled Duckling

Have the meat dealer prepare the duck for broiling by removing the backbone and the keel from the breastbone.

Place duck, skin down, on ungreased pan in preheated broiler. Broil 4 to 5 inches from moderate heat for 20 to 25 minutes. Turn duck and broil for same length of time on other side. For a rich brown color, brush skin side of duck with a mixture of 1 tablespoon honey and 1 teaspoon Kitchen Bouquet or soy sauce. Return to broiler for 2 minutes. Serve immediately.

The same mixture of honey and Kitchen Bouquet can be used to brush roast duckling 15 minutes before removing from oven.

Baked Duck Omelet

6 eggs	½ cup cooked carrots,
⅓ cup milk	finely diced
1 teaspoon salt	1 cup cooked duck meat,
⅛ teaspoon Tabasco	diced
sauce	Duck broth
½ cup cooked peas	

Beat the eggs slightly with the milk, salt, and Tabasco sauce. Stir in cooked peas, carrots, and duck meat. Pour into well-greased shallow baking dish. Place in slow oven (325°) and bake until omelet is just cooked through, about 35 minutes.

Cut into individual servings, topping them with sauce made from duck broth. *(Serves 4.)*

Duck Soup

Duck giblets and neck	½ cup celery, finely diced
2 tablespoons duck fat	½ cup carrots, finely diced
¼ cup onion, finely diced	Duck meat, shredded

Cook duck giblets and neck (see page 85). Drain off liquid. Allow fat to rise to the top and pour it off. Add enough water to make 2 cups broth.

Melt the duck fat in a saucepan and add onion, celery, and carrots. Cook over moderate heat for about 5 minutes. Add duck broth, giblets cut fine, and available duck meat.

Bring to a boil and simmer 5 minutes or until vegetables are barely tender. Correct seasoning if necessary.

TURKEY

When buying turkeys, estimate 1 pound per person. If there is turkey left over, there are so many things which can be done with it that it is welcome for several days after the initial serving.

In addition to birds for roasting, which vary from 8 to 30 pounds, it is now possible to buy small broiler turkeys. These range from 4 to 7 pounds and may be either split and broiled or stuffed and roasted.

Roast Turkey

Estimate an average of 1 cup of stuffing per pound, or a little less. Stuffing should not be forced in and packed too tightly, or the bird may split during the cooking process or the stuffing may be hard and thick, and not light and pleasantly dry. (See page 192.)

A piece of dry stale bread placed in the vent of the bird after it has been stuffed will help to keep the juices inside and avoid the inconvenience of sewing up the vent.

When the bird is stuffed, take a long piece of white twine and wrap it well around the legs at the joint. Then wrap it around the tail and cross the string. Carry it back and around the wings (which have been folded and skewered under the bird). Cross the string again and tie it around the piece of skin which is left when the neck bone is removed, and return it to the original spot and tie the string to the legs again. Trussing holds the turkey in shape and makes the bird more attractive for serving.

There are differences of opinion about procedure in roasting a turkey. It is my feeling that a bird should be well buttered and roasted in a moderate oven (350°) until done. The only really dependable method for determining the state of doneness is to try the meat of the thigh with a fork. If the juice runs red, it is not done. When it no longer runs red, the turkey is ready. Turkey that is overdone is dry and stringy. A perfect roasted bird is juicy and well grained.

An easy method of roasting is to cover the breast and legs of the bird with several thicknesses of cheesecloth saturated in olive oil or vegetable oil and roast the turkey without basting, removing the cheesecloth for the last 20 minutes or half hour so that the skin becomes crisp and brown.

There is also the searing method. Butter the turkey well and place it in a very hot oven (475°) and roast, basting frequently, for a half hour. Reduce the heat to moderate (350°) and continue basting until turkey is done. Allow about 18 to 20 minutes per pound for roasting turkey this way.

Small turkeys will cook in much less time and should be basted frequently, for they do not have the fat that the older birds have. A broiler-sized turkey should roast in a moderate oven (350°) 1 to 1½ hours.

Broiled Turkey

A broiled turkey will take approximately 50 minutes to cook under the broiler. Only young birds of 4 to 7 pounds are appropriate for broiling. They should be split, cleaned, rubbed well with butter or other fat, and placed skin side down on the rack in a broiler preheated to 350°. Broil for 20 or 25 minutes, or with a larger bird, for 30 minutes. Turn, baste with butter, season with salt and pepper, and continue broiling for approximately 20 minutes longer, basting frequently during the process. Do not broil the skin side of the turkey under too hot a flame or it will blister.

VARIATIONS

With Paprika: Add 2 teaspoons paprika to the fat with which you rub the turkey.

With Giblets: Add finely chopped giblets to basting fat for last 10 minutes of cooking.

With Parsley: Sprinkle turkey heavily with chopped parsley when it is removed from broiler.

Mabelle's Turkey Casserole

7- or 8-pound turkey	½ pound bacon, cut in tiny
Flour	slivers
Salt and pepper	½ cup chopped shallots or
¼ pound fat	green onion
	2 cups broth

Singe, clean, and cut turkey into serving pieces. Dredge with flour, salt, and pepper.

Melt fat in a large skillet and brown pieces of turkey in it, a few pieces at a time. Transfer the pieces to a large casserole. Add bacon and chopped shallots or green onion. Add broth, made from the neck and giblets and the chopped giblets. Cover the casserole and allow to simmer in a moderately slow oven (325°) for 1½ to 2 hours or until turkey is tender.

Taste for seasoning and serve with hot corn bread and succotash. If you want a thicker sauce, drop little balls of flour and butter into the broth 10 minutes before serving.

(Serves 8.)

Grilled Turkey Legs

Remove legs from a roast turkey. With a sharp knife slit the flesh to the bone and cut it away from the bone so that the meat is in one piece. Stuff with leftover stuffing and tie securely. Dip in beaten egg and crumbs, and sauté in 4 tablespoons fat till nicely browned on all sides. Serve with tomato sauce.

G A M E

A N D   S P E C I A L   P O U L T R Y

PHEASANT

The pheasant is an upland bird which has a tendency to be dry-meated. This means that it needs careful attention and ample lubrication while cooking. It used to be the custom to hang pheasants until they were well decomposed, but nowadays those who prefer a strong gamey flavor seem to be in the minority.

You can tell a young pheasant by its short, rounded claws. The older and tougher birds have long and much sharper claws. In the Southern and midland sections of the country the bird that goes by the name of pheasant often is actually a ruffed grouse, a splendid native game bird. The bright-plumaged ring-necked pheasant is a native of Asia that was introduced into this country many years ago, where it has become mixed with the so-called English pheasant, also released here from abroad.

Singe, draw, and clean pheasants as you do chicken (see page 67). You may stuff them or place a square of butter in each bird. One pheasant will serve 3 to 4 persons, depending on the size.

Western-style Sautéed Pheasant with Cream Gravy

Pheasant	8 slices bacon
Flour	3 tablespoons flour
Salt and pepper	2 cups rich milk

This is a typical Western dish that has come down from the period of the settling of the West, when wild birds were one of the mainstays of families and were treated as everyday food rather than as delicacies.

Singe, clean, and cut a pheasant into convenient serving pieces. Dredge with flour, salt, and pepper.

Fry bacon in an iron skillet till crisp. Remove the bacon to a hot plate and place the pieces of pheasant in the hot fat. Brown quickly on both sides, salt and pepper to taste, and reduce the flame. Cover the skillet and allow the pheasant to simmer for 20 minutes, turning once during the cooking.

Add flour to the pan and blend well with the fat and juice from the pheasant. Add the milk slowly, stirring constantly. Stir till the mixture thickens. Salt and pepper to taste. Pass the sauce in a gravy boat.

Mashed potatoes and buttered cabbage are good with this dish. Add hot biscuits and honey and you have a good pioneer dinner.

Braised Pheasant with Sauerkraut

1 or 2 pheasants	Juniper berries
2 pounds sauerkraut	½ teaspoon caraway seeds
2 cups broth	½ cup butter or other fat
1 cup white wine	Salt and pepper

Drain sauerkraut and place in a deep earthenware casserole. Add broth, white wine, a few juniper berries, and the caraway seeds.

Cover and simmer for 1 hour.

Singe and clean the pheasant. Brown it well on all sides in butter or other fat. Turn it from side to side to get an even brown. Salt and pepper to taste and, when the bird is thoroughly browned, place it in the casserole with the sauerkraut. Cover and place in a preheated moderate oven (350°) until pheasant is tender—about 35 to 45 minutes.

Serve on a platter surrounded by the sauerkraut and fried hominy squares. *(Serves 4.)*

Broiled Young Pheasant

Tender young pheasant may be split and broiled. The broiling time should be 15 to 18 minutes. Butter the breasts well and baste frequently while broiling, or you will get a dry-meated bird. Salt and pepper to taste, and serve with fried hominy squares.

PIGEON

Pigeon, or dove, of which the wood pigeon is the most common variety, is well-flavored meat but has a great tendency to be exceedingly tough. Therefore it needs long, slow cooking to be at its best.

Casserole of Wood Pigeon with Tomatoes

4 wood pigeons	Basil
1 small onion	1 cup sliced mushrooms
Parsley	1 No. 2½ can Italian-style
6 slices bacon, cubed	tomatoes, or 1 qt. home-
1 clove garlic	canned tomatoes with 1
1 medium onion, chopped very fine	tablespoon brown sugar added
Thyme	

Singe, clean, and stuff pigeons with a small onion and several sprigs of parsley.

Try out 6 slices of bacon cut into cubes. Brown the pigeons in the fat very quickly with a clove of garlic cut rather fine.

Place the birds in a deep casserole with the following: chopped onion, sprig of thyme, pinch of basil, the sliced mushrooms, and the Italian-style tomatoes, or home-canned tomatoes to which you have added 1 tablespoon brown sugar. Cover casserole and place in a preheated moderate oven (350°) and simmer for 1½ hours.

Test the birds for tenderness and rectify the seasoning. Replace in the oven and cook until the birds are tender.

Serve with buttered noodles sprinkled with grated Parmesan cheese. *(Serves 4.)*

WILD DUCK

Although there are many varieties of wild duck in this country, the usual choice is among the mallard, the canvasback, and the teal. The latter is quite small, and people have been known to eat two or three teal at one sitting.

Wild duck is difficult to pick; it is likely to be covered with pinfeathers. Many people singe them and then pick the pinfeathers out with tweezers. Draw wild duck as you would any other bird.

Roast Wild Duck (I)

Dress and clean ducks. Place on a trivet in roasting pan and rub breasts with butter. Place in preheated very hot oven (475° to 500°) breast side up. Roast 15 to 20 minutes, depending upon the size of the ducks. Baste every 5 minutes with melted butter or a mixture of melted butter and red wine. Salt and pepper to taste, and remove to a hot platter.

The birds will be thoroughly rare; a rich, red juice will run out when a sharp knife is sunk into the breast. Stuff the duck with a sprig of parsley or, if you like, with a few juniper berries.

Fried hominy grits or wild rice is a traditional accompaniment to wild duck. A bottle of fine Burgundy is a fitting complement to this delicacy.

Roast Wild Duck (II)

Singe and clean ducks; stuff them if you wish. Close the vents and place them on a trivet in a roasting pan, breast side up. Rub the breasts well with butter or oil and place in a preheated moderate oven (350°), allowing 15 minutes to the pound. Baste with melted butter or red wine.

Broiled Wild Duck

Small young ducks may be split and broiled, or broiled whole if you prefer. They should be well rubbed with butter or oil, placed in a preheated 350° broiler—skin side down if split or breast down if whole—and broiled for 10 to 20 minutes, depending upon the state of doneness you prefer. Turn frequently, especially if you are broiling a whole bird.

QUAIL

There are many varieties of quail in the United States: in the East, the bob-white, called partridge in the South; west of the Rockies, the crested or California quail, which is a most delicious morsel, and various varieties of valley and mountain quail. A quail is a small bird, one usually being considered a portion. Quail should be quite fresh and should be well lubricated, for it has a tendency to be dry. The breasts need salt pork and almost constant basting.

Broiled Quail

Draw and clean the quail and split it down the back. Rub well with butter or oil and place a goodly amount of the fat in the hollow of the rib cage. Broil for 8 to 10 minutes in a hot (400°) broiler. Salt and pepper to taste. Serve with a spicy relish and perhaps curried rice.

Breast of Quail Sauté

12 quail	Salt and pepper
¼ pound butter	1 tablespoon foie gras or
12 mushroom caps	chopped livers
3 teaspoons chopped shallots	Curry powder

Clean and remove the breasts of the quail with a small, sharp knife. Sauté in butter for 5 minutes. Add 1 mushroom cap for each breast and ¼ teaspoon chopped shallots for each bird. Salt and pepper and cover. Simmer for 12 minutes and add foie gras and a dash of curry powder. Cover and simmer again for 5 minutes. Serve on toast. *(Serves 6 amply.)*

Sauté of Quail with White Grapes

6 quail	½ cup broth
Dry bread	3 ounces brandy
Butter	1 cup white grapes
Salt and pepper	

For serving this dish and any variations of it that may suggest themselves, make oval croustades of dry bread. Cut bread about 2 inches thick; just a bit larger than the quail. Cut out an oval cup into which the quail or other small bird will fit, and toast the croustade gently in a slow oven. Butter the cavity into which you place the bird.

Prepare the quail for sautéing. Brown the birds very quickly in butter, salt and pepper to taste, and add broth. Cover, reduce the heat, and simmer for 10 minutes.

Add brandy and blaze it. Add white grapes. Cover again and simmer for 8 minutes longer.

Serve in croustades and pass the sauce in a separate dish. *(Serves 6.)*

SQUAB

Squab, one of the more delicately flavored of the small birds, is considered formal party food but may be found a delicious morsel for the entire family. Squab will vary in weight from 10 to 21 ounces, the average weighing about 1 pound. One squab is considered a portion.

Broiled Squab

Singe and clean the squab and split them down the back; or have your butcher clean and split them for you. Rub well with butter or other fat, place in a moderately hot broiler, skin side down, and broil 25 to 30 minutes, turning once after 10 minutes. Salt and pepper to taste.

Whole squab may be broiled, but they must be turned often to get an even color on all sides. Give them 30 to 40 minutes in the broiler.

Chopped giblets which have been cooked in 1 cup boiling water and seasoned to taste may be mixed with the pan gravy and poured over the cooked birds.

Roast Squab

Singe, clean, and stuff squab, using one per person. Butter them well or cover the breasts with bacon, place in a preheated moderate oven (350°), and roast from 40 to 45 minutes or until tender. Salt and pepper to taste, and baste every 5 minutes with drippings from the pan. Serve on well-browned fried hominy squares.

Squab Sauté with White Wine and Herbs

4 small squab	1 cup white wine
6 tablespoons butter	2 tablespoons chopped
Salt and pepper	parsley
2 tablespoons chopped	1 tablespoon tarragon
shallots	leaves

Singe, draw, and split the squab.

Melt butter or other fat in a skillet and brown the halves over a brisk flame. Salt and pepper to taste.

Add chopped shallots and ½ cup white wine. Reduce the heat and cover the pan, and simmer for 15 minutes.

Uncover the pan, add chopped parsley and tarragon leaves, and leave the pan uncovered. Add a little more wine—about ½ cup—and cook for 5 minutes.

Serve on crisp buttered toast with the sauce spooned over. *(Serves 4.)*

GOOSE

Goose is a delicious, though not at all an economical, bird. Geese are exceedingly fat, and their rather complex bone structure and the comparatively small amount of meat make them rather expensive. A goose should be treated in much the same manner as a duck, using a tart, savory stuffing for goose. Apples, chestnuts, and prunes are welcome additions to a goose stuffing. If you should use a bread stuffing, be certain that the stuffing is dry, for goose is fat and juicy and lubricates the stuffing while it is cooking. Estimate 1 pound of goose per person.

Roast Goose

Place stuffed and trussed goose breast side up in a deep roasting pan on a trivet. Add 1 cup boiling water or broth. Cover pan tightly. Place in a very hot oven (475°) for 15 minutes. Remove the cover and brush the breast with butter or other fat, and reduce the heat to moderately hot (375°). Roast until well browned and tender, allowing 15 minutes to the pound. Baste three or four times during cooking. Salt and pepper to taste.

Or:

Place goose breast side up on a trivet in the roasting pan and put in a moderate oven (350°). Allow 18 minutes to the pound and baste two or three times with broth. Prick the skin with a fork to allow the fat to run out.

Sauce for Roast Goose

1 medium-sized onion, finely chopped	½ cup chopped mushrooms
3 tablespoons goose fat	1 cup broth
Chopped goose liver	1 cup cream
2 tablespoons chopped parsley	2 egg yolks
	2 tablespoons brandy

Sauté onion in goose fat. Add chopped goose liver, chopped parsley, and mushrooms. Sauté for 5 minutes.

Add broth and simmer for 3 or 4 minutes; then add cream mixed with egg yolks. Stir constantly till the mixture thickens, and add brandy. Taste for seasoning and serve with goose.

NEW YEAR'S EVE GOOSE

8- or 10-pound goose	Salt and pepper
Onion	2 tablespoons gelatin
Cloves	¼ cup cold water
Herb bouquet	½ cup white wine
1 cup wine vinegar	

Singe goose clean, and rub well with lemon. Place it in a kettle with an onion stuck with cloves, an herb bouquet—parsley, thyme, tarragon, bay leaf, garlic—and 1 cup of wine vinegar. Cover with boiling water and simmer till goose is tender—1½ to 2 hours. Salt and pepper to taste.

Remove the goose from the pot, allow it to cool, and skin it. The skin may be rendered for the grease, and the cracklings eaten for an hors d'oeuvre. Cut the bird into serving-sized pieces and arrange in a large mold.

Remove the fat from the broth, reduce it over heat to half its quantity, and strain. Add gelatin dissolved in cold water and white wine. Taste for seasoning and pour over the goose sections in the mold. Chill.

Unmold on a large decorated platter and serve with potato salad and mayonnaise.

(Serves 8).

PARTRIDGE

"Partridge" is a name applied to different birds in different parts of the United States. In the South, several kinds of small quail, and in the North the somewhat larger ruffed grouse, are so named.

Markets specializing in game and fine poultry offer the chicken partridge and sometimes other varieties flown or shipped frozen from Europe. These are widely available during winter and may be ordered from New York markets.

Partridge is one bird which needs hanging for several days before it develops much flavor. One-half an average-sized partridge is considered a serving, although with the smaller birds a whole partridge is sometimes served. As with other game, wild rice, mushrooms, or fried hominy grits are considered traditional accompaniments, and a fine-vintage burgundy finds worthy company in a partridge.

Broiled Partridge

Partridges (1 bird per portion)	1 onion
	Cloves
Butter	2 cups water
Salt and pepper	Toast

Singe, clean, and draw partridges. Split and rub well with butter. Place in a broiling rack in a 350° preheated broiler and broil for 15 or 20 minutes.

Broil the well-buttered birds skin side down for 8 minutes. Salt and pepper to taste. Turn, baste with butter, and broil till nicely browned and tender.

Cook giblets, with 1 onion stuck with cloves, in the water until tender. Chop fine and mix with 1 tablespoon butter and a little of the broth in which they were cooked.

Spread slices of crisp well-buttered toast with this mixture and place a partridge on each slice of toast. Pour over the drippings from the pan and serve.

Roast Partridge

Partridges (1 per person)	Bread sauce
½ lemon, or lemon juice	Salt and pepper
Salt pork or bacon	

Singe, clean, and draw partridges. Rub well, inside and out, with lemon juice or half of a lemon. Wrap salt pork or bacon around the breasts and secure with string. Push the legs toward the breast and secure them with a skewer pushed through the middle of the bird. Roast for 18 or 20 minutes in a hot oven (400°), basting twice.

Five minutes before the birds are done, remove salt pork and increase the heat to very hot (450°) to brown the breast well. Serve with buttered crumbs or with the bastings of the pan mixed with the precooked chopped giblets, and salt and pepper to taste.

VARIATIONS

With Cabbage: Shred 1 head cabbage, cut 4 carrots in small dice, and stick 1 medium onion with cloves. Place in a kettle with ½ pound ground fresh pork, 6 strips of bacon cut in tiny slivers, and 1 cup broth or water in which you have dissolved 1 bouillon cube. Cover and simmer for 1½ hours, adding ½ cup white wine after the first hour's cooking. Salt and pepper to taste. Serve roasted partridges on the cooked vegetables on a large heated platter. Pour over all the pan gravy mixed with the chopped precooked giblets.

With Sausages: Serve with grilled, well-seasoned sausages and watercress.

With Mushrooms: Serve with grilled mushroom caps.

VENISON

Venison, probably the most plentiful of all game flesh, is not a palatable dish eaten fresh. You should take your carcass to your butcher and have him hang it for you, anywhere from 6 days to 6 weeks, in his refrigerator, and then have him cut it, saving the legs, the saddle, the loin, and the tenderloin. The shoulder meat, from the shank and breast, may be boned and cut up and used for ragout or for chopped meat. Venison requires marinating for anywhere from 3 hours to 3 days. I include 2 recipes from Cicely Foster:

Ragout of Venison

3 pounds venison	⅛ teaspoon thyme
2 cups red wine	⅛ teaspoon wild marjoram
¼ cup red wine vinegar	(oregano)
2 cloves garlic, minced	½ cup salt pork, cut in fine
2 medium onions, chopped	strips
2 or 3 sprigs celery leaves	2 cups canned tomatoes
½ cup olive oil	(or 3 tablespoons tomato
3 juniper berries, ground	purée with 1½ cups meat
½ teaspoon fresh-ground	stock or water)
black pepper	1 tablespoon butter
1 lemon	2 tablespoons flour
1 small bay leaf	

Since venison flesh, whatever the cut, is rather dry, a marinade is desirable.

Cut 3 pounds meat in convenient-sized pieces—about 1 to 1½ inches—removing the gristle and the tough tissue. (The less choice cuts will do perfectly for this dish.) Prepare a marinade of the red wine (burgundy or Cabernet), red wine vinegar, garlic, onions, celery leaves, olive oil, juniper berries, black pepper, the juice and rind of a lemon, bay leaf, thyme, and wild marjoram.

Soak venison in marinade for 24 to 48 hours in a cool place, turning the meat occasionally to see that each piece is well coated. Always remember that the marinade is a tenderizing as well as a flavoring device.

At cooking time, render salt pork. Drain the venison from the marinade and brown it lightly in the pork fat, using a heavy metal pan or Dutch oven having a tight cover. Add the marinade to the browned meat together with the canned tomatoes (or tomato purée with meat stock or water). Simmer 1 to 1½ hours, or until tender. If the gravy needs moistening during the simmering, add a mixture of half red wine and half stock, as required.

When done, thicken with a paste made of the butter and flour. Taste for seasoning and serve very hot. *(Serves 4.)*

This dish can be served reheated the next day with no diminution of flavor.

The perfect accompaniment for venison ragout is egg noodles, as fresh as possible, sprinkled liberally with bread crumbs browned in butter. Red cabbage and a good burgundy complete the menu.

Roast Rack or Loin of Venison

4 pounds rack or loin of	1 teaspoon salt
venison	½ teaspoon fresh-ground
Salt pork or bacon strips	black pepper
2 medium onions, chopped	1 tablespoon parsley,
1 small carrot, sliced thin	chopped
1 large clove garlic, minced	1 large lemon
¼ teaspoon dried thyme	½ cup olive oil
¼ teaspoon wild marjoram	1½ cups red wine
(oregano)	2 tablespoons flour
¼ teaspoon basil	½ cup concentrated meat
4 juniper berries, crushed	stock

Choose a rack or loin of well-hung venison weighing a good 4 pounds. Saw through the backbone so that each rib may be cut through without obstruction when carved. At regular intervals of about 2 inches make incisions with knife or larding needle and insert thin strips of salt pork or bacon. In addition, cut in thin strips 2 slices of bacon or the equivalent in salt pork for additional flavor, and lay it over the top of the venison.

Make a marinade by mixing together the following: the onions, carrot slices, garlic, thyme, wild marjoram (oregano), basil, juniper, salt, pepper, parsley, the juice and rind of the lemon, and olive oil.

Mix all ingredients well, pour the mixture over the venison in an earthenware dish, and set in a cool place. The length of marinating should be not less than 24 hours and not more than 48 hours, unless a very gamey flavor is desired: the longer the marinade, the gamier the flavor. The meat should be turned every few hours so that all surfaces of the meat are evenly exposed to the marinade and are kept well moistened.

At cooking time, place the venison in a roasting pan in a moderately slow oven (325°). Pour the marinade over the meat, without the lemon rind, and roast uncovered, basting frequently. Allow 20 minutes to the pound for rare venison, 22 minutes for medium rare. But remember that game, unless very young, is active, and therefore potentially tough. Meat is more tender either rare or very well done than in its intermediate stages of cooking. After the first half hour, add 1 cup heated red wine (burgundy or Cabernet) and continue to baste frequently. When done, remove venison to heated platter and keep warm.

Into the roasting pan stir the flour until very smooth, mashing and blending in the herbs. Add, gradually, concentrated meat stock —made from game trimmings or beef, or beef consommé, or 1 teaspoon meat glaze (glacé de viande) dissolved in ½ cup hot water— and ½ cup heated red wine.

Blend all together smoothly, being careful to dislodge all the good bits clinging to the pan. Strain, if a very smooth sauce is desired; otherwise the little bits of vegetable taste very good. Taste and correct the seasoning, if necessary.

Pour the sauce over the meat and serve very hot, carving slices not too thin and letting the juices from the meat mingle with and enrich the sauce. Potato dumplings or pancakes, buckwheat groats (kasha), or samp (whole hominy) is an excellent complement, and a favorite member of the cabbage family such as kale provides color as well as accent in texture and flavor. Wine of the same type as that used in the gravy makes the whole a feast. *(Serves 6.)*

Venison Hamburger

The less choice portions of the meat may be ground coarsely and seasoned to taste with onion, thyme, and salt and pepper. Shape into small patties, wrap each one with a strip of fat bacon, and secure with a skewer or toothpick. Broil or fry as you do hamburger steaks. Small patties may be used for sandwiches and prepared on an outdoor grill.

BEEF

Good beef has a bright red color. The flesh is firm, fine-grained, and well marbled or streaked with fat. The fat surrounding the flesh should be brittle or crumbly and a creamy white.

STEAK

Allow ¾ to 1 pound of meat per person and trim away all excess fat. This may be saved to cook with potatoes, to which it imparts a rare flavor. The steak should be cut 1 to 2½ inches thick.

Score the fat on the edges of the steak so that it will not buckle or warp in cooking. Let stand at room temperature for an hour.

Preheat the broiler until very hot. Or, if you are using a charcoal grill, achieve a fine bed of glowing coals. Steak should cook about 3 inches from the flame or coals.

If you like your steak well browned on the outside and rare in the center, maintain a constant high heat during the broiling process. Never try to broil a piece of meat less than an inch thick. Those are better sautéed or panbroiled.

Grease the broiling rack lightly, place your steak on the rack, and place the rack 3 inches from the heat. A 1½-inch steak should take about 18 to 20 minutes for rare cooking. Allow 8 to 10 minutes before turning the steak. Salt and pepper before turning and after. Many authorities say you will ruin a

steak by testing it with a knife for doneness, but that is being overly fussy. If you are uncertain whether the meat is well enough done, make a small incision near the bone. You will be able to tell at once whether or not you need return it to the broiler.

Serve your steak at once on a hot platter, and with hot plates. Place a generous piece of butter on the meat and, if you wish, pour over the juices from the broiling pan.

If your steak is over 2½ inches thick, sear it well on both sides in the hot broiler and then reduce the heat to moderate (350°) so that the steak will cook through.

The most popular accompaniments for steak are either a baked Idaho potato or French fried or sautéed potatoes. If you are fond of onions and like them French fried, serve them with a baked potato. If you wish fried potatoes, serve some sautéed mushrooms with the steak. Crisp French bread, a green salad, and a good ripe piece of cheese are ideal accompaniments to a steak dinner. A fine red wine or good ale helps, too. No catsup, please. If you must have sauce, a Béarnaise or a Marchand de Vin is especially suited to the dish.

VARIATIONS

Pan-broiled or Sautéed: Using a heavy skillet, melt 2 tablespoons butter or fat from the steak. Increase heat, place steak in very hot pan, and sear quickly on one side. Reduce the heat a little and allow a 1½-inch steak to cook 8 to 9 minutes before turning. Salt and pepper before turning steak. Brown well on the other side and cook until done. Serve with butter and the sauce from the pan poured over steak.

Barbecued: Brush your steak well with a paste made from 1 teaspoon salt, 2 teaspoons dry mustard, and enough water to make a thick paste. Allow to stand ½ hour before broiling.

Minute: Minute steaks are cut from the loin or the sirloin and may be anywhere from $\frac{3}{16}$ to ½ inch thick. They should be pan-broiled or sautéed very quickly and served at once. If you like them rare, merely a quick searing on each side will be sufficient.

Minute, Brazilian: This is an ideal dish to cook at table if you are blessed with one of the alcohol table stoves. Otherwise, prepare it in the kitchen and rush it to the table.

Melt ½ cup butter in a large, heavy-bottomed skillet. Add the steaks, sear them very quickly on both sides, and place them on a very hot platter. Now to your pan add 2 tablespoons shallots, chopped very fine; 1 teaspoon salt, ½ teaspoon coarse black pepper, 2 tablespoons finely chopped parsley, and 2 tablespoons steak sauce. Allow to cook together for 2 minutes. Add 6 tablespoons red wine, let the sauce heat through thoroughly, and pour at once over the steaks.

Chopped: Use top round or top sirloin for chopped steak and have it ground to order without fat. Allow ½ pound per person. Form into cakes with the hands, and either broil as you would a steak, or sauté in butter, salting and peppering the steaks as they cook. Or, you may form the meat into flat cakes and sauté very quickly in butter, adding a finely chopped clove of garlic to the pan. A little barbecue sauce added to the pan just before serving makes a tangy barbecued hamburger that is out of the ordinary.

Tartare: This is raw chopped round or sirloin, which should be very fresh. Steak tartare should be dressed with finely chopped onions or green onions, raw yolk of egg, salt, freshly ground pepper, and capers. Arrange patties on each plate and make a small indentation for the egg yolk. Arrange chopped onion, capers, and if you like, a little chopped parsley around the edges. Decorate with capers. This is a delicious luncheon dish, particularly stimulating in summer. Plenty of English mustard with it, please.

Good beef is bright red, firm, and fine-grained.

OSAGE COUNTY

FAIR

STOCK

WHILE U WAIT!

3 FOR 25¢

TAKE ONE HOME

FOR THE FOLKS

ROAST BEEF

Standing Ribs of Beef

In this country the most popular roast is the standing rib roast, preferably the first four ribs. Choose beef that is well marbled with fat. In the cooking process, these fine particles will melt and tenderize the firm flesh to make a better roast.

All excess fat and the protective coating over the ribs should be trimmed by the butcher, who should also remove the bone at the end or base of the ribs to make carving easier. You may or may not cut through the ribs just below the fleshy part of the roast, as you prefer.

Allow the roast to stand at room temperature for at least an hour before roasting— or, better, several hours. Wipe with a damp cloth and season with salt and pepper.

Place the roast, fat side up, in an open roasting pan. If you are using a meat thermometer, which is most efficient for roasting, insert in the fleshiest part of the roast, making sure that the bulb of the thermometer does not touch the bone. Place the roast in a preheated, moderately slow oven (325°) and roast, without basting, until thermometer reads 140° for rare meat, 160° for medium, or 170° for well-done beef.

If you do not plan to serve the roast until 15 or 20 minutes after it has finished cooking, remove it when thermometer is several degrees below the required temperature. The roast continues cooking after it leaves the oven; in removing it before it has reached the desired internal heat, you allow for this.

Timetable for Searing Method

450° for 20 minutes, then turn back to 300°.

Rare	16 to 18 minutes per pound
Medium	18 to 22 minutes per pound
Well done	23 to 28 minutes per pound

Timetable for Roasting with Thermometer

(Oven at 325°)

	Minutes per pound 3 to 5 pounds	Minutes per pound 6 to 8 pounds
Rare	26 minutes	22 minutes
Medium	30 minutes	26 minutes
Well done	35 minutes	33 minutes

I believe that low-temperature cooking at a constant heat is preferable for all roast meats. There is less shrinkage, the meat is more evenly done, and less fat gets spattered about the inside of the oven. Nevertheless, many people prefer the old-fashioned two-heat or searing method for meats, as follows:

Prepare roast as above. Place, fat side up, in a very hot oven (450-500°) for 20 minutes. Reduce oven heat to slow (300°), leaving the oven door open for a few minutes to reduce the temperature more quickly, and continue roasting. (See table below.)

Rolled Ribs of Beef

Place the roast on a rack in the roasting pan, fat side up if possible, and insert thermometer. Roast as you do a standing rib roast, allowing an additional 5 to 10 minutes per pound. This is because the bone in a standing roast transmits heat and consequently the meat roasts more quickly than a boned cut.

Sirloin of Beef

In England the sirloin cut is much preferred to the ribs for roasting. Roast it in the same way as a standing rib roast in a moderately slow oven (325°). For a meat thermometer, if you are using one, follow the table below.

OH, THE ROAST BEEF

Accompaniments for Roast Beef

The traditional accompaniments for a roast of beef are browned potatoes and/or Yorkshire pudding. I prefer the juices from the pan poured over the roast rather than the all-too-common brown gravy. Horseradish, either plain or mixed with sour cream and English mustard, is exceedingly popular.

A fine roast of beef, especially if your dinner is a gala affair, deserves your finest wines. A magnificent claret of good vintage, a noble burgundy, or one of the fine reds of the Rhone would be perfection.

Browned Potatoes

Peel potatoes, allowing 1 large potato per person. Halve them or quarter them (if they are the large Idahos) and place in the pan with the roast 1 to 1½ hours before serving time. Salt and pepper them and turn once or twice during cooking so that they become nicely browned on all sides.

Yorkshire Pudding

Beat 2 eggs with a rotary beater for 3 minutes. Add 1 cup milk and continue beating for another minute. Add, a little at a time, ¾ cup sifted flour and 1 teaspoon salt. Continue beating until smooth. Pour into a shallow pan in which you have put about ¼ cup drippings from the roast beef. Place in a hot oven (400°) and bake about 30 minutes. Cut into squares and serve with the roast.

(Serves 4)

LEFTOVER ROAST BEEF

Cold Roast Beef

Cold beef is far more palatable and flavorful when it has not been too thoroughly chilled in the refrigerator. Either allow the cold roast to stand in a cooler or remove it from the refrigerator an hour or two before serving. Serve slices of rare beef, all excess fat removed, with salad (potato or vegetable salad is an excellent accompaniment). Or combine slices of beef with other cold cuts for luncheon or for a buffet supper.

Deviled Beef Bones

Men are usually very fond of the rib bones —with some meat left on them, of course! The bones are dipped in beaten egg and rolled in dry bread crumbs, and cooked very quickly in butter in a large skillet until nicely browned on all sides. Serve with devil sauce.

Deviled Beef Slices

Slices of rare roast beef, prepared as deviled beef bones are, will be most delicious for dinner on a roast's second or third day.

ROAST BEEF TENDERLOIN

The tenderloin of beef, which usually weighs 4 to 6 pounds, is considered by many to be the choicest of all cuts. It has a tendency to be stringy and rather dry, although exceedingly tender. It slices perfectly because there is no tendon or bone, and is, although expensive per pound, a truly economical cut. Count on about ½ pound per person.

Tenderloin should be larded before cooking. Run strips of very fat salt pork through the flesh with a larding needle or have the roast thoroughly wrapped and tied with flattened pieces of beef suet. Place the tenderloin on a rack in a roasting pan and roast in either a very hot oven (450°), allowing 13 minutes per pound, or a moderately slow oven (325°), allowing 18 minutes per pound.

Tenderloin on a Spit

This is a dish for cooking outdoors. Lard the tenderloin. Secure to a roasting spit and toast over the coals, allowing about 15 minutes per pound.

It is a good idea to slice the meat thin and serve on large French rolls or pieces of toasted French bread with a pungent barbecue sauce.

This is an ideal way to serve a large number of people outdoors. A 6-pound tenderloin will serve 12 people easily.

POT ROASTS OF BEEF

A pot roast is one of the less tender cuts of beef. Pot roasts are covered and then cooked very slowly in liquid (water, wine, or stock) on top of the stove or in the oven. It may be marinated before cooking. The meat is always served well done and has tenderness and flavor. It is hearty fare and one that is relished by all who are blessed with good appetites.

The best cuts for pot roast are top round, rump, chuck, or bottom round. There should be an ample amount of fat on the meat.

Allow 1 pound per person, for a pot roast will shrink.

Wipe the roast well with a damp cloth. Brown quickly on all sides in hot fat. Season. Place in a heavy, covered kettle or pot, add liquid, and simmer on top of stove or in a slow oven until tender. Allow about 25 minutes per pound for a pot roast.

Plain Pot Roast

Choose a piece of beef weighing 4 to 6 pounds. Have it larded or not, as you wish.

Dredge the meat with flour, pepper, and salt. Melt 4 tablespoons butter in a deep kettle and sear meat on all sides very quickly until nicely browned. Add ½ to 1 cup liquid. (This may be water, stock, wine, or tomato juice.)

Reduce the heat, cover tightly, and simmer slowly for 25 minutes per pound or until meat is tender. The meat should be tender enough to cut easily, but not stringy and mushy. If the liquid evaporates, add more. *(Serves 4 to 6.)*

VARIATIONS

Italian Style: Stud the meat with thin slivers of garlic, using 2 cloves for a 5-pound piece of meat. Sear in 4 tablespoons olive oil until nicely browned. Add 2 large onions, sliced; a bay leaf, ½ teaspoon thyme, 1 teaspoon salt, 1 teaspoon pepper, a sprig of parsley, ½ cup tomato purée, and ½ cup stock or water in which you have dissolved a bouillon cube. Cover and simmer for 25 minutes per pound or until tender.

Remove pot roast to a hot platter and skim excess fat from the sauce. Add an extra cup of tomato purée and bring the sauce to a boil, stirring well. Serve with buttered noodles.

With Wine: Choose a 4- to 6-pound pot roast. Wipe with a damp cloth and season with salt and pepper. Lard the meat well with ¼-inch strips of salt pork. Sear in 4 tablespoons butter until nicely browned on all sides. Pour over it 6 tablespoons cognac, and blaze. Extinguish the flame and add 1 clove garlic, 1 bay leaf, a pinch of thyme, and 1 cup red or white wine. Cover and simmer for about 25 minutes per pound or until tender.

Add 12 small white onions, peeled, and 4 or 5 carrots, peeled and cut in strips. If you need additional liquid, add another ½ cup wine. Continue simmering until the meat and vegetables are tender. Just before serving, add ¼ cup finely chopped parsley and stir it into the sauce. Arrange vegetables around the meat on a hot platter and pour the sauce over. Buttered noodles or potatoes mashed with butter and cream are excellent with this. *(Serves 4 to 6.)*

Hungarian: Choose 4 to 6 pounds of beef larded with ¼-inch strips of salt pork. Sear the pot roast well in 4 tablespoons butter or olive oil and, when nicely browned, add 1 teaspoon salt, 1½ teaspoons Hungarian paprika, ¼ teaspoon nutmeg, and ½ cup stock. Cover and simmer until tender—25 minutes per pound—adding more liquid if needed.

Remove meat to a hot platter and then skim excess fat from sauce. Add another teaspoon paprika and 1 cup thick sour cream, and stir well until the sour cream is blended with the sauce and just heated through. Serve with buttered noodles generously sprinkled with parsley.

(Serves 4 to 6.)

BRAISED BEEF

The distinction between pot roast and braised beef is very small, but certain dishes are more justifiably placed in the latter category.

Braised Beef, Peasant Style

4 to 6 pounds beef (round, top sirloin, or rump)	1 knuckle bone of beef
2 pounds veal neck	2 cloves garlic
Salt pork for larding	13 small onions
6 carrots	½ teaspoon thyme
1 bay leaf	1½ teaspoons salt
6 tablespoons cognac	4 tablespoons butter
2 cups red wine	Parsley
	2 quarts water

Place the veal neck and the beef bone in a soup kettle with 1 onion stuck with 2 cloves, a bay leaf, and a generous sprig of parsley. Add the cold water and allow it to come to a boil.

When it has boiled briskly for 10 minutes, skim off any scum that has risen to the top. Cover, and allow to simmer for 2 hours, adding 1½ teaspoons salt after the first hour. Remove cover and let broth reduce by a third.

While making the broth, lard the beef (if you have not had your butcher do so) and stud it with garlic. Sear it on all sides in 4 tablespoons butter. Blaze with the brandy. Place beef in a Dutch oven or casserole, and add the veal neck and the beef bone. Add the thyme and enough of the broth to cover about three-fourths of the meat. Cover and simmer gently, about 2½ hours, then add 12 small peeled onions and 6 peeled and halved carrots. Add more broth if necessary and continue cooking until the beef is tender.

Remove cooked meat and vegetables to a hot platter and reduce the broth very quickly. Serve with boiled potatoes. *(Serves 4 to 6.)*

If you have some beef left, place it in a deep bowl and pour the reduced and strained broth over it. It should jell, and will give you a wonderful cold dish the next day.

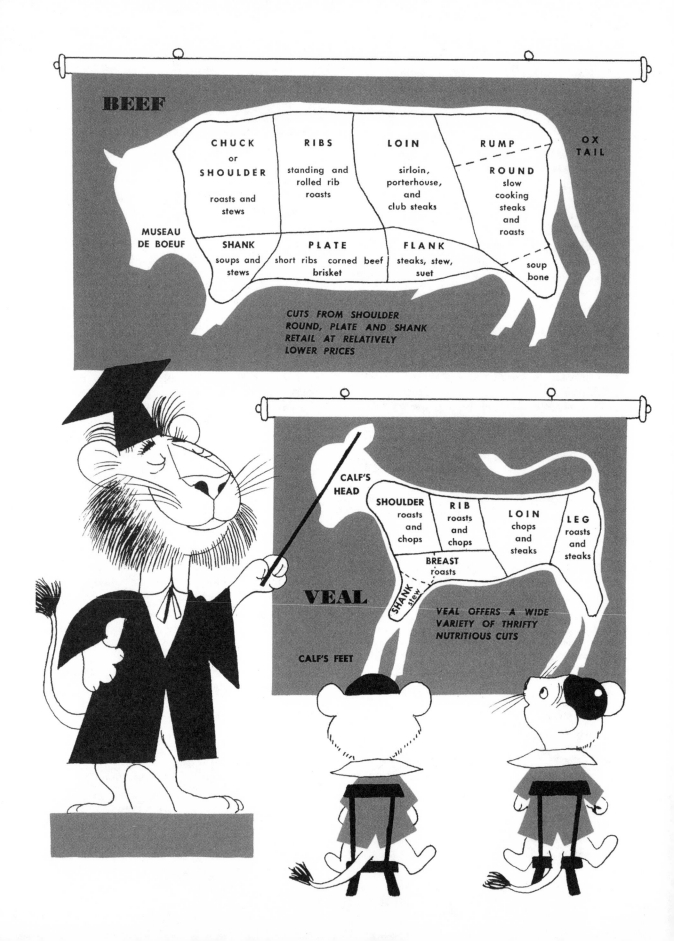

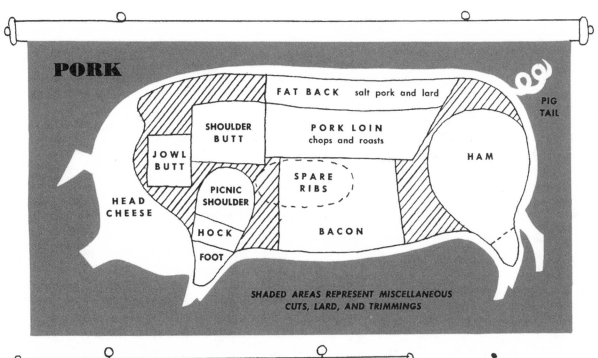

PORK

FAT BACK   salt pork and lard

PIG TAIL

SHOULDER BUTT

PORK LOIN
chops and roasts

JOWL BUTT

HAM

HEAD CHEESE

PICNIC SHOULDER

SPARE RIBS

HOCK

BACON

FOOT

SHADED AREAS REPRESENT MISCELLANEOUS CUTS, LARD, AND TRIMMINGS

LAMB

NECK

RIB
roasts and chops

LOIN
roasts and chops

SHOULDER
roasts steaks

LEG
roasts and steaks

SHANK
stew

BREAST
roasts

*NECK for braising, broth, and stew
SHANK for broth and stew*

SHEEP'S TROTTERS

INSP'D US & PAS'D

THIS STAMP MEANS THE MEAT HAS BEEN INSPECTED AND PASSED BY THE GOVERNMENT

BOILED BEEF DISHES

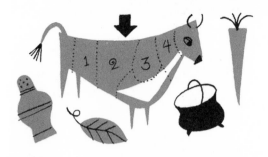

One may use a variety of cuts for boiling. Brisket, plate, short ribs, rump, and bottom round are all good. A 5-pound piece will serve 6 amply with some left over.

Boiled Beef

Beef	Bay leaf	1 onion
Salt	Parsley	1 carrot

Place the meat in a deep kettle and add salt—½ teaspoon per pound—a bay leaf, an onion, a carrot, and a sprig of parsley. Add enough hot water to cover about half the meat. Cover and simmer—do not boil—until tender. A 4- to 5-pound piece of beef will take 3 to 4 hours to cook. The meat should be tender enough to cut into even slices, but not mushy and stringy.

Serve hot with horseradish sauce, a piquant sauce, or a tomato sauce, and with whole carrots and onions which have been cooked in the kettle with the meat during the last hour.

If the meat is to be served cold, allow it to cool in the broth. When cool, place in a bowl or casserole with a little of the broth. Cover with a plate and place a weight of some kind on the plate to press the meat into form. This will make it slice better.

Beef with Potato Balls

Cold boiled beef (about 3 pounds)	4 tablespoons butter
3 large potatoes	Salt and pepper
	Parsley

Peel the potatoes and cut them into balls. Cook in the butter in a skillet, shaking the pan so that they brown evenly. When almost cooked, remove to a hot plate, leaving the butter in the pan.

Cut medium-thin slices of cold beef and then cut each slice into 1-inch strips. Sauté quickly in the butter in the pan, adding salt and pepper if needed.

When the beef is heated through, add the potatoes and allow them to cook together for a few minutes until they are piping hot and the potatoes quite done.

Arrange on a hot platter and sprinkle generously with chopped parsley. *(Serves 4.)*

Beef with Tomato Sauce

Cold beef slices	1 teaspoon Worcestershire
2 cloves garlic	sauce
4 tablespoons butter	½ teaspoon dry mustard
½ cup tomato purée	Salt and pepper

Sauté the beef slices in the butter with garlic, cut in thin shreds, until beef is thoroughly heated and lightly browned. Add tomato purée, Worcestershire sauce, and dry mustard. Salt and pepper to taste. Cook until sauce is thoroughly blended.

Beef with Potato Salad

Cold boiled beef slices	Celery, finely cut
Cold potatoes, sliced	French dressing
Onions, sliced	Hard-cooked eggs, sliced
Chopped parsley	Peeled tomato wedges

Cut slices of cold boiled beef into 1-inch squares. Place in a salad bowl with cold sliced potatoes, thin slices of onion, chopped parsley, and some finely cut celery. Toss with French dressing and garnish the salad bowl with sliced hard-cooked eggs and wedges of peeled tomatoes. This dish, with pickled beets or a string-bean salad, makes a delicious summer luncheon or supper.

Beef for Buffet Platter

Cold boiled beef slices	Hard-cooked eggs, sliced
Onion rings	Tomatoes, sliced
Sliced cold potatoes	Pickled beets
French dressing	Endive stalks, quartered, or
Chives, chopped	romaine wedges
Parsley, chopped	Vinaigrette sauce

A variation of the same dish is good for a buffet supper. Arrange thin slices of beef in the center of a large platter and garnish with onion rings. Surround the meat with sliced cold potatoes which have been marinating in a good French dressing made with chopped chives and plenty of chopped parsley. Garnish with quarters of hard-cooked eggs, sliced tomatoes, pickled beets, stalks of endive cut in quarters, or wedges of romaine. Vinaigrette sauce poured over the beef improves this dish.

CORNED BEEF

The brisket and the rump are the preferred cuts for corned beef; it is well to buy a piece without too much fat on it. Purchase ½ to ¾ pound per person. (If you plan on a pound per person, you will have some left for corned-beef hash, one of the most delicious leftover dishes in the world.)

Place the corned beef in a deep kettle and cover about ¾ of the meat with water. Simmer, covered, for 1 hour; then pour off the water and add fresh water.

Continue simmering until beef is tender. A 5-pound piece of corned beef will take approximately 4 hours to cook. Serve with plain boiled potatoes and cabbage, and accompany the meat with English mustard or horseradish sauce.

Many people relish their cabbage cooked in the pot with the beef during its last half hour. Do this if you wish, though it tends to become a bit greasy that way. If you cook it separately, it will taste much better. It makes a pleasant change to serve cole slaw instead of hot cabbage with your corned beef.

Corned Beef Hash

Corned beef	Fresh-ground pepper
Boiled potatoes, chopped	Pinch of nutmeg
1 small onion, chopped	4 tablespoons butter
Salt	

Home-made hash can be a triumphant dish, especially if you use a fine piece of corned beef that is flavorful and finely textured.

Chop the corned beef fine. Add ⅓ of that amount of chopped boiled potatoes and, if you wish, 1 small onion, finely chopped. Blend the ingredients and taste for seasoning. You probably will not need additional salt, but you may wish to add some freshly ground pepper and a pinch of nutmeg.

Melt 4 to 6 tablespoons butter in a skillet. Add the hash and press down into the pan. Cook over slow heat until the hash has formed a crust on the bottom. Fold over as you would an omelet and serve at once.

Baked Corned Beef Hash

Pack hash into a buttered casserole and dot with butter. Bake in a moderate oven (350°) until nicely browned on top.

Corned beef hash may be served with the traditional poached egg or with scrambled eggs mixed with plenty of chopped parsley. This is perhaps the one dish that requires chili sauce, but be sure it is slightly warm, for a cold sauce on hot meat is most unappetizing.

MISCELLANEOUS BEEF DISHES

Braised Beefsteak (Swiss Steak)

3 pounds round steak	Salt and pepper
1-1½ cups flour	Onion, thinly sliced
3 tablespoons butter or bacon fat	1 cup liquid (water, stock, tomato juice, or red wine)

For this dish, sometimes called Swiss steak, one should buy a thick slice of round steak. For 4 people select a 2-inch piece of steak weighing about 3 pounds.

With a heavy knife or the edge of a plate pound flour into the meat. Brown the steak very quickly in butter or bacon fat, and season well with salt and pepper. You may brown an onion cut in thin slices with the steak, if you wish.

Add liquid and cover the pan tightly. Simmer over a low flame or bake in a slow oven (325°) until very tender. This should take about 2 hours.

Serve with plain boiled potatoes or with steamed rice. If you wish, add peeled potatoes and peeled carrots to the pan for the last hour of cooking.   (Serves 4.)

Braised Short Ribs of Beef

Short ribs	Bay leaf
Salt and pepper	Thyme
4 tablespoons fat	Water or stock
1 clove garlic	Flour
8 small peeled onions	Butter
4 carrots, scraped and halved	Chopped parsley

Short ribs are a delicious cut if cooked thoroughly and seasoned well. There is a good deal of fat in this cut, and this should be taken into consideration when you purchase it. Average 1 pound of short ribs per person.

Cut ribs into serving pieces. Season with salt and pepper, and brown very quickly in a large skillet or Dutch oven in the fat, together with a clove of garlic.

Add onions, carrots, a bay leaf, and just a pinch of thyme. Pour in 1 cup liquid, cover, and simmer on top of stove, or cook in a moderately slow oven (325°) approximately 2 hours. Potatoes may be cooked along with the short ribs.

If you wish to thicken the sauce, add balls of well-blended flour and butter to the liquid just a few minutes before serving. Sprinkle with chopped parsley and pass the sauce separately.

VARIATIONS

With Tomato Sauce: Add 1 cup tomato purée and 1 cup stock to the pan. Serve with buttered macaroni or spaghetti, using the sauce for the paste as well as for the meat.

With Wine: For liquid, use half red wine and half stock, in addition to the seasonings given above. This will add a pleasant blend of flavors.

Beef Stews

Stews are ideal foods for party service—informal parties, of course—because continued cooking doesn't seem to hurt them. Use any of the less tender cuts for stew, but you will find that if you use very fat, gristly cuts you may have a less pleasing result than if you use good cuts of less tender parts. Chuck, round, rump, and shin all are good stewing cuts, and one should remember not to have too much fat on the meat. Three pounds of beef will serve 6 people amply and should leave some for the next day.

Cut meat for stew in 2-inch cubes, or smaller. Brown on all sides in fat in a Dutch oven or a heavy covered skillet and then cover with liquid, which may be water, stock, or a mixture of water or stock and red wine. Seasonings—garlic, onion, parsley, a bay leaf, and a pinch of thyme—are added and the whole brought to a boil.

When the boiling point is reached, the heat is immediately reduced and the stew allowed to simmer, covered, for the entire cooking process—1½ to 2 hours.

About 40 minutes before the stew is ready for the table, the vegetables are added and allowed to cook with the meat.

Almost any combination of vegetables may be added. Small onions, carrots, celery, peas, green beans, lima beans, potatoes, leeks, salsify—practically any vegetable is good. The only ones which should be used with caution are turnips and parsnips; but the less said about these two vegetables the better. If turnip has one claim to fame, it is its ability to smother any other flavor. If you include tomatoes, it is wiser to add them in purée, or else to seed the tomatoes beforehand.

You may thicken the stew, if necessary, with small balls of butter and flour mixed together and dropped into the kettle. Allow the liquid to boil for 1 minute. You may remove the meat and vegetables before thickening and replace them afterward if you find it easier to blend the sauce this way.

Many people like dumplings with stew. Some prefer boiled rice, others noodles.

Beefsteak and Kidney Pie

3 pounds rump or round steak	¼ teaspoon thyme
Flour	1 large onion, chopped
Salt and pepper	Water or stock
6 or 8 lamb kidneys	3 tablespoons butter
Beef suet	Pastry dough
	1 egg yolk

Cut steak into strips about 3 inches long and 1 inch wide. Dredge well with flour and season with salt and pepper. Skin, clean, and slice thin the lamb kidneys.

Render the fat from the beef, together with a little beef suet cut in tiny cubes, in a skillet. Brown the beef very quickly in the hot fat. When it is nicely browned, add thyme, onion, and enough water or stock to just cover the meat.

Allow this to simmer until the meat is tender, which should take 1 to 1½ hours.

When the meat is almost ready to remove from the stove, brown the kidneys very quickly in 3 tablespoons butter, but do not let them cook after browning.

Fill a 2-quart casserole with separate layers of meat and kidneys, and add the liquid from the cooked beef, letting it come to an inch from the top. It is wise to place a custard cup or jelly glass in the center of the casserole to hold up the crust (one may find special gadgets in the shops which are most efficient for this purpose).

Cover the casserole with a rich pastry dough. Make several slashes in the pastry so that the steam will escape, and brush with lightly beaten egg yolk.

Place in a very hot oven (450°) for 10 minutes, reduce the temperature to moderate (350°), and bake until the crust is nicely browned and cooked through—about ½ hour.

Serve with plain boiled potatoes and a green salad. *(Serves 4 to 6.)*

VARIATIONS

With Mushrooms: Add a few sliced, sautéed mushrooms to the pie.

With Biscuit Crust: Use a biscuit crust instead of pastry and bake in a hot oven (425°) for 15 minutes.

Leftover Meat Pie: Use leftover roast beef for the pie. Mix 2 tablespoons fat—butter or beef drippings—and 2 tablespoons flour over low heat until well blended. Add 3 cups stock, or water in which you have dissolved 3 bouillon cubes. Stir until thickened and add 1 tablespoon Worcestershire sauce. Pour over the meat, add 1 large onion chopped and sautéed in 3 tablespoons butter, and a tablespoon of chopped parsley.

Beefsteak and Kidney Pudding
Suet Crust

2 cups flour	⅓ teaspoon salt
¾ cup beef suet, chopped or ground very fine	Water

To the flour add the suet and the salt. The suet should be almost of a powdery consistency. Blend well and add just enough water to make a stiff paste. Roll.

The Pudding

2½ pounds rump steak	Salt and pepper
6 or 8 lamb kidneys	Water or stock

Line a deep bowl, which has a substantial rim, with the suet crust. Cut steak into 1-inch squares and dredge with flour.

Clean, skin, and slice 6 or 8 lamb kidneys. Fill the bowl with alternate layers of beef and kidneys, salting and peppering each layer. Add water or stock to within 2 inches of the top of the bowl. Cover the bowl with suet crust, moistening the edges of the crusts and pressing them tightly together so that the juices do not escape during cooking.

Wring out a large, clean cloth in hot water, flour it, and arrange it over the pudding, tying it securely around the bowl. Put the pudding in a large kettle of boiling water and cook for 4 hours. The pudding bowl should be covered for the entire cooking period, and you may have to replenish the water several times.

When you remove the cloth from the bowl before serving, be certain to slash the crust to allow the steam to escape, lest the pudding burst. *(Serves 4 to 6.)*

Beef Tongue

Smoked Tongue: It is preferable to soak a smoked tongue in cold water for 2 or 3 hours before cooking it. The tongue is a highly developed muscle and requires long, slow cooking to tenderize it.

Place the smoked tongue in a deep kettle with 4 or 5 peppercorns, a bay leaf, and an onion stuck with 2 cloves, and cover with cold water. Salt will not be needed.

After the water has boiled 5 minutes, remove any scum that has come to the surface. Reduce the heat to simmering and cook until the tongue is tender—about 50 minutes to the pound.

Allow the tongue to cool in the stock until you are able to handle it comfortably. Remove the tongue from the stock and skin it, using a sharp knife. You can pull off the skin fairly easily with your fingers. Tongue should be sliced very thin, against the grain.

Serve either hot or cold with a horseradish sauce, a mustard sauce, or a sweet-and-sour sauce.

Fresh Tongue: Prepare fresh tongue in the same way as smoked tongue, omitting the soaking period. Wipe well with a damp cloth, place in a kettle, and proceed as above, adding ½ teaspoon salt per pound.

Beef Kidney

Beef kidney	1 tablespoon finely chopped
Flour	shallot or green onion
Butter	1 tablespoon finely chopped
Salt and pepper	parsley
	½ cup red wine

Soak the beef kidney in acidulated water for 2 to 3 hours.

Remove and trim off excess fat and gristle. Slice thin and dredge with flour.

Melt 3 tablespoons butter in a skillet. Place slices of kidney in pan and sear very quickly on both sides. Salt and pepper well and add 1 tablespoon finely chopped shallot or green onion and 1 tablespoon finely chopped parsley.

When nicely browned, add ½ cup red wine and reduce the heat. Allow the kidney to simmer for 10 to 15 minutes. Serve at once.

Oxtail Ragout

2 ox tails	1 bay leaf
2 pounds shin of beef with	Water (about 3 quarts)
bone	3 carrots
1 large onion stuck with 2	Sprig of celery
cloves	Salt and pepper

Have the butcher cut up the ox tails for you. Place them in a kettle with the piece of shin (for a richer stock) and the seasonings. Cover with cold water and simmer for 3 to 4 hours or until tender. It is well to make this part of the dish the day before so that the meat and the broth will have a chance to cool thoroughly.

When they are cooled, remove the fat from the top and remove the pieces of ox tail and the piece of shin. Reheat the broth and strain. Broth may be used for a clear soup or reserved for other dishes.

For the ragout:

1 clove garlic	½ cup red wine
6 carrots	3 tablespoons chopped
10 small onions	parsley
½ cup diced celery	2 tablespoons flour
4 tablespoons butter	Sections of ox tail
3 cups broth	

Wash and peel carrots and cut in halves or quarters. Peel small onions and cut up celery. Melt butter in deep kettle or large skillet and brown the vegetables, including the garlic, in the butter. Sprinkle with flour; mix well.

Reduce heat. Mix in broth and red wine, and bring to a boil. Add ox tail and simmer for 25 to 30 minutes or until vegetables are tender and pieces of ox tail hot.

Add chopped parsley and taste for seasoning. Serve with boiled potatoes. *(Serves 6.)*

VEAL

Veal, which has less fat than any other meat, needs long, slow cooking and usually some striking flavor to complement it. It is delicate in texture and in flavor. The leg or rump is probably the choicest cut. It is used for roasts, cutlets, steaks, and pot roasts. The shoulder, which should be boned and may be stuffed, is an excellent cut for roasting or braising.

The loin or rib sections are used for chops and for roasting, although I feel that a roast from the leg is far more tender and delicious. Breast of veal is good stuffed and roasted. Veal produces many other delicacies—calf's liver (which is unsurpassed), sweetbreads, calf's head, calf's feet, and calf's tongue. These are less expensive cuts, except for the liver and the sweetbreads, but they are delicious. The very finest veal is the milk-fed variety, which is practically white in its raw state. Otherwise the flesh has a pinkish hue that is unmistakable. Since there is very little fat on veal, it is better to have it larded by the butcher for roasting or braising, or you may do the larding yourself. Allow about ¾ pound veal to a person when purchasing. Veal bones have a high gelatin content and make exceptionally good broth, so never allow the butcher to throw away any bones he may remove from the meat.

ROAST VEAL

Use leg, boned shoulder, rib, or loin. Allow ¾ pound meat per person. If you do not have the meat larded, cover the roast well with strips of salt pork, bacon, or suet. If you use a meat thermometer, insert it in the heaviest part of the muscle.

Roast the veal, uncovered, in a slow oven (300°). The meat thermometer should register between 165° and 170° when the veal is cooked. If you have larded the meat or covered it well with fat, it will need no basting. Otherwise you should baste often with a mixture of half butter and half broth. This will give a pleasant glaze to your finished roast.

Use the juices from the pan for sauce, and you may add a little heavy cream or sour cream. If you wish the gravy thicker, add balls of butter and flour, well blended, after removing the veal. Salt and pepper to taste.

Serve with noodles which have been boiled, drained, and tossed with butter and a little basil. This dish is exceedingly good with roast veal.

Stuffed Shoulder of Veal

5 to 6 pounds veal shoulder, boned	10 anchovy fillets with oil
2 cloves garlic, finely chopped	2 tablespoons parsley, chopped
1 cup dry bread crumbs, finely rolled	10 to 12 ripe olives
	Salt
	Bacon or salt pork

Have the butcher remove the shoulder bone and ask him to leave a pocket for stuffing.

Combine garlic with bread crumbs, anchovy fillets and the oil in which they are packed, parsley, and ripe olives seeded and cut into slices. Taste this stuffing before salting it, because the salt in the anchovies may make additional seasoning unnecessary.

Stuff the pocket of the veal and tie the roast securely with heavy white twine. Wrap bacon or salt pork around the roast to lubricate it, place it uncovered in a slow oven (300°), and cook until the roast thermometer (which you have inserted in the fleshiest part of the meat) registers 165°. If you do not use a thermometer, allow about 35 minutes per pound for the roast.   *(Serves 6.)*

VARIATIONS

With Pork Stuffing: Use a stuffing made as follows: Sauté 2 medium onions, finely chopped, in 3 tablespoons butter. Blend with ½ pound ground fresh pork, 1 teaspoon salt, 1 teaspoon coarse black pepper, 2 tablespoons chopped parsley, ½ teaspoon thyme, and ⅓ cup dry bread crumbs. Bind with 1 egg. Stuff the veal pocket. Roast as above.

With Ham Stuffing: For stuffing, combine 2 medium onions, finely chopped, with 1 cup finely ground ham, ½ cup dry bread crumbs, ½ cup pine nuts, salt and pepper to taste, and 2 eggs to bind. Season with ½ teaspoon thyme and 2 tablespoons chopped parsley. Stuff and tie the veal. Sear the veal in butter or olive oil in a deep pan. When it is nicely browned on all sides, add 1 cup dry white wine, cover, and simmer very slowly for approximately 2 hours, turning the meat once or twice during the cooking. Salt and pepper the meat during the last hour of cooking. Remove to a hot platter and season the sauce to taste. Add 2 teaspoons paprika and blend it well with the sauce in the pan. Add, stirring constantly, 1 cup heavy cream mixed with 2 egg yolks and stir until mixture thickens. Do not allow it to boil. Serve with the roasted veal and accompany the meat with buttered noodles to which you have added tiny croutons fried in butter until they are crisp.

Stuffed Breast of Veal

This is a most economical cut; though you do not get much meat with your stuffing, it is tasty and it is fun to pick the bones.

Have a pocket cut in the breast of veal at the large end. Stuff with any type of stuffing (those given above for veal shoulder are excellent). Fasten the edges with skewers and place the meat on a rack in a roasting pan. Butter it well or lay a few strips of bacon over the top and roast, uncovered, in a slow oven (300°), allowing 30 minutes per pound.

Serve with a tomato sauce or with merely the juices from the pan. You will need only a green vegetable or a fine salad to follow this, for there is an ample amount of starch in your stuffing to take care of that part of the meal.

Veal Loaf

2 pounds ground veal	1 pound ground ham
1 clove garlic, ground	2 medium onions, ground
1 green pepper, finely chopped	2 teaspoons salt
	2 eggs

Mix ingredients until they are completely and smoothly blended. Form the mixture into a loaf and place in a baking pan or on a rack in the pan.

Cover the top with a few strips of bacon or salt pork, place in a moderate oven (350°), and bake 1 to 1½ hours. Baste with the drippings in the pan once or twice during the cooking.

The loaf may be eaten hot or cold. In summer it is delicious served cold with a salad and a hot vegetable.   *(Serves 6.)*

VARIATIONS

With Olives: Instead of green pepper, add 10 or 12 sliced stuffed olives.

With Mushrooms: Add, instead of green pepper, 1 cup finely chopped mushrooms and proceed as above.

VEAL CUTLETS

Veal cutlet or veal steak is usually cut from the leg and has the small round leg bone in it. It is either breaded or dredged in flour, browned in butter or olive oil, and then simmered with seasonings and liquid until tender. Often it is served with a sauce to which cream or sour cream has been added, and on other occasions with tomato sauce. It is sometimes stuffed and rolled, in which case it is called a roulade or a veal bird.

Veal, being most amenable to flavorings, offers a good opportunity for imagination in respect to the seasonings and sauces used.

Serve with boiled, drained noodles to which you have added a clove of garlic, 3 tablespoons olive oil, and ½ cup grated Parmesan cheese. Mix well and sprinkle with a little chopped basil, fresh or dried. *(Serves 4.)*

Veal Cutlet Paprika

2 pounds veal cutlet about	6 tablespoons butter
¾ inch thick	1 tablespoon paprika
Salt and pepper	½ cup dry white wine
Flour	1 cup sour cream

Season cutlet with salt and pepper and dredge with flour. Sauté slowly in 6 tablespoons butter until nicely browned on both sides. Add 1 tablespoon paprika, sprinkling it over the surface of the meat. Add ½ cup dry white wine, cover the skillet, and simmer slowly until veal is tender—about ½ hour.

Remove the meat to a hot platter, add another teaspoon paprika, and stir in 1 cup sour cream, being careful that the sour cream does not curdle. Pour the sauce over the veal and serve at once with buttered noodles.
(Serves 4.)

Breaded Veal Cutlet

2 pounds veal steak, cut	Bread or cracker crumbs
¾ inch thick	5 tablespoons butter
Salt and pepper	½ cup heavy or sour cream
Flour	½ cup tomato purée
1 egg, beaten	

Season the cutlet with salt and pepper. Roll it in flour, dip in beaten egg, and roll in bread or cracker crumbs. Press the meat into the crumbs so that they adhere.

Melt butter in a large skillet. Sauté the meat very slowly until nicely browned, turning once. When it is well browned, cover and allow to simmer until tender, about 30 minutes. You may need to add more butter if the crumbs have absorbed all the butter in the pan. In a heavy-bottomed skillet no liquid need be added.

When the meat is tender, remove to a hot platter and add heavy cream or sour cream or the same amount of tomato purée to the pan. Blend well with the crumbs which will be lurking there. Rectify the seasoning and serve with the veal cutlet.

Veal Cutlet with Peppers

2 pounds veal steak	Salt and pepper
¼ cup olive oil	2 or 3 green peppers, cut
2 cloves garlic, shredded	in long strips
Flour	Lemon juice

Heat the olive oil in a large skillet. Lightly sauté garlic, cut in shreds. Dredge the steak in flour and season it well with salt and pepper. Sauté slowly in the olive oil until nicely browned on both sides. Add green peppers cut in long strips to the pan, cover, and simmer over a low heat until the veal is tender and the peppers are cooked through.

Remove the meat to a hot platter, add a few drops of lemon juice to the pan, and mix with the peppers. Place the peppers on the veal and serve with mashed potatoes which have been whipped with butter and cream and seasoned with a little paprika. *(Serves 4.)*

Sauté slowly in olive oil until nicely browned on both sides. Add garlic, finely chopped, and cover and cook for 10 minutes, simmering over low heat.

Add tomatoes and red wine. Cover again and allow to simmer until tender.

Just before removing from the fire, add chopped parsley and ripe olives. Remove the meat to a platter, and mix the sauce well and pour over the veal. *(Serves 4.)*

Serve with rice baked in the oven.

Veal Cutlet Provençale

2 pounds veal steak	½ cup red wine
½ cup olive oil	2 tablespoons parsley,
2 cloves garlic	chopped
2 tomatoes, peeled, seeded,	12 ripe olives
and finely chopped	

Season veal steak and dredge with flour.

SCALLOPINI OF VEAL

Scallops of veal are slices from the leg which are pounded very flat. They are either breaded or dredged with flour and cooked very quickly, and are usually served with a sauce. Allow ⅓ to ½ pound per person.

Pan-fried Scallopini of Veal

2 pounds veal cutlet,	Flour
cut in thin scallopini	Salt and pepper
(rounds or ovals)	Paprika
2 eggs, well beaten	¼ pound butter
2 tablespoons water	Lemon juice
Dry bread or zwieback	
crumbs	

About an hour before you wish to cook the scallopini, beat 2 eggs well and add 2 tablespoons water. Roll out dry bread crumbs or zwieback crumbs. Dip the pieces of veal into flour which has been seasoned with salt, pepper, and paprika, then into the beaten egg and roll in crumbs. Place the scallops in the refrigerator until ready to cook.

Unless you have two skillets working, you will not be able to cook all the scallops at one time. So have a pan or dish where the cooked ones may be kept hot without drying out too much.

Melt ¼ pound butter in a large skillet and sauté the scallops quickly, browning them nicely on both sides. Remove to the hot dish or plates and sprinkle with salt, pepper, and lemon juice.

When scallops are all cooked, arrange them on a hot platter with either buttered noodles or rice. Garnish with slices of lemon.

(Serves 4.)

Scallopini with Mushrooms and White Wine

2 pounds veal, in thin	3 or 4 shallots or small
scallops	white onions
Flour	1 cup mushrooms, sliced
Salt	½ cup white wine
Black pepper	1 tablespoon parsley,
Paprika	chopped
4 tablespoons butter	Few leaves tarragon

Dredge scallops with flour seasoned with salt, freshly ground black pepper, and paprika. Sauté the scallops slowly in the butter, and when they are nicely browned place them in a hot casserole or pan to keep warm.

When all the scallops are cooked, add to the butter in the pan the shallots or onions, finely chopped, and sauté for 2 minutes. Add sliced mushrooms and blend well with the onion or shallots. Add ¼ cup white wine and allow it to cook down for a few minutes.

Add parsley and tarragon.

Finally, add another ¼ cup white wine and allow all to boil up for 1 or 2 minutes before pouring over the scallops.   *(Serves 4.)*

VARIATIONS

Polonaise: Dredge scallops with flour seasoned with salt and pepper. Sauté in 4 tablespoons butter and place in a hot dish. Add to the pan 2 small onions, finely chopped, and 3 tomatoes, peeled, seeded, and chopped. Allow to cook down for 3 or 4 minutes; then add ¼ cup white wine and a tablespoon chopped parsley, and simmer for a few minutes. Stir in 3 or 4 tablespoons sour cream and allow the cream to just heat through before pouring the sauce over the meat.

Herbed: Sauté scallops of veal, which you have dredged in seasoned flour, until nicely browned and cooked through. Transfer to hot dish. Add 2 tomatoes, seeded, peeled, and chopped to the pan with ¼ cup white wine, and allow to cook down very quickly, stirring the while. Add 1 tablespoon chopped fresh basil or a teaspoon of the dried basil and blend well with the tomato. Add another ¼ cup white wine and allow it to cook up for a minute before serving the sauce over the hot scallops.

In Wine: Sauté the scallops as above. Add ½ cup sherry, Madeira, or Marsala to the pan. Cover, and simmer for 5 minutes. Arrange on hot platter, pour the sauce over the meat, and serve at once.

Madeira: Sauté scallops as above, remove to a hot platter, and add ¼ cup Madeira and ¼ cup strong consommé or bouillon to the pan. Cook for 3 or 4 minutes and add 1 teaspoon butter which has been mixed with 1 teaspoon flour. Blend well, pour over the scallops, and sprinkle with chopped parsley.

You may serve with this mushrooms sautéed in butter, to which you have added more of the same wine used in cooking the scallopini.

VEAL CHOPS

Veal chops, cut from the loin or the ribs, may be prepared in the same way as veal cutlets. And veal cutlets may be prepared the same way as veal chops, but they are listed here separately, with a few different recipes under each heading.

Veal Chops Parmigiana

4 veal chops, 1 inch thick (loin chops preferred)	1 egg, beaten
Flour	Dry bread or zwieback crumbs
Salt and pepper	¼ cup olive oil
Paprika	Tomato sauce
¼ cup Parmesan cheese, grated	4 slices mozzarella

For this dish you will have to find, in addition to Parmesan cheese, some mozzarella, which is a soft, quick-melting cheese used a great deal in Italian cooking.

Roll chops in seasoned flour (add salt, pepper, and paprika), then in beaten egg, and lastly in dry bread or zwieback crumbs which have been mixed with Parmesan cheese. Prepare the chops about 1 hour before you wish to cook them and allow them to chill in the refrigerator.

Prepare a tomato sauce as follows: Sauté 1 clove garlic in 3 tablespoons olive oil. Add 1 cup tomato purée. (The Italian style made from the small Italian tomatoes and flavored with basil is the best. If that is unavailable, add a small amount of basil to the tomato purée which you have on hand.) Allow the tomatoes to cook with the garlic over low heat for 10 to 15 minutes, stirring often to prevent sticking or burning. Taste for seasoning; often there is not enough salt in the commercial product.

Heat olive oil in a large skillet and sauté

the breaded chops until they are nicely browned on each side. Transfer the chops to a shallow casserole or baking dish with a little of the tomato sauce. Top each chop with thin slices of the mozzarella and place in a moderate oven (350°) for approximately 15 minutes or until cheese is melted and lightly browned and chops are cooked through. Serve with additional tomato sauce.

You may bake and serve the chops in individual casseroles, if you wish. *(Serves 4.)*

Stuffed Veal Chops

Veal chops, 1½ inches thick	Crumbs
Italian ham (prosciutto), sliced	¼ cup olive oil
Flour	½ cup white wine
1 egg, beaten	2 tablespoons parsley, chopped

Have veal chops (1 per person) cut 1½ inches thick. Cut a small pocket in each one and stuff with thin slices of Italian ham (prosciutto) or thin strips of Virginia ham.

Dredge chops in seasoned flour, dip in beaten egg, and then roll in crumbs.

Heat olive oil in a large skillet. Sauté the chops until well browned on each side. Add ¼ cup white wine, cover the pan, and simmer slowly over a low heat until the chops are tender. Test them with a fork or skewer. Turn once or twice during the simmering process.

Remove the chops to a hot platter, add ¼ cup white wine and the chopped parsley to the pan, and let it cook up briskly for a minute, stirring the while. Pour the sauce over the chops and serve at once.

MISCELLANEOUS VEAL DISHES

Veal Sauté

2 pounds veal in stewing pieces	½ cup stock or bouillon
Flour	12 white onions, small, peeled
¼ cup olive oil	6 to 8 small carrots, scraped
4 tablespoons butter	½ pound mushrooms, sliced
3 shallots, finely chopped	Italian parsley, coarsely chopped
1 cup dry white wine	

Have your butcher cut the veal into pieces for stewing. Shoulder, neck, or leg is good.

Dredge the veal in seasoned flour. Heat olive oil and butter in a large skillet and brown the pieces of veal quickly. When nicely browned, reduce the heat and add chopped shallots, dry white wine, and stock or bouillon. Bring just to the boil and reduce the heat to simmering. Add white onions and carrots. Cover and cook for about 45 minutes.

Add sliced mushrooms and continue simmering until the meat is tender. Add Italian parsley.

Remove the meat and vegetables to a serving dish and pour the sauce over them. If you wish to thicken the sauce, drop small balls of blended butter and flour in the liquid and stir until thickened. *(Serves 6.)*

VARIATIONS

Red Sauté: Proceed as above, adding 3 or 4 tomatoes, which you have peeled, seeded, and cut in small pieces, to the sauté. In this case do not add the carrots.

Farm Style: Use either bacon or salt pork finely diced and tried out until crisp. Remove crisp bits and sauté the veal in a combination of the bacon or pork fat and olive oil.

Blanquette of Veal

2 pounds breast or shoulder of veal	1½ teaspoons salt
13 small white onions	½ pound mushroom caps
2 cloves	5 tablespoons butter
1 carrot	½ cup broth or water
Sprig of parsley	2 tablespoons flour
Pinch of basil	1 cup heavy cream
2 egg yolks	Lemon juice

Use veal cut into pieces for stewing.

Place in a deep saucepan or a heavy-bottomed skillet with enough water to cover the meat. Bring the liquid to a boil and skim it. Reduce heat to simmering and add 1 onion, stuck with cloves, carrot, parsley, and a pinch of basil. Cover and simmer for ½ hour.

Add salt and continue simmering until meat is tender—approximately 1¼ hours. You may, if you wish, add peeled onions to the pot after the meat has cooked 45 minutes.

While the veal is cooking, sauté mushroom caps in 2 tablespoons butter for 3 or 4 minutes, add broth or water, and cook for 5 minutes. Let the mushrooms stand in the liquid.

In a skillet or the top of a double boiler melt 3 tablespoons butter. Blend well with flour. Add salt. Keep warm over hot water.

When the veal is tender, remove it from the broth and place it in a casserole or dish to keep warm. Strain the sauce, remove the small onions, and place them with the veal in the casserole. Add the cooked mushrooms to the veal and onions, and combine the mushroom liquor with the strained veal broth. Add 2½ cups of the veal and mushroom broth—there should be just about that much—to the mixed butter and flour gradually, stirring constantly, and heat until thickened.

When it is smooth and thickened, add to the sauce, gradually and stirring constantly, heavy cream mixed with egg yolks. Let this heat through but do not let it boil or it will curdle. Remove from heat at once. Taste for seasoning. Add a few drops of lemon juice to sauce and pour over veal. Serve with broiled rice or buttered noodles.   *(Serves 6.)*

Calf's Head

Calf's head	2 teaspoons salt
1 onion	2 cups water
Cloves	¼ cup white wine
Parsley	Peppercorns
Bay leaf	½ teaspoon salt

Have the butcher bone a calf's head for you and remove the brain. Reserve the brain.

Soak the head and the tongue in cold water for 2 hours. Clean the brain by removing the membrane and any blood clots, and soak in cold water for 2 hours.

Place the calf's head in a deep kettle, add onion stuck with cloves, a little parsley, and half a bay leaf. Cover with water, bring to a boil, and cook for 5 minutes. Remove any scum that forms on the top. Add salt and simmer until tender—1½ to 2 hours.

Meanwhile cook the brain in water with white wine, a few peppercorns, salt, half a bay leaf and a few sprigs parsley. Simmer about 20 minutes and allow it to cool in the liquor.

When the head is cooked, remove the tongue, cool under cold water, and remove the skin. Arrange pieces of the calf's head on a platter, slice the tongue and the brains,

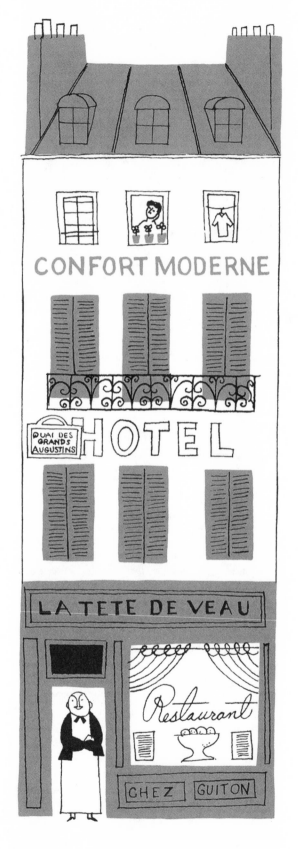

and serve with vinaigrette sauce or same sauce as for blanquette of veal (page 122). For a vinaigrette sauce add to a basic French dressing 1 tablespoon each of chopped parsley, chives, tarragon, sour pickle, and capers, and 1 hard-cooked egg, finely chopped.

Ossi Bucchi

Shank bones of veal	Olive oil
Rice	1 cup water
Veal broth or chicken broth	½ cup white wine
Saffron	1 clove garlic
Flour	½ teaspoon basil
3 or 4 tomatoes	2 medium-sized onions
Parsley	

This favorite Italian dish is most delicious. Serve it with rice baked in the oven with either veal broth or chicken broth. Flavor the rice with a pinch of saffron.

Have the butcher cut veal shank into serving pieces 3 inches long. Use one piece for each serving. Dredge the pieces in flour and sear in hot olive oil until nicely browned. Add water and white wine and bring to a boil. Cover and simmer for 20 minutes.

Add garlic, basil, tomatoes (peeled, seeded and cut in small pieces), onions (finely chopped), and a sprig of parsley. Continue simmering until tender—1½ to 2 hours.

Remove the meat to a hot dish or casserole and allow the sauce to reduce by cooking it uncovered for 5 minutes. If you wish a thicker sauce, knead together butter and flour and drop into the sauce, stirring the while. Correct seasoning and pour sauce over meat.

CALF'S LIVER

Calf's liver is one of the most delicate of all meats and is in great demand for certain diets as well.

Calf's Liver Sauté

Have slices of calf's liver cut very thin. Dredge with flour and sauté in either butter or olive oil, turning and browning quickly. Season with salt and pepper and serve at once. Liver should be slightly rare in the center for perfection. Allow ½ pound per person.

VARIATIONS

With Bacon: Sauté bacon (3 rashers per person) until crisp. Drain on absorbent paper. Serve with sautéed liver, which you may sauté in bacon fat mixed with butter.

Pungent: Sauté 2 or 3 shallots, finely chopped, or thinly sliced scallions for a few minutes in the butter or olive oil in which you are to sauté the liver. Sauté the liver quickly and add a generous handful of chopped parsley to the pan while the liver is cooking.

Deviled: Sauté liver very quickly in butter, remove to a hot plate, and add 1 teaspoon dry mustard and 1 tablespoon Worcestershire sauce to the pan. Allow it to cook with the butter and seasonings about 2 minutes. Pour over liver and serve at once.

With Onions: Sauté liver quickly in olive oil. Add chopped parsley at the last moment and remove to a hot platter. Garnish with either sautéed onions, lightly browned, or with French fried onion rings.

Broiled Liver

Liver for broiling—or "liver steak"—should be cut ⅓ to ½ inch thick. Oil or butter well, season with salt and freshly ground black pepper, place in broiler 3 inches from heat, and broil 4 to 5 minutes, turning once. Steamed or broiled new potatoes are excellent with this.

Liver Julienne

1 pound calf's liver	1 clove chopped garlic
Flour	½ cup dry white wine
Salt and pepper	2 tablespoons chopped
Paprika	parsley
2 tablespoons olive oil	¾ cup heavy sour cream
2 tablespoons butter	

Cut calf's liver into thin slices and cut these in strips about ½ inch wide. Dredge with flour seasoned with salt, pepper and a little paprika.

Heat olive oil and butter in a large skillet. Sauté garlic in the fat and add the liver strips. Cook very quickly, turning with a spatula so that all strips become uniformly browned and cooked. This should take about 2 minutes.

Remove liver to a hot platter and add white wine and parsley to the pan. Shake the pan well so that the wine rinses the pan thoroughly. Add heavy sour cream, stir into the other ingredients, and heat thoroughly. Do not let it boil. Taste and rectify the seasoning.

Remove the pan from the heat, return the liver strips to the pan, and mix well with the sauce. *(Serves 4.)*

Serve with buttered noodles or boiled rice.

VEAL KIDNEYS

Grilled Veal Kidneys

Kidneys	Salt and pepper
Butter	Bacon
Olive oil	

Allow approximately 1 kidney to a person. Slice the kidney in ½-inch slices and remove the core, leaving the outer coating of suet. Brush with melted butter or olive oil, and grill very quickly under a hot flame. Season with salt and pepper; serve with crisp bacon.

Veal Kidney Sauté with Red Wine

4 veal kidneys	4 tablespoons butter
8 or 10 mushrooms	Salt and pepper
4 or 5 chopped green onions	½ cup red wine

Slice veal kidneys and remove hard core and excess fat or suet. Clean and slice mushrooms. Sauté kidneys quickly in butter in a skillet 5 minutes or until nicely browned. Salt and pepper to taste. Be sure not to overcook.

Add green onions and the sliced mushroom caps. Cook 5 minutes longer, shaking pan to mix ingredients well. Add red wine; cook another 4 or 5 minutes. Serve on fried toast.

VARIATION

Flambé: Proceed as above. After adding mushrooms and onions, pour 1½ ounces brandy over ingredients. Blaze in pan after extinguishing flame of stove. Or prepare in a chafing dish at table.

Kidney Sauté Piquant

4 veal kidneys	Basil
½ cup olive oil	Salt
2 tablespoons wine vinegar	Freshly ground pepper
2 tablespoons chopped parsley	4 tablespoons butter
	1 clove garlic
Chopped chives (or chopped green onions)	Escoffier Sauce Diable
	¼ cup red wine

Clean and slice veal kidneys. Allow them to marinate for 2 hours in olive oil mixed with wine vinegar, parsley, chives (or green onions), a pinch of basil, and salt and freshly ground pepper to taste.

Melt butter in a medium-sized skillet. Sauté garlic lightly and add kidneys, being certain to mix them well with marinade before adding to pan. Sauté very quickly for 5 minutes. Add 2 or 3 tablespoons marinade, reduce heat, and cook kidneys 5 minutes.

Add 2 tablespoons Escoffier Sauce Diable and red wine. Allow to cook another 5 or 6 minutes or until the kidneys are just tender.

Rectify the seasoning and serve on crisp fried toast. Sprinkle with chopped parsley before serving. *(Serves 4.)*

SWEETBREADS

Sweetbreads are usually bought in pairs. A pair serves 1 or 2 persons. Soak them in cold water for ½ hour, then simmer in salted water for 20 minutes. Cool in cold water and remove membrane, tubes, and excess fat.

Broiled Sweetbreads

2 pairs sweetbreads	Salt and pepper
Butter	Lemon

Prepare sweetbreads for cooking. When they are ready to be broiled, split them crosswise. Brush well with melted butter and place under broiler, 3 or 4 inches from flame. Broil about 10 minutes, turning them once and brushing with butter during the process.

Season with salt and pepper, and serve with a slice of broiled or fried ham or with crisp rashers of bacon. Serve quarters of lemon with the sweetbreads. *(Serves 4.)*

Sautéed Sweetbreads

2 pairs sweetbreads	Salt and pepper
4 tablespoons butter	Lemon

Prepare sweetbreads as above. Cut in serving pieces. Melt 4 tablespoons butter in a skillet. Season sweetbreads with salt and pepper, and sauté until they are nicely browned on both sides. Serve with lemon quarters. *(Serves 4.)*

VARIATIONS

With Madeira: Dredge sweetbreads in flour and season with salt and pepper. Sauté in 6 tablespoons butter until lightly browned. Add ¼ cup Madeira to pan and cook 1 or 2 minutes. Serve at once on fried toast.

With White Wine: Sauté sweetbreads as above. Add 1 tablespoon chopped parsley and ¼ cup dry white wine to the pan. Serve on a slice of grilled ham.

With Bacon: Sauté bacon rashers, allowing 2 or 3 to a person, until crisp. Remove the bacon to absorbent paper. Sauté the sweetbreads in 2 tablespoons bacon fat and 2 tablespoons butter. Salt and pepper to taste, and serve the sweetbreads with the bacon.

Sweetbreads en Brochette

2 pairs sweetbreads	Butter
18 to 20 mushrooms	Salt and pepper
4 or 5 rashers bacon	Chopped parsley

Cut prepared sweetbreads in 1-inch squares. Wash and remove stems from mushrooms. Cut bacon in 1-inch pieces and sauté for a few minutes until partially cooked. Drain on absorbent paper.

Alternate pieces of sweetbread, mushroom caps, and squares of bacon on medium-sized skewers, allowing one skewer for each serving. Brush well with butter, sprinkle with salt and pepper, and broil, turning frequently until the sweetbreads are nicely browned and the mushrooms cooked. Sprinkle with chopped parsley and pour a little melted butter over each skewer before serving.   *(Serves 6.)*

VARIATIONS

You may use small cubes of ham with the sweetbreads, or use the tiny plum or cherry tomatoes for a change of flavor.

PORK

Pork has a popularity all over the world that perhaps puts it in the number one place for honors in the meat family. Each country seems to have a few of its own particular favorite cuts and methods of preparation. Although pork enjoys popularity in this country, it has never become—with the exception of ham, of course—one of the stylish or featured meats. This is a pity, because no other animal offers such a variety of dishes. Literally every part of the pig is delicious and edible, from the ears to the tail.

Pork has a soft, grayed-pink color and white fat. It is wise to buy meat cut from medium-sized hogs rather than the very large ones, as a general rule, because the texture and flavor will be found much more palatable and there will be less fat. Allow about $\frac{1}{2}$ pound per person. When buying a fresh ham or shoulder of pork, be certain to have the skin kept on, for this, scored and roasted, makes a most delicious crisp tidbit that to my taste is the best part of the roast.

Pork should be very thoroughly cooked. This means slow, low-temperature cooking. Roasts should be cooked in a moderately slow oven (325°) until thoroughly done, and chops and steaks should be braised or baked to insure tenderness and the best flavor. There is a distinctive, rich flavor to pork that is enhanced by slow cooking.

Corned pork, which is wet-cured or pickled, needs a soaking period of 6 to 8 hours before preparation.

ROAST PORK

The leg, or fresh ham; the shoulder; and the loin—the rib half, the loin half, or the entire loin—are used for roasting. The meat should be kept at room temperature for an hour before placing it in the oven. Preheat the oven to moderately slow (325°). Season the meat before placing in the oven. If it is a fresh ham or a shoulder with the skin attached, score the skin with a sharp knife in diamonds or squares and rub with salt and pepper and, if you like the flavor, a little thyme; for thyme and pork complement each other. Loins or ribs should be rubbed with salt and pepper and the (optional) thyme. Loin roasts should have the bones cracked for easier cooking, and the bone which attaches the ribs to the spinal column should be either removed or cut away from the flesh so that it may be removed after cooking. This assures you of even slices.

For a small fresh ham up to 5 pounds, allow 45 to 50 minutes per pound. For a larger ham allow 40 minutes per pound.

For a rib or loin roast allow approximately 35 minutes per pound; slightly more for small roasts.

A shoulder roast requires 40 minutes per pound.

No basting is necessary, for with slow cooking pork bastes itself. If you wish to barbecue your roast of pork—and a fresh ham may be cooked very successfully this way—brush it with a barbecue sauce before placing in the oven and continue applications of the sauce every 20 minutes or so during the cooking.

Accompaniments for Roast Pork

Pork needs something sharp to contrast with its richness. Apple sauce is the accepted relish. A pleasant change is a mixture of apple sauce and horseradish, either freshly grated or the prepared type, which should be drained before being combined with the apple sauce. Dill pickles are pleasant with roast pork, especially pickles with garlic added.

Potatoes may be roasted in the pan with the pork. Allow about an hour for them to cook. Lentils, simmered till tender and sautéed with onion and parsley, are another complementary food, although heavy. Or try cornbread or polenta.

Follow the pork with a green vegetable or a salad which has crispiness and a certain tartness, and let your final course be either fresh or cooked fruit. Pork is heavy and rich and should be accompanied by light foods. Wine, with the exception of vin rosé, does not seem to go well with pork dishes. A glass of good beer is far more satisfactory.

Pork Chop Suey

½ pound lean pork (shoulder)	½ cup chopped celery leaves
2 tablespoons fat	1 cup sliced onions
3 cups beef stock, or 3 cups water and 3 bouillon cubes	⅔ cup sliced green pepper
	1¼ teaspoons salt
	¾ teaspoon Worcestershire sauce
1 cup (¼ pound) sliced mushrooms	3 tablespoons quick-cooking tapioca
1½ cups thinly sliced celery	

Cut pork in small pieces and brown in fat. Add half of stock and continue cooking until meat is tender. Then add remaining stock, vegetables, and seasonings. Cover and simmer until vegetables are tender but still crisp.

Drain off stock, measure, and add water to make 2¼ cups. Add stock and tapioca to meat mixture and cook over low or medium heat until mixture comes to a boil, stirring constantly. Serve hot with rice or noodles.

(Serves 4 to 6.)

PORK CHOPS

Chops cut from the loin are the choicest, for they have a little of the tenderloin. Chops cut from the ribs or the shoulder are usually the economical cut and are not so delicate or delicious. Chops need slow cooking: baking or braising. One may broil them as well, but this method of cooking hardens the fibers and tends to toughen the meat and dry it out.

Pan-fried Pork Chops

In a preheated, heavy-bottomed pan place pork chops seasoned with salt, pepper, and a little basil or thyme (both of which have an affinity for pork). Add a very little olive oil to the pan as a safeguard against burning; it will lubricate the meat until the fat of the pork begins to melt. Let the chops cook very slowly for about 15 minutes before turning. Turn and allow the chops to brown on the other side, and cook until thoroughly tender. This will take 30 to 40 minutes, depending upon the size and thickness of your chops. Serve at once. Allow 1 to 2 chops per person.

VARIATIONS

Polish Style: Season loin pork chops with salt, pepper, and a little chopped fresh dill. Cook slowly in small amount of olive oil until nicely browned and cooked through. Remove to a hot platter. Pour off fat from pan, leaving 2 tablespoons. Add 1 teaspoon finely chopped dill, 1 tablespoon chopped parsley, and ½ cup sour cream, and stir till cream is just heated through. Do not let the sour cream come to a boil. Pour over the chops and serve at once with plain boiled rice and chilled apple sauce.

Breaded: Season pork chops with salt and pepper. Dip in flour, beaten egg, and rolled toasted crumbs. Place in warm, oiled pan and cook slowly for 15 minutes or until nicely browned on one side. Turn and brown on the other side and cook until tender—approximately 35 minutes. Remove to hot plate. Pour off all but 2 tablespoons fat. Add 3 tablespoons Escoffier Sauce Diable and 1 tablespoon Escoffier Sauce Robert. Allow to blend with the fat and add 2 more tablespoons Sauce Diable and 1 teaspoon dry mustard. Serve with chops.

With Apple Rings: Pan-fry chops as above. Wash, core, and slice tart apples. Do not peel. Roll in brown sugar and sauté lightly in 3 tablespoons butter. Handle apple rings carefully, for they are fragile when cooked. Serve the chops topped with apple rings.

Braised Pork Chops

Braised pork chops or pork steak cut from the leg or the shoulder should be slow-cooked, as should all pork. Chops and steaks cooked this way should be cut fairly thick—½ to ¾ inch.

Season the chops with salt, pepper, and if you desire, herb seasoning. Thyme or basil are the herbs to use—or oregano. Brown the chops over a low flame in a lightly oiled skillet from 10 to 15 minutes on each side. When meat is browned, add a small amount of liquid (broth, tomato juice, apple juice, or cider) and cover the pan. Simmer approximately 30 minutes or place in a casserole in a moderately slow oven (325°) for the same length of time.

VARIATIONS

Barbecued: Sear chops quickly. Reduce heat and cover pan. Simmer for about 10 minutes. Next add ½ cup barbecue sauce and cover and simmer for 20 minutes, being certain to turn the chops once or twice during the simmering process.

Côte de Porc Charcutière: An excellent sauce for braised chops: Brown 2 or 3 onions in butter, stir in 1 tablespoon flour, and add 1 cup bouillon. Stir till smooth. Add 2 fresh tomatoes and 1 cup tomato paste. Salt and pepper to taste. Cook about 20 minutes. Add 1 tablespoon vinegar and 1 of English mustard, and a handful of gherkins, sliced thin. Pour sauce over chops.

Lyonnaise: Dredge chops with seasoned flour. Sear very quickly on both sides in a large skillet. When chops are browned, add 2 large onions cut in slices, and reduce the heat. Cook, uncovered, until onions are delicately colored. Cover the skillet and simmer for 20 to 25 minutes.

Italian style — green pepper and garlic

Italian: Sear thick chops in a lightly oiled pan very quickly. Season with salt and pepper, and add 1 clove garlic and 2 large or 3 medium green peppers—washed, seeded, and cut into thin strips. Cover skillet and simmer 35 minutes. Serve chops with peppers arranged over or around them.

Stuffed Pork Chops

4 double pork loin chops	Thyme
1 medium onion, finely chopped	2 tablespoons chopped parsley
3 tablespoons butter	½ cup toasted rolled crumbs
⅓ cup finely chopped mushrooms	Salt and pepper
	1 lightly beaten egg

Purchase one double loin chop for each person and have the butcher cut a pocket in each one. The chops should be 1 to 1½ inches thick.

Prepare a stuffing as follows: Sauté onion in butter. When just transparent, add mushrooms, a few leaves of thyme, parsley, and crumbs. Mix thoroughly and remove from heat. Salt and pepper to taste, and stir in egg. Stuff the pocket in each chop. Secure with small skewers or toothpicks.

Sear chops very quickly in a lightly oiled skillet. Turn the chops carefully so that you do not disturb the stuffing and the skewers. When chops are nicely browned, cover the pan and simmer for an hour or until tender. Or you may place the chops in a baking dish or pan and roast them in a moderately slow oven (325°) for one hour or until tender and nicely browned. Serve with a green vegetable or a salad.

SPARERIBS

Spareribs may be broiled, boiled, baked, or braised, and are most savory. Buy the meatiest ones, getting at least a pound per person, for the bone content is large.

Broiled Spareribs

Cut spareribs into serving pieces. Season with salt and pepper, and place on the rack of a preheated broiler. Place the rack 4 inches from the flame and broil for 20 minutes. Turn and continue broiling until spareribs are nicely browned and crisp and cooked through. Serve with a spicy sauce.

Baked Spareribs

Arrange seasoned spareribs in a lightly oiled baking dish or pan. Place in a preheated moderate oven (350°) and allow them to roast for approximately 1 hour.

VARIATION

Baked Spareribs with Sauerkraut: Lightly oil a large baking pan, or cover it with strips of bacon. Arrange 2 pounds of sauerkraut on the bacon or in the oil, heaping it up in the center. Arrange slices of Spanish onion on the sauerkraut. Over this, arrange cuts of seasoned spareribs. Place in a moderate oven (350°) and roast for approximately 1½ hours or until spareribs are nicely browned and thoroughly cooked. It is practical to prepare this dish in something which may be used as a serving dish as well.

Baked Stuffed Spareribs: For this dish you may use your favorite bread or crumb stuffing. Place the stuffing on a large side of spareribs and top with another side. Tie

Basil and thyme have an affinity for Pork

them together securely with white cord and roast in a moderate oven (350°) 1½ hours. Serve with a heated barbecue sauce.

Barbecued: Brush spareribs well with barbecue sauce. Then arrange them in a baking pan, place the pan in a moderate oven (350°), and bake for one hour. Baste frequently with the barbecue sauce and turn the spareribs during cooking. Serve with additional heated barbecue sauce.

Boiled Spareribs with Sauerkraut

4 pounds spareribs	1 to 2 quarts drained
Bay leaf	sauerkraut
1 large onion stuck with	Grated fresh horseradish
2 cloves	Sour cream
Thyme	Dry mustard

Cut spareribs (count 1 pound per person) into serving pieces. Season and place in a deep kettle with a bay leaf, onion, and a little thyme. Cover with water and bring to a boil, covered. Allow the spareribs to simmer for ½ hour. Add sauerkraut and cook uncovered for ¾ hour. Drain and arrange on a serving platter or in a deep serving dish. Serve with horseradish mixed with sour cream and flavored with dry mustard. *(Serves 4.)*

PORK TENDERLOIN

Pork tenderloin is deliciously tender and, although more expensive, an economical cut to buy and prepare because one buys absolutely no waste. The tenderloin must be lubricated somewhat in cooking because of its lack of fat. Tenderloin has a great tendency to become dry and stringy.

Roast Pork Tenderloin

2 pork tenderloins	Grated raw beet
Salt and pepper	½ teaspoon salt
Pinch of thyme	½ teaspoon black pepper
2 or 3 strips bacon	Sour cream
Grated fresh horseradish	2 teaspoons wine vinegar

Season tenderloins well with salt and pepper and just a pinch of thyme. Place in a baking pan and top with strips of bacon for flavor and lubrication. Place in a moderately slow oven (325°) and allow about 35 minutes per pound roasting time.

If you wish, you may parboil sweet potatoes, peel, and brown them with the roasting tenderloins.

Serve with horseradish mixed with grated raw beet in equal proportions and with enough sour cream to bind the two. Add salt, black pepper, and wine vinegar to the mixture before adding the sour cream. *(Serves 6.)*

Braised Pork Tenderloin

2 pork tenderloins	3 tablespoons olive oil
Salt and pepper	½ cup heavy cream
Thyme	1 teaspoon paprika

Season tenderloins with salt, pepper, and thyme. Sear very quickly in a heavy skillet in 3 tablespoons olive oil. When nicely browned on all sides, cover pan and simmer 30 minutes. Add heavy cream and allow meat to simmer another 20 minutes or until tender.

Remove the tenderloins to a hot platter, add paprika to the sauce, and pour the sauce over the meat.

Serve with baked sweet potatoes and apple sauce with grated nutmeg added.

Pan-fried Pork Tenderloin

Cut slices of pork tenderloin 1½ inches thick. Place them between two pieces of waxed or butcher's paper and flatten them with a mallet or wooden potato masher. Or ask your butcher to do this.

Pan-fry the flattened slices of tenderloin very slowly in a lightly oiled skillet. Salt and pepper well, and serve with apple rings and mashed and buttered sweet potatoes.

VARIATION

Polonaise: Dredge tenderloin slices in flour and sear them quickly in 3 tablespoons butter. Add to the browned slices 2 tablespoons finely chopped onion, and salt and pepper to taste. Cover and simmer for 20 minutes. Add 1 tablespoon chopped fresh dill and ½ cup heavy cream. Cover and simmer for 10 minutes. Serve with boiled rice and a cucumber salad.

PIGS' FEET AND PIGS' HOCKS

No other pork seems to me so delicious as pigs' feet and hocks. But never serve them to guests who have inhibitions about using their fingers as implements!

Allow 1 pig's foot per person.

Boiled Pigs' Feet

Pigs' feet should be washed and brushed and, if there are bits of bristle left on them, scraped. Place in a deep kettle, cover with cold water, bring to a boil, and simmer slowly for about 3 or 4 hours. When the water begins to boil, add about ½ teaspoon of salt to each quart of water.

A useful trick (for which I am indebted to Jeanne Owen) is to wrap each foot in cheesecloth before placing it in the water.

When the pigs' feet are cooked, roll them out of the cloth into a fairly deep platter or bowl and cover them with the broth from the cooking process. The wrapping tends to keep the feet from splitting and maintains their shape perfectly. Allowing them to cool slightly in the broth makes them easier to handle. If you cook the feet beforehand, leave them in the broth and reheat, when it is time to serve them, in a small amount of the liquor.

Pigs' feet are served hot with sauerkraut or with a vinaigrette sauce.

Grilled Pigs' Feet

Chill the pigs' feet in the refrigerator, remove, and either split or keep them whole. Roll well in crumbs and broil under a medium flame so that they brown nicely on all sides. Serve with pungent sauce.

Pungent Sauce

6 shallots, finely chopped	1 tablespoon Worcestershire
3 tablespoons butter	sauce
1 tablespoon wine vinegar	1 teaspoon dry mustard
	3 tablespoons Escoffier
	Sauce Diable

Sauté shallots in butter. Add wine vinegar, Worcestershire sauce, mustard, and Escoffier Sauce Diable. Stir well in the pan and allow to come to the boiling point. Rectify the seasoning and serve hot in a sauceboat with the grilled pigs' feet.

Pig Hocks

Pig hocks are boiled in the same manner as pigs' feet and are served hot with horseradish sauce or mustard sauce. They are usually accompanied by boiled potatoes and sauerkraut.

These dishes are at their best when washed down with draughts of good cold beer.

HAM

Nowadays there are many kinds of cured pork —hams, smoked shoulders, and smoked butts. Virginia and similar types of ham which are cured and smoked for a long period need soaking and must be boiled or roasted with seasonings to be at their best. Tenderized hams have been processed so that they need only the addition of seasonings and a brief time in the oven. It is wise to inquire about or read carefully the directions on the wrapper of the ham you buy before cooking. I have seen tenderized hams reduced to dry shreds by being boiled for long periods.

Ham is a most economical and pleasant dish for large parties. A 10-pound ham will give you approximately 20 to 22 servings, and a 15- or 18-pound ham will serve close to 40.

Boiled ham is used for cold cuts and for various dishes calling for ham as a base. Baked ham is served hot or cold and may be dressed in a variety of ways. Aged hams are usually served hot as a main course or cold with a selection of cold cuts; very often at a formal dinner a slice of cold Virginia ham is served with the salad course.

Prosciutto or Parma ham is served in paper-thin slices as an hors d'oeuvre and is often combined with melon or with figs for a first course. Westphalian ham is served the same way. These hams require no cooking and are usually bought sliced from the dealer. Canned ham, which is boned, requires merely heating and glazing, or may be sliced and served cold just as it comes from the tin.

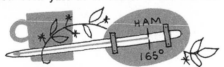

You may purchase half hams which are practical for a small family. Picnic shoulders and smoked butts are also available and are more economical cuts which bring, naturally, a smaller price. They may be treated the same way as ham.

Baked Ham

Most high-grade commercial hams need no parboiling. Scrub the ham well with a stiff brush and place, rind and fat side up, in a baking pan or roaster. If you use a meat thermometer, make an incision and place the thermometer in the fleshiest part of the ham.

Bake the ham in a slow oven (300°), allowing approximately 20 to 22 minutes per pound for a small ham (10 to 12 pounds); 18 to 20 for a larger ham (12 to 15 pounds); and 15 to 18 minutes per pound for the large hams (15 pounds and over). The thermometer should read around 165° when the ham is cooked.

Remove the ham from the oven and remove the rind with a sharp knife or with kitchen scissors. The easiest method is to cut the rind and then pull it off with the hands, aided by a small sharp knife.

Score the fat in diamonds, making rather deep cuts in it, or cut it in a pinwheel design. Glaze the ham with one of the following:

(1) 1 cup brown sugar mixed with 1 teaspoon dry mustard and ½ teaspoon ground cloves. Mix with a little of the fat from the pan to make a stiff paste.

(2) 1 cup brown sugar mixed with ½ cup dry toasted crumbs and ½ teaspoon ground cloves. Moisten with enough Madeira or sherry to make a paste.

(3) Rub ham with dry mustard and ground cloves, and drizzle strained honey over the mixture.

(4) Rub ham with dry mustard, ground cloves, and brown sugar. Place pineapple rings on the ham and sprinkle the pineapple with brown sugar. You may omit the ground cloves and stud the ham with whole cloves, but the ground cloves give more flavor and also keep the carver from having to cut his way through a pattern of cloves.

Place the ham in a hot oven (400°) for 15 minutes to glaze and brown it well. Serve hot or cold with mustard or horseradish sauce.

VARIATION

Place uncooked ham in roasting pan and proceed as above until 1 hour before ham is done. Remove rind, score, and glaze with brown sugar. Add any of these:

1 pint Madeira or sweet sherry	1 cup honey (in this instance omit the brown sugar)
1 pint champagne	
1 pint claret	1 pint cider
1 cup pineapple juice	

Return to oven at same temperature, and baste frequently. Increase temperature for last 15 minutes to brown the glaze.

AGED HAMS

The directions below apply to all hams which are country cured and aged before they are sent to the consumer. These include Virginia hams, Smithfield hams, Kentucky hams, and all others which are classed as aged hams. There are a few of these hams sold under a year old; these are not mature. If they are properly cured and stored, they will keep for a number of years. I know of hams that have kept for over six years and, while there is a certain amount of shrinkage and will be more when cooked, the hams lose none of their distinction or flavor.

A friend of mine, who has had vast experience in cooking aged hams, has developed a rule for such cooking that is absolutely foolproof. You also may apply it to corned beef and cured tongues and other similar foods which require soaking and careful cooking:

Soak the ham, or other cured meat, in enough water to entirely cover it overnight or from 12 to 18 hours. Remove, drain, and cover the meat with fresh cold water. Bring it to the simmering point—not the boiling point—and allow to simmer for just 2 hours. No matter what the size or weight, the rule is the same—just 2 hours.

Remove the kettle from the stove and allow the ham or other meat to cool in the liquor in which it cooked. If you cook your ham the day before, let it rest in the broth overnight and bake it the next day; the flavor will be much better.

After the ham is thoroughly cooled, remove the skin and glaze and bake the ham in any way you desire. It is my belief that a fine aged ham needs practically no embellishment save a little sugar or honey glaze, which is more for the appearance than for flavor. Perhaps a touch of clove is desirable, but, please, no orange marmalade or cranberry jelly with fine aged ham!

Serve aged ham hot or cold, sliced in paper-thin slices. It is rich and flavorful and deserves careful treatment.

Baked Ham Slice

Ham slice	1 cup liquid (milk, broth,
1½ teaspoons dry mustard	pineapple juice, cider,
2 tablespoons brown sugar	or wine)

Select a cut 1 to 2 inches thick, cut from the center of the ham. Make a paste of mustard, brown sugar, and just enough water to blend. Spread this over the ham slice, place in a lightly oiled baking pan, pour over 1 cup liquid, and bake in a moderate oven (350°) until ham is just tender. The time depends on the kind of ham you are using. It should take about 1 hour for a cured ham and half that time for a tenderized ham.

Note: If you use an aged ham slice for this recipe, you should simmer the slice for 20 minutes and allow it to cool in the water before you bake it.

VARIATION

Spiced: Choose 2 or 3 ½-inch slices of ham. Place in a baking dish with slices of pineapple between them or with the following mixture: ½ cup dry bread crumbs combined with 1 teaspoon dry mustard, ¼ cup chopped raisins, a few grains of ground cloves, and enough maple syrup to bind the mixture. Spread each slice with the mixture, add to the pan 1 cup liquid—pineapple juice is a good choice for this—and bake in a moderate oven (350°) about 1 hour or until just tender.

FRIED AND BROILED HAM

Aged ham slices should be parboiled or soaked in lukewarm water before cooking. Other ham need not be.

Fried ham slices should be about ½ inch thick. Rub a pan well with bits of ham fat and cook the ham very slowly so that it cooks through and browns lightly. Tenderized ham merely needs heating through and browning on each side.

Serve fried ham in any of the following ways:

With Eggs: You may fry the eggs in the ham fat or separately in butter. Two eggs per person is the general rule.

With Slices of Sautéed Pineapple: The pineapple slices may be cooked in the pan with the ham fat or sautéed in butter.

With Sautéed Mushroom Caps: 4 to 6 caps per person, served on the ham.

Barbecued: Rub ham slice with dry mustard before cooking. When ham is almost cooked, add a mixture of 1 tablespoon chili sauce, 1 tablespoon Escoffier Sauce Diable, a few grains of cayenne, a teaspoon of brown sugar, and a pinch of thyme. Mix this with ¼ cup red wine or Madeira. Pour over the ham and allow to cook over low heat for 3 or 4 minutes, turning the ham slice several times during the process.

With Fresh Asparagus: Serve with either hollandaise sauce or butter and grated Parmesan cheese.

Broiled ham may be served in any of the ways given for fried ham.

SCALLOPED HAM

Scalloped Ham and Cabbage

4 cups coarsely shredded cabbage	⅛ teaspoon pepper
½ teaspoon salt	3 tablespoons quick-cooking tapioca
⅛ teaspoon paprika	2 cups milk
2 tablespoons butter	1¼ cups (½ pound) chopped cooked ham
½ cup fine bread crumbs, buttered	

Cook cabbage in boiling salted water 2 minutes. Drain.

Combine tapioca, salt, pepper, paprika, and milk in saucepan. Place over low or medium heat and cook until mixture comes to a boil, stirring constantly.

Remove from heat. Add butter, cabbage, and ham and mix well. Turn into a greased 1½-quart baking dish. Cover with crumbs. Bake in moderate oven (350°) 20 minutes, or until crumbs are browned. *(Serves 4 to 6.)*

PORK SAUSAGE

Commercial sausages and sausage meat vary so greatly in quality that one must investigate carefully to find the ideal product or make one's own mixture, which is not hard to do.

Have your butcher grind fresh pork for you from the loin or the shoulder and tell him just what percentage of fat you want in the meat you are having ground. When you get it home, season it to your own taste; decide what you like and keep the formula for the next time. Coarse salt, freshly ground pepper, and just a touch of thyme added to the pork give it what seems to me the right flavor. Have about 1 pound fat included with every 4 pounds lean pork or sausage.

Sausage meat should be pan-fried very slowly so that it browns on both sides and is well cooked yet moist in the center.

Link Sausages

Of the many types of sausage on the market, some have much cereal mixed with the meat, others are overly fat and will shrink considerably, and others are lightly smoked and require soaking or parboiling before they are pan-fried or broiled or baked in the oven.

For the best results, cook links in boiling water 5 to 10 minutes, and then pan-fry slowly until nicely browned and cooked through. Turn often or shake the pan well from time to time, for the sausages have a tendency to stick.

The hot Italian sausages usually need parboiling in the same manner before pan-frying. Or they can be pan-fried until nicely browned, then combined with a tomato sauce and poached in the sauce until they are thoroughly cooked.

Sausage Rolls

Parboil 20 sausages for 5 to 7 minutes. Drain. Make up a recipe for plain pastry, or use the frozen pastry, and roll out very thin. Cut into squares, roll a sausage in each piece of pastry, prick each roll, and brush with beaten egg. Bake in a hot oven (425°) 15 to 20 minutes or until pastry is nicely browned. Serve hot or cold. These are excellent with cocktails.

BACON AND SALT PORK

Pan-broiled Bacon

Place sliced bacon in a cold skillet. Cook very slowly over extremely low heat. Turn the bacon and shake the pan slightly from time to time. If you want crisp bacon, pour off the fat as the bacon cooks. Drain bacon on absorbent paper before serving.

Broiled Bacon

Broil slices of bacon on a rack or in a shallow pan about 3 to 4 inches from the heating unit. Turn the bacon so that it cooks evenly.

Canadian Bacon

Canadian bacon may be pan-broiled in the same way as ordinary bacon. If the bacon is very lean, butter the pan slightly before placing the bacon slices in it. Sauté gently over a low flame.

Baked Canadian Bacon

Whole Canadian bacon may be scored and glazed in the same manner as ham. It needs no parboiling. Score and use any of the glazes listed for ham. Bake in a moderate oven (350°), allowing 20 minutes per pound. This meat slices excellently and is delicious hot or cold. It is a good substitute for baked ham for small families.

LAMB AND MUTTON

There is an almost universal—or, at any rate, national—tendency to overcook lamb and mutton. Most timetables for cooked meats and meat-thermometer temperature charts specify temperatures that are too high for lamb, which should be faintly pink and juicy. Lamb that is cooked to a leathery grayish brown falls from the bones or dries up completely. Another fault of lamb service is the notion that lamb should be accompanied by currant jelly or mint sauce or pineapple (though I love pineapple in its place). A vinegary mint sauce or a commercial mint jelly, tradition notwithstanding, is abhorrent to anyone who really appreciates the flavor of good meat, well cooked.

ROASTS OF LAMB

Lamb leg is considered the choicest cut for roasting, although a boned shoulder or a rack of lamb is delicious. Legs are usually sold with some of the loin chops attached, which you may or may not have removed to use for another meal. They range in weight from 5 to 10 pounds according to the size and age of the lamb. Allow ¾ to 1 pound per person, for there is a good deal of bone in a leg roast.

You may have the leg prepared three different ways for your cooking. A French leg has the shank bone left in and trimmed. In an American leg the shank bone is removed, and the meat turned under and either tied or secured with a skewer. If you have trouble carving a leg of lamb, have the shank bone left in, the other bones removed, and the roast rolled and tied. This gives you even slices and presents no trouble at table to the carver.

To carve lamb correctly, one should cut off a slice of the less fleshy side of the leg and stand the roast on the platter with the fleshy cushion side up. Then cut these slices to the bone and run the blade along the bone to loosen slices. Others prefer slicing from the top of the roast, but there is less economy in this method.

Roasting

Rub the roast with salt and pepper, and place it in a roasting pan or on a rack in the pan. If you use the meat thermometer, insert it in the thickest part of the roast, being careful it is not next to the bone. Cook the roast in a preheated slow oven (300°) until the thermometer registers 165°, if you like your lamb just pink and juicy and tender. If you must have it dry and thoroughly well done, let

the thermometer rise to 175° or 180° (but don't blame me!). If there is a nice layer of fat on the leg, you will not need to baste the roast at all while cooking. Approximately 22 to 25 minutes per pound is right for medium well-done lamb.

If you prefer the method of searing the lamb first, butter or oil it and sear it in a hot oven (350° to 475°) for 15 to 20 minutes. Open the door of the oven and reduce the heat to slow (300°). When the temperature in the oven has dropped, close the oven door and continue cooking till lamb is done. Allow 20 to 24 minutes per pound.

Serve lamb on a hot platter and on hot plates. Nothing is more unappetizing than a slice of lamb on a cold plate with congealed fat. Serve the juices from the pan over the roast.

You may roast potatoes in the pan with the meat, and most delicious morsels they are. Peel and quarter Idaho potatoes and add to the pan about 1 hour before removing the roast. Salt and pepper them well and turn them once or twice during the cooking process so they will brown nicely. Serve the browned potatoes with the lamb and a good bottle of wine—no jelly, if there is wine. Afterwards braised celery, perhaps, and a green salad and cheese—a perfect dinner for the family or for company.

VARIATIONS

With Garlic: Stud the lamb with shreds of garlic, piercing the flesh in several places and inserting thin slices of the bud. Allow it to stand an hour or two before roasting.

Marinated: Marinate the lamb for 24 hours before cooking. Use plenty of herbs, for lamb is exceedingly friendly to all sorts of herb flavoring. For a leg of lamb use ½ cup olive oil, 2 teaspoons salt, 1 teaspoon black pepper, the juice of 2 lemons, 1 clove garlic, a healthy infusion of thyme, parsley, and oregano, and onions and a bay leaf. Add to this a pint of wine, either red or white, and allow the roast to absorb all the goodness of the mixture. Turn several times during the marinating period.

There are two schools of thought on roasting marinated lamb. Some say it should be roasted in the marinade in a slow oven (300°), and basted with the marinade while cooking. Others insist it should be cooked in a very hot oven without basting. In either case, I believe that the results are about the same, and they are exceedingly good. Allow the same roasting time and meat temperatures as for plain roast lamb.

You may treat the boned shoulder roast the same way as a leg of lamb.

Roast Crown of Lamb

A crown roast is usually served for a dinner party because of its attractive appearance and the generally festive quality it presents when sent to the table.

Your butcher will arrange the roast for you. It is made from the rack and usually contains 12 to 16 chops. Some people stuff the center with a savory stuffing before roasting, but it is my opinion that it is simpler and in the long run more delicious if it is not stuffed. However, it is wise to place something inside the crown while roasting to insure the shape of the roast. A casserole or a piece of glass or metal which exactly fits the space will do.

The ribs are trimmed at the ends, and are usually served with paper frills, as decoration. Place bits of salt pork or other fat on the rib ends so that they will not be charred and blackened during the cooking process.

Roast the crown in a slow oven (300°) and only for about 1¼ to 1½ hours, for it will cook far more quickly than a leg or shoulder. Serve on a hot platter with the center filled with tiny potato balls which have been French fried and drained on absorbent paper. Or fill the center with fresh peas which are tender and buttery. Sprinkle with chopped parsley.

(*About 2 chops per person.*)

Racks and Loins of Lamb

Both the rack and the loin are ideal for roasting, especially if yours is a small family and you do not want a leg that may last forever. Proceed as for roast leg or shoulder, allowing about 22 minutes per pound for either cut.

LAMB CHOPS OR STEAKS

Lamb chops are usually cut from the ribs or the loin.

Rib Chops are cut from one to three ribs in thickness and may be "Frenched," or trimmed so that there is a good deal of the bone exposed which may be decorated with a paper frill when served.

Loin Chops are the most substantial and, to my mind, the best. Double chops, 1½ to 2 inches thick, are the choicest.

English Chops are cut from the double loin or saddle, and are usually cut thick and have kidney wrapped or skewered into the chop.

Saratoga Chops are cut from the boned shoulder and are usually held together with a skewer.

Steaks are cut from the leg and should be cut about 1 inch thick.

All these chops and the steaks can be cooked in the same way.

Broiling Chops

Preheat the broiler. Oil or rub the broiling rack with fat and arrange chops. Place the chops so that they cook about 3 inches from the flame. Brown chops quickly on both sides under intense heat. Reduce the heat and allow them to cook slowly until they arrive at the desired degree of doneness. This should take from 5 to 8 minutes per side according to the thickness of the chops.

Serve at once on hot platter and transfer to hot plates. One cannot be too emphatic about the necessity of having hot plates for lamb at all times. Lamb chops need only salt and pepper to enhance them, although English mustard is always a welcome addition. English mutton chops or lamb chops are excellent served with shoestring potatoes and are very often accompanied by cole slaw.

Sautéed Lamb Chops and Steaks

Lamb chops and steaks may be sautéed on top of the stove in sufficient butter merely to grease the pan. Or, if you use a heavy-bottomed pan, they may be started in the warm pan without fat. They should cook slowly, the fat being poured off as it collects in the pan. Turn chops on edge to cook fat.

BREAST OF LAMB

Navarin or Braised Lamb

2 pounds breast of lamb	Pinch of thyme
3 tablespoons olive oil	½ cup red wine
Salt and pepper	2 onions
2 cloves garlic	2 or 3 carrots
1 cup tomato purée	

Have lamb cut in serving pieces. Heat olive oil in a skillet and sear the pieces of lamb in the hot fat until well browned on all sides. Season with salt and pepper. Add garlic cut in small pieces, tomato purée, thyme, and red wine. Cover and simmer for 45 minutes. Add onions cut in thin slices and carrots, scraped and cut in slices. Cover again and simmer until the vegetables and meat are tender—about 45 minutes. Serve with freshly cooked snap beans. (*Serves 4.*)

Deviled Breast of Lamb

2 pounds breast of lamb	2 eggs
1 onion stuck with 2 cloves	2 tablespoons water
1 bay leaf	2 cups dry bread crumbs
1 sprig thyme	or zwieback crumbs
1 teaspoon dry mustard	Few grains cayenne
Flour	Butter
1 teaspoon salt	

Have lamb cut into serving pieces. Place in a saucepan and cover with water. Add onion, bay leaf, thyme, and salt, and cover. Simmer until the meat is tender.

Remove from the broth and pull out the small rib bones. Place the lamb on a deep platter or bowl, cover it with a plate, and weigh it down.

Beat eggs with water. Prepare bread crumbs and mix with dry mustard and cayenne.

Remove the weight and plate from the cooked lamb. Dip each piece in flour, egg, and crumbs. Either sauté in butter until nicely browned or grill them under a low flame in the broiler until nicely browned. Serve with Escoffier Sauce Diable. (*Serves 4.*)

Rolled Stuffed Breast of Lamb

2 breasts of lamb	Salt and pepper
1 pound pork sausage	2 cloves garlic
Chopped parsley	12 or 14 tiny white onions,
2 tablespoons chopped	peeled
onion	3 or 4 carrots, scraped
Thyme	1 cup red wine
Butter or olive oil	Flour

Have lamb boned at the butcher's. Spread with pork sausage to which you have added a little parsley, onion, and a little thyme. Roll and tie securely.

Brown the lamb in butter or olive oil. Season with salt and pepper and add garlic, onions, and carrots. Add wine, cover, and allow the meat to simmer until tender, about 1½ hours.

Remove the meat and vegetables and add, if necessary, another ½ cup wine. Add 2 tablespoons chopped parsley and several teaspoons of butter and flour, well mixed. Stir over a brisk flame until well blended and slightly thickened.

MISCELLANEOUS LAMB DISHES

Lamb Patties

Lamb patties are ground lamb formed into cakes and usually wrapped with bacon secured with small skewers. They may be broiled in the same manner as lamb chops, but should be lubricated well with butter or oil during the cooking process. Lamb patties should not be overcooked, or they will become as uninteresting as old hay.

Kebabs or Shashlik

2 to 2½ pounds lamb	1 teaspoon salt
½ cup olive oil	1 bay leaf
1 cup red wine	2 cloves garlic, crushed
3 tablespoons wine vinegar	Parsley, chopped
Thyme	Oregano

From Persia to New York there are many different combinations of lamb and accompaniments that take their place on skewers, brochettes, sticks, or imitation swords and are broiled over charcoal or under gas or electricity. Lamb thus cooked is nearly always marinated.

The meat should be cut in squares or cubes 1 to 2 inches square. You may use wire or steel skewers; the size varies according to the type. I suggest fairly substantial ones about 9 or 10 inches long.

For the marinade, mix salt, olive oil, red wine, wine vinegar, bay leaf, crushed into small pieces, garlic, parsley, thyme, and a little oregano.

Soak the lamb in the marinade for several hours; the longer the better. If you are planning the dish for evening, prepare the marinade first thing in the morning and allow the lamb to soak all day.

Arrange the squares of seasoned lamb on the skewers. Alternate the lamb with bacon or salt-pork squares and with tiny onions or tomatoes if you wish.

Broil quickly under a brisk flame or over hot coals. Turn frequently so that the meat becomes evenly cooked. You may for variety use mushrooms, kidneys, or other seasonings with the lamb.

Serve at once with baked rice. *(Serves 6.)*

Chopped Lamb Kebabs

1½ pounds chopped lamb	1 teaspoon salt
½ cup pine nuts	1 teaspoon black pepper
¼ cup chopped parsley	Pinch of thyme
¼ cup finely chopped onion	2 eggs
Butter or bacon	

Mix together lamb, nuts, parsley, onion, salt, pepper, and thyme. Blend with eggs and form into long sausage-shaped cakes around skewers. Brush well with butter or wrap with bacon. Broil as you do the kebabs, but under a slower heat.

You may serve the kebabs on the skewers, or, with a deft knife or fork, push the cooked meat and garnishes from the skewer to the plate, keeping them in good order. *(Serves 4.)*

Braised Lamb Shanks with Lentils

Lamb shanks	½ cup water or broth
Butter or olive oil	1½ cups quick-cooking lentils
Salt and pepper	1 onion stuck with 2 cloves
2 cloves garlic	Bay leaf
1 sprig thyme	1½ teaspoons salt

Allow 1 lamb shank per person. Sear the shanks in butter or olive oil until nicely browned. Add salt and pepper to taste, 1 clove garlic, thyme, and water or broth. Cover and simmer over low flame for 1 hour, adding more liquid if necessary.

Wash lentils and place in a saucepan with enough water to cover them by an inch. Add onion, bay leaf, 1 clove of garlic, and 1½ teaspoons salt. Allow lentils to simmer until just tender but not mushy. Do not boil.

Place lentils and lamb shanks in a casserole and cover with the lentil liquid and what liquid is left from the shanks. Place in a moderate oven (350°) for ½ hour or until the lamb is perfectly tender and the lentils well flavored with the lamb. Add more liquid if the casserole cooks dry.

Lamb Loaf

2 pounds ground lamb	1 clove garlic, finely
1 cup dry bread crumbs	chopped
¼ cup finely chopped onion	1¼ teaspoons salt
¼ cup finely chopped	1 teaspoon dry mustard
parsley	2 eggs
Bacon strips	

Mix together lamb, bread crumbs, onion, parsley, garlic, salt, mustard, and eggs. Form into a loaf and top with bacon strips. Bake in a moderate oven (350°) for approximately 1 hour. Serve with French fried onion rings and a green salad. *(Serves 4.)*

Lamb Kidneys

Lamb kidneys should be split in two and the white membrane and cord removed. Soak them in milk or acidulated water for a short time. Estimate 2 to 3 lamb kidneys per person.

Sautéed Lamb Kidneys

Lamb kidneys	Salt and pepper
4 tablespoons butter or	Worcestershire sauce
olive oil	

Sauté kidneys in butter or olive oil for 8 or 10 minutes. Season with salt and pepper. Turn frequently and add 1 or more teaspoons Worcestershire sauce just before serving.

VARIATIONS

(1) Dip kidneys in flour, beaten egg, and crumbs. Sauté in butter until nicely browned on both sides. Serve with Escoffier Sauce Diable.

(2) Cut kidneys in small thin slices. For 6 kidneys, clean and slice ½ pound mushrooms. Sauté mushrooms and kidneys together in 6 tablespoons butter. Add 1 tablespoon grated onion and 2 tablespoons chopped parsley. Cook 6 minutes. Add ¼ cup Madeira or sherry and ½ cup heavy cream. Allow cream to cook 2 minutes, correct seasoning, and serve on fried toast.
(Serves 2.)

(3) Clean and slice 6 kidneys. Sauté 1 finely minced onion in 4 tablespoons olive oil, add kidneys, and cook quickly. Add 1 teaspoon salt and 1 teaspoon dry mustard. Blend well. Add 2 tablespoons Escoffier Sauce Diable and 1 tablespoon chili sauce when kidneys are fully cooked. Blend with kidneys. Serve on toast.

Broiled Kidneys en Brochette

Lamb kidneys may be broiled en brochette very successfully. Combined with bacon, they make a perfect Sunday breakfast dish.

Clean and halve lamb kidneys, allowing 2 to a person. Attach a rasher of bacon to a skewer, then a half kidney, then the bacon again, and so on, so that the bacon runs ribbon-fashion on the skewer and will lubricate the kidneys during the broiling process. Sprinkle with salt and pepper, and broil about 3 inches from flame until cooked all over.

BENEDICTINE

POA CHED

FLORENTINE

CODDLED

WITH TOMATO

HARD BOILED

WITH HAM

EASTER

EGGS
AND CHEESE DISHES

EGGS

Boiled Eggs

(1) Place in a saucepan enough water to cover the eggs. Bring the water to a simmer, not a boil. Place the eggs in the saucepan with a spoon and allow the eggs to simmer for 3½ minutes or more depending on the degree of softness desired.

(2) Cover eggs with cold water. Place them over medium heat and allow the water to come to a full boil. Remove the eggs at once.

(3) Put the eggs in boiling water. Allow 1 minute of boiling and then remove the pan from the heat and let the eggs stand 3 minutes in the hot water.

Hard-Cooked Eggs

Allow eggs to boil, completely covered with water, for 8 to 10 minutes. Remove from heat and plunge into cold water. If you crack the shells slightly before cooling, the eggs will peel with greater ease.

Poached Eggs

A skillet or flat saucepan is the best utensil for poaching eggs, unless you have a patented poacher of one type or another. You should have water deep enough to cover the eggs. Add a little salt and a tablespoon of vinegar to the water. When it is boiling rapidly, break the eggs and drop them in carefully or slide them from a saucer and let them cook until set. Lift them out with a large perforated spoon or skimmer.

Eggs may be poached until fairly hard for use in salads or jellies or for a first course.

Eggs Benedict

For each person toast 1 English muffin split in half. Top each muffin half, which has been well buttered just at serving time, with a round slice of sautéed or boiled Virginia ham.

Top the ham with poached eggs and cover with Hollandaise sauce. Sprinkle with chopped parsley and serve.

Eggs Italian

Place poached eggs on crisp buttered toast, allowing 2 eggs per person. Add Italian tomato sauce, sprinkle liberally with grated Parmesan cheese, and put under the broiler for a few minutes to brown. Serve at once.

Eggs in Nest

Boil 8 ounces of fine noodles until just tender. Drain and mix with 4 tablespoons butter, salt, and pepper to taste, and 4 truffles, finely cut. Sprinkle liberally with chopped parsley. Form into nests on serving plates or platter and add 1 poached egg to each nest. Dot with softened butter and sprinkle liberally with finely chopped truffles. *(Serves 4.)*

Eggs Mornay

Poach 2 eggs per person and place the cooked eggs in a shallow baking dish. Cover the eggs with sauce Mornay, sprinkle liberally with grated Parmesan cheese, and put under the broiler for a few minutes to brown. Serve at once.

Eggs California

Soak artichokes, 2 to a person, in acidulated water for ½ hour. Cook artichokes until tender. Remove leaves and choke. Scrape the leaves and mix the pulp with melted butter. Sauté the artichoke bottoms in butter until heated through. When the artichoke bottoms are cooked through and hot, stuff them with the purée from the leaves. Top each artichoke with a poached egg and top this with Hollandaise sauce.

Eggs Florentine

Cook 1 pound spinach (or 1 package quick-frozen spinach) for each 4 persons. Salt and pepper to taste and chop the spinach or put it through a food mill. Make a thin bed of spinach in the bottom of an oval or round shallow baking dish and top with poached eggs, allowing 2 to a person. Pour sauce Mornay over this and sprinkle liberally with grated Parmesan cheese. Place under the broiler for a few minutes to brown.

Eggs with Spinach

Make a bed of chopped spinach as above. Place poached eggs, 2 to a serving, on the spinach and top with mushroom caps which have been lightly sautéed in butter and to which you have added sour cream and chopped parsley. For 4 people you will need 12 mushroom caps and 3 tablespoons sour cream. Salt to taste.

Eggs with Tomatoes

Sauté large tomatoes which have been peeled and sliced in ¾-inch slices, allowing 1 slice for each egg. Sauté them in olive oil flavored with garlic and a little basil. Arrange tomato slices on hot plates and place 1 poached egg on each slice. Top with a tomato sauce or with grated Parmesan cheese.

SCRAMBLED EGGS

To avoid tough and lumpy scrambled eggs, certain rules must be followed:

(1) Use plenty of butter in the pan. It should be hot when the eggs are added, but not smoking or browned.

(2) Allow 2 eggs per person and an extra "for the pan."

(3) Mix the eggs slightly before adding to the pan. Add 1 tablespoon water or cream for each egg. Water will make exceedingly fluffy eggs; cream will make a richer, smoother mixture.

(4) If you wish to have really fluffy or creamy scrambled eggs, allow the eggs to "set" slightly after you put them in the pan and then stir constantly with a fork, being certain to run the edge of the fork around the edges and into the center of the pan. Good scrambled eggs need constant and careful attention.

(5) You may add seasonings when mixing the eggs or while they are cooking, or you may prepare seasonings first and pour the eggs over them and scramble them with the precooked seasonings.

Scrambled Eggs with Herbs: Beware of prepared herb mixtures for eggs. They are usually dry and, if so, will make your eggs taste as though they have been flavored with hay, or the eggs will be pungent beyond belief. If you wish to use herbs, be certain to use fresh ones. The most agreeable herbs are parsley, chives, chervil, and tarragon. They should be chopped exceedingly fine and added to the egg mixture either before or during cooking. Additional chopped herbs may be sprinkled over the eggs just before serving. Or you may blend the chopped herbs with butter and add this mixture to the cooked eggs when you serve them.

Pungent Scrambled Eggs

Add freshly ground black pepper, Worcestershire sauce, and a few grains of cayenne to the eggs before cooking. Sprinkle with paprika during cooking and add a few drops of lemon juice just before removing from the heat.

Curried Scrambled Eggs

Slice 6 mushroom caps and sauté them lightly in 4 tablespoons butter. Break 9 eggs into a bowl and add 6 tablespoons water. Season with 1 teaspoon salt, 1 teaspoon black pepper, and 1 teaspoon (or more if it is to your taste) curry powder. Pour the egg mixture over the mushrooms and scramble the eggs. Serve on toasted English muffins.

(Serves 4.)

Scrambled Eggs with Anchovies

Heap hot scrambled eggs on thin, well-buttered slices of crisp toast striped with anchovy fillets. It is wise to determine how salty the anchovies are before adding salt to the eggs.

Scrambled Eggs with Ham

Chop or grind ¾ cup ham. The ends of a baked ham are ideal for this. Sauté the ham in 3 tablespoons butter or ham fat for just a few minutes to heat it through. Pour 9 eggs mixed with 6 tablespoons water or cream over the ham and scramble. Taste for seasoning before serving. *(Serves 4.)*

Scrambled Eggs with Smoked Salmon

Cut 4 or 5 thin slices smoked salmon into thin strips. Heat the salmon in 4 tablespoons butter but do not cook it. Add 9 eggs, slightly beaten, with 6 tablespoons water or cream. Scramble. Add freshly ground black pepper and salt to taste (be certain to determine beforehand whether the salmon is salted). Just before removing from the fire, add a few drops of lemon juice and a little chopped parsley. *(Serves 4.)*

Summer Scrambled Eggs

Cut 5 or 6 small green onions, with some of the green part included, in small pieces. Peel, seed, and cut into small dice 2 ripe tomatoes. Chop enough parsley to make ¼ cup. Stone and cut into small slivers 5 or 6 ripe olives.

Sauté the onion in 3 tablespoons butter until just transparent but not browned. Add the chopped tomato and allow it to blend and cook 3 or 4 minutes. Season to taste with salt and pepper.

Mix 9 eggs and pour them over the mixture. Add no water or cream to the eggs. Scramble in the usual fashion, adding the parsley and olives when the eggs begin to blend and cook. Serve with crisp bacon. *(Serves 4.)*

OMELETS

Omelets require a heavy skillet—iron or tin-lined copper is best. If the pan is never used for anything else and never washed, but merely rubbed clean with salt, your omelets will rarely stick—but you will also have one more utensil to find space for. Small omelets are much easier to make and usually more delicate than large ones. It is better to make two small omelets than one large one.

Plain Omelet

Allow 2 eggs per person. Break eggs into a bowl. Add 2 teaspoons water or milk for each egg, if desired. Otherwise add only salt and beat the eggs slightly.

Melt 2 or 3 tablespoons butter in the omelet pan and let it get very hot but not smoking. Pour in the eggs, which will set at once. Loosen the edges of the omelet with a spatula, letting the uncooked egg run underneath. When the omelet is creamy, but not hard, fold it over with the spatula or roll it. Slide it onto a hot platter and serve at once.

When you serve sauces or other additions to the omelet, it is customary to fold the flavor addition into the omelet or to pour it over. In some instances, as in the case of Omelet Fines Herbes, the finely chopped herbs are added to the egg mixture before cooking. Very often an omelet to which other things have been added is cooked like a pancake. It takes a deft hand and courage to flip the omelet while it is cooking, so my advice is to try it several times by yourself before attempting it for guests.

VARIATIONS

Omelet Fines Herbes: Mix finely chopped parsley, chives, and chervil with eggs before pouring into the omelet pan.

Potato Omelet: Place in omelet pan potatoes which have been cooked in their jackets, sliced, and browned in butter. Pour eggs over the potatoes.

Mushroom Omelet: Fold either creamed or sautéed mushrooms into omelet when cooked and add more to the top when served.

Onion Omelet: Sauté onion rings or green onions in butter until lightly browned and tender. Add egg mixture and cook.

Kidney Omelet: Fold sautéed lamb or veal kidneys in omelet or serve them on the side and decorate the top with sautéed mushroom caps.

Country Omelet: Sauté small pieces of bacon until crisp and combine with boiled potatoes which have been sliced or diced and then lightly browned in butter with a small amount of onion and chopped parsley. Pour eggs over this mixture and cook pancake-fashion, turning once. For a 4-egg omelet, 6 to 8 slices of bacon and 1 cup sliced or diced potatoes are ample.

Tomato Omelet: Peel, seed, and cut into small dice 2 ripe tomatoes. Cook them in 2 tablespoons butter and flavor with a tiny bit of garlic. When the tomatoes are cooked

FINES HERBES MUSHROOM TOMATO ONION

through, but not mushy, add the eggs and proceed in the usual fashion. Or you may cook the tomatoes separately and fold them into the omelet when it is cooked.

Watercress Omelet: Add 2 or 3 teaspoons finely chopped watercress to the egg mixture and surround the cooked omelet with fresh watercress.

Chicken Omelet: Fold either chicken hash or creamed chicken into omelet and add additional chicken to the serving platter. Decorate top of omelet with sautéed mushroom caps.

Cheese Omelet (I): Prepare a plain omelet, as above. Just as the eggs have set in the pan, add ½ cup grated cheddar cheese and allow it to cook until omelet is ready to fold and serve.

Cheese Omelet (II): Proceed as above, but substitute ¼ cup finely grated Parmesan cheese for the cheddar.

Cheese Omelet (III): Mix ¼ cup grated Parmesan cheese with the eggs and add an additional ¼ cup while the omelet is cooking.

Chicken Liver Omelet: Sauté ½ pound chicken livers in 4 tablespoons butter until cooked but not mushy. Add salt to taste, 1 tablespoon finely chopped onion, 1 tablespoon finely chopped parsley, and 1 teaspoon black pepper. Fold the omelet over the chicken livers. Or roll the omelet, place on a hot platter, and serve surrounded with chicken livers.

Fluffy Omelet

2 tablespoons quick-cooking tapioca	¾ cup milk
	1 tablespoon butter
¾ teaspoon salt	4 egg yolks
⅛ teaspoon pepper	4 egg whites

Combine tapioca, salt, pepper, and milk in saucepan. Place over low or medium heat and cook until mixture comes to a boil, stirring constantly. Add butter. Remove from heat and allow to cool slightly while beating eggs.

Beat egg yolks until thick and lemon-colored. Add milk mixture and mix well. Fold mixture into stiffly beaten egg whites. Turn into hot, buttered, 10-inch skillet and cook over low heat 3 minutes. Transfer to a moderate oven (350°) and bake 15 minutes.

Omelet is sufficiently cooked when a knife inserted comes out clean. Cut across at right angles to handle of pan, being careful not to cut all the way through. Fold carefully from handle to opposite side and serve on hot platter. *(Serves 4 to 6.)*

VARIATIONS

Apricot Omelet: Make fluffy omelet, spreading with apricot jam before folding. Fold as directed and dust with confectioner's sugar.

Cheese Omelet: Make fluffy omelet, adding ½ cup grated American cheese with the butter. Stir until cheese is melted.

Orange Omelet: Make fluffy omelet, reducing salt to ½ teaspoon and milk to ½ cup. Omit pepper. Add ¼ cup orange juice and 1 tablespoon grated orange rind with the butter.

CHEESE DISHES

Cheese is one of the most delectable and versatile of foods. It may be eaten in its natural state and may be combined with many foods to make delicious dishes. Soups, salads, casserole dishes, pastries, vegetable sauces—all are enhanced by cheese.

Ernest Oldmeadow has this to say of cheese: "Both wine and cheese represent man's effort to transmute the perishable into the durable. For a while—perhaps for thousands of years—our ancestors could refresh themselves with the juice of the grape only where the vine grew and its fruit ripened. Often must they have longed, in parched wastes and under brutal suns, for the grape's cool freshness; but at last somebody's carelessness or inquisitiveness left alone a bowl of pressed grapes long enough for nature's miracle of fermentation to produce the first wine. Likewise with cheese. To draw from some tamed mammal—a cow, a goat, a sheep, a mare— the food beverage which we call milk meant great progress in civilization; but milk, like grape juice, was as perishable as the daily manna of the wandering Israelites, until its controlled souring and curding made it durable and easily portable. In other words, both grape juice and milk tend to 'go bad'; but human skill can make them 'go good' in the forms of wine and cheese." *

There are four cheeses which may be called the stand-bys of cookery. Swiss, cheddar (including the American cheddars and cheddar types), Parmesan, and mozzarella are the mainstays of the cheese world. American Swiss is a delicious cheese to eat as a cheese course, but years of experimenting prove that for recipes calling for Emmenthal or Gruyère, the Switzerland Swiss gives the most successful results,

For additional information on the kinds and uses of cheese, see the section SALADS AND CHEESE in this book.

Basic Cheese Soufflé

3 tablespoons butter	½ cup grated sharp cheddar
2 tablespoons flour	cheese
1 cup scalded milk	4 egg yolks
1 teaspoon salt	4 egg whites
Cayenne pepper	

Melt butter in upper part of the double boiler. Add flour and stir with a wooden spoon until well blended and smooth. Gradually add scalded milk, stirring constantly, and stir until mixture thickens and becomes smooth. Add salt, a few grains of cayenne, and cheese. Continue stirring until cheese is melted.

Beat egg yolks until light and lemon-colored and pour the slightly cooled cheese mixture onto the egg yolks, stirring constantly. Cool for a short time.

While the cheese mixture is cooling, beat egg whites very stiff; then fold into the mixture. Pour into buttered casserole and bake in a moderately hot oven (375°) until light and well browned—35 to 45 minutes.

Be certain to have everyone ready, for this dish should be served at once. *(Serves 4.)*

* Reprinted by permission from *A Concise Encyclopedia of Gastronomy*, published by The Wine and Food Society, 28 Grosvenor Gardens, London, S.W. 1, England.

Parmesan Cheese Soufflé

4 tablespoons butter	1 cup grated Parmesan
3 tablespoons flour	cheese
1 cup milk	1 teaspoon salt
5 egg yolks, well beaten	½ teaspoon black pepper
	5 egg whites

Melt butter in the upper part of a double boiler, add flour and blend until smooth. Gradually add milk, stirring constantly, and continue stirring until the mixture is thickened and smooth.

Remove mixture from heat and mix with the well-beaten yolks of 5 eggs, the cheese, salt, and pepper. Blend well. Fold in the stiffly beaten egg whites. Pour into a buttered casserole and bake in a moderately hot oven (375°) for about 35 minutes or until well risen and firm. *(Serves 4.)*

Swiss Cheese Soufflé

¼ cup butter	4 egg yolks, well beaten
½ cup flour	½ pound grated Swiss
1 cup scalded milk	cheese
½ teaspoon salt	4 egg whites
Nutmeg	

Melt butter in the upper part of a double boiler and stir in flour. Add scalded milk to which you have added salt and a little nutmeg. Cook over hot water, stirring constantly, until smooth and thick.

Remove from fire and cool slightly. Blend with the well-beaten egg yolks and with the cheese. Fold in the egg whites, stiffly beaten, and pour into a buttered casserole. Bake in a moderately hot oven (375°) until risen and set—about 30 to 40 minutes. Serve at once. *(Serves 4.)*

Cheese Ramequin

Swiss cheese slices	2 cups milk
White bread slices	½ teaspoon salt
2 eggs	¼ teaspoon nutmeg

Butter a deep casserole and line with alternate layers of sliced Swiss cheese and slices of white bread. Allow the cheese slices to overlap the bread slices by about ½ inch. Beat eggs until very light and mix with milk, salt, and nutmeg. Pour this mixture over the slices of bread and cheese.

Place the casserole in a pan of hot water and bake in a moderately hot oven (375°) for approximately 30 minutes.

VARIATION

The same dish may be prepared with cheddar or American cheese. Substitute 1 teaspoon dry mustard for the nutmeg when blending the milk and eggs, or use 1 tablespoon Worcestershire sauce.

Cheese Charlotte

3 tablespoons butter	½ teaspoon salt
3 egg yolks	Nutmeg
1½ tablespoons flour	½ cup cream
2 cups diced bread	3 egg whites
½ pound grated cheese	White bread slices
(Swiss or cheddar)	Milk

Cream the butter. Blend in the egg yolks one at a time, add flour, and blend well. Add diced bread which has been soaked in milk, and add the cheese, salt, and a few grains nutmeg. Mix well with cream. Fold in the egg whites, stiffly beaten. Line a casserole with slices of bread soaked in milk and pour over them the cheese mixture. Bake in a moderate oven (350°) for 30 to 35 minutes. Serve at once. *(Serves 4.)*

Cheese Pie

Pastry	1 cup rich milk or light
1 cup grated Swiss cheese	cream
4 eggs	½ teaspoon salt
	Cayenne pepper

Line a 9-inch pie pan with pastry and brush pastry with milk. Add cheese. Beat eggs until light and lemon-colored and blend with the rich milk or light cream, salt, and a few grains of cayenne. Pour this mixture over the cheese and bake for 10 minutes in a hot oven (400°).

Reduce the heat to moderate (350°) and bake until the custard is set except for the center, which will continue cooking when removed from the oven. Serve either hot or cold. *(Serves 4.)*

VARIATION

Proceed as above but add to the egg mixture small bits of bacon which have been partially cooked and drained on absorbent paper. Bake in a hot oven (450°) for 10 minutes and then in a moderately slow oven (325°) for about 30 minutes.

Swiss Cheese Tartlets

Pastry	½ pound grated Swiss
Egg white	cheese
1 very small white onion,	2 eggs, well beaten
finely chopped	1 cup light cream
1 tablespoon butter	½ teaspoon salt
	Cayenne pepper

Line small tart pans or muffin tins with pastry and flute the edges nicely. Brush the pastry with egg white. Sauté the onion in butter until transparent. Mix with cheese, beaten eggs, and light cream. Season with salt and a few grains cayenne.

Fill tartlet shells half full and bake in a hot oven (400°) until done and crust is lightly browned.

VARIATIONS

Custard Cheese Tartlets (I): Line tart pans or muffin tins with pastry and flute. Sprinkle 1 teaspoon grated Swiss cheese in each shell and fill with custard mixture for cheese pie. Bake the tarts in a moderately hot oven (375°) until nicely browned and custard is set. Do not overcook.

Custard Cheese Tartlets (II): Prepare a stiff pastry with 1 cup flour, 4 tablespoons butter, ½ teaspoon salt, and 2 tablespoons ice water. Chill dough in refrigerator for an hour; then roll out. Line tart shells with pastry; prick the bottoms Mix 4 eggs well with 1 cup grated cheese, 1 teaspoon flour, salt, few grains nutmeg, and black pepper. Gradually beat in ¾ cup milk and blend thoroughly. Fill shells two thirds full and bake in a hot oven (425°) for 12 to 15 minutes.

Welsh Rarebit (I)

1 tablespoon butter	1 egg, slightly beaten
1 pound sharp American	½ teaspoon salt
or cheddar cheese,	Cayenne pepper
grated	1 teaspoon dry mustard
1 cup ale or beer	Toast points or toasted
	muffins

Melt butter in upper part of double boiler or in a chafing dish. Add cheese and, as the cheese begins to melt, add ale or beer gradually, stirring constantly until the mixture is well thickened and smooth. Add egg, salt, a few grains of cayenne, and mustard. Serve at once on toast points or toasted muffins.

The rarebit must not be allowed to overcook or become cool and leathery. Be certain that plates and toast are hot. More beer to drink with this is an absolute necessity.

(Serves 4.)

Welsh Rarebit (II)

2 tablespoons butter	1 tablespoon Worcestershire
½ pound sharp American	sauce
or cheddar cheese,	½ teaspoon salt
grated or shredded	Grated horseradish
2 egg yolks	1 cup beer or ale
2 egg whites	Toast
1 teaspoon dry mustard	

Melt butter in a heavy saucepan. Add cheese and allow it to melt until smooth and creamy. Mix egg yolks with mustard, Worcestershire sauce, salt, and a little grated horseradish. Beat the egg whites very stiff. When the cheese is completely melted, add the yolks of eggs, stir in well, and thin with beer or ale. When the ingredients are well blended and the rarebit almost at the boiling point, fold in the beaten egg whites. Serve at once on toast.

(Serves 4.)

White Monkey

1 cup bread crumbs	½ teaspoon salt
1 cup milk	½ teaspoon dry mustard
2 tablespoons butter	Cayenne pepper
1 cup sharp American	1 egg, slightly beaten
or cheddar cheese,	Crisp toast
shredded	

Soak bread crumbs in milk. Melt butter in upper part of double boiler and add cheese. When cheese is melted, add soaked bread crumbs, salt, mustard, and a few grains of cayenne. Stir in beaten egg and allow the mixture to cook for several minutes. Serve on crisp toast on hot plates. *(Serves 4.)*

Swiss Cheese Fondue

1 clove garlic	1½ teaspoons cornstarch or
1½ pounds Swiss cheese,	potato flour
shredded	Salt and pepper
1 cup dry white wine	Nutmeg
	¼ cup kirsch

Rub an earthenware casserole which will stand top-of-stove cookery with a clove of garlic. Add cheese and wine and allow cheese to melt and blend with the wine. When the mixture is creamy, add cornstarch or potato flour and blend with the cheese. Season with salt, pepper, and a little nutmeg. As the mixture starts to boil, add kirsch. Serve in the casserole over an alcohol flame at table.

This dish is traditionally accompanied by small pieces of French bread, which each person uses on the end of a fork for dunking into the hot cheese mixture. If the fondue becomes too thick, thin with kirsch. *(Serves 4.)*

VARIATION

Melt 2 tablespoons butter in a casserole, add 3 tablespoons flour, and blend well. Add 2 cups milk gradually, stirring constantly. When slightly thickened, add 1 pound shredded Swiss cheese. Stir constantly with a fork until melted. Season with salt, pepper, and a few grains nutmeg. Serve as you do fondue, above.

French Toasted Cheese Sandwiches

3 eggs, well beaten	Butter
1 cup milk	American or cheddar cheese
½ teaspoon salt	slices (1 for every 2 bread
Cayenne pepper	slices)
Bread slices a day old	Batter (optional)

To beaten eggs add milk, salt, and a few grains cayenne. Spread slices of day-old bread (2 slices per person) with butter, cover half the slices with sliced cheese, top with another slice of bread, and press together. Dip in egg-and-milk mixture and sauté in butter until golden brown on both sides and cheese is melted. Or dip in batter and fry in deep fat 3 to 4 minutes or till bread is browned and cheese melted. Drain on absorbent paper.

VARIATIONS

With Tomatoes: Add 2 or 3 slices tomato to the sandwich.

With Bacon: Before cooking, to the sandwich add bacon which has been cooked until almost crisp.

With Mustard: Spread cheese with a mixture of dry mustard and water blended to a thick paste.

Super Cheese Sandwich

6 shallots, finely chopped	1 cup Béchamel sauce
3 tablespoons butter	Salt and pepper
½ cup smoked ham, cut	Buttered toast
in small pieces	Swiss cheese slices
8 mushroom caps, sliced	Grated Swiss cheese

Sauté chopped shallots in butter until lightly colored and soft. Add smoked ham and mushroom slices. Simmer the mixture until mushrooms are tender, combine with Béchamel sauce, and season with salt and pepper.

Arrange slices of buttered toast in a large flat baking dish and top each slice with a thick slice of Swiss cheese. Pour the sauce between the slices of toast, sprinkle with grated cheese, and brown under the broiler until cheese is melted and lightly browned. Serve at once.

Toasted Cheese Sandwiches

½ pound sharp American or cheddar cheese, shredded	½ teaspoon salt
	½ teaspoon dry mustard
	2 egg yolks
2 tablespoons chives, chopped	2 egg whites
	Bread slices
	4 tablespoons butter

Blend shredded cheese with chives, salt, mustard, and the egg yolks. Fold in whites of eggs, stiffly beaten. Spread slices of bread well with mixture and top each with another slice. Butter both sides of sandwiches liberally and sauté in butter in skillet till bread is nicely browned and cheese mixture fully cooked.

Fromage en Brochette

White bread	2 eggs, well beaten
Swiss cheese	1 cup milk
Flour	Deep fat

Cut slices of white bread (with the crusts removed) into small triangles. Cut slices of Swiss cheese into matching triangles. Alternate slices on skewers, using bread for the first and last pieces. Roll in flour and dip in a mixture of beaten eggs and milk (2 eggs to 1 cup milk) and fry in deep fat (375°) until nicely browned. Serve at once.

Cheese Croquettes

4 tablespoons butter	½ pound sharp American or cheddar or Swiss
5 tablespoons flour	
1 cup milk	3 egg yolks, well beaten
4 tablespoons cream	Bread crumbs

Make a thick white sauce, using table butter and flour blended with milk. Stir until thickened. Stir in cream and add cheese. When cheese is melted and smooth, cool slightly, correct the seasoning, and blend with the beaten egg yolks. Pour the mixture into a shallow pan and chill thoroughly in the refrigerator.

When ready to cook, immerse the pan in hot water for a minute or so to loosen the cheese mixture, and turn out on a board. Shape into croquettes or rolls. Dip the croquettes in flour and in beaten egg and roll in crumbs. Fry in a very hot fat (390°) until golden brown. Drain on absorbent paper and serve with a tomato sauce or devil sauce.

(Serves 4.)

Molded Swiss Cheese

2 cups Béchamel sauce	¼ cup grated Parmesan cheese
1 envelope unflavored gelatin	1½ cups stiffly whipped cream
¼ cup water or milk	
¼ cup grated Swiss cheese	Greens
	Cheese slices
	Pickle

To Béchamel sauce add gelatin which has been dissolved in ¼ cup water or milk. Add cheese. Let the mixture cool and fold in stiffly whipped cream. Pour into individual molds and chill thoroughly. Unmold on a bed of greens and top each mold with thin slices of cheese and thin slices of pickle.

(Serves 4.)

VARIATION

You may add chopped chives and a bit of dry mustard to this recipe if you wish.

VEGETABLES

The subject of this chapter is one of my favorites. I strongly believe that the vegetable has never had its due in this country and I am determined to do something about it. The key to successful vegetable cookery is a minimum of water and cooking time in order to retain maximum flavor and texture.

Vegetables are a most important part of our diet, as far as nutrition and vitamin content are concerned. Further than that, they are among the truly delicious foods and should be treated with care. In addition to tasting better, the well-prepared vegetable retains more of its nutrients and vitamins than the poorly prepared one. If one eats good food, diversified and well prepared, one is healthfully and intelligently fed and need not fear nutritional deficiencies.

In many countries vegetables are served as a course in themselves. Asparagus, broccoli, green beans, and artichokes are really important enough to deserve a special spot on the menu. It is often pleasant to savor a well-prepared meat or poultry course by itself, with a vegetable selection following. These remarks do not apply, of course, to rice or noodles or potatoes which are part of the main dish.

There are many vegetable dishes important enough to be a main course at dinner or luncheon. Others may be served as hors d'oeuvres, and in such cases a vegetable course may be dispensed with. Vegetables à la grecque or vegetables vinaigrette are wonderful spring and summer dishes and need no additional vegetable to follow them. Dishes with dried beans or lentils take their place as main dishes and need a salad or a perfectly prepared green vegetable to follow them.

A few suggestions for vegetable dishes which may be served as a main course:

Asparagus with egg and grated Parmesan cheese (page 157)
Spinach with polenta and grated cheese (page 175)
Spinach in casserole with mushrooms (page 175)
Mushroom pie or broiled mushrooms (page 170)
Artichokes stuffed in various ways (page 156)
Asparagus with ham (page 157)
Eggplant casserole (page 168)

COOKING

Vegetables must not be overcooked. Those which are boiled are much better if cooked in a little water and only long enough to give them a degree of softness. Many vegetables are excellent steamed, a process which results in better color and a fresher appearance. Or they may be cooked solely in butter in a heavy kettle with a tight-fitting cover. Others are baked or sautéed or scalloped. Others, notably some of the leafy vegetables, are cooked with only the water which adheres to the leaves after washing. Dried vegetables such as beans, lentils, corn, and peas are cooked after soak-ing, except for those which are sold as "quick-cooking," which means they have been steamed or processed before packaging.

Pressure cookers have completely changed vegetable cookery in a great number of homes. Since different styles and makes of cookers require different treatments and timing, the manufacturers' directions should be consulted. Frozen vegetables, which will be treated more thoroughly in another part of this book, should be prepared according to the directions on the package.

GLOBE ARTICHOKES

The globe—sometimes called the French—artichoke is in reality the bud of a thistle-like flower which is as decorative as the bud is palatable. A choice artichoke should have bright green leaves rather closely packed. Rusty spots or widely separated leaves indicate age or injury. The very small artichokes may be trimmed for artichoke hearts or used as small cups to hold hors d'oeuvres or hot foods.

Most artichokes grown commercially in this country come from the northern California coast. They are at their best during early winter and reach their peak of plenty in March and April.

One artichoke per person (unless the artichokes are very small) is usually ample.

Soak the artichoke in acidulated water for half an hour before cooking. With a sharp knife, trim the bottom stem so that the artichoke will stand erect when served. Remove a few of the outside leaves and plunge again into the acidulated water to prevent discoloration. If you are going to stuff the artichoke, you may wish to cut off the tops of the leaves before cooking.

Artichokes should be plunged into enough boiling water to cover. Add salt, 2 or 3 peppercorns, and a slice of lemon to the water. Cook uncovered for 25 to 45 minutes, depending on the size of the artichoke. When cooked, the bottom core or heart should offer no resistance to a fork and the outside leaves should pull off easily. Remove from water and drain upside down so all water can run out.

Artichokes may be served hot or cold. Serve hot artichokes with melted butter, lemon butter, Hollandaise, or cheese sauce. Cold artichokes may be served with French dressing, vinaigrette sauce, mayonnaise, or Russian dressing. An artichoke should be served separately, either as an hors d'oeuvre or as a vegetable course. In the latter case it would not be followed by a salad.

When beans are
in flower — the
Fools are in
power

VARIATIONS

Cold Stuffed Artichokes: A delightful summer luncheon or supper dish. Gently spread apart the center leaves of cooled, cooked artichokes without tearing them from the core. With the aid of a spoon or a small knife, remove the small center leaves and the "choke," or small spindles, inside the heart of the artichoke. You will now have a cup formed by the outer leaves and the heart. This may be filled with any fish or poultry salad, such as crabmeat, shrimp, lobster, chicken, or turkey. Serve on a bed of greens and pass additional dressing so that one may have something in which to dip artichoke leaves after eating the salad.

Hot Stuffed Artichokes: Prepare these in the same way, using hot seafood mixtures such as lobster Newburg, creamed shrimp, curried shrimp, or barbecued crabmeat.

Stuffed Artichokes: Prepare 4 large artichokes as above and cook until just tender enough so that the leaves can be separated. Drain and cool enough so that they can be handled. Prepare a stuffing as follows:

Melt 3 tablespoons butter in a small skillet. Add 1 chopped clove garlic and sauté lightly. Add 6 mushroom caps, finely chopped, and 3 tablespoons ground smoked ham, and blend well. Add ⅔ cup dried bread crumbs and blend thoroughly. Taste for seasoning. Add salt and pepper to taste, and 3 tablespoons chopped parsley. Remove from heat and stuff small spoonfuls of the mixture between the leaves of the artichokes. Sprinkle with grated Parmesan cheese. Press leaves back into shape. You may tie the artichokes after stuffing so that they will hold their shape.

Brush artichokes with olive oil. Place in a casserole with 1 cup broth or 1 cup hot water in which you have dissolved 1 bouillon cube. Bake in a moderate oven (375°) for 30 minutes, basting every 10 minutes with the broth in the pan.   *(Serves 4.)*

ASPARAGUS

Most asparagus that one finds in the markets is green, although in certain parts of the country it is still possible to find the white variety with the delicately tinted tips. Green asparagus is at its best when the tips are firm and tightly closed and the stalk is green to the end or when there is just an inch or two of white at the bottom. If the tips are spread and not firm and there is a great deal of white on the stalk, the asparagus is old and not tender. In Eastern markets asparagus is usually sold in bunches weighing 2½ to 3 pounds. In the Middle West and the West it is more generally sold loose or in 1-pound bunches.

From ½ to ¾ pound of asparagus per person may be considered adequate.

Remove the tough end of the stalk with a sharp knife. Scrape or peel each stalk to remove scales and the somewhat tough outer skin. Wash well in cold water. It is convenient to tie the asparagus in serving-size bunches before cooking. Use plain white twine and do not tie too tightly.

Asparagus should be cooked in a small amount of boiling water. The tips of the stalk will become tender much more quickly than the ends of the stalks, so it is wise to cook the asparagus in an upright or semi-upright position, so that the stems will cook first and the tips remain out of the water until the stems have begun to tenderize. Young stalks will take about 12 minutes to cook, older ones 15 to 20. If you cook only the short tip section, they will cook in from 5 to 10 minutes. Remove bunches from the water and drain well. Remove strings before serving.

Hot asparagus may be served with melted butter, Hollandaise sauce, browned butter, fried crumbs, grated Parmesan cheese, cream sauce, or cheese sauce. Cold asparagus may be served with French dressing, vinaigrette sauce, or mayonnaise.

VARIATIONS

With Egg: For a luncheon or supper dish, serve a bountiful helping of freshly cooked asparagus with melted butter and either a poached egg or a fried egg and grated Parmesan cheese.

With Ham: Another pleasant luncheon or supper dish is fresh asparagus with a slice of grilled ham and Hollandaise sauce or melted butter and chopped hard-cooked eggs.

Baked: Oil an oblong baking dish with olive oil. Place 2 to 3 pounds freshly cooked asparagus in the baking dish. Add either

⅓ cup melted butter or a like amount of olive oil and a generous sprinkling of freshly grated Parmesan or Swiss cheese. Sprinkle with buttered bread crumbs and place in a preheated hot oven (400°) until cheese is slightly melted. Serve at once.
(Serves 4.)

Sautéed: Heat ⅓ cup olive oil in a large skillet over medium heat. Beat 2 eggs very well and beat in 1 tablespoon heavy cream. On a large sheet of waxed paper or cooking parchment, sprinkle 1 cup corn meal. Peel and slice 1 large clove garlic and sauté in the olive oil. Dip freshly cooked asparagus stalks in the egg mixture and roll in corn meal. Add to olive oil and cook until nicely browned. Drain on absorbent paper and serve with grated Parmesan cheese.
(Serves 4.)

Italian Style: Cook 1 large bunch asparagus stalks cut in 4-inch lengths until just tender. Drain well. Melt 4 tablespoons butter in a large skillet and arrange asparagus tips in the pan. Beat 4 eggs lightly and add ½ cup grated Parmesan cheese. Pour this over the asparagus tips and allow to cook until the eggs are set. Place under broiler flame for a minute to brown the top, and serve at once. *(Serves 4.)*

Vinaigrette: Marinate freshly cooked asparagus tips in a vinaigrette sauce for 2 hours. Arrange on a bed of watercress and place a serving of chicken mayonnaise on each plate. This, with the addition of crisp rolls and some fresh fruit, is a thoroughly delightful summer supper.

LIMA BEANS

In my opinion, the only lima beans worth cooking are the baby ones. In general, these may be bought more readily frozen than fresh.

Two pounds of lima beans in the pod will serve 4.

Shell fresh beans as shortly before cooking as possible. Fresh beans in the pod are much to be preferred to beans already shelled because the skins of shelled beans have a tendency to toughen and vitamin content is apt to disappear.

Cook in boiling salted water—just enough to cover the beans—from 20 to 30 minutes, according to size and age. It is better to cook

them in a covered pot. Drain and serve with either melted butter or browned butter.

VARIATIONS

With Mushrooms: Combine cooked lima beans with sautéed mushrooms before serving.

Succotash: The old familiar stand-by, succotash, is a combination of freshly cooked baby limas and corn kernels in equal amounts. To 1 cup lima beans and 1 cup corn kernels, add ¼ cup melted butter and mix well. *(Serves 4.)*

Succotash with Cream: To vary succotash, add ½ cup heavy cream and a generous sprinkling of paprika.

In Casserole: For a more elaborate variation, combine equal quantities of freshly cooked lima beans, corn kernels, and freshly cooked snap beans, shredded lengthwise, in a casserole. Cover with 1 cup sauce Mornay. Sprinkle with buttered crumbs and grated Parmesan cheese and place in a hot oven (400°) for a few minutes before serving.

SNAP BEANS OR GREEN BEANS

Green beans must be young and fresh, or they are not worth the time it takes to prepare them. Buy young beans which are crisp, tender, and without bumps, which denote maturity. The fresher the bean, the more delicate it is when cooked. Since most beans now raised commercially are stringless, one usually does not have to worry about stringing them.

Break or cut both ends and pull off strings if any are present. Leave the beans whole, break or cut them into inch lengths, or French them with a sharp knife or bean slicer. Frozen green beans are sold sliced lengthwise as "Frenched" beans. Cook the beans, covered, in a small amount of boiling salted water until just tender with a bit of crispness left in them. This should take from 12 to 25 minutes. Drain at once. Serve with butter and, if you like, with crisply fried bits of bacon.

VARIATIONS

With Almonds: Melt 6 tablespoons butter in a skillet. Add ¼ cup slivered, blanched almonds and allow them to sauté gently in the butter. Add 1 pound cooked Frenched beans, mix well with almonds, and correct the seasoning. Serve at once. *(Serves 4.)*

With Cheese: Cook 1½ pounds whole beans until just tender. Drain. Melt 4 tablespoons butter in a large skillet and add beans. Sauté for 5 minutes and add ⅓ cup freshly grated Parmesan cheese. Toss the beans well so that the cheese mixes with the butter and the beans. Arrange in serving dish, add a squeeze of lemon juice, and serve at once. *(Serves 6.)*

Steamed: Heat ⅓ cup olive oil in a skillet which has a tight cover. Add 1 pound raw Frenched beans and 1 clove garlic, minced. Cover tightly and allow to cook over a low flame until tender. Add ½ teaspoon salt, 2 tablespoons chopped parsley, and ⅓ cup grated Swiss or Parmesan cheese. Mix well and serve at once. *(Serves 4.)*

With Parsley and Mushrooms: Wash, clean, and French 1½ pounds beans. Cook in boiling salted water, covered, until just tender. Sauté ½ pound sliced mushroom caps in 4 tablespoons butter. Add drained beans and 2 tablespoons chopped parsley to the mushrooms. Salt and pepper to taste and add 1 tablespoon finely chopped chives. Sprinkle with lemon juice and serve at once. *(Serves 6.)*

With Bacon: Prepare 1½ pounds beans and leave them whole. Cook, covered, in boiling salted water until just tender. While beans are cooking, fry 5 strips fat bacon cut into small pieces. When bacon is crisp, remove from pan and pour off all but 3 tablespoons of the fat. Sauté 1½ tablespoons finely chopped onion in remaining bacon fat. Drain cooked beans, add to onion and bacon fat, and toss well. Correct the seasoning if necessary. Remove to a hot serving dish and sprinkle crisp bacon bits over the beans. *(Serves 6.)*

Cold Beans

Cook whole green beans in boiling salted water until just tender. Drain and cool. Serve with vinaigrette sauce or with small artichoke hearts (these may be purchased in jars). Arrange whole beans on a bed of greens, surround with artichoke hearts, and serve as a salad course with French dressing. Or combine beans with thinly sliced green onions and thin rings of green pepper or slices of pimiento, and serve with French dressing.

Cooked green beans may be combined with a well-flavored mayonnaise and used either as a salad or on the hors d'oeuvre tray.

Note: Wax beans may be prepared in any of the ways described above.

BEETS

Young beets are much preferred to the older and larger ones which linger in the markets throughout the year. Older beets have a tendency to be woody and strongly flavored. Beets are always cooked with the skin and 1 or 2 inches of the top. If you peel a beet and remove the top before cooking, both color and flavor will escape.

Young beets should be washed well and have all but 1 or 2 inches of their tops cut off. They should be cooked, covered, in boiling salted water to cover from 30 to 45 minutes, or until just tender. Older beets will require from 50 to 90 minutes.

When beets are cooked, drain and cover with cold water, and remove skins and tops as soon as they can be handled. Cool or re-heat with any desired seasonings. Hot beets may be served with butter, or may be sautéed with butter and finely chopped onion and sprinkled with chopped parsley.

Tiny young beets are very often served whole. Larger beets should be sliced, diced, or grated.

Two pounds beets will serve 4 to 6.

VARIATIONS

Buttered: Melt 4 tablespoons butter in a skillet. Slice 1 medium-sized onion and sauté in the butter until transparent. Add 2 pounds thinly sliced cooked beets and 1 tablespoon finely chopped parsley. Cover and allow the beets to heat thoroughly. Serve with a sprinkling of lemon juice.
(Serves 4 to 6.)

Herbed: Melt 4 tablespoons butter in a skillet. Add 2 pounds sliced beets, and salt and pepper to taste. Mix beets thoroughly with the butter and allow them to become heated through. Add 1 tablespoon chopped chives, 1 tablespoon chopped parsley, and ½ pint heavy sour cream. Mix well and allow the cream to heat through, but do not let it boil. Serve at once. *(Serves 4 to 6.)*

With Egg: Sauté 2 pounds diced cooked beets in 4 tablespoons melted butter. Correct the seasoning and serve garnished with sliced hard-cooked eggs and chopped parsley. *(Serves 4 to 6.)*

Cold Beets

Cold beets have many uses in hors d'oeuvres and salads:

Marinated: Combine ½ pound sliced cold beets and ½ pound sliced sweet onions. Add ⅓ cup olive oil, ¼ cup vinegar, 1 clove, and salt and pepper to taste. Allow the beets to marinate for several hours before serving.
(Serves 4.)

Beet-and-Egg Salad: Shred cold beets and allow them to marinate in French dressing for 2 hours. Drain and combine with finely chopped onion and hard-cooked eggs. Garnish with slices of hard-cooked egg and chopped parsley.

Polish Style: Slice 1½ pounds small beets into even slices. Combine with chopped onion and chopped hard-cooked egg. Mix with a dressing prepared as follows: To ¼ pint sour cream, add 1 teaspoon dry mustard and 2 teaspoons grated horseradish; salt and pepper to taste. Blend well and mix with the beet mixture. *(Serves 4.)*

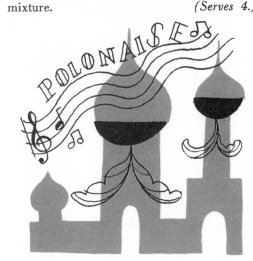

BROCCOLI

Broccoli belongs to the cabbage and cauliflower family and was once a much neglected vegetable, though in the last few years in this country it has come into great demand. It should be a deep green, closely headed, with both small and large clumps of heads on the stems. If the heads have started to open and flower, the broccoli will be tough, woody and flavorless.

Cut off the lower portion of the stalks and scrape the stalks well, removing any large wilted leaves. If there are both large and small stalks in the bunch, split the large ones for uniformity of size and cooking time. Freshen the broccoli in lightly acidulated water for a half hour before cooking.

Drain broccoli after soaking. Cook in a very small amount of boiling water from 8 to 15 minutes, being cautious to keep the heads out of the water. This may be achieved by tying the broccoli in a bunch and standing it in a deep kettle which may be covered. It is cooked when the stems can be pierced with a fork. Drain, remove strings, and serve with melted butter, browned butter, buttered crumbs, Hollandaise sauce, or grated Parmesan cheese and butter.

One pound broccoli will serve 2 people.

VARIATIONS

Sautéed: Drain 2 pounds cooked broccoli heads. Sauté very quickly in ¼ cup olive oil in which you have sautéed 1 clove of garlic. Serve with a generous sprinkling of freshly grated Parmesan cheese, buttered crumbs, and freshly ground black pepper.
(Serves 4.)

Deep-fried: Dip raw broccoli flowerettes into fritter batter and fry in deep fat (375°) until well browned on all sides. Drain on absorbent paper.

Cold: Cool cooked broccoli stalks. Serve with mayonnaise or vinaigrette sauce.

With Bacon: Serve cooked broccoli with browned butter, crisp crumbled bacon, and finely chopped parsley and chives.

In Casserole: Arrange slices of cold chicken, turkey, or smoked turkey in a casserole. Place cooked broccoli stalks on the chicken slices, cover with a sauce Mornay, sprinkle with freshly grated Parmesan cheese and buttered crumbs, and brown in a moderate oven (350°) 10 to 15 minutes.

Italian Style: Melt 4 tablespoons butter in a large skillet. Place 2 pounds cooked broccoli stalks in the skillet and pour over this 5 eggs lightly beaten with ⅓ cup Parmesan cheese. Cook until the eggs are set.
(Serves 4.)

Puréed: Cook 2 pounds broccoli until just tender, and force through a purée sieve or vegetable mill. Season with salt, pepper, 4 tablespoons melted butter, and 2 tablespoons heavy cream. One tablespoon finely chopped onion may be added if desired.
(Serves 4 to 6.)

Soufflé: Melt 4 tablespoons butter in the upper part of a double boiler. Add 4 tablespoons flour and blend well. Add 1 cup rich milk and stir until thickened. Beat 4 egg yolks well and mix with the cream sauce. Correct the seasoning and add 1½ cups puréed broccoli. Mix thoroughly and fold in the stiffly beaten whites of 4 eggs. Pour into a buttered soufflé dish and bake in a moderately hot oven (375°) 30 to 35 minutes or until the soufflé has risen.
(Serves 4.)

BRUSSELS SPROUTS

Brussels sprouts are in season throughout the winter months and are usually sold in pint or quart baskets. One quart will serve 6.

Trim off the browned outer leaves and the lower part of the stem with a sharp knife. Soak the sprouts in salted cold water for 30 to 45 minutes before cooking.

Cook in a small amount of boiling salted water in a covered kettle for 10 to 15 minutes or until just tender but not mushy. Drain and serve with melted butter, browned butter, Hollandaise sauce or butter, and grated Parmesan cheese.

VARIATIONS

Sautéed: Melt 4 tablespoons butter in a skillet. Add 1 quart Brussels sprouts which have soaked in salted water and ½ teaspoon salt. Cover the skillet and cook over a low flame until sprouts are just tender. A tablespoon of grated onion may be added to this if desired. Garnish with chopped parsley.
(Serves 6.)

With Mushrooms: Combine 1 quart cooked and drained Brussels sprouts with ½ pound mushroom caps which have been sautéed in 5 tablespoons butter. Sprinkle with chopped parsley, and season with salt, freshly ground black pepper, and lemon juice. *(Serves 6.)*

Country Style: Try out 6 strips bacon cut in small bits. Remove crisp bacon to absorbent paper and pour off all but 3 tablespoons bacon fat. Sauté 1 small white onion, finely chopped, in bacon fat; add 1 quart cooked and drained Brussels sprouts, toss well, and add crisp bacon bits.

CABBAGE

There are usually three varieties of cabbage on the market the year round. Especially good eating are the young green heads of the common cabbage, freshly cut. Available all year are the larger white heads from which the wilted outer leaves have been removed. Then there is the curly-leafed savoy cabbage, much more delicate in flavor than the ordinary variety. Lastly, there is red cabbage.

A 2-pound head of cabbage will serve 6.

Trim off wilted outer leaves, quarter or shred cabbage, and soak in salted water for ½ hour before cooking or serving.

It used to be the custom to cook cabbage for hours, often with a piece of bacon or ham or salt pork, which must have been the cause of the doubtful reputation it acquired for odor and indigestibility. It is now considered one of the vegetables that can be cooked in a very short time.

Shredded or chopped cabbage should be cooked in a covered kettle in a small amount of boiling water for from 3 to 8 minutes.

Quartered cabbage cooked in the same fashion takes slightly longer, from 5 to 12 minutes.

Savoy cabbage, which has much more loosely developed heads and is generally a more delicate vegetable, needs only 5 minutes' cooking.

Red cabbage will take 8 to 15 minutes to become tender. Some acid—either vinegar or a slice of lemon or a little wine—should be cooked with red cabbage to preserve its color.

Serve cabbage with butter, creamed, or baked with a cream sauce, grated cheese, and crumbs.

VARIATIONS

In Casserole with Sausage: Line a casserole with slices of bacon. Place washed cabbage quarters on the bacon strips, add 1 small onion, ½ teaspoon salt, ½ teaspoon black pepper, and ½ cup bouillon. Top with pork sausages or several slices of bacon and place, covered, in a preheated moderate oven (350°) and cook until cabbage is tender—about 1 hour.

Hot Slaw: Shred 2 pounds young cabbage very fine. Soak in cold salted water for 1 hour. In a double boiler heat ½ cup vinegar and ½ cup water with 6 tablespoons sugar. Add 4 tablespoons butter which you have blended well with 1 tablespoon flour. Lastly, add 2 well-beaten eggs and stir until sauce is thickened. Correct the seasoning and pour over the raw cabbage, which has been well drained. Mix thoroughly and serve hot. *(Serves 6.)*

Béchamel: Remove the outside leaves from 1 good-sized head of savoy cabbage. Shred the cabbage very coarsely and cook, covered, for 5 minutes in a very small amount of salted boiling water. Remove the cabbage and drain well. Chop the cooked cabbage coarsely and add 2 tablespoons butter. Place in a glass or earthenware casserole and pour over 1 cup Béchamel sauce. Mix well. Sprinkle with buttered crumbs and grated Parmesan cheese and place in a moderately hot oven (375°) for 10 to 15 minutes or until the top is nicely browned. *(Serves 4.)*

Sautéed Red Cabbage: Clean and remove outside leaves from 1 2-pound red cabbage and shred it medium-fine. Freshen in cold water for half an hour. Place 3 tablespoons goose fat or pork fat (bacon or sausage fat will do) in a large skillet, and when it is melted add 1 medium onion finely chopped and sauté until lightly browned. Add the cabbage and toss until well mixed. Add ½ teaspoon salt, ½ teaspoon black pepper, and 1 cup red wine, and allow the cabbage to simmer for 10 minutes. Add 2 very tart apples finely diced, 2 tablespoons brown sugar, and 1 tablespoon vinegar. Allow this to simmer until apples and cabbage are well blended and tender—about 15 minutes. Add more wine if necessary. This is an excellent dish with pork or duck. *(Serves 4 to 6.)*

Red Cabbage with Caraway: Remove outside leaves from, and cut into wedges, a 2-pound red cabbage. Cook in a little boiling salted water to which you have added 1 tablespoon vinegar (to retain the color) and 2 teaspoons caraway seeds. Cover the kettle and cook 8 to 12 minutes or until just tender. Serve with plenty of melted butter. *(Serves 4 to 6.)*

CARROTS

Leonie de Sounin says of the carrot in her delightful book *Magic in Herbs:*

"So delicate is this vegetable that it is predestined by nature just to be taken from its cool ground and eaten right on the spot, crisp and fresh. Yet if you take it home and cook it, then please don't scrape this lovable rosy thing of charm. Just place it in a little boiling water. After a while the skin comes off easily and the carrot underneath looks just as alluring as in its original state." *

The larger, older carrots do need a deal of scraping, but the flavor of young carrots is held in and the texture is much more delicate if they are cooked in the skin.

Carrots should be cooked, covered, in a very small amount of boiling salted water. Young whole carrots should cook in 15 to 18 minutes. Whole mature carrots will take from 20 to 30 minutes; if you slice them or cut them in strings or shreds, they will take from 10 to 18 minutes.

Very young whole carrots may be steamed in butter, and very good they are when done this way. Simply melt 2 or 3 tablespoons butter in a kettle with a tight-fitting lid and cook the carrots over a low flame in the melted butter—covered, of course.

Serve cooked carrots with butter or with herb butter. Parsley, chives, chervil, and oregano will enhance the flavor. Creamed carrots are scarcely an inspired choice for any meal, and the eternal combination of carrots and peas is, to my taste, better forgotten.

Two pounds carrots will serve 6.

VARIATIONS

Glazed: To 1½ pounds cooked, drained carrots add 2 tablespoons butter, 2 tablespoons strained honey, and 1 tablespoon chopped parsley. Cook over a low flame for several minutes so that honey and butter become well blended. Add just a touch of lemon juice before serving. *(Serves 4.)*

With Onions: Combine cooked, buttered carrots with an equal amount of tiny white onions which have been boiled until just tender. Add butter and chopped chives.

* From *Magic in Herbs* by Leonie de Sounin. Published by M. Barrows and Company, Inc., New York.

CAULIFLOWER

Cauliflower is available most of the year and is one of the most popular and also one of the most misused vegetables on the market. It comes by the head, ranging from tiny ones weighing well under a pound to huge ones weighing 4 or 5 pounds. A 2-to 3-pound head is ample for four people. Buy only the white compact heads. Avoid those which are spotty or bruised and those in which the flowerets are badly spread out.

Cut off all the green leaves and trim the stalk. Leave the head whole, or cut it into quarters or into flowerets. The latter are the small clumps which are attached to the main stem by auxiliary stems.

It is important to soak the cauliflower in salted water for a half hour before cooking to free it from any insects which may be lurking in the body of the head.

Cook cauliflower in boiling salted water in a covered kettle. A whole head weighing 2 to 3 pounds should cook in 25 to 30 minutes, and flowerets in 15 minutes. Be careful not to over cook cauliflower, for then it becomes mushy and turns yellow.

Drain and serve with any of the following:
Melted butter and slivered blanched almonds lightly sautéed in butter
Cheese sauce
Melted butter
Hollandaise sauce
Browned butter

Or chill and serve with:
Russian dressing
Vinaigrette sauce
Mayonnaise

Baked Cauliflower

1 head cauliflower broken into flowerets, cooked, and drained	Grated Parmesan cheese ½ cup crumbs
4 tablespoons butter	Salt and pepper

Cook cauliflower flowerets as above. Drain and arrange in a casserole. Dot with butter and sprinkle liberally with grated Parmesan cheese, and season to taste with salt and black pepper. Sprinkle with crumbs and additional grated cheese. Place in a moderate oven (375°) for 10 minutes or until lightly browned. *(Serves 4.)*

VARIATIONS

Swiss: Arrange drained, cooked cauliflower flowerets in a casserole. Pour over them 1 cup heavy cream, and sprinkle with coarsely ground black pepper. Add grated Parmesan and Swiss cheese plentifully to the top and place in a hot (450°) oven until nicely browned and cheese is melted.

Cheesed: Drain a whole head of cauliflower which has been cooked until just tender. Place it in a casserole and dot heavily with butter. Stud with small squares of sharp American cheese. Place in a hot (400°) oven till cheese melts.

Farmer Style: Drain a 2- or 3-pound head of cauliflower which has been cooked until just tender. Place it in a casserole and sprinkle liberally with buttered crumbs and bits of bacon which have been cooked until crisp and drained on absorbent paper. Sprinkle liberally with chopped chives and chopped parsley. Place in a hot (425°) oven for 5 minutes.

French Fried Cauliflower

Cook cauliflower flowerets in boiling salted water until just tender. Drain. Dip into fritter batter and fry in deep hot fat (370°) for 3 to 5 minutes or until nicely browned. Serve as a separate course plain or with a tomato sauce.

Cold Cauliflower

Polonaise: Cook and drain a large head of cauliflower. Chill thoroughly. Arrange on a bed of greens and cover with the following sauce:

1 cup sour cream	4 tablespoons red caviar
1 tablespoon finely chopped onion	Salt and pepper
2 teaspoons capers	3 tablespoons chopped parsley

Blend the ingredients together and taste for seasoning. Allow it to stand for 1 hour before pouring over chilled cauliflower. *(Serves 6.)*

Cauliflower Buffet Dish: Drain and cool a large head of cauliflower which has been cooked until tender. Arrange on a bed of watercress and curly chicory, on a large platter. Surround with whole green beans which have been cooked until tender and marinated in French dressing for 3 hours. Garnish the platter with artichoke hearts and radishes. Just before serving, cover cauliflower with a mayonnaise which has been flavored with dry mustard. Sprinkle with chopped chives and chopped parsley. *(Serves 8.)*

Raw Cauliflower: Raw cauliflower flowerets are excellent mixed with other raw vegetables for hors d'oeuvres. A few tiny flowerets of raw cauliflower may be added to a green salad for a pleasant change.

CELERIAC OR KNOB CELERY

This member of the celery family is comparatively strange to a great number of people and deserves far better treatment than it gets. It is a delicious vegetable when served hot with various dressings, and when served cold it has a fascinating flavor. It is a strange-looking root slightly suggestive of stunted celery.

Whether knob celery is to be used raw or cooked, its preparation is the same. Cut off the roots and top, and peel it carefully. Plunge in cold salted water for half an hour. If you are to use it raw, shred it with a coarse shredder or grater. You may shred it for cooking as well, but it is more often diced or cut into slices.

Cook knob celery in a very small amount of boiling salted water in a covered kettle. Or steam it in butter in a covered kettle over a low flame. Ten to 15 minutes' boiling time is all that is needed; slightly more if it is steamed in butter. Drain and serve with butter, browned butter and crumbs, Hollandaise sauce, or cheese sauce, or grated Parmesan cheese and butter.

VARIATIONS

Herbed: Grate 2 celery roots which have been peeled and soaked in cold salted water. Combine with 3 tablespoons mayonnaise, 1 teaspoon dry mustard, 1 tablespoon finely chopped onion, 1 tablespoon finely chopped parsley, and a few leaves of tarragon. Mix thoroughly and correct the seasoning. Garnish with slices of hard-cooked egg. Serve as an hors d'oeuvre or a salad. *(Serves 4.)*

Vinaigrette: Trim and peel 2 or 3 celery roots. Cut into even slices and soak in cold salted water for ½ hour. Drain. Cook in boiling salted water for 15 minutes or until just tender. Drain, remove to a serving dish, and cover with a vinaigrette sauce. Serve cold. *(Serves 4 to 6.)*

Deep-fried: Cook slices of celery root until just tender, as directed. Dip cooked slices in fritter (also known as "dipping") batter and fry in hot fat (380°) till nicely browned.

Parmesan: Cut celery roots in thin slices. Melt 4 tablespoons butter in a skillet and arrange slices of celery root in the butter. Cover and cook over gentle heat until the celery is just tender. Salt and pepper to taste and add grated Parmesan cheese. *(Serves 4.)*

CELERY

There are two types of celery on the market, both presented in various ways. The white or blanched celery is sold either in single stalks or in bunches of three or four "hearts," which means the tender succulent center sections with all the coarser leaves removed. These leaves are often sold in bunches for cooking or for soup. The green or Pascal celery is by far the more desirable. It is more tender, less stringy, and has a texture that the blanched product has never achieved. Sometimes the stalks of Pascal celery reach startling proportions, but even these gargantuan stalks are tender and delicious.

Celery should be thoroughly washed and brushed with a vegetable brush, for a good deal of dirt adheres to the heads and between the branches as they mature. You will need to remove the stringy fibers that are on the larger outside stalks and, in the case of Pascal celery, you may want to split some of the branches. Don't throw away the tops of the celery—they are good either cooked or raw. Added to a green salad they are delicious, and they are a natural part of a celery salad. They may be used for flavoring in cooking as well.

For boiled celery, cut the branches into 1- or 2-inch lengths and soak in salted cold water for half an hour. Cook in a small amount of boiling salted water for 15 to 18 minutes or until the celery is just tender. You may serve this dish with melted butter, with a cream sauce, or with Hollandaise. This dish is delicious also when served cold with vinaigrette sauce.

(One large head will serve 4 people.)

VARIATIONS

Braised: Cut in half, lengthwise, celery stalks from which you have removed the outside branches. Do not remove the root section or the stalks will not hold together. Soak in cold water for half an hour and drain. For 4 halves (2 stalks) melt 4 tablespoons butter or heat 4 tablespoons olive oil in a skillet. Brown the celery halves over a medium heat. When nicely browned, add ¾ cup bouillon or the equivalent amount of water in which you have dissolved one bouillon cube. Cover and allow the celery to cook until just tender. Serve as a separate course. *(Serves 4.)*

With Mushrooms: Proceed as above, combining with 1 cup sautéed mushrooms.

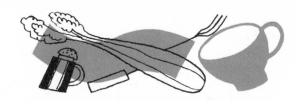

Stuffed: This may be used for an hors d'oeuvre or as a garnish for salads or cold plates. The center branches of the celery are used, and the stuffing may be any cream or cottage cheese mixture, a blend of Roquefort and cream cheese seasoned with Worcestershire sauce, mashed highly seasoned avocado, seafood mixtures, etc. When stuffing the tender center stalks, be certain to leave some of the leaves on the branch.

CHAYOTE

This pear-shaped vegetable is comparatively unknown in this country, but in Latin American countries it is one of the stand-bys. In fact they joke about it a great deal in Brazil, where it is called "Xuxu" (pronounced "shoo-shoo")—something that is used for practically every purpose. The chayote is probably a member of the squash family. The skin is a pale green and the seed is edible.

One pound chayote will serve 4.

Peel, split, and cut into strips or dice. Cook in a small amount of boiling salted water, covered, about 20 minutes, or until just tender. Serve with butter or with grated Parmesan cheese and butter, or cool it and combine with other vegetables or seafood or salad. It combines well with other vegetables such as lima beans, snap beans, green pepper, and tomato.

VARIATION

Xuxu: Combine equal quantities of cooked, well-seasoned shrimp and cubes of cooked, cooled chayote. Serve arranged on watercress and topped with rémoulade sauce. This is a delightful first course or a main dish for summer luncheon. Call it "Shrimps Xuxu."

CORN

The most common table varieties of corn are Golden Bantam and Golden Cream. There is midget corn on the market as well, and very good it is. Of the varieties of white corn, Country Gentleman is by far the best. Shop for the youngest ears of any corn and insist on seeing the husk turned back a bit, to be certain you are getting fully formed, tender ears. Never buy corn that is ready-husked.

Of course the ideal way to eat green corn is to gather it, husk it, and cook it all within about ½ hour. City dwellers cannot indulge in such practice. But I do find that keeping corn in the refrigerator for several hours before cooking seems to give it freshness.

Remove husks and silk from the ears and cut off stem end and undeveloped tip.

The less corn is cooked, the better it is. I like to put it in cold water and bring it just to the boil. Or plunge the ears in rapidly boiling water and cook 3 to 6 minutes. No salt, please. If the corn looks overly mature, the addition of a teaspoon or so of sugar helps the flavor. Serve, wrapped in a linen napkin, with plenty of butter and salt and freshly ground pepper.

VARIATIONS

Roasted: Strip husks back, but do not remove from stem. Remove all silk and replace husks. Dip in cold water and roast in a hot oven (400°) or on an open grill, turning occasionally, from 10 to 15 minutes. Remove husks and serve.

Sautéed: With a small sharp knife, remove the kernels from 8 or 9 ears of corn. Sauté very gently in 4 tablespoons butter for approximately 5 minutes, stirring while cooking so that the corn does not stick to the bottom of the sauté pan. Season with salt and pepper and, if you wish, add ⅓ cup heavy cream and a generous sprinkling of paprika before serving. *(Serves 4.)*

With Peppers: Sauté 1 large or 2 small green peppers, which have been cut in fine dice, in 4 tablespoons butter or olive oil. Add 2 cups corn kernels and sauté for 5 or 6 minutes, stirring so as to mix the two vegetables well. *(Serves 4.)*

Mexican Corn: Add finely cut pimiento and a bit of chopped onion to the above dish and mix the vegetables together well. Add a little chopped parsley just before serving.

With Bacon: Cook 3 or 4 strips of bacon cut in tiny bits until the bacon is crisp. Remove the bacon to absorbent paper and pour off all but 3 tablespoons of fat. Sauté 2 cups cut corn, cooked or uncooked, in the fat for 5 minutes, stirring constantly. Add the bacon bits and serve at once. *(Serves 4.)*

CUCUMBERS

Cucumbers, which many people think of only as a salad vegetable, make a very pleasant change from other cooked vegetables, although they are best served occasionally for variety than as a regular part of the diet.

Cucumbers should be carefully peeled and cut in slices or in quarters lengthwise. Cucumbers require very little cooking and should never be boiled. They should be simmered in chicken or beef stock for 5 to 10 minutes and served with a sauce made by adding 1 cup cream mixed with 2 egg yolks to the liquid left from cooking. This should be stirred very carefully and not allowed to boil, else it will curdle. Remove from heat when mixture coats spoon. Add a few drops of lemon juice, and salt and pepper if desired.

VARIATIONS

Hollandaise: Cucumber fingers may be poached or simmered in stock and served with Hollandaise sauce.

Polish Style: Cut 2 or 3 cucumbers into thick slices and dredge with flour. Season with salt, pepper, and fresh dill, finely chopped, and sauté in 3 tablespoons butter until delicately browned. Add 3 tablespoons sour cream to the mixture and heat it through but do not cook it.
(Serves 4 to 6.)

Florentine: Slice 2 or 3 cucumbers in medium-thick slices. Sauté 1 clove garlic, finely cut, in 4 tablespoons olive oil. Dredge cucumbers with flour, season with salt and pepper, and brown the cucumbers on both sides in the flavored oil. Add ½ cup tomato purée, 1 tablespoon finely chopped parsley, and a few sprigs of basil, either fresh or dried. Cook for 4 or 5 minutes and serve.
(Serves 4.)

EGGPLANT

Eggplant is not only one of the most beautiful of vegetables; it is also one of the most delicious and accommodating ones. There are many varieties, from the very large, bell-shaped ones to small, almost finger-shaped fruits. Choose those which are well formed and free from bruises. A medium-sized eggplant (1½ pounds) will serve 4 people.

For most dishes one peels eggplant before cooking it, but you will find occasional recipes which call for the entire vegetable. It is cooked either in thin slices or in cubes.

Sautéed Eggplant

Pare and cut a 1½-pound eggplant into ¼- to ½-inch slices. Dredge with flour, season with salt and pepper, and sauté in hot olive oil or butter until tender and delicately browned on both sides. You should have a hot casserole or pan to hold the cooked slices, for it is impossible to prepare all of them at one time. Serve as a separate course.

VARIATIONS

Barbecued: Serve eggplant sautéed as above as a main course for luncheon with a spicy tomato sauce or a barbecue sauce, and top it with grated Parmesan cheese.

Sandwich: Serve slices of sautéed eggplant sandwich-fashion with slices of grilled tomato and sautéed onion rings between. Sprinkle top with grated Parmesan cheese.

With Poached Egg: Serve sautéed eggplant with crisp bacon and top with a poached egg sprinkled with grated cheese.

Grilled: Arrange slices of sautéed eggplant in a shallow baking dish. Top with grated cheddar cheese or a mixture of grated Swiss and Parmesan. Place under grill just long enough to melt the cheese. Serve at once.

Eggplant Casserole

Au gratin:

1 large eggplant	Chopped parsley
2 Spanish onions	Bread crumbs, toasted
Flour	Butter
Olive oil	

Pare and slice the eggplant and onions. Dredge the slices of eggplant lightly in flour and brown very quickly in olive oil. Brown the slices of onion in the hot oil as well. Arrange alternate layers of eggplant and onion, seasoned to taste, in a casserole. Sprinkle the top with chopped parsley and cover with toasted bread crumbs. Dot the top with

butter and place in a moderate oven (350°) for 20 to 25 minutes. Serve at once.

(Serves 4 to 6.)

With Tomato:

Eggplant	Green pepper, thinly
Olive oil	shredded
Onions, sliced	Salt and pepper
Tomatoes, peeled and	Butter
sliced	Parmesan cheese

Arrange slices of eggplant lightly browned in olive oil, slices of onion, slices of peeled tomato, and thin shreds of green pepper in alternate layers in a baking dish. Salt and pepper to taste. Dot each layer with butter and add ¼ cup olive oil to the casserole. Place this in a moderate oven (350°) and bake for 30 to 35 minutes or until tender. Sprinkle with grated Parmesan cheese and return to oven for 5 minutes.

French Fried Eggplant

Pare and slice a 1½- to 2-pound eggplant in ¾-inch slices. Cut these slices into ¾-inch fingers. Dip fingers of eggplant first in flour, then in beaten egg, and then in bread crumbs, and fry in deep hot fat (380°). Drain on absorbent paper. Season well with salt and pepper.

(Serves 4.)

Stuffed

1 large eggplant
3 tablespoons chives, chopped
3 tablespoons parsley, chopped
1 cup bread crumbs, toasted
1 cup cooked chicken, cubed
½ cup pine nuts
Butter

Cut the eggplant in half lengthwise and parboil in boiling salted water for 10 to 15 minutes. Scoop out the pulp of the eggplant, leaving about half an inch of shell. Chop the pulp very fine. Add chopped chives, chopped parsley, toasted bread crumbs, cubed cooked chicken, and pine nuts. Mix all ingredients together and fill the shells. Sprinkle the top with toasted crumbs and dot heavily with butter. Bake in a moderately hot oven (375°) for 20 minutes. *(Serves 4.)*

Eggplant Appetizer

1 large eggplant
1½ cups water
⅓ cup olive oil
Juice of 1 lemon
½ teaspoon salt
½ teaspoon fresh-ground pepper
1 clove garlic
Sprig of parsley
Pinch of thyme

Peel and cube the eggplant. Mix together in a kettle water, olive oil, lemon juice, salt, pepper, garlic, parsley, and thyme. Bring to a boil and simmer 5 minutes. Add eggplant and cook 10 to 15 minutes or until eggplant is tender. Allow it to cool in this sauce. Serve chilled as an hors d'oeuvre. Add French dressing if desired. *(Serves 6.)*

LEEKS

Leeks are a much-neglected vegetable and one that has as distinctive and different a flavor as any member of its family. Leeks vary in size from about ½ inch in diameter to 1½ inches. All are good, but when you are shopping for them try to find those of uniform size.

Cut off the roots and the green tops to within 1 inch of the white section and remove the outer layer of fiber. Soak the leeks in salted water for at least half an hour and hold the top ends under the tap, for a great deal of grit collects in the top.

Leeks should be cooked, covered, in a very small amount of boiling salted water until just tender. The cooking time will vary according to the size of the leeks. Serve them with melted butter, Hollandaise sauce, buttered crumbs, or browned butter.

VARIATIONS

A la Grecque: Cook 10 to 12 leeks in 1½ cups water, ⅓ cup olive oil, the juice of a lemon, ½ teaspoon salt, ½ teaspoon freshly ground pepper, one clove garlic, a sprig of parsley, ½ teaspoon tarragon, and a pinch of thyme. Bring this to a boil and simmer for 5 minutes. Add the leeks and cook 20 to 25 minutes or until just tender. Allow the leeks to cool in this sauce. Serve chilled as an hors d'oeuvre. *(Serves 4.)*

Parmesan: Cook leeks in boiling salted water until tender. Drain and place in a buttered baking dish. Add melted butter, sprinkle well with grated Parmesan cheese, and place in a moderately hot oven (375°) for 5 minutes. Serve at once.

Vinaigrette: Serve cooked leeks hot or cold with a vinaigrette sauce.

Béchamel: Arrange cooked leeks in a serving dish and cover with a Béchamel sauce made with chicken broth and flavored with a little of the liquid in which the leeks were cooked.

MUSHROOMS

Mushrooms are most adaptable. Use them as a main course, as seasoning, as vegetables, in salads, or as an hors d'oeuvre, or to add distinction to many dishes. Sautéed caps, sliced or whole, combine well with vegetables and add much to steak or roast beef. Raw mushroom slices enhance many salads. A few sliced or whole mushrooms with other ingredients in chicken or meat pie, stews, and other mixed casserole dishes are excellent.

Mushrooms lose flavor if peeled. But old and tough skins must be scraped off. Peeled stems will flavor many dishes and may be put in the kettle when making broth. For mushroom stock for use in sauces or soups, add peelings and stems to 2 cups water and simmer 20 minutes. Add salt, pepper, and parsley.

Sautéed Mushrooms

Use 1 pound caps, whole or cut in pieces. Sauté in 5 tablespoons butter over very low flame until just tender—6 to 10 minutes. Season with salt and pepper.　　　*(Serves 4.)*

VARIATIONS

With Cream: Sauté 1 pound sliced mushrooms as above. Add 2 tablespoons chopped parsley and ¼ cup heavy cream, and allow to heat through.

Polonaise: Sauté 3 shallots, finely chopped, in 5 tablespoons butter, and add 1 pound sliced mushrooms. Add 3 tablespoons chopped parsley and 1 cup sour cream. Stir well. Heat through, but do not boil.

Country Style: Cut 4 strips of bacon into fine pieces and sauté slowly until bacon is crisp. Sauté 1 pound mushroom caps in 2 tablespoons bacon fat and 2 tablespoons butter until just tender. Salt and pepper to taste. Mix with bacon bits, sprinkle with chopped parsley, and serve at once.

Pungent: Sauté 1 clove garlic, sliced, in 4 tablespoons olive oil. Add ½ pound mushroom caps and sauté slowly until just tender. Salt and pepper to taste. Add 1 teaspoon Worcestershire sauce.

Broiled Mushrooms

Use large mushroom caps for broiling and do not peel. Brush the caps well with melted butter or olive oil, sprinkle with salt and pepper, and place on broiling rack, cap side up, about 3 inches below the heating unit. Broil approximately 10 minutes and serve on fried toast. Use 4 to 6 mushrooms per person.

Mushrooms à la Grecque

Cook mushroom caps or very small whole mushrooms in sauce à la grecque for 6 to 8 minutes or until just tender. Serve cold.

Jeanne Owen's Mushroom Pie *

"This should be made in a 1½ quart glass or earthenware baking dish.

"Trim, wash, and dry 2½ pounds of firm fresh mushrooms. Put 2 ounces (4 tablespoons) of butter in a large saucepan, and when the butter is melted, add the mushrooms. Cover the pan and cook the mushrooms for 10 minutes over a lively flame, shaking the pan so that mushrooms will cook evenly. Set aside, covered to keep it warm.

"Prepare a Madeira-flavored sauce. . . . .

"Melt 2 ounces of butter in a pan; when melted, add 3 tablespoons of flour. Blend well over a slow fire and then add slowly—constantly stirring—1 cup chicken broth and 1 cup milk which have been mixed and heated. Keep beating the sauce with a spoon to make it light. Then add the juice from the pan in which the mushrooms have been cooked and a generous ½ cup of Madeira—heated, but not boiled. (Sherry may be used, but the flavor of Madeira is finer with mushrooms.)

"Season the sauce with salt, a pinch of ground nutmeg, and a touch of cayenne. Put the mushrooms in a buttered baking dish, piling up toward the center to keep the crust high. Pour the sauce over the mushrooms and cover with pie crust. Ornament the top with extra-fancy cut leaves of pie crust—always remembering to brush the crust with beaten egg first, then again after the "leaves" of dough have been added—and make tiny openings in the crust to allow the steam to escape.

"Bake in a preheated oven (450°) for about 15 minutes, then reduce the heat and cook for 10 or 15 minutes longer, or until the crust is cooked through. Serve immediately.

"Note: Mushrooms vary in size. If you have too many for the baking dish and if there is sauce left over, heat the mushrooms in the sauce and serve separately."　　*(Serves 6.)*

* Reprinted from *Lunching and Dining at Home* by Jeanne Owen, by permission of Alfred A. Knopf, Inc. Copyright 1942 by Jeanne Owen.

Stuffed Mushrooms

For stuffed mushrooms you will want caps of uniform size, not peeled. A basic mixture, to which you may add various things, is:

½ cup dried bread crumbs	1 tablespoon onion, finely chopped
2 eggs	
1 tablespoon parsley, finely chopped	½ teaspoon salt
	½ teaspoon black pepper, coarsely ground

To this you may add any one of the following:

½ cup crabmeat	2 hard-cooked eggs, finely chopped
½ cup tiny shrimp or large chopped shrimp	
	½ cup lobster meat
½ cup chopped chicken	½ cup raw mushroom caps, finely chopped

Mix the ingredients well and fill the mushroom caps. Sprinkle with additional crumbs, dot with butter, and top with grated Parmesan or Swiss cheese. Arrange the mushroom caps in a lightly oiled baking dish and place them in a moderately hot oven (375°) for 15 to 20 minutes or until mushrooms are just tender. Serve on fried toast as a main course for luncheon or as a first course for dinner. This recipe will stuff 16 to 24 mushroom caps.

ONIONS

This section does not attempt to deal with the entire onion family. We have mentioned elsewhere chives, shallots, and garlic, which are used mainly for seasoning, and leeks. We deal now with the four or five main types of onions used generally in cooking: white onions, small and large; the yellowish-skinned Bermuda onion; the red-skinned, red-meated sweet Italian onion; and the very large globular Spanish onion. The very tiny white onions are used for flavoring and in combination with other vegetables. The Spanish onion is used for flavoring, is used raw in salads and sandwiches, and is delicious when cooked. Red onions are a delight when served raw and are good for cooking as well.

Onions should be peeled just before they are used, and kept in cold water until they are cooked.

Boiled Onions

It is difficult to specify the number of onions to a serving because of the tremendous variation in the sizes of the bulbs. You'll want two medium-sized, three small-sized, or one large-sized onion per person. They should be boiled in a very small amount of water in a covered kettle for from 18 to 35 minutes or until just tender. Drain and season with salt and pepper, and serve with melted butter or creamed.

Sautéed Onions

Twelve medium-sized onions or 4 large Spanish onions are ample for 6 persons.

Peel onions, cut in very thin slices, and soak in salted cold water for 30 to 45 minutes. Dry on absorbent paper. Sauté in ¼ cup olive oil, 5 tablespoons butter, or a combination of butter and bacon fat. This will take approximately 18 minutes. The onions should be stirred frequently and allowed to brown very lightly. Salt and pepper to taste.

French-fried Onion Rings

Peel and slice 4 or 5 large Spanish onions in ½-inch slices and break into rings. Dip the onion rings first into cold milk, then in flour which has been seasoned with salt and pepper. Fry in deep hot fat (380°) a few at a time until lightly browned—from 4 to 6 minutes. Drain on absorbent paper, salt again, and serve at once.   *(Serves 4 to 6.)*

Baked Onions

Peel medium-sized Spanish onions—1 per person. Place in a buttered casserole that can be tightly covered. Salt and pepper well. Add ½ cup beef bouillon or consommé. Dot the top with butter, cover, and place in a moderate oven (350°) for approximately 1 hour or until onions are just tender. Remove cover, sprinkle liberally with grated sharp American cheese, and return to oven or place under the broiler until cheese melts. Serve at once.

Stuffed Onions

Parboil 4 large onions for 20 minutes in boiling salted water. Drain and remove the center portion of the onion with the aid of a sharp knife and a fork. Fill with well-seasoned sausage meat or with link sausages. Place in a buttered casserole and bake in a moderately hot oven (375°) for 20 minutes or until sausage is thoroughly cooked.   *(Serves 4.)*

Grilled Onions

Slice large Spanish onions into ¼-inch slices. Arrange on broiling rack, brush well with melted butter, and sprinkle with salt and pepper. Place under broiler 3 inches from flame and allow onions to brown lightly. Turn carefully, using a spatula or pancake turner; brush with butter and brown on the other side. Onions cooked in this fashion will not be thoroughly tender, but are delicious served with hamburger or in hot meat sandwiches.

PARSNIPS

The parsnip is probably the most unpopular of all vegetables, and we are not going to spend very much time with it. There used to be a superstition that parsnips were not good until they had been in the ground through frost, but that has been discredited. What you do with them makes little difference in their flavor.

Wash and peel or scrape 8 parsnips. Cook parsnips in a small amount of boiling water in a covered kettle until tender—about 25 to 35 minutes. Drain and split the parsnips, and if the core is woody, as it frequently is, remove it. Cut the cooked parsnips into dice and serve them with butter and salt and pepper, or you may serve them with a light cream sauce. *(Serves 4.)*

VARIATIONS

Mashed: Mash or rice 8 cooked parsnips and combine with 2 tablespoons butter, and salt and pepper to taste. Beat well with a wire whisk or with a wooden spoon. Add 2 or 3 tablespoons heavy cream and continue beating until well blended. *(Serves 4.)*

Sautéed: Cut 8 cooked parsnips into small dice or fingers. Sauté slowly in 3 tablespoons butter until nicely browned on all sides. Salt and pepper to taste. *(Serves 4.)*

Deep-fried: Cut 8 cooked parsnips into even-sized fingers. Dip in flour, then in beaten egg, and roll in crumbs. Fry in deep hot fat (380°) 3 to 5 minutes. Drain on absorbent paper. *(Serves 4.)*

PEAS

Fresh peas should be shelled and cooked as soon as possible after they are picked to achieve the utmost in flavor. Those who live in cities will find the frozen variety a good substitute when fresh peas are not to be had.

Peas have been commonly made to do duty as a "company" vegetable and for that reason become something of a bore served eternally with chicken, steak, and roasts. Use imagination; don't just roll a spoonful of boiled peas around the plate the next time you serve them.

Two pounds of peas in the shells serve 4.

Shell peas just before cooking. Never shell peas early in the day and let them stand all day in water, for they will lose their flavor completely if you do.

Cook peas in a very small amount of boiling salted water in a covered kettle. If they are older peas, add ½ teaspoon sugar to the water. Peas take from 8 to 12 minutes to cook. Add plenty of butter, salt, pepper, and, if you desire, a little heavy cream.

VARIATIONS

With Onions: Combine freshly cooked peas with tiny white onions which have been boiled until just tender. Add butter, salt, and pepper.

With Bacon: Add to cooked peas crisp bits of bacon which have been cooked very slowly and drained on absorbent paper.

French Style: Melt 4 tablespoons butter in a pan. Add 2 cups freshly shelled peas and cover with large leaves of lettuce which have been freshened in cold water. Add no water. Cover the peas with the lettuce leaves and cook slowly over very low heat until peas are just tender. *(Serves 4.)*

Deep-dish Pea Pie *

"For this dish make the pastry first. Sift together 1½ cups of pastry flour with ½ teaspoon of salt. Work in with the fingertips ¾ cup of butter. Moisten the flour and butter with a few drops of tepid water, and mix with a large fork until it holds together. Form it into a flat ball, wrap in wax paper, and chill several hours.

"Shell 8 to 10 pounds of peas, discarding the large tough ones. Wash the peas, put them in a large enamel pan, add a pinch of bicarbonate of soda and 1 teaspoon of salt, and cover with rapidly boiling water. Skim carefully. Cook about 20 to 25 minutes. When done, drain, saving the juice. Put the peas in a deep dish in which has been placed ¼ pound of butter and pour over just enough juice barely to cover the peas. Season to taste with salt and freshly ground black pepper, and allow the peas to cool in their juice.

"When ready to assemble and bake the pie, roll out a small piece of pastry to form a band about an inch wide and long enough to edge the rim of the dish—a 1½ quart deep-dish pie casserole—in which the pie is to be cooked. Paint the rim with beaten egg, then press the strip of pastry securely around the edge. Fill the dish level with peas and their juice. Roll the rest of the pastry to form a circle large enough to cover the dish and overhang about ¾ inch. Paint the strip of pastry around the rim with more egg; then place the top over all, pressing the edges together with floured fingers. Work quickly. Brush the top with egg and make a hole in the center of the crust for the steam to escape.

"Place in the refrigerator for a few minutes; then bake in a preheated, very hot oven (450°) for 15 minutes. Reduce the heat a little and continue cooking about 15 minutes longer, or until the juice in the pie is boiling hot and the crust cooked through. Serve at once."

PEPPERS

Green peppers are used too seldom as a vegetable and too often merely for garnish or for color. As a vegetable, they are delicious.

Cut sweet green or red peppers across the stem end and remove the seeds. Wash out the peppers to rid them of stray seeds.

Sautéed Peppers

Seed and cut 4 or 5 peppers into ½-inch strips and soak in cold water ½ hour. Heat ¼ cup olive oil in a saucepan or a small skillet and add pepper strips. Add garlic to oil if desired. Cook, uncovered, over a very low heat for 10 minutes. Salt and pepper to taste, cover, and continue cooking slowly until peppers are just tender. Just before removing from fire, add a teaspoon of wine vinegar and let it blend well with peppers and oil. This dish may be served hot or cold.   (Serves 4.)

Fried Peppers

Sear the peppers over the open flame before seeding them. Attach the peppers to a fork and hold over the flame, turning frequently. Then scrape the skin from the peppers and wipe with a damp cloth. Allow 1 or 2 to a person. Fry quickly in olive oil, turning once or twice during the process. Use ½ cup oil for 6 or 8 peppers. Remove to a serving dish. Sprinkle with grated Parmesan cheese.

Stuffed Peppers

Parboil peppers for stuffing. Fill with one of the stuffings listed below. Place in a casserole or baking dish and bake in a moderately hot oven (375°) for 25 minutes. If you like, serve a Spanish or tomato sauce.

With Corn: Mix 2 cups fresh or cooked corn kernels with ¼ cup melted butter, and salt and pepper to taste. Fill pepper shells with mixture and top with buttered crumbs.

With Hash: Add 1 medium onion, chopped fine; 1 tablespoon chopped parsley; and 1 teaspoon dry mustard to 2 cups corned beef hash (canned or frozen). Fill peppers with mixture and place in casserole.

With Leftover Meat: Mix 1½ cups leftover chicken or cold meat with ½ cup dry bread crumbs, 1 medium-sized onion, finely chopped, ½ teaspoon chopped parsley, and 2 well-beaten eggs. Fill pepper shells. Cover with crumbs and dot with butter.

With Curried Shrimp: Mix 1 cup cooked rice with 1 cup cooked shrimp, 1 tablespoon chopped onion, salt and pepper to taste, and 2 teaspoons curry powder. Moisten with heavy cream and fill peppers with mixture. Dot with butter and place in casserole.

* From *June Platt's Plain and Fancy Cooking* (Houghton Mifflin Co., Boston). Reprinted by permission.

SPINACH

The preparation of spinach, which is a great deal of trouble, may be simplified by purchasing either the cleaned spinach sold in cellophane bags or the quick-frozen product.

Two pounds of leaf spinach serves 6 people.

If you buy root spinach you must remove the roots, the tough stems, and the wilted and dried leaves, and wash it under running water until all the sand and dirt disappears. Begin the washing with warm water, to loosen sand. Rinse in at least 2 waters.

Put the washed and rinsed spinach in a saucepan, cover, and cook without water over slow heat until just tender. Drain off excess water, add salt to taste, pepper, and either butter or olive oil. If you prefer spinach chopped or puréed, chop with a heavy knife or put it through a food mill. Serve at once.

VARIATIONS

With Garlic: Add finely chopped garlic to cooked spinach and flavor with olive oil, salt, and pepper.

Herbed: To 2 pounds chopped cooked spinach add 2 tablespoons finely chopped chives, 2 tablespoons melted butter, 1 tablespoon fresh or ½ teaspoon dried tarragon leaves, and a few drops of lemon juice. Salt and pepper to taste. *(Serves 6.)*

Creamed: Chop cooked spinach very fine, return to saucepan with 2 tablespoons butter, and reheat slightly. Salt and pepper to taste and fold in 3 tablespoons heavy cream.

With Polenta: Add 2 tablespoons butter and salt and pepper to chopped, cooked spinach. Place in a baking dish and press down. Cover with polenta, sprinkle with grated Parmesan cheese, dot with butter, and brown under the broiler.

With Egg: Chop cooked spinach very fine, add 2 tablespoons butter, salt and pepper to taste, 1 tablespoon finely chopped onion, and 2 hard-cooked eggs, finely chopped. Garnish with slices of hard cooked egg.

Timbales: Chop soaked spinach very fine, add 2 tablespoons melted butter, ½ teaspoon salt, and 2 eggs, well beaten, which have been combined with 1 cup light cream. Mix well, add a few grains of nutmeg, and pour into greased individual baking cups. Place in a pan of hot water and bake 25 to 30 minutes in a moderate oven (350°). Unmold and serve at once.

Spinach Soufflé

Melt 3 tablespoons butter in upper part of double boiler. Blend in 3 tablespoons flour, stirring constantly. Add, still stirring, 1 cup milk and continue stirring until mixture thickens. Season with ½ teaspoon salt. When mixture has cooled slightly, add beaten yolks of 4 eggs and blend well. Fold in 1 cup chopped, cooked spinach; then gently fold in the beaten whites of 5 eggs. Place in a 2-quart baking dish. Bake in a moderately hot oven (375°) for 35 to 50 minutes or until soufflé is lightly browned and well puffed. Serve at once.

This dish is delicious served with sautéed mushrooms. *(Serves 4.)*

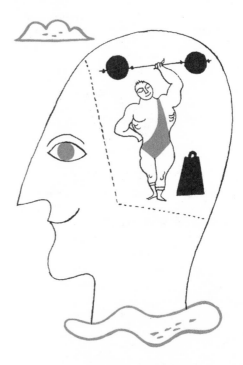

Spinach Casserole with Mushrooms

Place 2 cups chopped, cooked spinach in a greased 2-quart dish. Add 2 tablespoons melted butter, 1 teaspoon chopped or dried tarragon, ½ teaspoon salt, and a few drops of lemon juice. Cover with sautéed mushroom caps. Over this pour very gently 4 well-beaten eggs which have been mixed with ½ cup grated Parmesan cheese. Place in a moderate oven (350°) until egg and cheese mixture is set. Serve at once.

SQUASH

There are two kinds of squash—summer and winter. Winter squash usually means Hubbard or the small acorn or Danish squash. Summer squash include the white, scalloped variety, the long-necked yellow squash, and the dark green Italian zucchini. The latter is least likely to have large seeds and be watery.

Winter squash are good baked or steamed. For baking, do not remove rind; cut in serving pieces. Remove seeds and stringy portions. For steaming, cut off rind with a sharp knife.

Baked Acorn Squash

One small or half of a large acorn squash makes a serving. Halve the squash, remove seeds, brush interior with butter, and bake in a moderate oven (350°) 45 to 50 minutes or until tender. Season with salt, pepper, and additional butter, and serve in the shell.

Baked Hubbard Squash

Cut 2 pounds Hubbard squash into 2-inch squares, sprinkle with salt and pepper, and dot with butter. Place in a flat baking pan and bake 45 to 50 minutes or until soft in moderate oven (350°). Serve in rind. *(Serves 4.)*

VARIATIONS

Hubbard with Bacon: Bake cleaned and buttered squash until soft—about 50 minutes. Remove from shell, add 3 tablespoons butter, and mash well. Serve with crisp strips of bacon. Two pounds will serve 4.

Acorn with Bacon: Brush halves with butter, place a small piece of bacon in each, season with salt and pepper, and bake.

Spiced: Brush inside of halved squash with melted butter, sprinkle with brown sugar and few grains nutmeg. Midway in cooking add ½ teaspoon melted butter to each half.

Boiled Summer Squash

This applies to all varieties except zucchini. Cook slices in very little boiling salted water in a covered saucepan until tender—10 to 15 minutes. Drain. Season with salt and pepper and ample melted butter.

Sautéed Summer Squash with Sour Cream *

Peel 4 pounds summer squash and cut in matchlike strips. Sprinkle with 2 teaspoons salt and let stand 1 hour. Drain well and sauté in ¼ cup butter 15 minutes, or until almost soft. Stir 2 tablespoons flour to paste with a little sour cream. Add with more sour cream to squash, using 2 cups sour cream in all. Add 2 onions, chopped fine, and simmer 5 minutes, stirring carefully. Serve at once. One teaspoon paprika may be added. *(Serves 6.)*

Steamed Hubbard Squash

Split and clean squash and cut in 4-inch squares, or cut in quarters. Place in a perforated steaming pan over hot water and steam until tender—30 to 45 minutes. Cool and scrape squash from shell. Purée or wash it. Serve with butter, pepper, salt. Or use for squash pies or casserole dishes.

Steamed Zucchini

Slice (do not peel) 1 pound zucchini into ¼-inch slices. Soak in cold water 15 to 20 minutes. Cook in a very small amount of boiling salted water in a covered saucepan 10 to 20 minutes. Drain. Serve with butter or Hollandaise sauce. Do not overcook. *(Serves 4.)*

* Courtesy Mrs. Ella Russell.

Sautéed Zucchini

Cut 2 pounds zucchini in quarters and soak in cold water for 15 to 20 minutes. Sauté slowly in ¼ cup olive oil with 1 or 2 cloves garlic. Turn during cooking to brown it lightly all over. Do not overcook. Remove garlic. Salt and pepper to taste, and serve at once.

If you prefer the zucchini softer, cover the skillet after adding the zucchini and allow it to cook covered for 6 to 8 minutes or until just soft. Proceed as above. *(Serves 4 to 6.)*

VARIATION

With Tomatoes: Add 2 peeled, seeded tomatoes in small dice to pan while cooking.

Zucchini with Cheese

Cut 4 or 5 small zucchini into ¼-inch slices. Place in a large skillet containing ¼ cup heated olive oil and sauté gently 5 or 6 minutes. Beat 4 eggs well, add ½ teaspoon salt, 1 teaspoon coarsely ground black pepper, and ½ cup grated Parmesan cheese. Pour over zucchini and cook very slowly until eggs are set. To brown lightly, place under broiler 2 or 3 minutes. Serve hot or cold. Cut in wedges. *(Serves 4.)*

VARIATIONS

Herbed: Add 1 or 2 cloves of garlic to the olive oil before adding the zucchini and add ¼ cup finely chopped parsley and a little chopped basil to the egg mixture.

With Prosciutto: Add prosciutto slices (Italian-style ham) to pan, placing over zucchini just before adding egg mixture.

Casserole: Line small ovenproof molds with slices of prosciutto. Add sliced zucchini-and-egg mixture. Bake in moderate oven (350°) until eggs are set. Serve hot or cold. If molds are buttered well, you may serve unmolded on a plate.

TOMATOES

Tomatoes, both raw and cooked, play such a tremendous part in our diet that it is hard to believe that they have been in the general category of edible vegetables for only about a hundred years. We shall concern ourselves here with a few of the more unusual ways to prepare the tomato.

If you wish to peel tomatoes, hold them over a gas flame, turning constantly, or blanch them in boiling water for 1 minute. When cool, the skins will slip off without any trouble. Remove the stem ends. If you are planning to use the tomatoes for seasoning a dish, cut in quarters and remove the seeds. This means that you will have the essence of the tomatoes without the additional liquid that results from the cooking of the seeds.

Stewed Tomatoes: For stewed tomatoes, cut peeled tomatoes into quarters, season with salt and pepper, and cook very slowly until they are just tender. Add butter and, if tomatoes are too tart, a small amount of sugar.

VARIATIONS

With Onion: A small amount of onion sautéed in 2 tablespoons butter may be added to cooked tomatoes.

With Basil: A few leaves of basil are a natural ally of tomatoes in any form.

With Bread Crumbs: Buttered crisp bread crumbs may be added to tomatoes if you wish them thickened.

Grilled Tomatoes

Allow 1 tomato per person. Cut tomatoes in halves crosswise. Dot with butter, sprinkle with salt and freshly ground black pepper, and grill under moderate flame until lightly browned. This should take 2 to 4 minutes.

VARIATIONS

With Crumbs: Add a coating of buttered crisp crumbs to each half before broiling.

Provençale: Chop 1 clove garlic and 1 small onion very fine. Mix with 1 tablespoon finely chopped parsley, a few leaves of finely chopped basil, and 3 or 4 finely chopped, seeded, ripe olives. Mix this to a paste with 2 or 3 tablespoons olive oil. Add ½ teaspoon salt and a sprinkling of freshly ground black pepper. Spread over 6 to 8 tomato halves and broil under a very low heat so that the flavor will have a chance to permeate the tomatoes.

Pennsylvania Dutch Tomatoes

Slice firm tomatoes (1 per person), either ripe or green, in thick slices. Dredge with flour and sprinkle with salt and pepper. Cook very slowly in a skillet in 4 tablespoons butter. Sprinkle each slice with brown sugar before turning and after turning. Cook slowly so that the sugar, butter, and flour blend but do not burn. When tomatoes are lightly browned, add ⅔ cup heavy cream and cook until cream is heated and lightly thickened. Pour this sauce over tomatoes when serving.

Stuffed Tomatoes

Wash tomatoes. Do not peel. Remove stem ends and center pulp and seeds. Fill tomatoes with any of the stuffings listed below and place in a buttered baking dish. Bake in a moderately hot oven (375°) about 20 minutes. Use 1 large beefsteak tomato per person.

VARIATIONS

With Crabmeat: Combine 1 cup crabmeat with ⅔ cup dry, buttered bread crumbs, 2 well-beaten eggs, 1 tablespoon chopped parsley, 2 tablespoons chopped chives or shallots, ½ teaspoon salt, and a pinch of dry mustard. Fill 4 large tomato shells, sprinkle with buttered crumbs, and bake. *(Serves 4.)*

With Shrimp or Lobster: Substitute cooked shrimp or lobster for crabmeat.

With Rice: Sauté 1 cup chopped mushrooms in 3 tablespoons butter for 1 minute. Combine with ½ cup cooked, buttered rice, 1 tablespoon finely chopped onion, 1 teaspoon Worcestershire sauce, ½ teaspoon salt, and 1 tablespoon chopped parsley. Fill 4 tomato shells, sprinkle with buttered crumbs, and bake. *(Serves 4.)*

Mexican: Sauté 2 medium-sized green peppers, finely chopped, in 3 tablespoons olive oil. Add ½ teaspoon salt and ½ teaspoon freshly ground black pepper, and combine with 1½ cups cooked or raw corn kernels, 1 tablespoon butter, and 1 tablespoon finely chopped onion. Mix well. Fill 4 tomato cups, sprinkle with buttered crumbs, top with bits of bacon, and bake. *(Serves 4.)*

TURNIPS

Turnips and rutabagas, having a strong flavor, are considered by some highly complementary to meat and game. In some regions mashed rutabagas are traditional in Thanksgiving menus. Others prefer white turnips with certain game.

Two pounds of turnips or rutabagas serve 6. Scrub, pare, and cut them in large pieces or dice. Tiny young turnips may be scraped or pared and cooked whole. Cook turnips or rutabagas in covered saucepan in a little boiling salted water till just tender—15 to 18 minutes. Drain and add butter or a mixture of butter, cream, salt, and pepper; or mash and add plenty of butter. Or serve them creamed.

POTATOES, BEANS, RICE, AND SPAGHETTI

Add salt, black pepper to taste, and scalded cream or rich milk, little by little, beating constantly until potatoes are light and smooth. Remove to a hot dish, put another piece of butter in the center, and sprinkle with paprika.

VARIATIONS

With Parsley: Add chopped parsley to potatoes when whipping them. Sprinkle additional chopped parsley on top.

With Chives: Add chopped chives (quantity according to taste) to potatoes when whipping them. Sprinkle chopped parsley on top.

With Cheese: Sprinkle mashed potatoes with grated Parmesan cheese and dot with butter. Brown under broiler for few minutes before serving.

Mashed Potato Cakes

Cold mashed potatoes may be formed into cakes and cooked slowly in butter, turning once, until they are brown and crusty on both sides.

Baked Potatoes

Choose large Idaho potatoes, or similar ones, for baking. Scrub well and cut out any imperfections. Rub well with olive oil or butter. Make 1 or 2 slits in each potato with a knife, or prick it with a fork. Place in a moderately hot oven (375°) and bake until just soft when squeezed. (Because potatoes are not uniform, it is impossible to specify exact cooking time; it varies from 35 to 60 minutes.) Split and butter, season with pepper and salt, and serve at once.

POTATOES

Mashed Potatoes

Mashed potatoes, probably our most popular potato dish, are seldom prepared so that they are light and fluffy. They should be.

Peel and cut in quarters 1 large or 2 medium-small potatoes for each person. Boil in salted water, covered, until just tender and mealy but not mushy. Drain. Put drained potatoes through a potato ricer, coarse sieve, or food mill. Return to a kettle and add 1 tablespoon butter for each potato. Mix well with a wooden spoon or a wire potato masher.

Stuffed Baked Potatoes

Butter	Chopped parsley
Cream	Chopped chives
Salt and pepper	Grated Parmesan cheese

Cook potatoes as above until just soft. With a small, sharp knife cut a slice off one side of each potato to make long, boat-shaped shells or barquettes. Remove insides of potatoes and put through a ricer or food mill. Combine with 1 tablespoon butter and 1 tablespoon cream for each potato, and salt and pepper to taste. Beat well. Add 1 tablespoon parsley and 1 tablespoon chives. Beat again.

Refill potato shells, sprinkle with grated Parmesan cheese, and dot with butter. Return to oven just long enough for potatoes to heat through and cheese to brown lightly.

VARIATION

Cheese Potatoes: Proceed as above, but add 2 tablespoons grated sharp cheese for each potato, and omit parsley and chives. Add ½ teaspoon paprika for each potato. Return potato to shells, sprinkle with additional grated sharp cheese, and return to oven until cheese has melted.

OVEN-COOKED POTATOES

Potatoes Anna

Peel and thinly slice 4 large potatoes or 6 medium-sized ones. Butter a baking dish very well and place a layer of sliced potatoes evenly on the bottom. Sprinkle with salt and pepper and dot liberally with butter. Add another layer of potatoes, and repeat the process until all potatoes are used. Dot the top liberally with butter and bake in a hot oven (400°) 40 to 50 minutes or until the potatoes are tender when tested with a toothpick. Before serving, invert baking pan on a hot plate so that the nicely browned and crusty potatoes on the bottom will come out on top.   *(Serves 6.)*

Scalloped Potatoes

Peel and slice thinly 1 medium-large potato for each person to be served. Butter a baking dish well, arrange a layer of potatoes on the bottom, add salt and pepper, and dot with butter; then another layer of potatoes, seasoning and butter until all the potatoes are used. Add milk to nearly cover and dot the top liberally with butter. Cover casserole or baking dish and bake in moderately hot oven

(375°) 30 minutes. Remove cover, test for tenderness, and continue cooking uncovered until done.

VARIATIONS

With Herbs: Sprinkle each layer with chopped parsley and chives, mixed, and sprinkle with salt. Proceed as above.

Parmesan: Sprinkle each layer with grated Parmesan cheese and dot with butter. Top with grated Parmesan and butter. Bake as above.

With Onion: Alternate layers of potatoes and thinly sliced onion. Bake as above.

With Ham: Alternate layers of potatoes and cubes of ham, sprinkle each layer with chopped parsley, and mix 1 teaspoon dry mustard with the milk before pouring it over potatoes.

Curried: Alternate layers of potatoes and onions. Mix 2 teaspoons curry powder with the milk before pouring it over the potatoes. Bake as above.

FRIED POTATOES

Raw Fried Potatoes

Peel and slice thinly 1 large potato per person. Potatoes should be cooked medium fast in an ample amount of fat to keep them from sticking to the pan. Toss the potatoes frequently during cooking so that they do not stick together and those on the bottom do not become crisp and those on the top soggy. For fat you may use butter, bacon fat, or oil, or:

(1) Render small bits of beef suet from a steak or roast until the pieces are crisp. Cook potatoes in this fat, leaving some of the crisp bits of suet in the pan to mix with the potatoes.

(2) Cut 5 or 6 rashers bacon into small pieces and fry until crisp. Remove to absorbent paper. Fry potatoes in the bacon fat. Top potatoes with crisp bacon pieces when serving.

French Fried Potatoes

Fat: Use oil, lard, or rendered beef fat. It is simple to buy beef suet and render it yourself, and it gives potatoes and other vegetables a really wonderful flavor.

Heat: For most potatoes, excepting julienne or shoestring, the heat of the fat should be 375°. The fat, if you have no thermometer, should be hot enough to brown a 1-inch cube of bread in 25 to 30 seconds.

Cutting Potatoes: Peel the potatoes. (Large Idahos are preferred for this type of cookery.) Cut them in slices the long way and then into strings or strips of any width you desire. Soak in cold water 30 minutes and dry between towels or absorbent paper. Julienne or shoestring potatoes are cut in very thin slices and thin strings.

Frying: Be sure the fat is the right temperature. Test with a thermometer or cube of bread. Cook potatoes a few at a time in a frying basket, shaking the basket from time to time. Drain potatoes in frying basket, turn on absorbent paper, and add salt and pepper. Keep hot in a warm oven until all potatoes are cooked. If potatoes get soft, return them to hot fat again for a minute or so to crisp them. Most French fried potatoes will cook at proper temperature in approximately 4 minutes.

Pommes Soufflé

The first secret of pommes soufflé is to have two pans of fat—one heated to about 280° and the other to 400° or 410°. The second secret is to have even slices of potato. Use medium-large potatoes and cut them in ⅛-inch slices, either the long way of the potato or diagonally. Slices must be of uniform size. Soak in cold water 30 minutes and dry carefully. Place a few at a time in a frying basket and cook 3 to 4 minutes in the low-heat kettle. Remove, drain, and plunge basket into the high-heat kettle. The potatoes will puff immediately and should cook 1 or 2 minutes longer to be perfectly crisp. Transfer cooked drained potatoes to a pan and keep hot in a warm oven until all potatoes are cooked. Salt and serve at once.

Fried Boiled Potatoes

Peel and slice cold boiled potatoes—1 or 2 potatoes to a person, according to size. Melt 3 or 4 tablespoons butter in a skillet, add potatoes, and sauté slowly, turning often so that potatoes brown nicely on all sides. Salt and pepper to taste.

VARIATION

Lyonnaise Potatoes: Proceed as above. When potatoes are brown, remove to a hot dish. Sauté in the fat 1 onion, finely chopped, until brown. (Another tablespoon of butter may be added to the fat if desired.) When onions are lightly browned, return potatoes to pan and mix well. Sprinkle with chopped parsley. If you prefer more onion, use 2 or 3. I like to cook a good bit of chopped parsley with the onion as well, and add additional parsley when serving.

Hashed Brown Potatoes

Peel and chop very fine 8 or 10 medium-sized potatoes. Melt 5 tablespoons butter in a skillet, add potatoes, and press down with a spatula. Sprinkle with salt and pepper, and let potatoes cook until they have formed a brown crust on the bottom. Run the spatula around the edge and under the crust to loosen, and invert the pan on a hot platter or plate, so the potatoes come out with the brown crust on top.

VARIATIONS

Browned in Cream: When potatoes are about half cooked, add ½ cup heavy cream and mix potatoes with a spatula so that bits of brown crust on the bottom are mixed in. Allow another crust to form on bottom and invert pan on a hot plate or platter.

Herbed: Mix potatoes with chopped chives and chopped parsley before placing in pan.

Creamed Potatoes

In 3 tablespoons butter heat potatoes, covered, in upper part of double boiler over hot water. Add salt and pepper to taste. When potatoes are heated through, add ½ cup or more heavy cream and mix well. Cook until done. Sprinkle liberally with paprika.

New Potatoes Steamed in Butter

Wash and clean small marble-sized new potatoes. Peel a strip around each one about ⅜ inch wide. Melt 4 tablespoons butter in a saucepan. Add new potatoes, cover tightly, and simmer over a low flame, shaking pan occasionally, until potatoes are tender. Salt and pepper to taste. Add chopped parsley or chives.

Sautéed New Potatoes

Wash and scrape new potatoes of uniform size. Cook in salted boiling water until just tender. Drain. Melt 3 tablespoons butter in a skillet and sauté 1 small onion until just transparent. Add potatoes, salt and pepper to taste, and cook until potatoes are lightly browned. Sprinkle with chopped parsley or with paprika. Serve at once.

New Potatoes with Bacon

Wash and scrape small new potatoes. Cook in boiling salted water until tender. While potatoes are cooking, cut 5 or 6 slices bacon in small pieces and fry until crisp. Remove to absorbent paper. Drain potatoes and add 2 tablespoons butter and some freshly ground black pepper. Mix with crisp bacon bits and serve at once.

BEANS AND LENTILS

We have become so wedded to the Boston baked bean that it is difficult to remember there are many other delicious ways of preparing the great variety of dried beans and lentils offered in the markets. There are many such dishes, excellent for buffet suppers and for winter or fall meals which require a hearty main dish to satisfy large appetites.

BEANS

White pea or navy beans, tawny pinto beans, red kidney beans, and dried lima beans are those most often used in our bean dishes. Most may be bought in packages marked "quick-cooking" — that is, processed and cleaned. These are a great help, for they save the nuisance of long soaking and long cooking. Most cook in approximately 30 minutes. Those not processed often take long, slow cooking with more or less constant attention.

Baked Beans, New England Style

3 cups quick-cooking white pea beans	½ cup brown sugar or molasses
1 teaspoon salt	2 teaspoons dry mustard
1 medium-sized onion	1 teaspoon black pepper
1 pound salt pork	

Wash beans and cover with water, allowing water to reach 2 inches above the top of the beans. Add salt and simmer until beans are just tender.

Place onion in the bottom of a bean pot or large earthenware casserole with a tight-fitting cover. Add a layer of the cooked beans. Cut salt pork, which you have soaked 3 hours and drained, in thick slices and cut each slice into several pieces. Place a layer of salt pork on the beans, add another layer of beans, and top with more pork. Mix together brown sugar or molasses, dry mustard, and black pepper, and pour this over the beans and pork. Cover with boiling water and place, covered, in a slow oven (250°) and bake 4 to 5 hours. Add boiling water from time to time so that the water is always even with the top of the beans and pork.

Bake 1 hour longer, uncovered, without adding more water. This gives the pork a chance to brown and lets the liquid cook down. *(Serves 6.)*

If you do not use quick-cooking beans, soak beans overnight and pick them over carefully to remove any bits of stone or pod. Cover with water and simmer slowly until just tender but not mushy. Proceed as above.

VARIATIONS

With Molasses: If you like the dish sweeter, add additional molasses or brown sugar.

Maple-flavored: Substitute maple sugar or maple syrup for the molasses and brown sugar.

With Tomato: Add ½ cup catsup or chili sauce to the bean mixture.

White Beans, Country Style

3 cups quick-cooking white pea beans	1 finely chopped green pepper
2 teaspoons salt	3 ripe tomatoes, peeled, seeded, and chopped
1 clove garlic	
1 bay leaf	½ teaspoon oregano
½ teaspoon black pepper	3 tablespoons chopped parsley
2 medium-sized onions	
6 tablespoons butter	

Wash quick-cooking beans. (Or soak a similar quantity of regular variety overnight.) Drain and cover with water and add salt, garlic, bay leaf, and pepper. Simmer until tender.

Sauté onions in 4 tablespoons butter. Add green pepper and tomatoes, and allow mixture to cook down for several minutes. Flavor with oregano and parsley. Mix with the cooked beans and add 2 tablespoons butter.

(Serves 6.)

Herbed White Beans

2 cups white pea beans	4 tablespoons chopped parsley
Bay leaf	
Onion	3 tablespoons chopped chives
2 cloves	
1 clove garlic	3 tablespoons chopped green pepper
3 tablespoons butter	

Wash beans. Add bay leaf, onion stuck with cloves, garlic, and salt. Cook until beans are tender. Drain beans and add butter, parsley, chives, and green pepper. *(Serves 4.)*

VARIATION

With Herbs: Allow beans to cool. Chill them in the refrigerator. Add chopped green pepper and herbs, and dress with a French dressing. Serve as a cold hors d'oeuvre or a salad with cold meats for a buffet supper or a summer luncheon.

Pinto Bean Casserole

3 cups quick-cooking pinto beans	1 clove garlic, cut in small pieces
½ pound smoked ham	2 green peppers, finely chopped
1 pound Italian or Spanish hot sausage	½ cup red wine
1 teaspoon oregano	Grated Parmesan cheese

Wash beans and cook in salted water until tender, following directions on package. Be sure they do not overcook and become mushy.

Cut ham into ½-inch cubes. Sauté Italian or Spanish hot sausage until nearly cooked. Mix ham, sausages, and beans in 2-quart casserole and add oregano, garlic, and green peppers. Cover with water in which beans cooked. Add red wine and place in a moderate oven (350°) for 1 hour. Sprinkle with grated Parmesan cheese and return to oven for 20 minutes. *(Serves 4.)*

Pinto Bean and Sparerib Casserole

3 pounds spareribs	2 medium-sized onions, coarsely chopped
Salt and pepper	
2 cups pinto beans	3 tablespoons butter
	½ teaspoon thyme

Cut spareribs in serving-sized pieces and sprinkle with salt and pepper. Broil under brisk flame 20 minutes so they brown lightly on both sides and some fat is cooked out.

Wash and cook beans until just tender. Sauté onions in butter till delicately browned.

Combine spareribs, beans, and onion with thyme and salt and black pepper to taste in 2-quart casserole. Cover with bean liquid and bake in a moderate oven (350°) approximately 1 hour or until spareribs are tender. Add additional liquid if needed. *(Serves 6.)*

Pinto Beans with Chili

2 pounds chopped round steak	1 teaspoon salt
5 tablespoons butter	1 tablespoon sweet chili powder
1 large Spanish onion cut in coarse pieces	½ teaspoon oregano
3 cups broth or canned consommé	2 cups pinto beans
	Chopped parsley

Roll round steak into small balls about 1 inch in diameter. Brown very quickly in butter and remove to a hot plate or casserole. In the same fat sauté the onion. Add broth or consommé, salt, sweet chili powder, and oregano. Simmer 15 minutes.

Wash and cook beans until tender. Drain. Combine with sauce and bake in moderate oven (350°) 20 minutes. Top with the tiny meat balls and sprinkle with chopped parsley. Add additional chili powder if you desire a strong chili flavor. *(Serves 6.)*

Kidney Beans and Herb Casserole

2 cups kidney beans	1 teaspoon salt
1 large Spanish onion, finely chopped	1 teaspoon black pepper
2 cloves garlic, finely chopped	1 bay leaf
	½ teaspoon thyme
1 green pepper, finely chopped	¼ cup chopped parsley
4 tablespoons olive oil	2 tablespoons chopped chives
4 or 5 tomatoes, peeled, seeded, and chopped in small pieces	Grated Parmesan cheese

Wash and prepare kidney beans or use 2 cans of the prepared variety. Sauté Spanish onion, garlic, and green pepper in olive oil. When vegetables are just tender, add tomatoes. Flavor with salt, black pepper, bay leaf, and thyme. Cover and simmer 30 minutes.

Mix the sauce with the cooked or canned kidney beans. Add chopped parsley and chopped chives. Bake in a moderate oven (350°) 35 to 40 minutes or until sauce is cooked down and well blended with beans. Sprinkle with grated Parmesan cheese and let the cheese brown lightly before serving.

(Serves 6.)

Kidney Beans Baked with Salt Pork and Tomato Sauce

3 cups kidney beans	½ cup concentrated tomato purée
1 pound salt pork	
1 large Spanish onion	½ teaspoon basil
½ cup stock or water	1 teaspoon dry mustard

Prepare kidney beans. If you use the quick-cooking type, wash and cook until just tender; soak the regular type overnight and simmer until just tender. If you use the canned ones, you will need 3 cans.

Soak salt pork 3 hours. Cut in ½-inch slices. Peel onion and slice thin. Place a layer of beans in a casserole which has a tight-fitting cover. Place pieces of the salt pork and slices of onion on the beans. Cover with tomato purée which has been mixed with stock or water. Add basil and dry mustard. Add another layer of beans and another layer of the pork, onion, and tomato mixture. Top with beans.

Cover casserole and bake very slowly in a slow oven (250°) until sauce has blended thoroughly with beans. Remove cover and return to oven to brown the top slightly. Baking time: 3 to 4 hours. *(Serves 6.)*

Kidney Bean Casserole

2 medium-sized onions	Salt and pepper
3 tablespoons butter	1 tablespoon chopped parsley
2 cans red kidney beans	
Slices of prosciutto (Italian ham)	½ teaspoon oregano
	Grated Parmesan cheese

Kidney beans may be purchased in cans already prepared for casserole dishes or for general service. This makes it possible to prepare a buffet or a supper dish on very short notice.

Sauté onions in butter until golden. Mix with the kidney beans from the cans. Line a glass or earthenware casserole with slices of prosciutto. Add to this a layer of the beans. Salt and pepper the beans. Add parsley and oregano. Then place a layer of thinly sliced salami on the beans and cover with another layer of beans.

There should be enough liquid in the canned beans to keep this dish moist throughout the cooking period. If there is not, add stock or red wine to the casserole, and replenish it if necessary. Bake in a moderate oven (350°) 30 to 40 minutes. Sprinkle with grated Parmesan cheese before serving. *(Serves 6.)*

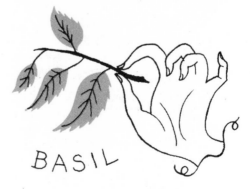

BASIL

Brazilian Bean Dinner

1 quart pinto or red kidney beans (unprocessed, long-cooking beans)	3 pounds beef brisket
	1½ teaspoons salt
	2 cloves garlic
3 pounds loin of pork	1 teaspoon oregano
4 or 6 pigs' tails	2 onions
1 pound Italian or Spanish sausages	1 bay leaf

Use the unprocessed, long-cooking beans for this dish—either pinto or red kidney beans.

Soak beans overnight. Pick out any stems or stones. Place beef, pork, and beans in a large kettle with salt, garlic, oregano, onions, and bay leaf. Cover with water, bring to a boil, and boil 10 minutes. Skim the scum from the top of the kettle and reduce heat to simmering. Simmer 3 to 4 hours or until meat and beans are tender. Test meat from time to time for tenderness with a fork or toothpick. If liquid cooks down too much, add more boiling water. Add sausages the last half-hour of cooking.

Correct seasoning, remove meat to a platter or board, and cut beef and pork loin in slices. Remove onion, garlic, and bay leaf from the pan and discard them. Pile beans in the center of a platter and surround with sliced meat, pigs' tails, and sausages. Serve with boiled rice and a very sharply flavored mustard or horseradish sauce. Follow with a green salad. *(Serves 8.)*

Cassoulet

4 cups white pea beans	1½ teaspoons salt
2 quarts water	1 large onion stuck with cloves
2 pounds pork, fat goose, mutton, and fat bacon in pieces	Sprig of thyme
	Bay leaf
2 pounds Cervelat sausages	1 cup thick tomato purée or sauce
6 to 8 peppercorns	

After soaking beans overnight in the water, simmer 3 hours in same water. Meanwhile, sauté pieces of meat and the sausages lightly in frying pan. Add other ingredients with enough hot water to cover. Simmer 2 hours, turning meat occasionally.

Put cooked beans and meat mixture in large casserole. If there is not enough liquid to cover, add vegetable stock or more tomato purée or sauce. Cover and cook slowly in 300° oven about 1½ to 2 hours, uncovering casserole toward the end to let surface brown. Serve in casserole. *(Serves 6 to 8.)*

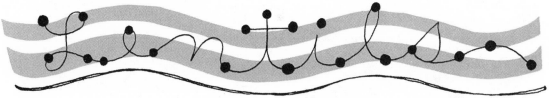

Lentil Casserole

2 cups quick-cooking lentils	1 teaspoon salt
1 onion stuck with 2 cloves	1 pork chop per person
	Salt and pepper
1 bay leaf	Bacon strips

Use the quick-cooking variety of lentils for this dish and its variations. Place lentils in a saucepan with onion, cloves, and bay leaf. Add salt, cover with cold water, and bring to a boil. Allow lentils to simmer, watching them carefully, until just tender. Take care that they do not burst and become mushy.

While lentils are cooking, brown 1 pork chop—thick loin chops are the choicest—for each person. Salt and pepper to taste.

Remove onion and bay leaf from lentils, and place a layer of lentils on the bottom of a 2-quart glass or earthenware casserole. Place pork chops on lentils and cover with another layer of lentils. Pour lentil liquid from the saucepan over the casserole and bake in a moderate oven (350°) 1 hour. If liquid cooks down too much, add additional water to the casserole. Cover top with strips of bacon during the last 20 minutes of cooking.

(Serves 4.)

VARIATIONS

Virginia: Use thin slices of baked Virginia ham with the lentils. Add 1 teaspoon dry mustard to the lentil liquid before pouring over lentils and ham.

With Duck: Combine lentils with pieces and slices of cold roast duck. Add ¼ cup finely chopped onion, lightly sautéed in 3 table-spoons butter; 2 tablespoons chopped parsley; and ¼ teaspoon thyme. Blend lentil liquid with 1 cup red wine and add to casserole. Bake as above.

With Hot Sausage: Combine lentils with slightly cooked Italian or Spanish hot sausages and bake as above. Sprinkle top of casserole with grated Parmesan cheese 15 minutes before removing from oven.

With Salami: Place a layer of cooked lentils in the bottom of a casserole, then a layer of thinly sliced imported salami, another layer of lentils, and another of salami, and top with lentils. Cover top with strips of bacon and bake in a moderate oven (350°) 30 minutes.

With Pork Sausage: Combine lentils and pork sausages which have been parboiled for 10 minutes. A layer of salami in the center of the casserole is a good addition.

With Ham: Combine cooked lentils with 1 cup diced cooked ham, ½ cup finely chopped onion, and 1 finely chopped clove of garlic, all of which have been sautéed lightly in 3 tablespoons butter. Add ¼ cup chopped parsley and ½ teaspoon dried thyme. Cover top with strips of bacon and bake 30 minutes in a moderate oven (350°). Add ½ cup red wine to the liquid in which lentils were cooked and pour over lentils before placing in oven. If the liquid cooks down, add additional red wine.

Sautéed Lentils *

2 cups quick-cooking lentils	8 green onions, finely chopped
Salt	Finely chopped parsley
6 or 8 strips bacon	Paprika

Place lentils in a saucepan and cover with cold water. Add 1 teaspoon salt. Bring to a boil and reduce heat at once so that lentils will just simmer. Simmer until just tender; be careful that the lentils do not break up and become mushy. Drain.

Chop bacon and fry slowly in a heavy frying pan. When fat is melted, add onions. When onions are slightly cooked, add lentils, parsley, salt to taste, and paprika. Mix well with bacon and onions, and cook over a slow fire with a cover on the skillet for 15 to 20 minutes.

(Serves 4.)

* From *Lunching and Dining at Home* by Jeanne Owen, by permission of Alfred A. Knopf, Inc. Copyright 1942 by Jeanne Owen.

RICE

The long-grained variety of rice will be found the best for flavor and texture for all rice dishes.

Boiled Rice

1 cup rice	2 teaspoons salt
3 quarts boiling water	

There are many different recipes for boiling rice, but this one is as safe as any I know.

Add salt to the water in a deep kettle and bring it to a boil. When the water is boiling briskly, add the rice, a little at a time, so that the water never stops boiling. Cook 13 to 18 minutes, depending upon the degree of doneness you prefer. Rice which is slightly *al dente* —an Italian term signifying resistance to the teeth, or "bity"—is more desirable than rice cooked too soft. Drain the rice in a colander and, if you wish, pour boiling water over it.

If you wish to dry out the rice, place it in a flat pan and dry it out in a very slow oven (250°), being certain to stir it from time to time. Add butter to the hot rice before serving, and additional salt if needed.

Chinese Boiled Rice

Soak 1½ cups rice in lukewarm water in an earthenware casserole for 1 hour. Fill a large kettle with 4 quarts water and bring it to a boil. Add soaked and drained rice and allow it to boil 12 to 15 minutes. Drain and replace in a dry kettle. Place this over very low heat to dry out. *(Serves 6.)*

Baked Rice

4 tablespoons olive oil	1 quart beef or chicken
1 cup raw rice	stock
	1 teaspoon salt

Heat olive oil in a large skillet, add rice, and let it cook about 5 minutes over a low flame, stirring frequently. Heat beef or chicken stock to the boiling point. Pour over the rice and let it just come to a boil. Add salt. Transfer rice and liquid to a casserole or leave it in the iron skillet. Place in a moderately hot oven (375°) and bake about 25 minutes or until the rice has the desired degree of tenderness and the broth is cooked away. The liquid for this type of cookery should be about 2 inches above the rice when you put it in the oven, and should have cooked away completely by the time the rice is cooked.

This is a most satisfactory way to cook rice and practically assures having each grain separate. *(Serves 4.)*

VARIATIONS

With Garlic: Sauté 1 finely minced clove of garlic in the olive oil. Add 1 teaspoon salt and 1 teaspoon freshly grated black pepper to the oil before adding the rice. Add broth or stock and bake.

With Parsley: Sauté ¼ cup finely chopped onion in the olive oil and add the rice. Just before adding broth, add ½ cup finely chopped parsley and then the broth. Add 1 teaspoon salt and bake as above.

Saffron Rice: Add rice to the oil and sauté it for a few minutes. Add a few strings of Spanish saffron, then the broth, and mix thoroughly. Bake as above.

Paprika Rice: Sauté ¼ cup finely chopped onion in the olive oil before adding rice. Add rice and 2 teaspoons paprika, and mix well with oil. Add broth and bake.

With Pine Nuts: Add 1 clove finely chopped garlic to the olive oil and sauté lightly before adding rice. Cook rice 5 minutes and add, with the broth, ½ cup pine nuts, ½ cup finely chopped parsley, 1 teaspoon salt, and ¼ teaspoon thyme. Bake as above.

With Tomato: Sauté 1 finely minced garlic clove in the olive oil. Add rice and cook 5 minutes. Substitute boiling tomato juice seasoned with 1 teaspoon mustard, 1 tablespoon Worcestershire sauce, and 1 teaspoon freshly ground black pepper for the broth. Bake as above.

Sautéed Rice

4 tablespoons olive oil	1 teaspoon fresh-ground black pepper
1 cup raw rice	
1 teaspoon salt	3 cups chicken broth or stock

Heat olive oil in a skillet. Add raw rice and stir well with the oil. Add salt and pepper. Heat broth or stock to the boiling point. Add stock a little at a time until liquid is absorbed and rice cooked. This method takes fairly constant attention; you should add the broth a little at a time and let it cook almost dry before adding the next bit. Rice cooked in this way is much better *al dente* than soft.

Chicken broth is by far the best liquid to use. It adds a delicious flavor to the rice.

(Serves 4.)

WILD RICE

Wild rice is not strictly a rice but is a type of water grass grown in some parts of this country. It is especially delicious served with game and poultry, and is often used for stuffings for squab, chicken, duck, etc.

Boiled Wild Rice (I)

Wash 1 cup wild rice. Add it to 4 cups rapidly boiling salted water slowly, so that water never stops boiling. Cook until rice is tender but not mushy—20 to 30 minutes. Drain off excess water and serve with plenty of melted butter. *(Serves 4.)*

Boiled Wild Rice (II)

Soak 1 cup wild rice in cold water 3 or 4 hours. Drain, place in a kettle, and cover with boiling water to a depth of 2 inches above the rice. Add 1½ teaspoons salt, cover, and simmer until rice is tender. Drain off any excess water. Butter well and serve. *(Serves 4.)*

VARIATIONS

With Mushrooms: Sauté ½ pound mushrooms, coarsely cut or thinly sliced, in 5 tablespoons butter until just tender—about 5 minutes. Salt and pepper to taste, add to cooked wild rice, and mix lightly with a fork.

With Ham: Sauté 1 clove garlic, finely chopped, and 5 or 6 green onions, thinly sliced, in 4 tablespoons butter and 2 tablespoons chopped parsley. Add 1 cup Virginia

ham cut in thin strips and mix well. Blend with hot cooked wild rice. A few chopped sautéed mushrooms and a few pine nuts may be added to this dish as well.

Wild Rice Stuffing

2 cups rice, cooked and buttered	½ cup strips of cold smoked ham
1 medium-sized onion or 4 shallots	2 tablespoons chopped parsley
4 tablespoons butter	Thyme
	½ cup pistachio nuts

Combine cooked and buttered wild rice with chopped onion or shallots sautéed in butter, strips of cold smoked ham, and chopped parsley, thyme, and pistachio nuts. Use for stuffing game or squab.

POLENTA

Plain Polenta

Mix—a little at a time and stirring constantly with a wooden spoon—1½ cups water-ground corn meal with 3 cups boiling salted water. Continue stirring, so that mixture does not become lumpy, until smooth and very thick. Pour into a mold or in a thick cloth which is placed inside a round sieve or small colander, and steam over hot water for 3 hours or until firm. Serve, sliced and buttered, if you wish, with chicken dishes or with such dishes as curries, chili, or stews. *(Serves 4.)*

Gnocchetti di Polenta

12 slices cold polenta	Salt and pepper
Butter	3 tablespoons tomato purée
2 tablespoons olive oil	2 tablespoons broth or stock
1 small onion, 1 stalk celery, and 2 small carrots, finely chopped or ground together	5 or 6 dried mushrooms
	Grated Parmesan cheese

Cut cold polenta into ½-inch slices and cut each slice into small squares or rounds about 1 inch across. Melt butter with olive oil in a skillet. Sauté the mixture of onion, celery, and carrots. Salt and pepper to taste. Add tomato purée (Italian type), thinned with broth or stock, and dried mushrooms which have been soaked in cold water and chopped very fine. Let the sauce simmer ½ hour over a very low flame.

Arrange a layer of the small squares of polenta in a buttered flat baking dish. Butter them and spread with some of the sauce. Sprinkle generously with grated Parmesan cheese. Top with another and smaller layer of the polenta and add more butter, sauce and grated cheese. If you have more polenta, you may arrange another and smaller layer, top all with any remaining sauce, and sprinkle liberally with grated Parmesan cheese and dot with butter. Bake in a moderately hot oven (375°) 15 minutes. Serve at once.

(Serves 4.)

PASTES

There are dozens of different kinds and shapes of pastes that may be used for dishes of "pasta." The same basic principles apply to all. For spaghetti you may substitute the seashell macaroni, large elbow macaroni, the little bowknots of paste, or any shape you fancy.

NOODLES

Noodles, both green and white, are an admirable substitute for potatoes and are particularly complementary to certain foods. Most veal dishes are much better with noodles than with potatoes, and certain chicken dishes should always be served with noodles. You can purchase good noodles in packages, both the green (spinach) noodles and the white (egg) noodles. If you wish to make your own, it is not a difficult task.

White Noodles

2 eggs	1 to 1½ cups flour
1 teaspoon salt	

Beat eggs slightly and mix with salt and enough flour to make a very stiff dough. Turn on a floured board and knead 2 minutes. Roll paper-thin and let stand about 1 hour. Roll and cut into strips of any desired width.

Green Noodles

2 eggs, slightly beaten	1 teaspoon salt
½ cup finely chopped cooked spinach	Flour

Beat eggs slightly and mix with cooked spinach and salt. Add enough flour to make a very stiff dough, turn out on a lightly floured board, and roll paper-thin. Allow to stand 1 or 1½ hours. Roll and cut in ¼-inch strips. Allow noodles to dry in a warm place.

Boiled Noodles

A pound of dry noodles should serve 8 persons.

Cook noodles in plenty of boiling salted water. Cook rapidly for 8 to 10 minutes, depending upon the degree of softness you like. Drain. Serve in any of the following ways:

(1) With melted butter.

(2) With melted butter and grated Parmesan cheese.

(3) Return drained noodles to a pan with 1 clove garlic, 3 tablespoons olive oil, 1 teaspoon coarsely ground black pepper, and grated Parmesan cheese. Stir these together and allow noodles to heat 2 or 3 minutes before serving.

(4) Place cooked noodles in a buttered casserole, dot generously with butter, and sprinkle liberally with grated Parmesan cheese. Bake in a moderate oven (350°) 10 minutes.

(5) Heat 5 tablespoons olive oil in a skillet and sauté 1 clove garlic, finely chopped. Add drained cooked noodles and either fresh or dried basil—1 teaspoon of the dried or 6 or 7 leaves of the fresh cut in small pieces—1 teaspoon coarse black pepper, and 1 teaspoon salt. Let noodles cook in the oil until slightly crisp on the bottom, and turn out on a plate crisp side up. Sprinkle with grated Parmesan cheese.

(6) Dress boiled drained noodles with 4 tablespoons butter, coarse black pepper, and additional salt if needed. Sprinkle liberally with finely chopped parsley and top with small croutons fried in butter.

(7) Serve with any of the sauces given for spaghetti and macaroni.

Macaroni and Cheese

½ pound macaroni	1 cup grated cheddar or
2½ quarts boiling water	sharp American cheese
2 cups Béchamel sauce	Salt
	Paprika

Boil macaroni in water until just tender—about 9 minutes. Drain and transfer to a buttered casserole. Pour over it Béchamel sauce and the grated cheese.

Mix well and add salt to taste. Sprinkle top with additional grated cheese and paprika. Add buttered crumbs and bake in a moderately hot oven 20 minutes or until nicely browned.

VARIATIONS

(1) Substitute 1½ cups heavy cream for Béchamel sauce.

(2) Substitute 1½ cups sour cream for sauce and add 1 tablespoon Worcestershire sauce.

(3) Use 1 cup diced cooked ham with the Béchamel sauce and the cheese. Add 2 teaspoons dry mustard to the sauce when you make it.

SPAGHETTI

Cook spaghetti in plenty of boiling salted water 9 to 12 minutes, according to the degree of doneness you like. Drain. Pour boiling water over spaghetti and drain. Keep hot over boiling water. Arrange on a platter or individual plates, top with sauce, and serve, or pass the sauce separately. Allow each person to add cheese to taste, and additional salt and pepper.

Sauces for Spaghetti

Recipes for spaghetti sauces will be found on pages 233 and 235.

STUFFINGS

Basic Bread Stuffing

3½ cups stale bread crumbs or toasted crumbs	1 teaspoon thyme and marjoram, mixed
1 cup finely cut celery	¼ cup butter or other fat
1 medium onion, finely chopped	1 tablespoon chopped parsley
	Salt and pepper

Sauté the onion in 1 tablespoon butter till transparent. Blend with crumbs and seasonings and cut in the butter or fat. If you are fortunate enough to have a bird with a good deal of fat inside, use that, finely chopped, instead of the butter. Bacon fat adds a good flavor, too. *(Makes 5 cups stuffing.)*

Use approximately 1 cup stuffing per pound of bird.

VARIATIONS

(1) Add 2 tablespoons chopped green pepper or pimiento.

(2) Add 1 cup sliced mushrooms sautéed in 3 tablespoons butter.

(3) Add 12 small sausages, well browned.

(4) Add ½ cup diced smoked ham, sautéed in a little fat.

(5) Add ½ cup crisply fried bacon slivers.

(6) Add ½ cup blanched almonds.

(7) Add ½ cup salted peanuts.

(8) Add ½ cup coarsely chopped tart apple.

(9) Add the chopped giblets of the bird, sautéed in butter.

(10) Substitute cornbread for bread crumbs.

(11) Add 1 cup sausage meat, browned quickly in the skillet.

(12) Add ½ cup raisins soaked in sherry.

Chestnut Stuffing

1 pound chestnuts	½ teaspoon rosemary
1 large onion	Salt and pepper
4 tablespoons fat	3 cups dry bread crumbs
2 tablespoons chopped parsley	¼ cup melted butter, or other fat
½ teaspoon thyme	Chopped, sautéed giblets

Roast or boil chestnuts till tender. (Roasting is my preference.) Shell and skin them, and break them into bits.

Sauté onion in fat till transparent. Add chopped parsley, thyme, rosemary, and salt and pepper to taste. Blend with dry bread crumbs and mix with the chestnuts. Lubricate with melted butter or other fat, or the chopped fat from the bird you are to stuff. Chopped sautéed giblets may be added if desired.

Matzo Stuffing

3 tablespoons butter or fat from the birds	4 beaten egg yolks
Chopped giblets	Thyme and marjoram (about ¼ teaspoon of each)
2 finely chopped onions	Dash of nutmeg
Salt and pepper	Dash of ginger
5 to 8 matzos or dry water crackers	

Sauté in butter or fat from the birds the chopped giblets mixed with chopped onions. Salt and pepper to taste, and reserve the fat.

Soak matzos (or dry water crackers) in water. Drain, squeeze dry, and add to fat in the pan in which you have sautéed the giblets and onion. Stir well over a very low flame and add to the giblets. Add the eggs, thyme, and marjoram to taste, and the nutmeg and ginger. Blend well and correct the seasoning. *(Makes enough stuffing for a large chicken or small turkey.)*

Cornbread Stuffing

4 cups cornbread crumbs	½ teaspoon poultry seasoning, sage, or thyme
½ cup melted butter or savory fat such as bacon, sausage, or chicken	3 tablespoons chopped onion
½ teaspoon salt	Pepper
	1 egg, slightly beaten

Mix the following ingredients lightly with a fork: cornbread crumbs; melted butter or fat; salt; poultry seasoning, sage, or thyme; chopped onion; and pepper to taste. Taste and correct for seasoning. If a compact stuffing is desired, moisten with hot water or scalded milk and stir in egg, slightly beaten.

SALADS

AND CHEESE

SALAD GREENS

Green or tossed salad has become increasingly popular in this country. More people have come to know that there are other greens besides lettuce and that the salad course is often all one wants at the end of a meal, especially if it is accompanied by a piece of cheese and a roll or a biscuit.

LETTUCE

The green most commonly used for salad, but not necessarily the most delicious or most practical, is lettuce. There are several varieties.

Head Lettuce—Iceberg or California Head Lettuce: The tightly packed, crisp-leafed lettuce most common in American markets. Its color varies from dark green to almost white. It should be cut at the core and pulled apart and broken into bits for a green salad, or carefully pulled apart if you use it for bedding a salad or for a garnish.

Boston Lettuce: A loosely headed, medium-green lettuce, delightfully tender and delicious. Great care should be taken in the handling of Boston lettuce, for it bruises easily and cannot stand up under handling as iceberg can. Ideal for a green salad, it may be used for bedding and garnishing as well.

Leaf Lettuce: Somewhat coarser in texture and not headed at all. When the plant is young, it makes a tenderly succulent salad by itself.

Romaine or Cos Lettuce: Really the aristocrat of the family. The leaves are long and exceedingly crisp, the heads somewhat loosely packed. Romaine retains its texture and character better than any other member of the family and is ideal for green salad bowls or garnishes.

Garlic

Romaine

Chicory

Tarragon Chervil

Dill Basil

O Noble Salad Herbs

Iceberg Lettuce

Watercress

Escarole

A spendthrift for oil.

Endive

Onion

Cabbage

Cucumber

Boston Lettuce | Lamb's Quarters | Spinach | Leaf Lettuce | Avocado

Turnip Tops
Celery
Fiddle Heads
Nasturtium
Parsley

Four persons are wanted to make a salad—

A miser for vinegar,

A counselor for salt

And a madman to stir it all up

Dandelion

OTHER GREENS

Chicory or Curly Endive: This is a very frizzy green which grows in flat heads and is tied while maturing to give the center a blanched color. The leaves are tender and have a slightly bitter quality that makes this green a delicious complement to others in the salad bowl.

Endive or Belgian Endive: To my mind this is the most desirable of the larger greens for salad. The long white stalks are tightly headed, each being about the size of a small head of celery. This green is grown indoors and is carefully blanched and nurtured until ready for the market. For salad, the heads are usually quartered or halved or sometimes cut in ½-inch slices. Endive may also be used for garnish or for bedding other salads and is most decorative. Endive may be cooked as well. It is delicious when braised as celery is.

Escarole: This member of the chicory family has leaves that are sturdy and lightly curled, though broader than the chicory leaves. It, too, has a lightly bitter flavor that is pleasant mixed with other greens. Escarole is delicious when braised.

Field Salad or Lamb's Lettuce: This delicate green is found in most foreign markets outside of New York. In New York it is found almost everywhere. The soft, almost tongue-shaped leaves of sage green are a great delicacy. Use them with other greens or alone. This green is found in small heads and should not be broken or cut. It is one of the very choicest additions to the salad bowl.

Spinach: Raw spinach leaves are frequently used in salads. They should be very carefully washed in several waters or under a spray. Remove the coarse stems and either shred the leaves or break them into small bits.

Watercress: The tangy, peppery quality of watercress easily distinguishes it from any other green. It may be mixed with other greens or served by itself. It may also be used for a garnish or as bedding for a mixed salad that is to be served as a separate course.

Celery: Celery lends itself to salad, and the leaves are excellent when mixed either with the stalks or with other greens.

Miscellaneous: There are many other greens which may be added to the salad bowl for variety. Some are regional delicacies; others are seasonal. They include tender beet tops, turnip tops, wild fiddlehead fern sprouts, bean sprouts, heart of palm, and nasturtium leaves.

PREPARATION OF SALAD GREENS

All salad greens should be freshened in ice-cold water. Dry them on a clean towel and place in the refrigerator. Be certain that all grit and sand have been removed in the washing and that most of the water has been absorbed by the cloth or paper towel before the mixing of your salad.

To remain crisp and fresh, a green salad should be tossed or mixed at the last minute. "Made" salads may be mixed long in advance and kept chilled so that the flavors blend more thoroughly.

SALAD ACCESSORIES

There are many flavorings which one may add to green salad for pungency and for variety.

SALAD HERBS

Tarragon: The most pleasant salad herb. It seems to blend with all types of greens and is complementary to most other flavors commonly introduced in the salad bowl. Use the fresh herb if you can.

Chervil: Always welcome. It is delicate and subtle and when used should be the only herb added. Too frequently people mix many herbs together and lose the benefit that would be given by one alone.

Fresh Dill: May be bought in many markets most of the year. It is friendly to many salads, especially those with cucumber or cabbage.

Sweet Basil: Excellent in many salads, especially those with tomato, to which it is a natural complement.

The above four are the noblest of the salad herbs, although some people like to use a little thyme or rosemary.

Parsley: This adds much to many salad mixtures, although in a green salad it has perhaps less place.

VEGETABLES AND FRUIT TO ADD TO GREEN SALAD

Tomatoes: Always a good addition, tomatoes should be peeled and quartered, and if the salad is to stand longer than 10 or 15 minutes, the quarters should be seeded. Or you may use sliced tomatoes as a garnish for green salad. Tiny plum or cherry tomatoes are an attractive addition. The little yellow pear tomatoes are delicious mixed with greens.

Cucumber: Cucumber, if you are certain everyone likes it, is a cooling and pleasant addition to the salad bowl. Cucumbers have more flavor when they have marinated for an hour or two in the dressing before being added to the salad. Peel them or score the green skin with a fork and slice in rounds or in long strips. If the cucumbers are young and tender, the rind is a pleasant asset. If a cucumber is large, with coarse seeds, split it lengthwise, remove seeds, and cut the outer flesh in thin slices. Cucumbers need not soak for hours in water or salt, as was once believed. If cool and fresh, they may be eaten at once.

Avocado: Sliced avocado is delicious with salad greens. Peel and split the avocado and remove the pit. Cut in thin slices either at the moment of tossing the salad or when you mix the greens and arrange the bowl.

Grapefruit: Grapefruit segments add zest to a salad of greens, especially when the previous course has been a heavy one. After game or pork, the addition of the citrous quality seems to freshen the palate. Grapefruit segments may also be combined with avocado for another pleasant change.

Orange: Slices of orange in green salad when accompanied by rings of raw onion are a favorite with many people especially after seafood. The orange should be peeled and all the white pulpy layer removed. Cut the orange in thin slices and blend with the greens and the onion rings.

Mushrooms: Sliced raw mushroom caps are exceptionally good in salads. They are best if allowed to marinate in the dressing for a short time before the salad is mixed. Tiny pickled mushrooms are a good addition too.

Truffles: A few sliced truffles mixed with soft or rather delicate greens and a not-too-highly-flavored French dressing make a noble salad for a festive meal. Place a layer of truffles in the midst of the greens—Boston lettuce is ideal. Allowing the greens and truffles to stand for a half hour or so before adding the dressing will increase the flavor.

Almonds: A few blanched almonds will enhance many salads. In some cases the almonds should be toasted for a few minutes in the oven for extra flavor.

Pepper: Strips of red or green pepper or canned pimiento are often used in salads to good effect.

Carrots: Strips or shreds of raw carrot are another welcome addition.

The Onion Family: Garlic is the greatest salad flavoring of all. There are several ways to use it:

(1) Rub the bowl well with a clove of garlic. Sprinkle a little salt into the bowl and rub the garlic into the salt. This will extract more flavor than if you just rub the bowl.

(2) Grate the garlic on a fine grater and add to the dressing.

(3) Slice the garlic and add to the dressing. Do this only when serving people of whose taste for garlic you are absolutely sure. To have the unhappy experience of biting into a kernel or slice of garlic is more than many can stand.

(4) Use a *chapon*. This is the most subtle way to add garlic. Take a very stale piece of French bread or a stale roll with plenty of crust, rub it well with a clove of garlic, and add it to the salad bowl. You may leave it there while you toss the salad and when you serve it. Many people like to eat the *chapon* after it has become more or less saturated with the mixture of garlic and French dressing flavors.

Onion—the winter variety or the tiny green onions or scallions—may be used sliced, chopped, or. in the case of green onions, whole in green salads.

SALAD DRESSINGS

Basic French Dressing

3 or 4 parts olive oil   **1 part wine vinegar or**
Salt and pepper   **lemon juice**

Olive oil, for those who like the flavor, is by far the most satisfactory of all salad oils. If you do not care for it, the vegetable oils, notably peanut or corn or soy bean oil, are all acceptable, though they lack the flavor of olive oil.

Do not keep oil in the refrigerator, for cold affects oil and often ruins good oil. On the other hand, heat tends to turn oil rancid. So try to find a relatively cool place for oil during very hot weather.

Wine vinegar is, if it is true wine vinegar, much less strident in a salad than the other vinegars. Ready-flavored vinegars are "tricks." If one wishes a herb flavor, for best results one should introduce the herb or flavoring agent oneself.

Coarse salt, ground in a salt mill, is the best kind to use in a dressing. The same holds true with pepper.

Mixing the Dressing: Dressing should be made fresh each time you have a salad, not mixed in a jar or bottle and kept for weeks on end. In any case, do not let garlic, if you use it, stand in the dressing from one day to another, or it will give your dressing and your salad a disagreeable rank taste.

Combine oil and flavoring agents and stir well. If you are using herbs, either fresh or dried, the dressing should be mixed ½ to 1 hour before the salad course, so that the flavors have a chance to blend.

If you are using mushrooms, almonds, or other things of that type in the salad, it is often wise to allow them to marinate in the dressing in the salad bowl for a half hour or so before you add the greens and toss the salad.

VARIATIONS

Besides the flavoring agents added to the salad itself, there are certain spices which may be mixed with the dressing for variety.

With Mustard: Dry mustard is fine for certain salads. The amount to mix in will depend on your taste. A celery salad or certain fruit combinations can take a good deal of mustard to give a contrast of flavors.

With Curry: Curry powder gives zest to the dressing for various salads.

With Worcestershire Sauce: A little of this sauce is good in a dressing for any salad with tomatoes in it.

With Garlic: Garlic also makes a good addition to French dressing for certain salads.

Vinaigrette Dressing

Basic French dressing	Parsley
Onions, finely chopped	Hard-cooked egg, chopped
Chives	Dill or sour pickles, chopped

This, a variation of French dressing, is used for many vegetables and for certain seafood and meat dishes. Other herb flavors may be added according to how they suit.

Mayonnaise

2 egg yolks	1 cup olive oil
Salt	1 teaspoon vinegar
½ teaspoon dry mustard	Cayenne pepper

There are many new ideas for making mayonnaise, but the old method of using a silver fork and a flat dish (such as a large soup plate or vegetable dish) is best. The resulting dressing is a richer, heavier sauce and seems to be more flavorful.

Important things to remember:

(1) Use only the best olive oil and never chill it.

(2) Have the eggs at room temperature and have them fresh.

(3) Never add the oil too quickly, or the emulsion will curdle. If it does curdle, start with another egg yolk and a little oil and gradually stir in the curdled mayonnaise until smooth.

(4) If the emulsion becomes too stiff, cut it with the addition of a small amount of vinegar or lemon juice.

Place 2 egg yolks, a little salt, and ½ teaspoon dry mustard in a bowl and stir well with a silver fork. When they are well blended, begin adding olive oil. Add it gradually, beating well after each addition, until the dressing becomes thick and well emulsified. If the mayonnaise becomes too thick, add vinegar or lemon juice. Continue beating until you have used all the oil. Season with more salt, mustard, and lemon juice or vinegar. A little cayenne may be added, if desired.

VARIATIONS

With Lemon Juice: Use lemon juice, if you prefer, instead of the vinegar.

Green Mayonnaise: Add finely chopped parsley, spinach, chives, tarragon, and chervil to mayonnaise, and flavor with a little garlic.

Red Mayonnaise: Add a little tomato purée and a little basil.

Russian Dressing: To mayonnaise add chili sauce, finely chopped hard-cooked egg, chopped onion, parsley, and olives.

Tartar Sauce: Add finely chopped green onion, dill pickle, and parsley to mayonnaise. A little grated horseradish is often a pleasant addition.

Rémoulade Sauce: Add to 1 cup of mayonnaise 1 teaspoon dry mustard, 1 tablespoon finely chopped anchovies, 1 tablespoon chopped parsley, 1 tablespoon capers, 1 tablespoon finely chopped hard-cooked egg, grated garlic, fresh or dried tarragon, and a few chopped olives. Also add chopped green pepper, if you wish, and some horseradish.

For certain fish salads add to mayonnaise a teaspoon of anchovy paste, a tablespoon of finely chopped pickled onions, and chopped parsley.

SOUR CREAM DRESSINGS

Certain salads, notably cucumber and cabbage, are good with sour cream dressings.

Sweet and Sour Dressing

1 cup sour cream	½ teaspoon salt
1½ teaspoons sugar	½ teaspoon dry mustard
2 tablespoons vinegar	

Blend well the sour cream, sugar, vinegar, salt, and mustard. Taste for seasoning. The flavor should be a pleasant sweet-sour blend, but because of differences in vinegars and sour cream, you will have to establish the proper proportions for yourself by testing.

Sour Cream Dressing for Cucumbers

1 cup sour cream	1 tablespoon finely chopped
1 tablespoon chopped parsley	fresh dill
	1 teaspoon salt

Mix ingredients and blend well.

TOSSED SALADS

The preparation of a simple tossed green salad, and the greens and flavorings that may be included in it, are discussed in the opening pages of this chapter. However, other things may be added to a tossed salad for variety and a more elaborate course.

Chef's Salad

Many restaurants often serve what is called "chef's salad" for a main course. It is basically a green salad with certain additions which make it substantial enough for a summer luncheon or a Sunday night supper. In each of the following variations, the ingredients are added to the mixed greens, and the salad is dressed with a French dressing and tossed as usual.

VARIATIONS

(1) Add strips of cold boiled or baked ham, cold chicken, and Swiss cheese.
(2) Add thin strips of cold tongue, Swiss cheese, and hard-cooked egg.
(3) Add strips of cold turkey, slices of hard-cooked egg, and tiny cooked asparagus tips.
(4) Add cold cooked whole snap beans, artichoke hearts, and shreds of Swiss cheese.
(5) Add strips of cold chicken or turkey and blanched almonds.
(6) Add cold cooked shrimp and capers.
(7) Add crab legs or crabmeat and thin slices of avocado.
(8) Add peeled grapefruit segments and slices of avocado.
(9) Add thin slices of beet root, sliced hard-cooked egg, and thin slices of onion.
(10) Add cooked green peas, grated raw carrots, sliced radishes, and sliced hard-cooked eggs.

The above salads are excellent served with Melba toast or toasted hard rolls.

Anchovy Salad

2 small tins anchovy fillets	2 or 3 small white onions
2 medium-sized green peppers	1 tablespoon chopped parsley
2 tomatoes	3 tablespoons olive oil
	1 tablespoon wine vinegar

Place in a salad bowl the anchovy fillets with the oil in which they are packed. Add cleaned and seeded peppers cut into fine strips; tomatoes, peeled, quartered, and seeded; onions, peeled and cut in small dice; parsley; 3 tablespoons olive oil or more, depending on amount in anchovy tins; and wine vinegar. Mix ingredients well and allow them to blend for 2 hours or so before serving. This dish may be used as an appetizer or a salad, whichever you prefer. *(Serves 4.)*

Wilted Lettuce

Lettuce	1 teaspoon sugar
5 or 6 slices bacon	¼ cup wine vinegar
4 or 5 scallions	Black pepper

Break lettuce or other greens into a salad bowl. Cut bacon into small pieces and try out until crisp. Remove and drain on absorbent paper. Add scallions, finely cut; sugar; wine vinegar; and a sprinkling of black pepper. Allow bacon fat and vinegar to come to the boiling point. Pour over the greens and sprinkle with the crisp bacon bits. Serve at once. *(Serves 4.)*

Roquefort Cheese Bowl

Combine any types of greens you desire—romaine, endive, and escarole would be complementary. Add a generous quantity of crumbled Roquefort cheese to a French dressing, blend well, pour over salad greens, and toss.

VEGETABLE SALADS

Potato Salad (I)

6 or 8 medium-sized potatoes	½ teaspoon mustard
½ cup olive oil	½ teaspoon black pepper
2 tablespoons vinegar	Chopped parsley
1 teaspoon salt	Chopped chives (or small green onions or scallions)

New potatoes or the waxier varieties of old potatoes are best for salads. Mealy potatoes very often make salad mushy.

Boil 6 or 8 medium-sized potatoes (or 12 or 14 smaller ones) in salted water in their jackets. When just tender and pierceable, remove and drain. Plunge them into cold water so you can handle them at once. Peel while still hot and cut into even slices.

Pour over the potato slices olive oil mixed with vinegar, salt, mustard, and black pepper. Toss the potatoes with the dressing and allow to cool and chill. (It is better if you can make this dressing the day before using it.) When ready to serve, add generously chopped parsley and chopped chives. If chives are not available, use small green onions or scallions. If all the dressing has been absorbed by the potatoes, you may add additional dressing, made in the same proportions as before. Mix well and arrange in a salad bowl. Sprinkle with additional chopped parsley. *(Serves 6.)*

Potato Salad (II)

8 medium-sized potatoes or 12 small ones	2 tablespoons finely chopped parsley
1 cup dry white wine	½ cup olive oil
3 tablespoons finely chopped onion	2 tablespoons wine vinegar
1 tablespoon finely chopped raw carrot	2 tablespoons white wine
	Salt and pepper
	Hard-cooked eggs, sliced

Boil the potatoes in their jackets until tender and pierceable. Cool in water and drain. Peel and slice the potatoes while still hot. Pour over them dry white wine and allow to cool. When ready to serve, add onion, raw carrot, and parsley. Dress with a dressing made with the olive oil, wine vinegar, white wine, and salt and pepper to taste. Toss well, arrange in salad bowl, and garnish with sliced hard-cooked eggs.

Potato Salad (III)

6 medium-sized potatoes	12 almonds, blanched and shredded fine
Salt and pepper	1 tablespoon capers
¼ cup olive oil	2 tablespoons finely chopped parsley
2 tablespoons wine vinegar	
1 green pepper, seeded and finely chopped	3 or 4 stuffed olives, sliced
4 or 5 green onions, cut fine	Mayonnaise
	Stuffed hard-cooked eggs

Boil the potatoes in their jackets. Drain and cool. Peel and cut in slices. Sprinkle with salt and pepper, and marinate in olive oil blended with wine vinegar. When ready to serve, add green pepper, onions, shredded almonds, capers, chopped parsley, and olive slices. Mix with enough mayonnaise to bind the salad, arrange in a salad bowl, and garnish with stuffed hard-cooked eggs.

MIXED VEGETABLE SALADS

Arrange lettuce or romaine leaves in a large salad bowl and make an attractive arrangement of raw and cooked vegetables. The cooked vegetables should be cooked in boiling salted water and chilled and marinated in French or vinaigrette dressing. Dress and mix.

Suggested Combinations

(1) Fresh peas, whole string beans, shredded raw carrot, sliced beets. Garnish with tomato slices and green pepper rings.

(2) Cooked asparagus tips, raw cauliflower buds, cooked carrot slices, sliced tomatoes. Garnish with sliced hard-cooked eggs and pimiento strips.

(3) Whole cooked green beans, cooked peas, preserved artichoke hearts, sliced cucumber.

(4) Shredded raw carrot, finely shredded raw beet, cooked peas, cucumber slices. Garnish with tomato slices and finely chopped green onions, and flavor with fresh basil if available.

(5) Thin raw zucchini slices, cooked asparagus tips, tomato slices, thinly sliced onions, sliced raw mushroom caps. Garnish with green pepper rings and serve with watercress.

(6) Center bowl with whole cooked cauliflower. Sprinkle cauliflower with finely chopped chives and parsley. Surround it with a ring of tomato slices, a ring of cucumber slices, and a ring of highly flavored stuffed eggs. This makes an acceptable and attractive buffet dish.

(7) Broccoli flowerets carefully cooked and marinated, shredded raw carrot, whole beets, and leeks which have been cooked and marinated in French dressing for several hours. Garnish with artichoke hearts.

Italian Salad

In a large salad bowl which has been lined with romaine or Boston lettuce, arrange cooked carrots (whole or in slices), slices of cooked potato, whole cooked green beans, cooked peas, and asparagus tips. Dress with herbed mayonnaise and garnish with anchovy fillets, tomato slices, olives, and capers. Sprinkle with chopped parsley or chervil. Surround with quartered hard-cooked eggs.

Russian Salad

Russian salad is basically a mixed vegetable-

and-meat salad bound with mayonnaise and elaborately arranged. It may also be served molded in aspic.

Suggested Combinations:

(1) Cooked peas, diced carrots, diced potatoes, beans, pimiento, cubes of ham, and tongue.

(2) Cubed cooked carrots, beets, and potatoes; peas, diced raw celery, chicken cubes, ham cubes.

(3) Cucumber cubes, raw celery in small bits, diced cooked potatoes, raw carrots, peas, cubed cooked duck, chicken, ham, tongue.

Garnish with tiny whole peeled tomatoes, anchovy fillets, capers, quartered hard-cooked eggs, pimiento.

Asparagus Salad

Arrange on greens (watercress is good) the cooked, chilled asparagus, either fresh or canned, tips or long spears. Dress with any of the following:

(1) Vinaigrette dressing. Garnish with strips of green pepper.

(2) Mayonnaise. Garnish with pimiento and chopped parsley.

(3) Green mayonnaise. Garnish with slices of hard-cooked egg.

Cold asparagus vinaigrette and perhaps an egg dish make an ideal summer luncheon.

Beet Salad

Cooked beets may be used in a variety of ways in salads. They may be sliced, diced, shredded, or cut in julienne strips and used in any of the following combinations or by themselves.

(1) Sliced beets, flavored with chopped

chives and parsley and dressed with sour cream.

(2) Sliced beets with sliced onions dressed with French dressing to which you have added tarragon.

(3) Beets in julienne slices mixed with chopped onion and mayonnaise.

(4) Beets chopped coarsely and combined with chopped hard-cooked egg and mixed with either French dressing or mayonnaise.

(5) Sliced beets combined with sliced eggs and mayonnaise.

(6) Tiny whole beets combined with field salad (page 196) and dressed with French dressing.

(7) Sliced beets, sliced onion, and orange segments with French dressing.

Cauliflower Salad

Whole cooked cauliflower makes a pleasing salad and a most decorative one when combined with other vegetables. Be certain that the cauliflower is not overcooked, for mushy cauliflower with a dressing is something less than delicious.

Arrange cauliflower on a bed of greens. Watercress is particularly pleasant with this type of salad. Sprinkle with a little chopped parsley and dress with French dressing. Sprinkle with paprika.

VARIATIONS

With Blanched Almonds: Stud the head of cauliflower with blanched almonds, sticking the almonds into the creases between the flowerets of the vegetable so that they will stand and give it a spiky appearance when served. Dress with a curry-flavored French dressing.

With Tomatoes: Arrange a bed of watercress on a large plate or a shallow salad bowl. Place cooked head of cauliflower in center and surround with slices of peeled tomatoes and rings of green pepper. Sprinkle cauliflower with paprika and serve with

a bowl of mustard mayonnaise (made by adding 2 teaspoons dry mustard to a cup of mayonnaise).

With Greens: Mix tiny raw cauliflower flowerets with greens and thinly sliced cucumber and toss with French dressing which has had a good touch of tarragon added to it.

Pepper Salad

2 or 3 green peppers	3 or 4 radishes
1 pound cottage cheese	Chopped parsley
1 small onion, finely chopped	Chopped fresh dill
	Salt and pepper
1 clove garlic, finely chopped	Watercress
	Tomatoes

Clean and seed peppers. Blend together with a fork cottage cheese, onion, garlic, radishes cut in thin slices, plenty of chopped parsley, and a little chopped fresh dill. Salt and pepper the mixture to taste and stuff the peppers with it, pressing it in as tightly as possible. Slice the stuffed peppers in ⅓-inch slices and arrange them on a bed of watercress alternating with slices of ripe tomato. Pass French dressing in a sauceboat or bowl. You will need a flat spatula-like server for this so that the stuffing does not fall out of the pepper rings.

Cucumber Salad

Cucumber needs merely peeling or scoring with a fork and slicing. Mature cucumbers are sometimes better if seeded by splitting in half and removing the seedy section.

Slice cucumbers very thin, and salt and pepper to taste. Add 2 or 3 tablespoons sour cream and allow the cucumbers to stand an hour or more before serving.

VARIATIONS

(1) Add chopped dill to the sour cream and blend with the cucumbers.

(2) Add a grated garlic clove and chopped parsley to the sour cream.

(3) Add 1 tablespoon each chopped chives, chopped parsley, and chopped dill.

Cucumber and Onion Salad

Slice equal quantities of cucumbers and small white onions in very thin slices. Marinate for 2 hours in French dressing. Serve in French dressing with 1 teaspoon celery seed and 1 teaspoon mustard seed added.

Cucumber Cheese Salad

Peel, seed, and shred with a coarse shredder 1 good-sized cucumber. Combine with 1½ cups cottage cheese and 2 tablespoons chopped chives, and blend well. Serve on a bed of romaine and garnish with cucumber slices. Serve with a French dressing to which you have added a teaspoon of paprika.

(Serves 4.)

Cucumber Boats

Peel or score with a fork evenly shaped and matched cucumbers, using 1 cucumber per person. Cut a slice from one side of the cucumbers and remove the seeds and a small amount of the pulp. Sprinkle with salt, turn upside down, cover with a damp cloth and let stand for a half hour. When ready to serve, stuff with any meat, fish, or seafood salad, and arrange on a bed of greens and garnish.

Suggested Fillings: Crabmeat salad, lobster salad, sweetbread salad, chicken and almond salad.

TOMATO SALADS

Sliced Tomatoes

To many people a plate of sliced ripe tomatoes is the ideal salad dish. Many a luncheon I have enjoyed was nothing more than a fine array of peeled sliced tomatoes with salt, a little freshly ground pepper, olive oil and vinegar, and good crusty bread and butter.

VARIATIONS

(1) Alternate slices of fine beefsteak tomatoes with slices of Bermuda onion, garnished with cucumber slices. Serve French dressing or oil and vinegar separately.

(2) Quarters of romaine or Boston lettuce and tomato slices. Pass a condiment tray containing cruets of oil and vinegar and condiments, or serve with a French dressing.

(3) Whole small tomatoes, peeled and heavily dusted with a mixture of chopped parsley, basil, and chives. Serve with a tray of vinegar and oil cruets, pepper grinder and salt mill, and other condiments.

(4) Sliced peeled tomatoes, thin slices of avocado, and a sprinkling of finely chopped onion. Serve with condiment tray or with French dressing.

(5) Sliced tomatoes, chilled cooked asparagus spears, and sliced hard-cooked eggs arranged on a large serving plate. Pass a bowl of vinaigrette dressing with this for a perfect luncheon combination.

(6) Sliced tomatoes, sliced onions, and sliced green pepper rings arranged around a dish of anchovy fillets. Serve with a vinaigrette dressing, heavily flavored with garlic, to which capers have been added.

Stuffed Tomatoes

Peel ripe tomatoes of even size and remove a ¼-inch slice from the top. Remove seeds and pulp from inside of tomatoes and sprinkle with salt. Turn upside down and allow to chill in the refrigerator for 1 hour before serving. Fill with fish, seafood, or meat salad or with:

(1) A large piece of cold lobster, a cold egg which has been poached until the yolk is just barely set, and chopped chives. Dress with a garlic mayonnaise.

(2) Cottage cheese which has been blended with chopped chives, parsley, shredded cucumber, and sliced green olives, and seasoned to taste. Serve with French dressing.

(3) Cottage cheese mixed with finely chopped green pepper, chives, stuffed olives, and chopped walnut meats. Serve with French dressing.

(4) Diced avocado which has marinated in a French dressing heavily laced with garlic and tarragon.

SEAFOOD SALADS

For a seafood or fish salad, use only fish or seafood, crisp flavorful greens, and well-flavored dressing. Rather than a stretched salad, serve a vegetable or green salad.

Crabmeat Salad

Arrange crabmeat on a bed of crisp greens —romaine, watercress, endive, or Boston lettuce. Dress with either rémoulade or Russian dressing.

Garnish with any of the following:

(1) Sliced tomato.
(2) Sliced avocado.
(3) Blanched almonds.
(4) Capers.
(5) Slices of cucumber.
(6) Stuffed celery.

Lobster Salad

Remove meat from body and claws of a cooked lobster. On salad greens arrange good-sized pieces (pieces cooked in court-bouillon are good). Dress with mustard mayonnaise, rémoulade, or Russian dressing. Garnish with a piece of claw meat and any of these:

(1) Sliced hard-cooked egg.
(2) Ripe olives.
(3) Sliced tomato and sliced egg.
(4) Capers.
(5) Long strips of cucumber.
(6) Small cooked shrimps.

Shrimp Salad

Arrange cooked shrimp on bed of greens and dress with a mayonnaise or rémoulade or Russian dressing. Garnish with a few additional shrimp and any of the following:

(1) Sliced hard-cooked eggs and tiny peeled tomatoes.
(2) Chopped parsley and chives with cucumber slices or capers.
(3) Sliced avocado, chopped chives, and slices of tomato.
(4) Strips of green pepper and sliced ripe olives.
(5) Quarters of hard-cooked egg and anchovy fillets and capers.
(6) Stuffed celery and tiny peeled tomatoes.

VARIATIONS

With Anchovies: Arrange halves of hard-cooked egg in center of salad bowl lined with crisp greens. Cover eggs with Russian dressing and surround with cooked, chilled shrimp. Sprinkle with chopped parsley and garnish with anchovy fillets and capers.

Green Salad: Cold cooked shrimp may be added to vary a green salad dressed with French dressing.

Mixed Seafood Salad

Shrimp, crabmeat, and lobster may be mixed with a good mayonnaise or rémoulade dressing with plenty of chopped herbs and served with any of the garnishes suggested for other seafood salads.

VARIATIONS

(1) Any of these salads may be mixed with a green mayonnaise and sprinkled with additional herbs.
(2) Any of the salads may be used for stuffing tomatoes, avocado halves, cucumber boats, or green pepper cups.
(3) You may combine seafood of any kind in a green salad, dress with a well-herbed French dressing, and then toss it as you would a tossed salad. This type of salad adds variety to green salad and might be used for a main course at a summer luncheon.

MOLDED SALADS

Eggs and Vegetables in Aspic

1 envelope unflavored gelatin	8 cooked or canned asparagus spears
½ cup cold water	2 hard-cooked eggs, chopped
¾ cup hot water	
1 bouillon cube	½ cup cooked peas
½ cup tomato juice	¼ teaspoon salt

Soften gelatin in cold water. Add hot water, bouillon cube, and salt, and stir until dissolved. Add tomato juice. Pour gelatin mixture into mold to depth of ¼ inch. Arrange asparagus spears in mold. Chill until almost firm. Chill remaining gelatin until it has the consistency of unbeaten egg whites. Fold in eggs and peas, put on top of stiffened gelatin and asparagus. Chill until firm. Unmold and garnish with greens, and serve with mayonnaise or French dressing.   (Serves 6.)

Salmon or Tuna Fish Mold

1 envelope unflavored gelatin	1 teaspoon prepared mustard
1 cup milk	¼ teaspoon paprika
2 egg yolks	2 tablespoons mild vinegar or lemon juice
1 teaspoon salt	
2 cups flaked salmon or tuna fish	

Soften gelatin in cold milk in top of double boiler. Combine the egg yolks, salt, mustard, and paprika, and beat slightly. Add small amount of the milk to the egg yolk mixture and return to double boiler. Cook over hot, not boiling, water, stirring constantly, until mixture thickens. Remove from heat and cool. Stir in lemon juice and flaked fish. Turn into large or individual molds and chill until firm. Unmold and serve the dish with cucumber dressing.

Molded Chicken Salad

1 envelope unflavored gelatin	¾ cup mayonnaise or salad dressing
¼ cup cold chicken stock or bouillon	1 cup diced cooked chicken
½ cup hot chicken stock or bouillon	3 tablespoons minced green pepper
1 tablespoon lemon juice	¾ cup diced celery
	¼ teaspoon salt

Soften gelatin in cold chicken stock. Add hot stock and salt, and stir until gelatin is dissolved. Cool. Add salt, lemon juice, and mayonnaise. Stir in the chicken, green pepper, and celery. Turn into loaf pan or individual molds and chill until firm. Unmold on lettuce or other salad greens and garnish with tomato wedges and sliced hard-cooked egg.

(Serves 6.)

CHICKEN SALADS

CHICKEN SALAD

Cut the meat of a cold chicken in generous-sized cubes, being careful to discard all gristle, skin, and hard, dry portions of the meat. Add finely chopped celery in proportions of 2 cups diced chicken to 1 cup chopped celery. To serve traditionally, decorate with mayonnaise, sliced hard-boiled eggs, and capers.

One quart (4 cups) chicken salad will serve 5 people. If you are making it in quantity—for a large supper party, for instance—you may stretch it a bit with more celery or you may mix some veal with your chicken. Thus for 25 people you will want 3 quarts diced chicken and 2 quarts diced celery.

VARIATIONS

For 2 cups chicken:

(1) One-half cup celery, ½ cup sliced ripe olives, ½ cup shaved toasted almonds. Bind with mayonnaise and decorate with almonds and olives.

(2) One cup English walnut meats lightly toasted in the oven. Bind with mayonnaise and decorate with pimiento strips.

(3) One cup diced cooked sweetbreads and ½ cup diced cucumbers. Bind with mayonnaise and decorate with sliced cucumbers.

(4) One cup diced pineapple and ½ cup sliced toasted almonds. Bind with mayonnaise, decorate with whole almonds, and dust with grated orange rind.

(5) One cup diced avocado. Dress with Russian dressing and decorate with ripe olives.

Any of these salads may be made with turkey, duck, or any kind of game.

SALADS WITH CHEESE

There is nothing which so perfectly points up the flavor of cheese as does salad. A green salad and a ripe cheese make a splendid dessert. A well-aged natural cheese should have flavor and mellowness. It should be at room temperature, never served just out of the refrigerator.

Toasted cheese and French bread make a pleasant accompaniment. Many people enjoy cheese with fruit and coffee as dessert.

The Creamy Cheeses

Camembert: Comes in either a large cake or in individual portions wrapped in foil. It should be soft and creamy and should remain out of the refrigerator 1 or 2 hours before using.

Brie: Comes in large round cakes or smaller ones about the size of a camembert. Brie should be well ripened, rather strong in flavor, and creamy in texture. Keep it at room temperature 2 hours before serving.

Poona: A distinctive cheese made in New York State. It is unlike any other cheese made in this country and should be soft but not runny when eaten. Keep it at room temperature for several hours before serving.

Liederkranz: This American-made cheese should be quite soft and just a little runny to be right. It should be kept at room temperature 2 hours before serving.

The Firmer Cheeses

Cheddar: Although, technically, cheddar is a cheese from a certain part of England, the word has come into everyday usage and we find many native varieties of cheddar-type cheese. Canada, Wisconsin, New York State, Oregon, Vermont, and many other parts of the country prepare it. Aged cheddar which has a sharp quality is preferred by most people. The younger cheese has a bland flavor and is not as desirable for after-dinner service. Keep cheddar at room temperature 2 hours before serving.

Swiss: True Switzerland Swiss is one of the greatest of all cheeses. It has a distinctive flavor and texture which is superior to that achieved by others of its type, probably due to pasturage and aging conditions. It should be served at room temperature and should be well aged. Similarly with domestic Swiss.

Bel Paese: Both the imported and domestic are distinguished, somewhat bland but delightful to eat. Serve at room temperature.

Oka: A distinguished cheese of Canada, richly flavored. Serve at room temperature.

Provolone: An Italian cheese, dry but rich in flavor. Serve at room temperature.

Blue Cheeses

Roquefort: Officially only that which comes from the Roquefort district is entitled to this name. It is well aged, creamy, and crumbly. Serve at room temperature.

Bleu: Some distinguished Bleu cheese is made in this country.

Gorgonzola: There are both imported and domestic varieties. Both should be creamy and crumbly and highly flavored. Serve at room temperature.

There are dozens of other cheeses, some of them excellent local products which are not extensively distributed.

Always serve a plate of butter with cheese, for there are many people who enjoy butter and cheese together and like to make their own mixture at table.

FRUIT DESSERTS

APPLES

For cooking, the early Gravensteins, the Delicious, both golden and red, the MacIntosh, and the Yellow Newtown apples are all excellent. The Gravensteins are fairly early. The Delicious and MacIntosh are in the markets most of the fall and winter months, and the Newtowns carry over until spring.

Baked Apples

Baked apples may be served either hot or cold. Core the apples, preferably with a patented corer, and pare the top 1½ inches. Place apples in a baking dish. Fill cavities in the apples with sugar, using 1½ to 2 tablespoons for each apple. Dot with butter and add to the dish 1 cup or more water—to a ½-inch depth. Bake in a moderate oven (350°) 30 to 40 minutes or until apples are tender. Baste very often during the baking. Serve baked apples with heavy cream or, if desired, with sour cream.

VARIATIONS

(1) Fill cavities with maple sugar, sprinkle with cinnamon, dot with butter, and bake.
(2) Mix brown sugar and cinnamon and nutmeg, and fill cavities. Bake.
(3) Omit sugar. Add 1½ cups maple syrup and 1 cup water to pan. Pour syrup over apples. Bake.
(4) Mix 1 cup brown sugar with ½ cup chopped nuts and raisins, mixed. Fill cavities of apples, sprinkle tops with additional brown sugar, dot with butter, add water to pan, and bake as above. Add cinnamon or nutmeg if desired.
(5) Fill cavities with strained honey and add cinnamon and water to pan. Dot each apple with 1 teaspoon butter.
(6) Pare apples a third of the way down. Sprinkle lightly with sugar, add water to pan, and cover. Bake until apples are just barely tender, sprinkle the tops with an ample amount of brown sugar, dust with cinnamon, and dot with butter. Finish cooking, uncovered, in the broiler under a low flame until sugar is melted and bubbly.

Apple Sauce (I)

Peel, core, and slice 4 or 5 medium-sized tart apples. Combine with ½ cup water. Cover and allow to simmer until soft. Add sugar to taste (½ to 1 cup granulated, brown or maple sugar), mix well with apples, and allow to simmer another 15 minutes or until well blended and thoroughly cooked. To improve flavor, add ¼ teaspoon salt.

Apple Sauce (II)

Core apples, but do not peel. Cut out any blemishes on the skin. Cook apples rapidly with ½ cup water until just soft. Put through a fine sieve and add sugar to taste.

VARIATIONS

Spiced: Add spice to apple sauce when you add the sugar. Cinnamon, nutmeg, or mace are all very good with it.

Ginger: Add small slivers of candied ginger when apple sauce is removed from heat. Mix well with the hot sauce.

Brandy Raisin: Add ½ cup Sultana raisins which have been soaked 2 hours in just enough cognac or apple brandy to cover them.

Horseradish: For pork, mix apple sauce with drained or grated fresh horseradish to taste.

With Cream: Serve apple sauce with sweet or sour cream and sprinkle with cinnamon.

Sliced Apples

Ripe, juicy apples with a crisp texture are delicious when peeled and thinly sliced and served with sugar and heavy cream.

AVOCADO DESSERT

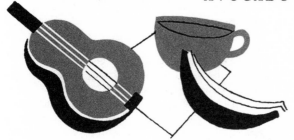

Select ripe, unblemished avocados, allowing ½ avocado per person, and put them through a food mill or sieve just before serving. Mix the puréed avocados with powdered sugar—approximately ½ cup for each avocado. Flavor with fresh lime juice and serve at once with wedges of lime.

APRICOTS

Fresh apricots, halved or peeled and sliced, may be served with sugar and cream or in a variety of other ways.

Slice or halve apricots and cover with sugar. Add kirsch (which is most complementary to all fruits), cognac, or apricot liqueur. Or combine apricots with strawberries; add sugar and kirsch.

To Peel: Dip apricots in boiling water for 1 or 2 minutes. The skin can then be taken off easily with a sharp knife.

Poached Apricots Flambée

Peel fruit but do not remove the pits. With a sharp knife cut into the flesh on one side.

Prepare a syrup of equal parts sugar and water and let it boil 5 minutes. Add apricots and allow them to poach in syrup 8 or 10 minutes. Do not boil. Remove from heat, allow to cool in syrup, and serve. Or serve warm, and just before serving add kirsch or cognac to taste, reserving 1 tablespoon to ignite the rest. Send to table ablaze.

Apricots thus cooked may be served cold or hot and with a variety of flavorings. They may also be halved, some of the pits cracked, and a few of the kernels from the pits added to the apricots.

BANANAS

Sliced Bananas

Sliced bananas may be varied by combining with other fruits. The addition of a little lemon juice will prevent bananas from discoloring.

(1) Combine sliced bananas and strawberries, either fresh or quick-frozen. If fresh strawberries are used, slice and sugar them before adding them to the bananas.

(2) Combine sliced bananas, pineapple— either fresh, canned, or quick-frozen—and the moist canned coconut for an unusual flavor balance.

Baked Bananas

Peel firm ripe bananas and place them in a buttered baking dish. Sprinkle lightly with brown sugar and a little lime or lemon juice. Dot with butter and bake in a moderate oven (350°) about 15 minutes or until bananas are soft but not mushy.

VARIATIONS

With Rum: When you remove bananas from the oven, pour over them 3 ounces Jamaica or Martinique rum. Ignite rum and carry to table at once, or ignite dish at table.

With Coconut: Peel bananas and place in a buttered baking dish. Sprinkle lightly with brown sugar and dot with butter. Cover with grated fresh or tinned coconut. Bake in a moderate oven (350°) until bananas are soft and coconut lightly browned.

BLACKBERRIES

Blackberries, good with cream and sugar, also combine exceedingly well with fresh peaches.

BLUEBERRIES

To vary blueberries:

(1) Combine with real maple syrup and cream.

(2) Combine with fresh or quick-frozen peaches and flavor with maple syrup.

(3) Pour port over cleaned and picked-over blueberries. Allow them to soak in the wine for an hour before serving. Unless you have a very sweet tooth, probably you will not need additional sugar.

CHERRIES

Fresh Cherries

Fresh cherries, either Royal Annes, Bings, or Lamberts, are best when served well chilled in a compote or fruit dish. Serve each person with small bowls of water, so they may dip the cherries before eating them.

Cherries Jubilee

For 4 people, use 1 No. 2½ can pitted Bing cherries. Drain cherries and measure out 1 cup juice (the remainder may be used for other purposes). Heat cherries and juice very slowly, being certain they come just to the simmering point without boiling. When ready to serve, place cherries in a large bowl or in individual flame-proof dishes. Add ¼ cup heated kirsch or brandy for each serving. Ignite just as the cherries are served.

VARIATION

With Ice Cream: Serve the flaming hot cherries over ice cream.

Cherries and Almonds

Serve Bing or canned Royal Anne cherries iced, with kirsch or brandy. Top with a few blanched almonds which have been lightly toasted in the oven for about 5 minutes.

FIGS

Fresh figs, either purple or white, should be perfectly ripe but not mushy. Peel, slice thin, and add sugar. Serve with heavy cream or sour cream or with port.

Brandied whole figs are available in jars. Serve with more brandy. Figs in syrup may also be served brandied or with heavy cream.

GRAPEFRUIT

Broiled Grapefruit

Sprinkle halves of grapefruit with brown sugar or spread with strained honey. Dot with butter, place on broiler rack 4 inches from flame, and broil very slowly. A little sherry or port may be added.

GOOSEBERRIES

Poached Gooseberries

Large English gooseberries may be poached in a syrup made of equal parts of sugar and water which has boiled 5 minutes before the fruit is added. Pick stems and blossoms off the berries and wash well. Poach in the syrup until tender and cooked through. Do not let them cook to a mush.

Gooseberry Fool

Wash and clean 1 quart gooseberries. Cook very slowly with ½ cup sugar and ¼ cup of water until tender enough to mash. Put through a sieve or food mill and add sugar to taste. Mix ½ pint heavy cream with ½ pint of milk and blend in the gooseberry pulp. Chill for several hours before serving.

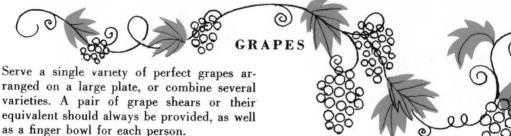

GRAPES

Serve a single variety of perfect grapes arranged on a large plate, or combine several varieties. A pair of grape shears or their equivalent should always be provided, as well as a finger bowl for each person.

MELONS

Melons in great variety, plentiful in the markets throughout summer and fall, are one of the most refreshing of fruits. Serve as they are, well chilled or iced, or in combination with other things.

The melons most widely available are cantaloupe and other muskmelons, honeydew, Persian, papaya, casaba, and watermelon.

Serve melons well iced. Always accompany slices or halves of melon with a wedge of lemon or lime for each serving, and pass salt, pepper, and powdered sugar. Everyone seems to have different tastes about the proper seasoning.

Combinations of melons, served in slices or in balls (which may be cut with a ball cutter from the pulp), are pleasant.

Melon Surprise

Choose a large, unblemished casaba or Persian melon. With a sharp knife cut a circular piece about 7 inches wide out of the top of the melon. Carefully remove all seeds and strings. With a ball cutter, cut balls of pulp from the interior of the melon. Combine melon balls with any other fruits you wish— bananas, cherries, pineapple, other melon balls, or grapes—sprinkle lightly with powdered sugar, and flavor with kirsch or Cointreau. Fill melon with the mixed fruits, replace piece cut from top, and chill thoroughly. Serve melon on a bed of chopped ice and garnish with leaves.

Melon Mélange

Choose a large watermelon. Split it the long way, remove seeds, and cut out flesh with ball cutters of various sizes. Fill shells with cracked ice to chill them. Combine watermelon balls with pineapple cubes, cantaloupe balls, cherries, firm ripe strawberries, apricot halves, and white grapes. Chill thoroughly.

When ready to serve, remove cracked ice and water. Arrange fruit on a large bed of crushed ice, and place a bed of strawberry or grape leaves around the edge of the shell. Fill shells with the chilled fruit and serve with either a flavoring of kirsch or a well-chilled bottle of champagne poured over it just before serving.

NECTARINES

Nectarines may be served in any of the ways described for peaches (below).

ORANGES

Sliced Oranges

Sliced oranges or orange segments served with the addition of a little curaçao make a delightful dessert after a heavy meal.

Ambrosia

Combine sliced oranges or orange segments with sugar to taste and grated coconut. The moist canned coconut is the best for this.

PEACHES

Fresh Peaches

Serve sliced peaches with cream and sugar. Or vary as follows:

VARIATIONS

With Maple Syrup: Serve sliced peaches with maple syrup to taste.

With Liqueur: Sugar sliced peeled peaches and add liqueur. Kirsch is highly complementary, as it is to all fruits. Curaçao and Cointreau are very good, and Triple Sec is another favorite. Cognac may be used. For another delicious dish, let the peaches stand in port for an hour or so before serving.

With Raspberries: Combine peaches with raspberries, either frozen or fresh, in equal amounts. If fresh ones are used, add sugar to taste. The frozen ones will be sweet enough to sweeten the peaches. Add kirsch or cognac to taste if you wish.

Peaches Poached in Syrup

If the peaches are fully ripe, they will usually peel easily. If not, plunge them into boiling water for 1 minute and remove at once. Then the skin will come off easily.

Choose 6 or 8 large ripe peaches. Peel, cut in halves, and remove pits. Make a syrup, using 1½ cups sugar to 1 cup water, and flavor very lightly with vanilla. (If you keep a special jar of sugar on your supply shelf with a vanilla bean in the jar, you will always have delicately flavored sugar for syrups and for dessert use generally.) Boil syrup 5 minutes. Add peach halves and allow to cool in the syrup. Serve flavored with kirsch or cognac. Or serve hot and blaze peaches just as you serve them. (I have had most delicious peaches prepared in this manner, flavored and blazed with bourbon whiskey.)

VARIATION

With Cream: Half or whole peaches prepared this way may be served cold with cream instead of being flavored with a liqueur.

Baked Peaches

Peel 6 or 8 ripe peaches and leave them whole. Cover with cold water to which you have added a bit of lemon juice to prevent discoloring.

Make a syrup with 1½ cups sugar and 1 cup water. Allow to boil 5 minutes.

Stick each peach with a clove. Arrange peaches in a baking dish. Pour syrup over them and bake about 25 minutes in a moderate oven (350°), basting every 5 minutes with syrup. Allow peaches to cool before serving. Serve with heavy cream.

Broiled Peaches

Choose fine halves of canned peaches in syrup. Drain and reserve syrup for other uses. Arrange peach halves on a broiling pan or rack with the pitted side up. Sprinkle a little brown sugar or maple sugar into the hole, dust with cinnamon, and dot with butter. Broil under a medium flame for 5 minutes or until fruit is well heated and butter and sugar are blended and bubbling. Serve at once with meat dishes or as a dessert course.

VARIATIONS

With Jam. Substitute a heaping teaspoon of raspberry jam for the sugar.

With Jam and Coconut: Use raspberry jam instead of sugar, cover jam with a mound of moist grated coconut, and broil until coconut is lightly browned.

PEARS

Bartletts in summer and early fall are delicious raw or cooked. After them come the Boscs, Anjous, and Comices.

Fresh Pears

Anjou or Comice pears are really so perfectly flavored that they are at their best served raw. Serve alone or with a cheese board, for pears and cheese are one of the most satisfying of combinations for dessert.

Or peel and slice the pears and serve with sugar, or sugar and heavy cream, or maple syrup, which is most satisfying with pears.

Pears Poached in Syrup

Prepare a syrup, using 1 cup water to 1 cup sugar. Bring to a boil and let it cook 5 minutes. For 6 pears use about 2 cups syrup.

Peel and halve the pears, or peel and leave them whole. Poach pears in syrup—basting frequently—about 15 minutes, or until tender and translucent. Allow pears to cool in the syrup and serve.

VARIATIONS

With Lemon: Add 3 or 4 slices lemon to syrup and poach pears in the syrup. Serve with a slice of the cooked lemon.

With Ginger: Add 3 tablespoons finely cut candied or preserved ginger to the syrup when the pears are added.

In Port: Add ½ cup port to the syrup when the pears have cooled.

Minted: When pears have cooled, add ¼ cup green crème de menthe to syrup and let pears stand until they have absorbed the flavor and are delicately tinted with the liqueur.

With Raspberries: Crush 1 pint fresh or frozen raspberries and add sugar to taste. Put through a sieve so as to remove all seeds. Pour over cooked pears just before serving.

Flambée: Flavor syrup with ¼ cup kirsch and serve pears flambée with additional kirsch. Or you may use ¼ cup cognac for flavoring and for blazing.

Baked Pears

Prepare a syrup with brown sugar and water, using 1½ cups sugar to 1 cup water. Boil 5 minutes.

Choose ripe firm pears; do not peel them. Cut in halves and remove seeds, or leave them whole. Arrange pears in a baking dish, stick each with a clove, and sprinkle lightly with cinnamon. Pour syrup over the pears and bake in a moderate oven (350°), basting frequently, about 30 minutes or until tender. Serve hot or cold with cream or flavor with cognac to taste.

VARIATION

With Ginger: Add finely cut pieces of candied or preserved ginger to the syrup in which you cook the pears.

PINEAPPLE

Sizes of pineapples vary, but size has nothing whatsoever to do with flavor. The very small sugar pineapples are among the most delicious of all. Quick-frozen pineapple, very useful in dessert-making, comes in cubes. Canned pineapple comes crushed and in cubes, fingers, and slices. Brandied pineapple is available in jars.

Fresh Pineapple

Cut the green top from the pineapple. Peel the fruit with a very sharp knife, removing all pines or small prickly bits with which the flesh is indented. Core the fruit and cut in round slices or in wedges, remove core, and cut in long fingers or slices; or cube the fruit and remove most of the core. Sprinkle lightly with sugar and chill. Since pineapples vary greatly in sweetness, taste before adding sugar. Brown sugar gives pineapple an excellent flavor.

Serve plain or with dark rum, kirsch, cognac, or Cointreau.

Or serve pineapple in combination with other fruits such as:

(1) Fresh or frozen strawberries, sweetened to taste.

(2) Fresh or frozen raspberries, sweetened to taste.

(3) Sliced bananas and grated coconut.

(4) Sliced fresh apricots, flavored to taste with kirsch or Triple Sec.

Pineapple Wedges

Cut a pineapple lengthwise in quarters or, if it is exceptionally large, in 6 pieces. Do not remove top, but cut through it when dividing the pineapple. With a very sharp small knife or a grapefruit knife cut along the underside of the core and around the skin to loosen the edible part of the fruit. Do not remove the core. Cut edible part in thin slices. With fingers, slide pieces of pineapple out on either side so they alternate, protruding slightly from the shell. Sprinkle fruit with sugar and add 1 ounce dark rum to each wedge. Allow wedges to chill for an hour before serving. Serve 1 wedge to a person.

VARIATION

Substitute kirsch for the rum.

Broiled Pineapple

Use the small sugar pineapples. Split them in half, reserving stems to use for a garnish for the plates. With a sharp knife or curved grapefruit knife remove core and cut flesh in small cubes, loosening it from the shell. Sprinkle pineapple with brown sugar and dot heavily with butter. Broil about 4 inches from the flame for about 10 minutes or until fruit is heated through and sugar and butter have blended with the fruit juice. Serve hot. Half a pineapple makes one serving.

Add dark rum to each half before serving if you wish.

Canned Pineapple

Canned pineapple may be served in any way that you serve the fresh, with the exception of dishes calling for a whole pineapple or large wedges. Canned crushed pineapple may be combined with many other fruits, fresh or canned, to great advantage. For example:

(1) With finely cut pears or apricots.
(2) With raspberries and kirsch.
(3) With grated coconut.
(4) With blueberries.

Broiled or Sautéed Sliced Pineapple or Pineapple Fingers

Broil slices or fingers of pineapple with a few dots of butter added to each piece, or sauté in butter with a little sugar or syrup added. Flavor with a little dark rum just before serving.

Stuffed Whole Pineapples

Cut tops from large pineapples, cutting about 2 inches below the stem. Reserve tops. With a very sharp knife or ball cutter, remove edible part and cut away as much of the core as possible. Add sugar to taste.

Stuff pineapple with large ripe strawberries with hulls left on. Replace tops and serve with a bowl of powdered sugar.

VARIATIONS

(1) Stuff pineapple with a combination of pineapple meat and sliced strawberries, sugared to taste, and flavor with kirsch. Replace tops and serve chilled in a bowl of crushed ice or, if you are serving more than one pineapple, on a bed of crushed ice on a large platter or plate.

(2) Stuff with a combination of pineapple, strawberries, bananas, and coconut.

(3) Fill pineapple shells with ice cream and serve the fresh fruit flavored with rum over the ice cream.

(4) Cut small pineapples in half lengthwise, top and all. Scoop out fruit and combine with strawberries, white grapes, and fresh peaches cut in thin slices. Sugar to taste, flavor with kirsch or Triple Sec, and fill pineapple shells with the fruit. Garnish with sprigs of mint dusted with powdered sugar. Serve on a bed of grape or strawberry leaves.

PLUMS AND PRUNES

Plums

Plums are most often eaten raw, for their delicate flavor and extreme juiciness are very refreshing. They may, however, be poached in syrup, made in the proportions of 1 cup water to 1 cup sugar. Prick the skin with a fork before adding the fruit to the syrup, and poach only 5 or 6 minutes. Flavor with cognac or with a little kirsch or Cointreau.

Prunes

The oval Italian prunes are delicious when poached halved, with pit removed, with sugar and a little cinnamon. They may also be baked.

Baked Prunes

Cut prunes in half and remove pits. Arrange in a baking dish and sprinkle with ground cinnamon. Pour over them a syrup made with 1½ cups brown sugar and 1 cup water. Dot with butter, sprinkle lightly with brown sugar, and bake in a moderate oven (350°) about 15 minutes, or until tender.

RHUBARB

Rhubarb, though it cannot rightly be called a fruit, is one of the most refreshing of plants.

Baked Rhubarb

Cut rhubarb in 4-inch lengths. Place it in a casserole and sprinkle heavily with brown sugar. Add no water. Cover casserole. Bake in a moderate oven (350°) till just tender.

VARIATIONS

With Strawberries: Serve poached or baked rhubarb with sliced and sugared fresh or poached strawberries. Or you may bake the berries with the rhubarb.

RASPBERRIES

Serve raspberries with sugar and heavy cream or sour cream.

Serve them with kirsch or, if you are lucky enough to find it, Eau de Vie de Framboise, which is a brandy made from raspberries.

Combine with other fruits (apricots, peaches, bananas, pineapple, pears, etc.).

With Pecans: When baking rhubarb, add ½ cup shelled pecan halves to the casserole.

Poached Rhubarb

Wash rhubarb stalks and, if they are mature and tend to be stringy, scrape them. Cut into 1-inch lengths and arrange in a shallow saucepan which has a cover. Cover with a syrup made from 2 cups sugar and 1 cup water boiled 5 minutes. Cover saucepan and poach rhubarb over very slow heat until just tender. Allow it to cool uncovered.

STRAWBERRIES

Combinations of strawberries with other fruits are mentioned elsewhere in this section. By themselves they may be served—

(1) With sugar and sweet cream, or with maple syrup and sweet cream.

(2) With honey butter (a commercial product).

(3) With kirsch.

(4) Sugared and soaked in port for an hour before serving. (Serve with whipped cream.)

(5) With sour cream.

(6) With a custard sauce.

(7) Without being hulled, if the strawberries are large and ripe. (They should be perfectly arranged in a bowl or on a plate covered with leaves and accompanied by a dish of powdered sugar, for dipping.)

(8) Covered with orange juice, with a tiny bit of the peel grated over the top.

FRUIT DESSERTS WITH ICE CREAM

Most fruits, raw or cooked, may be combined with ice cream. A few of the better-known fruit-ice cream specialties are given here.

Banana Caribbean

Use large, perfect bananas—1 to a person. Split skin lengthwise with sharp knife. Carefully pull it away from the banana so that the skin remains in one piece. Roll banana in grated coconut. Arrange skins on plates.

Now fill the skins with a layer of vanilla ice cream. Cut bananas in thick slices and arrange them on the ice cream, sticking each slice upright into the cream. Sprinkle with additional coconut and serve.

VARIATION

With Liqueur: You may add a little crème de banane (banana liqueur) to this dish before serving.

Cherries Jubilee with Ice Cream

Follow recipe for cherries jubilee (page 211). Pour the hot cherries over vanilla ice cream and add heated kirsch or cognac. Ignite liqueur before serving. Or serve in individual dishes and blaze when served.

Cantaloupe à la Mode

Fill centers of cantaloupe with ice cream and serve. Or fill with ice cream and cover with sugared fresh raspberries or strawberries. Flavor with kirsch, if desired.

Melon Surprise

Remove a wedge from a good-sized honeydew or casaba melon. Remove seeds and stringy pulp, and chill. Fill melon with ice cream, replace wedge, and secure with toothpicks if necessary. Cut melon at table in wedges or round slices. Serve with crushed sugared raspberries or strawberries.

Peach Melba

Arrange peach halves, which have been poached in vanilla-flavored syrup, in a serving dish. Add a scoop of ice cream for each 2 peach halves and dress with raspberry syrup or Melba sauce (obtainable in bottles).

Pear Melba

This may be prepared like peach melba, using pear halves instead of peaches.

Pear Hélène

Arrange pear halves, which have been poached in vanilla-flavored syrup, in a serving dish. Add a large scoop of vanilla ice cream for each 2 pear halves and serve a hot chocolate sauce separately.

Apricot Melba

This may be prepared as above, using apricots.

Pineapple Delight

Scoop out flesh from halves of small pineapples which have been cut with tops intact. Fill shells with ice cream, top with pineapple which has been sugared and flavored with kirsch, and sprinkle top with grated coconut.

Stuffed Pineapples

Remove pulp from 2 or 3 large pineapples from which you have removed tops with about 1 inch of the fruit. Sugar pulp to taste. Flavor shells with kirsch by sprinkling it over the interior. Place a layer of ice cream in the bottom, a layer of pineapple, a layer of ice cream, and a layer of crushed sugared strawberries. Arrange tops on pineapples and serve.

Strawberries Supreme

Wash, hull, and slice 1 quart ripe strawberries. Add 2 cups sugar and allow berries to stand an hour. Heat gently over low heat and allow berries to come to the boil and boil 1 minute. Remove from fire and allow to cool thoroughly. Serve with vanilla ice cream, and add whipped cream which has been flavored with orange curaçao.

Meringues Glacés with Fruit

Make good-sized meringues (page 225). Place a scoop of ice cream with 2 meringues in each dessert dish. Top with crushed raspberries or strawberries or sliced peaches or apricots or crushed or cubed pineapple. Top all with a little vanilla-flavored whipped cream.

Fruit Coupé

Combine fresh strawberries, sliced peaches, white grapes, diced pineapple, raspberries, and cubes of ripe pear. Sugar the fruit to taste and let it stand 2 or 3 hours.

Place vanilla or strawberry ice cream (vanilla is best with fruits) in a large compote dish. Cover with mixed fruits. Just before serving, add a half bottle of iced dry champagne.

PIES AND PASTRIES

Plain Pastry

2 cups flour   2/3 cup butter
1/2 teaspoon salt   Ice water

Sift flour and salt. Cut the butter in with a knife or pastry blender until the pieces of butter are the size of large peas. With a fork or the blender mix in ice water—just enough to moisten all the flour and no more: 4 to 5 tablespoons should be sufficient. Form pastry into a ball and wrap it in either wax paper or foil. Place in the refrigerator for 15 to 25 minutes.

Roll half the pastry out on a lightly floured board or cloth to about 1/8 inch thickness. Place in bottom of pie pan and trim edges so they are about 1/4 inch over the edge of the tin. Arrange filling in pan. Roll out the second half of the pastry for the top of the pie. Fold pastry over or roll it lightly, place on top of filling, and unfold or unroll. Press edges of the two crusts together and trim off excess. Use the fingers to flute the rim of the pie. Cut several gashes in the top crust to let steam escape. *(Makes one 2-crust pie.)*

Rich Pastry

2½ cups flour   1 cup butter
1/2 teaspoon salt   2 tablespoons sugar
1 egg   Ice water

Sift flour and salt onto a pastry board, making a crown of flour with a clear space in the center. Break an egg into the center and place butter, cut into small pieces, in the center with the egg. Cut in the butter and egg with a knife or blender until butter is the size of large peas. Add sugar and just enough ice water to moisten all the flour. Roll out on floured board, knead lightly for 3 or 4 minutes, and wrap in wax paper or foil. Chill for an hour or longer before rolling out. Roll out as you do plain pastry. *(Makes a 9-inch 2-crust pie or two 9-inch shells, or about 12 medium tart shells or 18 small tart shells.)*

Crumb Pastry

Roll out enough crumbs — zwieback, graham cracker, ginger wafer, vanilla wafer, or chocolate—to make 1¾ cups. Combine with ¼ cup sugar and 2/3 cup melted butter. Line a 9-inch pie plate with the mixture and press down firmly with spatula or spoon. Fill with cream fillings or cooked fruit fillings and top with cream or meringue or glaze.

Glaze for Fruit Pies

Heat apricot or raspberry jam. Force through a fine sieve and brush fruit pie with the hot jam purée.

Meringue for Pies

Beat 3 egg whites until stiff but not dry. Beat in, a little at a time, 6 tablespoons sugar and ¼ teaspoon salt. Beat thoroughly until well blended. Spread over top of pie, being certain to cover the edges, with a spatula. Bake in a very slow oven (325°) 15 to 20 minutes or until meringue is slightly browned.

FRUIT PIES

The basic preparation of fruit pies is the same, regardless of the kind of fruit used. A fruit pie takes 2½ to 4 cups fruit—sliced, diced, or whole, according to the fruit. Line a 9-inch pie plate with pastry dough. Mix with your fruit 1 to 1½ cups sugar (or to taste), 1½ tablespoons quick-cooking tapioca or flour, and a little lemon juice and grated rind. Let stand for about a half hour.

Brush pastry dough with slightly beaten egg white. Place mixture in pie shell, heaping fruit toward the center. Add any spice you wish and dot with butter. Moisten edge of pastry with cold water and adjust the top crust, crimping edges and cutting several vents for steam to escape. Bake in a hot oven (425°) about 20 minutes, then reduce to 350° and bake 25 to 30 minutes (depending on fruit) or until fruit is tender and crust done.

Suggested Fruits for Pie

(1) Apple, flavored with cinnamon or nutmeg and plenty of butter. Or apple with maple sugar and cinnamon.
(2) Blackberry and apple in equal parts.
(3) Apple and blueberry.
(4) Blueberry, with cinnamon flavoring.
(5) Apricot, with the kernels of apricot pits for flavoring.
(6) Cherry, with cinnamon.
(7) Cranberry.
(8) Loganberry.

(9) Rhubarb, with brown sugar and cinnamon.

(10) Peach, with cinnamon or clove.

(11) Prune, with cinnamon.

(12) Gooseberry. Be certain to sweeten well with sugar.

Raisin Pie

1½ tablespoons quick-cooking tapioca	2 cups raisins
¾ cup brown sugar, firmly packed	1½ tablespoons lemon juice
½ teaspoon salt	1½ teaspoons grated lemon rind
½ teaspoon cinnamon	Pastry for 1 pie
1½ cups water	1 tablespoon butter

Combine tapioca, sugar, salt, cinnamon, water, raisins, lemon juice, and rind. Let stand about 15 minutes.

Line 9-inch pie pan with pastry rolled ⅛ inch thick. Fill pie shell with raisin mixture. Dot with butter. Moisten edge of pastry with cold water. Adjust top crust, cutting several slits to permit escape of steam. Bake in hot oven (425°) 20 minutes; then reduce oven to 350° and bake 25 to 30 minutes longer.

Deep-Dish Pies

Deep-dish pies are made without the bottom crust and are baked in an earthenware or glass casserole deeper than the usual pie tin. Place a small cup or egg cup or one of the patented pie dish cups in the center of the dish to hold up the crust. Arrange in pie dish sliced or whole fruit which you have mixed with sugar and spices to taste. Dot with butter. Cover with ½ recipe for pastry (page 220), being certain to dampen edges of dish and pastry before placing it on. Adjust crust, brush top with milk, and cut one or two vents for steam to escape. Bake in a hot oven (425°) about 10 minutes, then at 350° for 30 to 35 minutes. If crust browns too quickly, cover with brown paper.

plain pastry

← 2 CUPS

Flour

½ tsp → SALT +++

BUTTER ← ⅔ CUP

3/4 ½ 1/4

4-5 TBS icewater

CREAM PIES

(1) Prepare ½ recipe plain pastry or rich pastry (page 220). Roll out dough and place it on back of a pie tin, or place it in tin and fill the shell with uncooked beans or rice. Bake in a hot oven (425°) until nicely browned but not burned. If shell has been baked on back of the pie tin, remove it and place in the tin; if baked with beans or rice in shell remove them and save for another baking. Fill shell with flavored cream filling (page 222), top with fruit, and glaze or top with meringue or whipped cream. If topped with meringue, return to slow oven (325°) for 15 minutes or until meringue is set and lightly browned.

(2) Make a crumb crust and line a pie tin with it. Add cream filling flavored as desired. Top with fruits and glaze or with meringue or whipped cream.

(3) Bake individual tart shells or make individual shells of crumb crust. Proceed as above.

Cream Filling for Pastry, Cream Pies, and Tarts

1 tablespoon butter	1 pint milk
⅓ cup flour	Vanilla (or other flavoring)
½ cup sugar	Apricot glaze or whipped
6 egg yolks	cream

Melt butter in upper part of double boiler. Blend in flour, sugar, and egg yolks. Mix well with wooden spoon or whisk and gradually stir in milk. Continue stirring and cooking over hot water until the mixture boils. Flavor with vanilla to taste or other flavoring. Allow to cool slightly and pour into the shells. Cool thoroughly before adding fruit. Halves of any kind of poached fruit—peaches, pears, apricots, or rings of pineapple—may be used. Or whole strawberries, raspberries, or bananas. Glaze top of fruit with apricot glaze (page 220) or cover with flavored whipped cream.

VARIATION

With Tapioca: The following filling makes a lighter pie. It is made with quick-cooking tapioca and does not have the heaviness of cream made with flour or cornstarch:

Beat 2 egg whites until stiff but not dry. Beat in, a little at a time, 4 tablespoons sugar. Beat until mixture peaks.

Mix 2 egg yolks with 1 cup milk in upper part of double boiler. Add 4 tablespoons sugar, ½ cup quick-cooking tapioca, ¼ teaspoon salt, and 3 cups milk. Cook over hot water, stirring constantly, until mixture boils. It will not thicken much in cooking, so take care not to overcook it.

Remove from heat; stir gradually into beaten egg whites. Flavor and cool. Pour into two 9-inch baked pie shells. Place fruit on top of cream if it is to be a fruit cream pie. Cover with whipped cream or glaze. For one pie shell use ½ recipe.

Suggested Flavorings for Cream Pies

Vanilla: Top with vanilla-flavored whipped cream.

Peanut Brittle: Cover filling, when cold, with crushed peanut brittle. Top with whipped cream. Decorate with more peanut brittle.

Cacao: Add ¼ cup crème de cacao to filling. Top with whipped cream flavored with cocoa.

Banana: Top filling with thin slices of banana and whipped cream.

Pineapple: Top with slices or cubes of pineapple and cover with whipped cream.

Peach: Top with poached peach halves and brush with raspberry glaze (page 220).

Apricot: Top with halves of poached apricots, and cover with apricot glaze (page 220).

Cherry: Top with canned or poached Bing cherries. Glaze with apricot glaze.

Tutti Frutti: Flavor cream filling with ¼ cup cognac. When partially cooled, fold in ½ cup chopped blanched almonds, ½ cup marrons (chestnuts) in syrup, in small pieces, ¼ cup candied cherries, and ½ cup seedless raisins which have soaked in a little brandy 2 hours. Top with whipped cream and sprinkle with shaved unsweetened chocolate.

Macaroon: Add 1 teaspoon almond flavoring to filling and, when partially cool, add 2/3 cup crushed macaroons. Top with whipped cream. Sprinkle with macaroon crumbs.

Ginger: Mix ½ cup finely cut preserved or candied ginger with filling and flavor with 1 teaspoon vanilla. Cover with whipped cream and sprinkle with shaved ginger.

Mocha: Add 2 teaspoons instant coffee to filling while it is still hot and stir in well. Top with whipped cream flavored with Dutch process cocoa.

Pear: Top filling with halves of poached or canned pears. Cover with apricot glaze.

Strawberry: Cover top of filling with hulled whole berries. Cover with apricot glaze.

Black Bottom: Use chocolate crumb crust. To 1/3 of the cream filling add, while hot, 2 squares of unsweetened chocolate melted over hot water. Flavor remaining two-thirds of the filling with ½ teaspoon vanilla and 1 jigger Jamaica rum. Pour chocolate-flavored filling into crumb crust and allow it to cool, keeping rum filling warm but not cooking. Pour rum-flavored cream over chocolate. Cool. When ready to serve, top with whipped cream and cover with shaved sweet chocolate.

Chocolate Cream Pie

Crumb crust (page 220)
3 squares unsweetened chocolate
½ cup sugar
¼ cup water
6 tablespoons flour
¼ teaspoon salt
2 cups milk
1 egg, well beaten
1 teaspoon vanilla
1 tablespoon butter
Whipped cream
Shaved sweet chocolate

Combine unsweetened chocolate with ¼ cup sugar and the water in a small saucepan and cook 5 minutes, stirring constantly. Combine, in top of double boiler, flour, ¼ cup sugar, and the salt. Stir the milk in gradually, and when well blended stir in the chocolate mixture. Cook, stirring constantly, until the mixture is thickened; continue cooking over hot water about 10 minutes, stirring occasionally.

Remove 4 tablespoons of the mixture and add to the egg, stirring vigorously. Then blend with the mixture in the double boiler and flavor with vanilla. Just before removing from the hot water, stir in butter. Cool the mixture, pour into crumb crust, and chill. Top with whipped cream and shaved sweet chocolate.

Custard Pie

½ recipe for pastry (page 220)
4 egg yolks, lightly beaten
½ cup sugar
2 cups milk
½ teaspoon salt
1 teaspoon vanilla
Nutmeg or cinnamon

Line a 9-inch pie tin with the pastry. Beat egg yolks lightly and gradually add sugar and milk. Add salt and vanilla, and pour the mixture into pie shell. Sprinkle with nutmeg or cinnamon and bake in a hot oven (425°) until the cream is set but not firm. Custard continues cooking when it is taken from the oven, so remove it when the center is not completely firm. Cool.

Lemon Meringue Pie

1 9-inch pie shell
4 tablespoons cornstarch or arrowroot
1½ to 2 cups sugar
1 cup boiling water
½ teaspoon salt
½ cup lemon juice
1 lemon rind, grated
2 tablespoons butter
4 eggs, separated

Bake the pie shell (page 220).

Combine, in a double boiler, cornstarch or arrowroot, 1 cup sugar, and boiling water. Cook, stirring constantly, until mixture thickens. Add salt, lemon juice, and the grated lemon rind. Continue cooking and stirring constantly until well blended.

Beat egg yolks until light and lemon-colored. Pour the hot mixture over the egg yolks, stirring constantly. Return to the hot water and cook 3 or 4 minutes.

Add butter and blend well with the mixture. Remove from hot water and allow the mixture to cool before pouring into the baked pie shell.

Beat egg whites until very stiff, gradually add 6 tablespoons sugar, and beat until it peaks. Spread over the lemon mixture with a spatula completely to the edges and bake in a slow oven (325°) for 15 minutes or until meringue is delicately browned.

SOUFFLES

SOUFFLES WITH A CREAM BASE

The first thing to do in preparing a soufflé is to banish the notion that soufflé making is something which only an expert should tackle. Half the soufflé failures are caused by over-anxiousness and nervous fussing rather than mistakes in cooking or preparation.

3 tablespoons butter
¼ teaspoon salt
3 tablespoons flour
1 cup hot milk
4 beaten egg yolks
½ cup sugar
4 stiffly beaten egg whites

The basic formula is as follows: Melt butter in upper part of a double boiler, blend in salt and flour, and gradually stir in hot milk. Stir constantly until mixture thickens and allow it to cook 2 minutes. Cool slightly. Pour over a mixture of egg yolks and sugar (¼ cup sugar if a sweet liqueur is being used). Add flavoring and fold in the stiffly beaten egg whites. Pour into a buttered soufflé dish (a 2- or 2½-quart ovenproof glass dish is good) which has been sprinkled with sugar.

Bake in a moderate to moderately hot oven (350°-375°) 35 to 40 minutes or until risen and nicely browned. Serve at once with whipped cream or a sweet sauce. *(Serves 4.)*

Suggested Flavorings

Liqueurs: Use ¼ to ½ cup. Any of the following are good additions: Grand Marnier, chartreuse, Triple Sec, Cointreau, crème de mandarine, raspberry liqueur, apricot liqueur, crème de cacao, crème de café, Benedictine.

Flavorings: Good flavorings include: vanilla; almond; and lemon juice and grated lemon rind. Also, ¾ cup finely cut candied ginger added to the cream; or 2 squares unsweetened chocolate melted over hot water with ¼ cup sugar; or 2 teaspoons instant coffee dissolved in 2 tablespoons warm water.

SOUFFLES MADE WITH TAPIOCA

⅓ cup quick-cooking tapioca	2 tablespoons butter
½ cup sugar	4 well-beaten egg yolks
¼ teaspoon salt	Flavoring
2 cups milk	4 stiffly beaten egg whites

This simple procedure makes a well-textured soufflé. Combine the tapioca with sugar, salt, and milk. Bring to a boil, stirring constantly. Add butter and blend well with the mixture.

Remove from the fire and cool slightly. Stir mixture into the egg yolks. Blend well. Add flavoring and fold in the egg whites. Pour into buttered and sugared soufflé dish and bake in a moderate oven (350°) 30 or 35 minutes.

Use any of the flavorings suggested above or use finely cut or puréed fruits. The amount of sugar given here will sometimes have to be reduced for certain flavorings.

FRUIT SOUFFLES

1 cup finely cut or puréed fruit—fresh, quick-frozen, or canned	Kirsch, cognac, or Triple Sec
Sugar	4 stiffly beaten egg whites

Put the fruit through a food mill or a fine sieve. Heat with sugar to taste and flavor with kirsch, cognac, or Triple Sec. Combine fruit pulp with stiffly beaten egg whites, pour into a buttered and sugared soufflé dish, and bake about 30 minutes in a moderately hot oven (375°). Serve with whipped cream or a sauce flavored with the fruit or a liqueur.

CUSTARDS AND MERINGUES

Baked Custard

1 quart milk	¼ cup sugar
6 lightly beaten egg yolks	1 teaspoon vanilla

Scald the milk. Allow it to cool slightly. Beat egg yolks lightly and add sugar and vanilla. Add hot milk gradually, mixing well with the egg and sugar. Pour into a buttered baking dish and place this in a pan of hot water. Bake in a moderate oven (350°) until the custard is set but not entirely firm. Cool.

Bake in individual molds if desired.

VARIATIONS

With Coconut: Add ½ cup grated coconut to the custard.

With Chocolate: For chocolate custard, melt 2 squares unsweetened chocolate with ¼ cup sugar and ¼ cup hot water. Add to the hot milk before adding it to the beaten eggs.

With Coffee: For coffee custard, add 2 heaping teaspoons instant coffee to the hot milk before adding it to the eggs.

Floating Island (Oeufs à la Neige)

2 cups milk	¼ cup sugar
4 stiffly beaten egg whites	1 teaspoon flour
¼ cup sugar	1 teaspoon vanilla or
4 lightly beaten egg yolks	almond

Scald the milk in the top of a double boiler. Beat egg whites until stiff and add sugar gradually. Drop several large spoonfuls of egg-white mixture into the hot milk. Cover and cook 4 minutes. Remove the puffs carefully with a perforated spoon and drain. Drop additional spoonfuls into hot milk until all the puffs are cooked. Beat egg yolks lightly, add sugar and flour, stir into the hot milk, and continue stirring until mixture thickens. Flavor with vanilla or almond, allow the custard to chill, and top with the puffs.

Rice Pudding

½ cup rice	½ cup sugar
3 cups milk	½ cup heavy cream
4 lightly beaten egg yolks	½ teaspoon nutmeg

Wash rice well and combine in top of double boiler with milk. Cook, covered, over hot water 1½ hours or until rice is thoroughly cooked. Combine egg yolks, sugar, heavy cream, and nutmeg. Blend with the cooked rice and milk and bake in a mold in a hot oven (400°) until browned and set—about 15 minutes. Serve in mold. *(Serves 4.)*

Baked Meringues

1 cup sugar	⅓ cup water
¼ teaspoon cream of	4 egg whites
tartar	1 teaspoon vanilla

In a saucepan combine sugar, cream of tartar, and water. Cover and bring slowly to a boil. Uncover and cook till syrup makes a long thread when a little drips from a spoon held high above saucepan—or until, when tested with a thermometer, temperature is 240°. Beat egg whites till stiff, using electric beater if you have one. Continue beating while pouring in syrup in a fine thread. At all times mixture should be stiff enough to stand in peaks. When all syrup is in, flavor with vanilla.

Moisten a heavy board and cover with heavy unglazed paper. Place tablespoons of meringue on paper, rounded side up; or shape with pastry tube into circles, barquettes, rings, etc. Sprinkle tops with fine granulated sugar and bake in very slow (250°) oven about 1½ hours. Do not let meringues color. When tops are crisp, remove from oven and, with a knife, slip them off the paper. Press in soft part at center of underside. Let cool. Serve filled with whipped cream, ice cream, or sliced and sweetened fruit. Do not fill till ready to use. *(Makes about 16 shells.)*

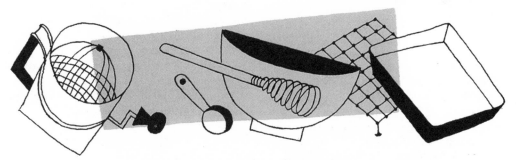

CAKES AND FRITTERS

No general cookbook can deal fully with the huge family of cakes. This section is limited to a number of those reliable and easy-to-make cakes that fill most basic needs.

Happy Day Cake

2¼ cups sifted cake flour	1½ cups sugar
2½ teaspoons double-acting baking powder	2 eggs, unbeaten
	1 cup milk
1 teaspoon salt	1 teaspoon vanilla
½ cup butter	

Sift flour once, measure, add baking powder and salt, and sift together three times. Cream shortening, add sugar gradually, and cream together until light and fluffy. Add eggs, one at a time, beating very thoroughly after each addition. Add flour alternately with milk, a small amount at a time, beating after each addition until smooth. Add vanilla.

Turn into 2 deep 9-inch layer pans which have been lined with paper and then well greased. Bake in moderate oven (375°) 25 to 30 minutes.

Continental Apple Cake

1 cup butter	Juice and rind of 1 lemon
2 cups flour	2 egg yolks, white of one
2 tablespoons sugar	

Filling

4 apples thinly sliced	½ cup sugar
1 teaspoon cinnamon	¼ cup raisins

Mix flour, butter, egg yolks, and sugar. Knead with hands. Add lemon juice and grated rind. When well blended and smooth, chill for several hours.

Roll ¼ inch thick. Divide in two parts. Line an oblong tin with half the dough and sprinkle with bread crumbs. Fill with sliced apples, sugar, and raisins. Sprinkle with cinnamon. Cover with the remaining dough. Brush top with slightly beaten egg white and bake at 350° 30 to 35 minutes or until apples are tender.

Dust with powdered sugar and cut in squares. Serve hot or cold with whipped cream. *(Serves 6.)*

Chocolate Roll

6 eggs	1 scant tablespoon flour
1 cup sugar	1 pint cream
3 tablespoons cocoa	

Beat egg whites until stiff but not dry. Beat yolks until foamy and add sugar gradually, beating constantly. Add cocoa and flour which have been mixed together, and lastly fold in the stiffly beaten egg whites.

Grease a long shallow pan very well and line it with buttered wax paper. Pour batter and spread over pan. Bake in a hot oven (400°) 12 minutes or until tester comes out dry. Turn on to a wet cloth. Roll, then unroll and spread with vanilla-flavored whipped cream. Roll again. Top with the following icing:

1 cup icing sugar	2 tablespoons strong black
2 teaspoons cocoa (or to	coffee
taste)	½ teaspoon vanilla

Blend the coffee with the sugar and flavoring ingredients, adding additional coffee if necessary. Icing should be smooth before it is spread over the roll. *(Serves 6.)*

Jelly Roll

4 eggs	Juice of 1 lemon
1 cup sugar	1 cup sifted cake flour
¼ teaspoon salt	Jelly or jam
1 teaspoon baking powder	Powdered sugar

Beat eggs with a rotary beater until light and lemon-colored. Gradually beat in sugar and continue beating until thickened and very light in color. Stir in salt and baking powder. Add lemon juice and fold in cake flour, adding a little at a time and folding only until the flour is absorbed. Line a large sheet pan with buttered paper. Pour in the mixture and bake in a hot oven (400°) 12 to 14 minutes. Remove cake from oven and turn on a sugared towel. Remove paper, trim edges, and roll in towel at once, rolling the towel in the cake. Let stand 10 or 12 minutes, unroll, remove towel, spread with jelly or jam, and roll again. Wrap in towel or foil and cool on a cake rack. Sprinkle with powdered sugar before serving.

Quick Butter Cake

1 heaping tablespoon	1 heaping teaspoon baking
butter	powder
6 tablespoons sugar	Pinch of salt
2 eggs	⅓ cup milk
Cinnamon	½ cup broken nut meats
1 cup flour	

Cream the butter with 2 tablespoons sugar. Add 1 whole egg and 1 egg yolk. Stir until creamy. Add flour, sifted with baking powder and a pinch of salt, alternately with the milk. Spread in a well-buttered layer tin. Brush with lightly beaten egg white and sprinkle with butter, remaining sugar, nut meats, and cinnamon mixed. Bake in a 350° oven 18 to 20 minutes or until golden brown. *(Serves 6.)*

Old-Time Pound Cake

1 pound (2 cups) butter	4 cups (1 pound) sifted flour
1 pound (2 cups) sugar	¼ cup brandy
10 egg yolks	½ teaspoon mace
10 egg whites	

Cream the butter. Gradually add sugar and stir continuously till creamy. Beat egg yolks till light and lemon-colored. Into sugar-and-butter mixture gradually beat the egg yolks, beating thoroughly for 5 minutes after each addition. Beat the egg whites until stiff. Add sifted flour and egg whites alternately to the egg-butter-sugar mixture, beating well each time. When egg white and flour are all in, beat well 5 minutes. Add brandy and mace.

Butter 2 loaf tins and line with heavy paper. Pour batter into tins and bake in a moderately slow oven (325°) about 1½ hours.

ICINGS FOR CAKES

Seven-Minute Frosting

2 unbeaten egg whites   2 teaspoons corn syrup
1½ cups sugar   Flavoring
5 tablespoons water

Combine egg whites with sugar, water, and corn syrup. Place over boiling water and beat vigorously with rotary or electric beater. Cook approximately 7 minutes or until the mixture peaks. Remove from the fire, add flavoring, and beat until mixture is of consistency for spreading. This will cover and fill two 9-inch layer cakes or about 24 small cup cakes.

Flavorings

Vanilla: 1 teaspoon.

Chocolate: 2 squares unsweetened chocolate, melted and added when frosting is removed from fire.

Coconut: Sprinkle shredded coconut on frosting while it is soft.

Caramel: Add 2 teaspoons caramelized sugar syrup.

Lemon: Omit corn syrup and add 1 tablespoon lemon juice when frosting is removed from heat.

Mocha Frosting

Add 1 teaspoon instant coffee and 1 tablespoon cocoa with the sugar.

Rum Frosting

Substitute dark rum for cream in thinning the frosting. Add no vanilla.

You may add artificial coloring for any of these frostings if you desire.

Martha's Chocolate Cake De Luxe

3 squares bitter chocolate
1 cup milk
4 eggs
1½ cups sifted granulated sugar

1 generous cup cake flour, sifted 3 times
2 teaspoons baking powder
1 teaspoon vanilla

Melt chocolate in milk over a very low flame, stirring constantly. Cool. Beat egg yolks until foamy, adding granulated sugar which has been sifted 3 times. Stir constantly. Slowly add cooled chocolate mixture. Stir in flour which has been sifted with baking powder. Add vanilla. Fold in egg whites beaten stiff but not dry. Bake in well-buttered spring form in moderately hot oven (350-400°) 35 to 40 minutes or until cake tester comes out dry. When cool, split cake in half and fill with whipped cream flavored with vanilla to taste. Cover with the following icing:

3 squares bitter chocolate
2 tablespoons butter
½ cup milk

¾ to ⅞ cup sugar
Vanilla to taste

Melt chocolate over a low flame. Remove from fire and add granulated sugar, stirring continuously. When thoroughly blended, replace over flame. Stir till mixture bubbles. Remove from fire and beat, adding butter and vanilla. Continue beating to get right spreading consistency. Pour over the cake.

(Serves 6.)

FRITTERS FOR DESSERT

Fritter Batter

2 eggs, slightly beaten
½ cup milk
2 tablespoons melted butter

1 teaspoon baking powder
1 cup flour
3 tablespoons sugar

Beat eggs slightly and add milk and melted butter. Sift together flour, sugar, and baking powder. Stir into the liquid with a wooden spoon and combine thoroughly.

Note.—When fritter batter is used for non-dessert dishes, omit the sugar.

Any of various fruits may be used—small fruits, such as cherries, or large fruit cut in small slices.

With Apples: Peel and slice, sprinkle with sugar and lemon juice, and let stand 1 hour.

With Pineapple: Cut in cubes or small diagonal-shaped pieces. Quick-frozen pineapple should be drained of all syrup.

With Apricots: Use halves. If apricots are canned, drain well.

With Peaches: Use halves, and cut them in two before dipping in batter.

Flavor fruit with a little kirsch or Triple Sec if desired. Drain well before dipping in batter.

Dip the fruit in the fritter batter and fry in deep hot fat 3 to 5 minutes. Temperature of fat should be 370°, or hot enough to brown a 1-inch cube of bread in 45 seconds. Drain the cooked fritters on absorbent paper. Sprinkle with sugar. Serve very hot with custard sauce or fruit sauce (pages 239-240).

WHITE OR CREAM SAUCES

A sauce is not, as is sometimes thought, an infallible sign that the cook is a master of his or her art, for no sauce, however carefully made, will disguise poorly cooked food. Nevertheless, a good sauce is the crowning achievement of a truly accomplished cook, for, with the aid of sauces, knowingly prepared, a cook may turn the humblest ingredients into appetizing fare.

The thickening agents or liaisons for sauces are flour, the most generally used; cornstarch; yolk of egg (which gives a far richer flavor to a sauce but which must be handled carefully); rice; and *beurre manié*—butter and flour blended together and dropped into liquids to thicken them. The proportions of butter and flour in *beurre manié* are about equal, or, sometimes, two parts flour to one of butter.

There are certain basic sauces to which other ingredients are often added for variations on the single theme. In France, these are called the "mother sauces" and they include a white sauce, or Béchamel (sometimes called sauce Allemande), brown sauce or Espagnole, and mayonnaise, which is a base for many other sauces.

Basic White or Cream Sauce

1 cup milk	2 tablespoons butter
½ teaspoon salt	2 tablespoons flour

Blend butter and flour in top of double boiler. (The mixture of butter and flour over heat, basic to most sauces, is called a "roux.") Stir milk in gradually, using a spoon or whisk. Continue stirring until mixture thickens and comes to a boil. Add salt and allow sauce to cook over hot water about 5 minutes.

Cream Sauce

Make the roux described above and add 1 cup cream instead of milk. Season to taste.

Béchamel Sauce

2 tablespoons butter	¼ bay leaf
2 tablespoons flour	4 peppercorns
1 cup chicken broth	Sprig of parsley
1 small onion, sliced	¼ cup heavy cream
1 small carrot, sliced	

Make a roux by combining flour and butter in top of a double boiler or in a saucepan. Simmer chicken broth 10 minutes with onion, carrot, bay leaf, peppercorns, and parsley. Strain broth and add it to roux, stirring constantly. Continue cooking until thickened. Stir in heavy cream and cook 5 minutes. To make a fish sauce, substitute for the broth 1 cup strained court-bouillon (page 53) in which you cooked the fish.

VARIATIONS

(1) Substitute milk for the chicken broth.
(2) When sauce is cooked, stir slightly beaten egg yolk into it, being careful it does not overcook.
(3) Add chopped parsley, chives, and tarragon, and a teaspoon of lemon juice.
(4) Sherry, Madeira, or other wines may be added to the sauce just before serving. In this case omit lemon juice.

Sauce Supreme (Sauce Velouté)

2 cups chicken broth	Large sprig parsley
3 mushrooms (or 6 or 7 stems)	Salt
1 small onion, sliced	4 tablespoons butter
¼ bay leaf	3 tablespoons flour
1 carrot, sliced	½ cup heavy cream
	Juice of ½ lemon

Simmer for 10 minutes the broth, mushrooms or stems, onion, bay leaf, carrot, and parsley. Salt to taste. Strain.

Blend in the upper part of the double boiler 3 tablespoons butter and the flour. When well blended, add, slowly, seasoned chicken broth, stirring constantly until it thickens. Then allow it to cook 5 minutes and add 1 tablespoon butter and the heavy cream, and blend well with a wooden spoon or wire whisk. Just before removing from the fire, add juice of lemon.

Sauce Mornay

1 cup basic white sauce	cheese plus 1 tablespoon
2 tablespoons grated Parmesan cheese, or 1 tablespoon grated Parmesan	grated Swiss cheese, well dried
	¼ cup heavy cream

Prepare the basic white sauce and add cream and cheese. Blend well.

Cheese Sauce

1 cup basic white sauce	⅓ cup grated American cheese
Cayenne pepper	

To basic white sauce add cheese and a few grains of cayenne pepper. Cook over hot, not boiling, water until cheese is melted.

Parsley Sauce

1 cup Béchamel sauce	¼ cup finely chopped parsley

Add parsley to sauce and mix well. This makes a good sauce for fish.

Caper Sauce

1 cup basic white sauce	1 teaspoon liquid in which capers are preserved
2 tablespoons capers	

To basic white sauce add capers with liquid. This sauce is good with certain fish dishes and with boiled leg of mutton.

Egg Sauce for Poached Fish

1 cup Béchamel sauce (made with fish stock or court-bouillon)	3 hard-cooked eggs, finely chopped
1 teaspoon dry mustard	¼ cup finely chopped parsley

To sauce add other items. Stir in parsley.

Mustard Sauce

1 cup basic white sauce	1 teaspoon prepared mustard
2 teaspoons dry mustard	

Add mustard to sauce. Blend thoroughly.

Sauce Vinaigrette

Olive oil	Garlic
Wine Vinegar	Parsley, chopped
Salt	Capers
Dry mustard	Hard-cooked eggs, chopped

To 4 parts olive oil and 1 part vinegar add other ingredients. Chopped chives or chopped shallots are welcome too, as is tarragon.

Horseradish Sauce

1 cup Béchamel sauce	½ cup grated fresh horseradish
Juice of ½ lemon	

Add horseradish to sauce. Blend well and add lemon juice. If you use bottled horseradish, be certain it is well drained before adding to sauce, and omit lemon juice.

Mushroom Sauce

12 medium-sized mushroom caps	5 tablespoons butter
2 cups chicken broth	3 tablespoons flour
Salt	6 tablespoons cream

Peel and slice thinly the mushroom caps. Combine peelings and stems with chicken broth, salt to taste, and simmer 15 minutes.

Make a roux of 3 tablespoons butter and flour. Stir in strained mushroom-flavored broth and, when sauce thickens, add cream.

Sauté the sliced mushrooms in 2 tablespoons butter 3 or 4 minutes. Combine sautéed mushrooms with sauce and allow to cook 5 minutes over hot water. Taste for seasoning. If sauce is too thick, dilute with a little cream.

Dill Sauce for Fish

4 tablespoons fresh dill, finely chopped	1 tablespoon chopped parsley
1 cup basic white sauce	

Combine dill with parsley. Blend with white sauce. Cook over hot water 4 or 5 minutes.

Sauce Poulette

2 egg yolks	Juice of ½ lemon
1 cup basic white sauce	Chopped parsley

Combine egg yolks with white sauce and blend well with a wooden spoon or a whisk. Season with lemon and parsley. Do not boil.

Sauce Parisienne

3 egg yolks   **Salt**
¼ cup cream   **Juice of ½ lemon**
  2 tablespoons tomato purée
  3 tablespoons butter
  ¼ teaspoon dry mustard

Blend, in upper part of double boiler, egg yolks, cream, and tomato purée. Stir constantly over hot water with a wire whisk until mixture thickens. Add butter, one tablespoon at a time, stirring well each time. Add salt to taste, lemon juice, and mustard.

BROWN SAUCES

Brown Sauce (Sauce Espagnole)

¼ pound butter	1 carrot, sliced
¼ pound lean ham, diced	1 bay leaf
¼ pound veal, diced	4 tablespoons flour
1 medium-sized onion	1 quart beef or veal stock
2 cloves	1 teaspoon salt

Melt butter in a heavy saucepan. Add ham and veal, onion stuck with cloves, carrot slices, and bay leaf. Cook until well browned. Add flour and blend well over a low fire, stirring constantly, until flour is browned. Add stock and salt and let mixture simmer, covered, for 1 hour. Taste for seasoning and strain through a fine sieve. This makes a basic sauce used mainly in combination with other flavorings.

VARIATIONS

For Roasts or Game: Flavor sauce with red wine.

For Beef: Flavor with freshly grated horse-radish.

For Other Meat Dishes: Flavor with sliced sautéed mushrooms.

For Use with Pastes or Leftover Meats: Add tomato purée and a finely chopped clove of garlic.

Quick Brown Sauce

½ cup butter	½ cup flour
Stock or tomato purée or pan gravy	2 tablespoons Kitchen Bouquet

This is a quickly made sauce approximating brown sauce, not so flavorful but useful in an emergency. Blend butter with flour and gradually add Kitchen Bouquet. This may be combined with stock or tomato purée or with pan gravy to make a sauce for meat. You need approximately 3 tablespoons for a cup of liquid. It may be stored in the refrigerator.

HOLLANDAISE SAUCES

Hollandaise Sauce (I)

¼ pound butter	Juice of a lemon or
3 egg yolks	1 tablespoon tarragon
½ teaspoon salt	vinegar

Cut butter into 3 equal parts. Combine 1 part with egg yolks in the top of a double boiler. Place over hot water and stir constantly with a wire whisk. Add the second piece of butter when the first is melted, and then the third, stirring constantly. Do not let the water under the sauce boil. Season with salt and lemon juice or vinegar. Serve at once.

If the sauce should curdle, beat in a little boiling water, very slowly, until sauce is emulsified again.

Hollandaise Sauce (II)

½ pound butter or 1 cup olive oil	2 teaspoons lemon juice
	½ teaspoon salt
3 egg yolks	¼ teaspoon dry mustard

Melt butter (or use olive oil) in upper part of double boiler and heat slightly over hot water. Beat in egg yolks, lemon juice, salt, and mustard with wire whisk or rotary beater. Beat until the sauce is thickened.

ESPAGNOLE

Sauce Mousseline

1 cup Hollandaise sauce   ½ cup heavy cream

To sauce add cream, stiffly whipped. Blend well and taste for seasoning. Serve with fish.

Sauce Béarnaise

3 shallots	4 tablespoons wine vinegar
1 sprig parsley	2 tablespoons water
1 sprig tarragon	4 egg yolks
1 sprig chervil	4 tablespoons butter,
(or use ½ teaspoon	softened
each dried tarragon	Salt
and chervil)	Cayenne pepper

Cook shallots, parsley, tarragon, and chervil in wine vinegar diluted with the water. Allow to boil 3 or 4 minutes and strain. Add strained liquid, a little at a time, to the egg yolks in the upper part of a double boiler, stirring constantly with a wire whisk. Cook over hot water, stirring constantly, until mixture thickens. Add, one at a time, 4 tablespoons softened butter. Blend well, salt to taste, and add a few grains of cayenne pepper. Chopped parsley and tarragon may be added. Serve with beefsteak, fish, or vegetables.

Sauce Parisienne

3 egg yolks	3 tablespoons butter
¼ cup cream	Salt
2 tablespoons tomato	Juice of ½ lemon
purée	¼ teaspoon dry mustard

Blend, in upper part of double boiler, egg yolks, cream, and tomato purée. Stir constantly over hot water with a wire whisk until mixture thickens. Add butter, one tablespoon at a time, stirring well each time. Add salt to taste, lemon juice, and mustard.

SPAGHETTI SAUCES

Oil and Garlic Sauce

⅔ cup fine olive oil	Fresh or dried sweet basil
3 cloves garlic	1 teaspoon salt

Heat olive oil with garlic cloves, which have been peeled and slightly crushed with a heavy-bladed knife or a wooden spoon. Add basil to taste, and salt. Press garlic cloves several times while the oil is heating, so that the essence of the garlic will distribute itself.

Arrange spaghetti on plates and add the garlic-flavored oil and basil—and bits of garlic as well, if desired. Sprinkle with freshly ground black pepper and a generous amount of freshly grated Parmesan cheese.

Mushroom Sauce

¾ pound mushrooms	1 teaspoon freshly ground
4 tablespoons olive oil	pepper
1 teaspoon salt	Juice of 2 lemons

Slice mushrooms very thin. Sauté in olive oil, adding salt and pepper. Cook quickly until just tender, remove from fire, and add lemon juice. Keep warm until ready to use.

Mario's Meat Sauce

3 stalks celery	1½-pound piece of lean beef
2 cloves garlic	cut from the round or
2 medium-sized onions	brisket
2 or 3 leeks	2 teaspoons salt
¼ cup pine nuts	Sweet basil leaves
4 or 5 sprigs parsley	2 cups thick tomato purée
4 tablespoons butter	Broth or canned consommé
1 cup thinly sliced	or 2 bouillon cubes dis-
mushrooms	solved in boiling water
1 thick loin pork chop	
(about 1 pound)	

Chop the following very fine or put through a fine grinder: celery with the leaves, if fresh; garlic; onions; leeks; pine nuts; and parsley—the Italian type if you can get it. Sauté this mixture in butter until just heated through. Add mushrooms (the dried Italian mushrooms, soaked in cold water, will add more flavor to this dish), pork chop, and piece of beef. Add salt, a few leaves of sweet basil, and tomato purée. Add enough broth to cover the meat. Bring the mixture to a boil and allow it to simmer 1 hour or until meat

is just tender. Remove meat and keep in a warm place. Continue simmering the sauce for another 1 or 1½ hours or until it is cooked down and quite thick. Correct the seasoning. Serve with freshly cooked spaghetti, thin slices of the cooked meat, and grated Parmesan cheese.

Spaghetti Sauce with Tuna

¼ pound dried Italian mushrooms	Salt
¼ cup olive oil	Black pepper
3 garlic cloves	Basil leaves
2 pounds fresh tomatoes	1 No. ½ can tuna fish

Soak mushrooms in water for 2 hours. Heat olive oil with cloves, peeled and lightly crushed. Drain mushrooms, add to the hot oil, and sauté for 4 minutes. Add tomatoes, peeled, seeded, and chopped very fine. Season with salt, black pepper, and a few leaves of basil, and let simmer until very thick—about 2 hours. Add tuna fish which you have flaked with a fork and cook with sauce 10 minutes.

Drain spaghetti and serve topped with sauce and plentifully sprinkled with chopped parsley and freshly ground black pepper.

Anchovy Onion Sauce

2 large or 4 medium-sized Spanish onions	Thyme Fresh or dried basil
4 tablespoons olive oil	1 cup tomato purée (Italian type)
10 anchovy fillets	¼ cup white wine
¼ cup chopped parsley	

Peel the onions and chop them fine. Sauté until delicately golden, but not brown, in olive oil. Add anchovy fillets, each cut in 2 pieces. Mix very carefully with the onions and add chopped parsley, a few leaves of thyme, and basil. Stir in tomato purée mixed with white wine and let the entire sauce cook down very slightly. Taste for seasoning, for whether you need additional salt depends upon the saltiness of the anchovies.

Pour sauce over spaghetti and add grated Parmesan cheese.

BUTTER SAUCES

Drawn Butter

Drawn butter really means melted butter. If you can find one, a small pipkin, or doll-size saucepan, is ideal for various butter sauces. Place the amount of butter you will need for the dish you are preparing in a small pan or pipkin and put it in a warm place where it will melt gradually, not cook.

Beurre Noisette (Browned Butter)

Heat butter in a small skillet or pipkin until it is a delicate brown but not burnt. Use on vegetable or fish.

Beurre Noir (Black Butter)

Heat 6 tablespoons butter until well browned and add lemon juice or wine vinegar to taste. Mix well and serve with fish, brains, or certain vegetables.

Sauce Amandine

Melt 6 tablespoons butter in a small skillet and sauté ⅓ cup blanched shredded almonds in the butter for several minutes or until almonds are delicately tinted. Serve with fish or sweetbreads.

Buttered Crumbs

4 tablespoons butter	Salt
⅓ cup very dry bread crumbs	Few grains cayenne pepper Paprika

Melt butter in a small skillet and sauté bread crumbs until nicely browned and crisp.

Season with salt, pepper, and a little paprika. Serve with fish or with vegetables or noodles.

You may substitute very small toasted croutons for the crumbs. Cut slices of bread into tiny cubes and toast well before sautéing.

Anchovy Butter (I)

5 tablespoons butter	1 tablespoon anchovy
Lemon juice	paste

Melt butter in a small skillet or pipkin and combine with anchovy paste (more than 1 tablespoon if you wish a stronger-flavored sauce). Add a few drops of lemon juice and serve with fish or with steak.

Anchovy Butter (II)

½ cup butter	Lemon juice
6 anchovy fillets or anchovy paste	1 teaspoon chopped parsley

Cream butter until quite light. Fold in anchovy fillets, finely chopped, or anchovy paste to taste. Add a few drops of lemon juice and parsley. Spread on fish or steak just before serving.

Parsley Butter

½ cup butter	Lemon juice
¼ cup chopped parsley	

Cream butter until soft and light. Add parsley and blend well. A few drops of lemon juice will add an extra dash of flavor to this sauce. Spread on fish just before serving or add to vegetables.

Herb Butter

½ cup butter
2 tablespoons parsley
2 tablespoons chopped
  chives
2 tablespoons chopped
  chervil
Grated garlic
Lemon juice

Cream butter until light and creamy. Add 2 tablespoons each of chopped parsley, chopped chives, chopped chervil (dried chervil if the fresh is not available), and just a flavoring of grated garlic. Add a few drops of lemon juice and blend well. Serve with fish or with chops or steak, or spread on halved French rolls. Place halves of rolls together and heat in a moderate oven (350°) until butter is melted and rolls are crisp.

Shrimp Butter

½ cup butter
3 tablespoons finely
  chopped cooked shrimp
Lemon juice
Cayenne

Cream butter until light. Add shrimp and blend well. Season with a few drops lemon juice and a few grains cayenne. Serve with fish, or use for a sandwich spread with cucumbers and sliced tomatoes.

TOMATO SAUCES

Spanish Sauce

1 medium-sized onion
3 tablespoons olive oil
2 tablespoons chopped
  green pepper
2 tablespoons finely
  chopped celery
1½ cups cooked or canned
  tomatoes
1 teaspoon salt
1 teaspoon black pepper

Sauté onion, finely chopped, in olive oil. Add pepper and celery. Add tomatoes, salt, and pepper. Let the sauce simmer ½ hour or until thickened. Use for omelets or meats, or over poached eggs.

Tomato Sauce (I)

2 cups canned tomatoes
Basil leaves
1 onion
Bay leaf
½ teaspoon salt
½ teaspoon black pepper
1 tablespoon butter

Cook tomatoes with a few leaves of basil, onion, and a small piece of bay leaf for 15 minutes over a very low heat. Strain, add salt and pepper, and simmer until sauce has cooked down by about ½ cup. Add butter and blend well. If a thick sauce is desired, add several balls of butter and flour, blended, and stir until thickened.

Tomato Sauce (II)

6 ripe tomatoes
½ teaspoon salt
1 small onion stuck with
  2 cloves
Few sprigs basil
½ cup chicken broth or
  consommé
1 tablespoon butter

Peel, quarter, and seed tomatoes. Place in a saucepan with salt, onion, and basil. Add chicken broth or consommé and simmer, covered, for 35 to 40 minutes or until tomatoes are well blended with seasonings. Strain through a fine sieve and reheat with 1 tablespoon butter. Correct the seasoning.

VARIATIONS

Tomato Cheese Sauce: Add ½ cup grated or diced cheese to tomato sauce and stir until melted. Use cheddar, mozzarella, or Swiss cheese.

Tomato Curry Sauce: Add 1 tablespoon curry powder to tomato sauce after it has been strained, and simmer 10 minutes. For a stronger curry flavor, add 2 tablespoons.

Creole Sauce

1 cup strained tomato
  sauce (see Tomato
  sauce [II])
1 green pepper, finely
  chopped
6 shallots, finely chopped
2 tablespoons butter
¼ cup dry sherry
Salt
Cayenne pepper

To tomato sauce, add shallots and pepper, sautéed in butter until well blended. Rinse the pan with sherry, add to sauce, and mix well. Salt to taste, add a few grains of cayenne pepper, and bring sauce to boiling point.

Barbecue Sauce

2 medium-sized onions,
  finely chopped
¼ cup olive oil
1 cup Italian tomato paste
1 teaspoon salt
1 teaspoon basil
½ cup steak sauce
¼ cup Worcestershire sauce
1 teaspoon dry mustard
½ cup strained honey
½ cup red wine

Sauté onions in olive oil until lightly browned. Add tomato paste, salt, basil, steak sauce, Worcestershire sauce, mustard, and honey. Allow to simmer 5 minutes, stirring constantly. Add red wine and allow sauce to come just to the boiling point. Taste for seasoning. Strain through a fine sieve.

For other barbecue sauces, see OUTDOOR COOKERY.

OTHER NON-DESSERT SAUCES

Currant Jelly Sauce

1 glass currant jelly	2 teaspoons prepared
4 tablespoons melted	mustard
butter	¼ cup port
½ teaspoon dry mustard	

Melt jelly over low heat. Add butter, prepared mustard, and dry mustard. Blend with wine and stir until smooth. Serve with venison or other game.

Chestnut Sauce for Turkey

12 or 15 chestnuts	1 teaspoon salt
2 tablespoons butter	1 tablespoon Kitchen
2 tablespoons flour	Bouquet
1½ cups consommé or turkey stock	

Roast chestnuts in the oven until mealy. Be certain to slit the hulls before roasting. When the chestnuts are roasted, peel and put through a ricer or food mill.

Make a roux of butter and flour and let it brown lightly. Add, stirring constantly, consommé or turkey stock and stir until thickened. Add salt, Kitchen Bouquet, and the puréed chestnuts. Stir until well blended and hot. Taste for seasoning. Serve with turkey.

VARIATION

With Turkey Giblets: Add turkey giblets which have been cooked in a little water, chopped fine, and sautéed in 2 tablespoons butter. Add ¼ cup chopped parsley before adding to the chestnut mixture. Stir in ½ cup heavy cream just before serving.

Giblet Sauce

Giblets of 1 turkey	2 tablespoons butter
1½ cups water	1 cup of broth
1 small onion stuck with clove	1 cup heavy cream
	2 egg yolks
Sprig of parsley	2 tablespoons chopped
½ teaspoon salt	parsley
3 or 4 shallots or 1 tablespoon minced onion	2 tablespoons cognac

Cook giblets in water flavored with 1 small onion, sprig of parsley, and salt. Remove, trim gristly parts from gizzard, and chop giblets or cut them in small dice. Strain the broth.

Sauté shallots or minced onion in butter and add the diced giblets. Add the broth in which you cooked the giblets and heat. Just before serving, add cream mixed with egg yolks and cook over hot water, stirring constantly, until mixture coats the spoon. Do not let it boil. Remove from fire, season with salt to taste, and stir in parsley and cognac.

Chasseur Sauce for Game

4 tablespoons butter	3 onions
2 tablespoons flour	Few leaves of celery
2 cups stock	3 ripe tomatoes
3 cups water	6 mushroom caps
1 teaspoon salt	2 ounces (¼ cup) red wine

Make a roux with 2 tablespoons butter and the flour, blending well.

Prepare stock made from trimmings of game birds. Cover wing tips, necks, and giblets with water seasoned with salt, an onion, and a stalk of celery. Simmer 1½ hours. Reduce to 1 cup.

Sauté 2 medium - sized onions, finely chopped, in 2 tablespoons butter until transparent. Add tomatoes which have been peeled, seeded, and diced, and mushroom caps, thinly sliced. Blend with broth and simmer 1½ hours, stirring occasionally. Just before serving, thicken with roux, add wine, blend well.

Devil Sauce (I)

6 shallots, finely chopped	2 tablespoons Escoffier
3 tablespoons butter	Sauce Diable
1½ teaspoons dry mustard	½ teaspoon salt
½ cup consommé	Cayenne pepper
½ cup white wine	Juice of ½ lemon

Sauté shallots or 1 small onion and 1 clove garlic in butter. Add mustard. Gradually add consommé and white wine, blending well. Add Escoffier Sauce Diable, and salt and pepper to taste. Just before serving add lemon juice.

Devil Sauce (II)

1 medium-sized onion, finely chopped	¼ teaspoon dry basil
	1 teaspoon salt
2 tablespoons butter	½ teaspoon crushed or
½ cup tomato purée	freshly ground black
2 tablespoons Worcestershire sauce	pepper
	2 tablespoons chopped
1 teaspoon dry mustard	parsley

Sauté the onion in butter until the onion is transparent. Add the tomato purée, Worcestershire sauce, mustard, basil, salt, and black pepper. Simmer for 10 minutes, stirring constantly. Add parsley and allow to come to a boil for 1 minute. Serve separately in a sauceboat.

VARIATIONS

With Mushrooms: Add to sauce 6 or 8 mushroom caps, thinly sliced and sautéed in 2 tablespoons butter for 5 minutes.

With Truffles: Add 2 or 3 truffles, thinly sliced, to the sauce.

Corn Relish for Cold Meats

1 cup whole kernel corn (canned or fresh)	2 tablespoons grated onion
2 tablespoons diced green pepper	1 teaspoon salt
	½ teaspoon black pepper
1 tablespoon chopped pimiento	½ teaspoon dry mustard
	4 tablespoons olive oil
½ cup finely chopped celery	1 tablespoon wine vinegar
	Few tarragon leaves

If fresh corn is used, cook 3 ears in enough cold water to cover until they boil. Allow to boil 1 minute. Cool and remove kernels from ear with a very sharp knife. Combine corn with pepper, pimiento, celery, onion, salt, pepper, mustard, olive oil, and wine vinegar, to which you have added tarragon. Blend well and allow mixture to stand an hour or two before serving.

Juliette Sauce

Mayonnaise
Whipped cream
Lemon juice

Salt
Watercress, finely chopped

Mix equal parts mayonnaise and whipped cream. Flavor with lemon juice and salt to taste. Just before serving, add ample watercress and sprinkle watercress on the top. Serve with salads or fish.

Soft Custard

3 egg yolks
4 tablespoons sugar
Salt

1 cup scalded milk
1 teaspoon vanilla or any liqueur

Combine egg yolks with sugar and a few grains of salt in the upper part of a double boiler. With a wooden spoon, gradually stir in milk and cook over hot water, stirring constantly, until mixture coats the spoon. Flavor with vanilla or with any liqueur you choose—chartreuse, Grand Marnier, Triple Sec, crème de cacao, etc. Serve with fruit or puddings.

Cucumber Sauce for Fish or Salads

1 cup sour cream
½ cup seeded grated cucumber
½ teaspoon salt

1 teaspoon finely chopped fresh dill
2 teaspoons finely cut chives
½ teaspoon black pepper

Combine cream with cucumber, salt, dill, chives, and pepper. Blend well and allow to stand in the refrigerator 1 or 2 hours before serving.

Cold Meat Sauce

1 tablespoon dry mustard
Dry white wine
1 tablespoon drained or freshly grated horseradish
2 tablespoons chili sauce

½ teaspoon salt
½ teaspoon paprika
½ teaspoon sugar
1 teaspoon Escoffier Sauce Diable

Combine mustard with enough white wine to make a stiff paste. Add horseradish, chili sauce, salt, paprika, sugar, and Escoffier Sauce Diable. Mix thoroughly and serve with any cold meat or fish. You may double or triple this recipe and keep the sauce in a jar.

DESSERT SAUCES

Chocolate Sauce

2 squares unsweetened chocolate
6 tablespoons water
Vanilla

½ cup sugar
Few grains of salt
3 tablespoons butter

Melt chocolate in water over a very low flame. Add sugar and salt and cook slowly, stirring constantly, until slightly thickened. Add butter and a little vanilla to flavor, and blend the butter into the sauce. Serve hot or cold.

VARIATIONS

With Cream: Whip ⅓ cup heavy cream and fold into ½ cup chocolate sauce. Sprinkle with grated chocolate before serving.

With Almonds: Combine ½ cup sauce with ¼ cup blanched, toasted almonds and serve with ice cream or other desserts.

Rum-flavored: Flavor ½ cup chocolate sauce with 1 tablespoon dark rum. Blend well.

Mint-flavored: Flavor with mint extract or with white crème de menthe.

Coffee-flavored: Melt chocolate with 6 tablespoons strong coffee instead of water and use additional coffee for flavoring if needed.

With Cinnamon: Add ¼ teaspoon cinnamon to sauce for subtle flavoring.

Foamy Sauce for Puddings

4 tablespoons brown	1 egg white
sugar	1 cup whipped cream
1 egg yolk	Jamaica rum or cognac

Combine half brown sugar with egg yolk and beat until light and well blended. Beat egg white until light and foamy. Add other half brown sugar to egg white gradually, beating well after each addition, and beat egg until stiff. Combine with yolk and add whipped cream. Flavor with Jamaica rum or cognac to taste.

Hard Sauce

| ½ cup butter | Brandy or liqueur |
| 1 cup confectioners' sugar | |

Cream butter until light. Gradually beat in sugar, beating until sauce is very smooth and light. Flavor with brandy or liqueur, beating in flavoring a little at a time until well blended. Chill thoroughly before using.

VARIATIONS

Orange-flavored: Flavor with orange juice or orange curaçao and beat in a little grated orange rind.

Lemon-flavored: Add grated lemon rind to the sauce before flavoring.

With Almonds: Add 3 tablespoons chopped almonds.

With Brown Sugar: Cream butter. Use brown sugar instead of confectioners' sugar, reducing amount to ¾ cup, and proceed as above. Flavor with Jamaica rum or brandy.

Ginger-flavored: Add finely cut crystallized ginger to hard sauce.

Brandy Sauce

4 tablespoons butter	⅔ cup heavy cream
½ cup confectioners' sugar	1 jigger cognac or other
2 egg yolks	brandy

Cream butter with sugar. Gradually work in egg yolks. Combine with cream and cook over hot water, stirring constantly, until mixture coats the spoon. Flavor with cognac or other brandy.

Caramel Sauce

| 1 cup of sugar | 1 cup boiling water |

Caramelize sugar by heating it slowly over medium heat in a heavy skillet or pan, stirring it constantly. The sugar should melt and develop a rich brown color. Add boiling water to the caramelized sugar and mix well. Bring mixture to a boil and let it simmer for 10 minutes. Cool and serve with custards, puddings, or ice cream.

Butterscotch Sauce

1¼ cups brown sugar	⅓ cup heavy cream
⅓ cup butter	Vanilla
Salt	

Combine sugar with butter, a few grains of salt, and cream. Cook in upper part of double boiler, stirring occasionally, 1 hour. Flavor with a few drops of vanilla. This sauce may be used with toasted, blanched almonds for ice cream or puddings.

Simple Fruit Sauce

1 cup fruit juices	Lemon juice
1 cup sugar	Grated lemon rind
½ cup water	Kirsch or Triple Sec
1 tablespoon cornstarch	

Mix fruit juices (use any combination of canned or fresh juices, or a single variety of fruit juice). Mix together sugar and water and blend with cornstarch. Heat over boiling water and stir until thickened. Simmer 5 or 6 minutes, remove from heat, and cool. Add fruit juice after mixture has cooled. Flavor with a little lemon juice and grated lemon rind or with a little kirsch or Triple Sec.

Raspberry Sauce

| 1 pint fresh ripe | ½ cup sugar |
| raspberries | |

Wash and force raspberries through a food mill or fine sieve. Add sugar and mix well. Bring mixture to a boil over a medium heat. Simmer until it forms a heavy syrup.

VARIATIONS

With Canned or Frozen Raspberries: May be used instead of fresh berries.

With Crème de Cassis: Combine cooled syrup with 2 ounces (¼ cup) Crème de Cassis before serving.

With Kirsch: Flavor syrup with a little kirsch.

With Whole Berries: If fresh whole berries are used, let them stand with the sugar for 2 hours before cooking.

BREADS

QUICK BREADS—
RECIPES WITH BASIC MIX

If you have storage room in the refrigerator, this basic dough recipe is the greatest possible boon for baking biscuits, muffins, shortcake, cobblers, coffee cake, or nut bread, or for making pancakes or waffles on short notice. The basic ingredients—flour, salt, shortening, and double-action baking powder—are combined in quantities that are easy to work with, easy to store, and easy to use. The recipe will make about 14 cups of the blend. To store, place in glass jars or bowls, cover lightly, and store in the refrigerator. It will keep well for 3 to 4 weeks.

Basic Mix

For the basic mix for biscuits, waffles, shortcake, coffee cakes, etc., you will need:

12 cups (3 quarts) sifted flour	**4 tablespoons double-acting baking powder**
2 tablespoons salt	**2 cups (1 pound) shortening**

Sift the flour once. Measure 3 cups at a time into sifter, adding 1 tablespoon baking powder and 1½ teaspoons salt for each 3 cups flour. Sift into large bowl. Repeat until full amount of dry ingredients has been sifted. Cut in shortening with a pastry blender or 2 knives until the mixture is finely divided and resembles coarse meal. This will make about 14 cups basic mix. Place in glass jars or crockery bowls and cover lightly with cloth or plate to allow circulation of air. Store in refrigerator or other very cool, dry place.

For a smaller amount, use 6 cups sifted flour, 2 tablespoons double-acting baking pow-

der, 1 tablespoon salt, and 1 cup (½ pound) shortening. For convenience, sift flour mixture 3 cups at a time, as above.

Biscuits

Measure 2 cups basic mix into a bowl. Add about ½ cup milk and stir until a soft dough is formed (use more or less milk, depending upon the quality of the flour). Turn out dough on a lightly floured board and knead 30 seconds. Pat or roll ½ inch thick and cut with floured 2-inch biscuit cutter, or cut in squares or diamonds with a sharp floured knife. Bake on ungreased baking sheet in a very hot oven (450°) 12 to 15 minutes.   *(Makes 10 to 12 biscuits.)*

Buttermilk Biscuits

Stir ¼ teaspoon soda into 2 cups basic mix. Substitute buttermilk for sweet milk and proceed as directed above.

(Makes 10 to 12 biscuits.)

Drop Biscuits

Measure 2 cups basic mix into a bowl. Add ¾ cup milk and stir until a soft dough is formed. Drop from teaspoon on lightly greased baking sheet. Bake in a very hot oven (450°) 12 to 15 minutes.

(Makes 10 to 12 biscuits.)

Muffins

2 cups basic mix	1 egg, well beaten
2 tablespoons sugar	¾ cup milk

Measure basic mix into a bowl and add the sugar, egg, and milk. Mix only until dry ingredients are dampened. Fill greased muffin pans two thirds full. Bake in a hot oven (425°) 20 minutes or until done.

(Makes 8 large or 12 medium muffins.)

VARIATIONS

Rich Muffins: For rich muffins, add 2 tablespoons melted butter after adding milk.

Marmalade Muffins: Omit sugar and mix 3 tablespoons orange marmalade with the milk. Before baking, top each muffin with ½ teaspoon marmalade.

Jiffy Pancakes

2 cups basic mix	2 eggs, well beaten
1¼ cups milk	

Measure the mix into a bowl. Combine the eggs and the milk, and add gradually to the mix, mixing only enough to dampen flour. The batter will be lumpy. Bake on a hot griddle. *(Makes 7 to 8 4-inch pancakes.)*

Quick Nut Bread

3 cups basic mix	1 egg, well beaten
¾ cup sugar	1 cup milk
1 cup finely chopped nut meats	

Measure basic mix into a bowl. Add sugar and mix well. Combine the egg and milk, and add to flour mixture. Mix just enough to blend. Fold in the nuts and turn into a buttered 9-inch loaf pan. Bake in a moderate oven (350°) about 1 hour. Cool, wrap in waxed paper, and store overnight before slicing.

Note: If desired, 1 teaspoon grated orange rind may be added to the batter.

QUICK BREADS—
RECIPES WITHOUT BASIC MIX

A good baking-powder biscuit should be well shaped and well baked, with a golden brown crust, a level top, and straight sides. It should be served piping hot and should be tender and flaky, never doughy.

Basic Baking Powder Biscuit

2 cups sifted flour	5 tablespoons shortening
2½ teaspoons double-acting baking powder	(butter, vegetable shortening, or butter substitute)
¾ teaspoon salt	¼ cup milk (approximately)

Note: If cake flour is used, use only 2 teaspoons baking powder and reduce milk to ½ cup.

Sift the flour, measure it, add baking powder and salt, and sift into a bowl. Cut in the shortening with a pastry blender or two knives until it looks like coarse meal. Add milk and stir until you have a soft dough.

Turn onto a lightly floured board and knead for 30 seconds. Pat or roll dough lightly ½ inch thick and cut with a 2-inch cutter. If you wish crusty, richer biscuits, pat or roll dough ¼ inch thick and dip each biscuit into melted butter before placing on baking sheet. Bake on a baking sheet in a very hot oven (450°) 12 to 15 minutes. *(Makes 12 to 15 biscuits.)*

VARIATIONS

Shortcake: For shortcake, add 2 tablespoons sugar to the flour mixture, divide dough into two parts, using ⅔ for the bottom and ⅓ for the top. Pat or roll the larger section on a floured board and shape evenly. Place on an ungreased baking sheet. Dot well with butter or brush heavily with melted butter. Bake in a very hot oven (450°) 12 to 15 minutes. Remove top section and place sweetened fruit on the bottom crust and cover. Serve with heavy cream or whipped cream.

Herbed Biscuits: Add 3 tablespoons chopped parsley and 2 tablespoons chopped chives to biscuit recipe. Roll, cut, and bake as directed.

Cheese Biscuits: Add 1 cup grated sharp cheese to the dry mixture in the recipe for baking powder biscuits. Add a tiny pinch of cayenne pepper. Proceed as above.

Corn Muffins

1 cup sifted flour	⅔ cup yellow corn meal
3 teaspoons double-acting baking powder	1 egg, well beaten
	¾ cup milk
2 tablespoons sugar	⅓ cup butter
¾ teaspoon salt	

Sift the flour and measure. Add baking powder, sugar, and salt, and sift. Add corn meal to the mixture. Combine the egg and milk and add to the flour and corn meal mixture. Add melted butter. Mix only enough to dampen the flour and meal. Fill buttered muffin tins two thirds full and bake in a hot oven (400°).

(Makes 6 large or 12 small muffins.)

Blueberry Muffins

2 cups sifted flour	Milk
3 teaspoons double-acting baking powder	1 egg, well beaten
	½ cup melted butter
3 tablespoons sugar	¾ teaspoon cinnamon
Salt	1 cup blueberries

Sift flour once and measure. Combine with baking powder, sugar, cinnamon, salt. Sift again. Combine milk and beaten egg; mix with dry ingredients. Add butter; mix until flour is dampened. Lastly, fold in the blueberries, fill buttered muffin tins two thirds full, and bake in a hot oven (400°) for 25 minutes.

(Makes 6 large or 12 small muffins.)

Sweet Milk Waffles

2 eggs	¼ cup melted butter
1½ cups milk	2½ teaspoons double-acting baking powder
2 cups sifted flour	
¾ teaspoon salt	

Beat eggs until light and lemon-colored. Add milk gradually and continue beating. Mix in sifted dry ingredients and mix until smooth. Fold in melted butter and blend with the batter. Bake in a hot waffle iron until steaming ceases. *(Makes 4 to 5 waffles.)*

VARIATIONS

Bacon Waffles: Add ½ cup crisp crushed bacon to the batter before baking.

Nut Waffles: Add 1 cup coarsely chopped walnuts to the batter before baking.

Chocolate Waffles: Add ¼ cup sugar and 2 tablespoons Dutch process cocoa to the batter.

Coconut Waffles: Add 1 cup shredded coconut to the batter.

Sour Cream Waffles

2 eggs	½ teaspoon soda
1 cup sour cream	¾ teaspoon salt
1½ cups flour	4 tablespoons melted butter
2 teaspoons baking powder	

Beat eggs until light and lemon-colored. Beat in sour cream. Sift flour, baking powder, soda, and salt, and add gradually to cream-and-egg mixture. Add 4 tablespoons melted butter. Blend well. *(Makes 4 to 5 waffles.)*

Note: This makes a much heavier batter, but it will be found to bake exceedingly light.

These waffles are delicious as a fruit shortcake base. Serve them with crushed raspberries, strawberries, or sliced peaches, and top with whipped cream. They may also be used for chicken or ham shortcakes.

Corn Meal Cakes

½ cup sifted flour	2 cups water-ground corn meal
1 teaspoon soda	
1 teaspoon baking powder	1 egg, well beaten
1 teaspoon salt	1 cup (or more) sour milk or buttermilk

Combine flour with soda, baking powder, and salt. Sift. Combine with corn meal. Mix egg with 1 cup buttermilk or sour milk, and combine with dry ingredients. Add more milk, if needed, to make a very thin batter. Bake on a hot greased griddle.

Buckwheat Cakes

½ yeast cake	1 teaspoon salt
2½ cups warm water	2 cups buckwheat flour
1 tablespoon brown sugar or 2 tablespoons maple syrup	½ cup water-ground corn meal
	1 teaspoon soda

Dissolve yeast in warm water. Add salt and brown sugar or maple syrup. Stir in buckwheat flour and corn meal. Mix well, cover, and allow to rise overnight in a warm place. In the morning stir the mixture well, add soda dissolved in a little warm water, mix again, and bake on a hot greased griddle.

Corn Bread

¾ cup corn meal	2 teaspoons baking powder
1 cup boiling water	
2 tablespoons butter	1 cup milk
Salt	1 tablespoon sugar
2 eggs, well beaten	

Scald corn meal with boiling water. Mix in butter and ½ teaspoon salt. Beat eggs until light and lemon-colored; combine with baking powder, milk, and sugar. Add to the corn-meal mixture and mix well. Pour into well-buttered baking pan and bake in a moderately hot oven (375°) about 25 minutes or until nicely browned and thoroughly cooked.

Buttermilk Corn Bread

2 eggs, well beaten	1 cup corn meal
2 cups buttermilk	¼ cup melted butter
¾ teaspoon soda	

Beat eggs until light and lemon-colored. Beat in buttermilk, in which you have dissolved soda. Gradually blend this with corn meal, stir until smooth, and add melted butter. Pour into well-buttered baking pan and bake approximately 30 minutes in a moderately hot oven (375°).

Corn Meal Spoon Bread

2 cups milk	4 tablespoons butter
1 cup corn meal	4 egg yolks, well beaten
1 teaspoon salt	4 egg whites, stiffly beaten

Heat milk in the upper part of a double boiler. When it is almost at the boiling point, add corn meal and stir until mixture is thickened and smooth. Add salt and butter, and blend well. Remove from the fire and pour onto the well-beaten egg yolks, beating well. Finally fold in the stiffly beaten egg whites and pour into a well-buttered casserole—the 2-quart size is best. Bake in a 375° oven 35 to 40 minutes or until well risen and nicely browned. Serve from the casserole with a spoon.

Mabelle's Snickerdoodle

1 cup flour	½ teaspoon cinnamon
1 cup sugar	½ cup milk
1 teaspoon baking powder	1 egg
¼ teaspoon salt	¼ cup melted butter
Granulated sugar	

Sift together the flour, baking powder, salt, sugar, and cinnamon. Mix with milk and egg. Blend well and stir in melted butter. Spread thinly in 9-by-12-inch baking-pan, sprinkle with granulated sugar, and bake in a hot oven (400°) about 25 minutes.

French Pancakes

1 cup flour	¾ cup milk
¼ cup powdered sugar	3 tablespoons heavy cream
Pinch of salt	1 tablespoon melted butter
2 eggs	1 teaspoon cognac
2 egg yolks	

Sift together flour, powdered sugar, and a pinch of salt. Beat eggs and egg yolks well and mix with the dry ingredients. Add milk and heavy cream, and stir until smooth. Finally, add melted butter and cognac. Strain this batter through a fine sieve.

It is better to let the batter stand for an hour or so before cooking. Cook these pancakes in a hot pan, lightly buttered. Pour in enough batter for 1 pancake and tilt the pan so that the batter will spread. Cook until lightly browned on one side, about 1 minute, and turn and brown on the other side. Fold or roll the pancakes, and keep them hot on a hot platter or in a hot baking dish.

VARIATIONS

With Jelly: Spread with jelly or jam. Roll and sprinkle with powdered sugar.

With Fruits: Spread with sugared fresh fruit, such as strawberries, raspberries, or peaches which have been flavored with a little kirsch or Cointreau. Roll and sprinkle with powdered sugar.

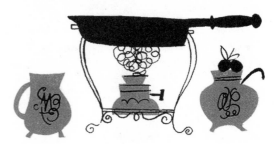

Crêpes Suzette: Have your pancakes baked and folded and on a hot platter. The final performance should be done at table on a table stove or in a chafing dish. Melt in the chafing dish or crêpes suzette pan 4 tablespoons butter which you have creamed with 4 tablespoons powdered sugar. Add to this the juice of half a small orange and the grated rind: enough to make 1 tablespoon. Stir into this 2 tablespoons orange curaçao and heat the folded pancakes in this mixture, basting them well with the sauce. You may add 1 or 2 tablespoons cognac at last minute and blaze crêpes before serving.

With Strawberries: Pancakes may be sprinkled with powdered sugar and rolled and kept hot. Serve with crushed strawberries mixed with sugar and topped with whipped cream.

Pancakes as an Entrée

Omit sugar and cognac from the recipe and bake the pancakes as above.

VARIATIONS

Parmesan: Roll with creamed chicken or mushrooms, top with grated Parmesan cheese, and brown briefly under broiler.

With Cheese: Roll the pancakes with a rich cheese sauce: a fine Béchamel sauce to which you have added grated Swiss, cheddar, or crumbled Roquefort cheese, and ½ teaspoon dry mustard and a few grains of cayenne. Sprinkle more grated cheese over the top and place under the broiler for just a moment.

With Sausages: Roll cooked sausages in French pancakes and arrange 2 or 3 to a serving on a hot platter or on individual plates. Serve for breakfast or luncheon with a little real maple syrup.

Breakfast: Sprinkle with powdered sugar and serve for breakfast with maple syrup or honey.

Brioche

1 yeast cake	6 eggs
½ cup lukewarm water	4 cups flour
2 tablespoons sugar	1 cup melted butter
1 teaspoon salt	

For the sponge: Dissolve the yeast cake in lukewarm water and add 1 cup flour. Mix until smooth and set aside in a warm place for about 2 hours, or until it doubles in bulk. Mix the other dry ingredients together and add 3 eggs, unbeaten. Mix until smooth, and gradually add the melted butter, beating it in as you go. Add the other 3 eggs, one at a time, beating after each addition. Add the sponge and mix it in thoroughly. When it is thoroughly mixed, cover and let it rise again in a warm place for about 3 hours. Deflate it by punching the dough down well, and place it in the refrigerator overnight or until ready to use. Cut off pieces, form into any desired shape, and place in buttered pans. The traditional pans are small fluted ones, and the traditional shape is a roll with a small topknot. Allow to rise again until almost double in bulk. Brush with beaten egg and bake in a moderately hot oven (375°) until delicately browned.

VARIATIONS

Brioche Crown: You may form a crown of brioche by working the dough into a large roll, laying it in the pan in a large circle, and topping with another and smaller roll.

Brioche Ring: Roll out the dough and cover with any desired filling, such as softened butter, sugar, and nuts or raisins. Roll and form into a ring, slash around the outer edges, and allow it to rise. Bake.

Brioche Loaf: Form the brioche into loaves and bake. This makes a delicate and delicious bread for sandwiches.

Braids: Form into three small rolls and braid. Bake plain or fill with a nut, butter, and sugar mixture and top with granulated sugar.

Popovers

2 eggs	1 cup milk
1 cup flour	1 tablespoon melted butter
¼ teaspoon salt	

Beat the eggs until light, add the flour, salt, milk, and melted butter, and beat for 2 minutes.

Butter ovenproof custard cups or muffin pans. If you use iron pans have them very hot. Fill the cups or pans about a third full and bake in a very hot oven (450°) about 20 minutes. Then reduce the heat to moderate (350°) and continue baking for another 20 minutes or so. *(Makes 6 popovers.)*

Popovers should not be a problem. It is the attempt to bake them too short a time and in an oven that is not hot enough that results in failure. A good popover should be crusty and crisp and well dried out inside. A wet, sticky popover has no place on the table.

WHITE BREADS

Bread and the art of bread-making are as old as time. But an opinion to which I have never been able to subscribe is that home-baked bread is the be-all and end-all of perfection. Though women have written rapturously of the thrill of getting their hands into the dough and the joy of smelling the bread baking in the oven, I have yet to taste any home-made bread that can equal that good crusty French or Italian bread made by the village baker or sold in a city side street. However, for those who must bake bread I will outline the procedure, which requires a good deal of time, care, and effort.

Your flour should be an all-purpose flour. Soft cake flours are for delicate baking.

There are several kinds of yeast. Compressed yeast, which is quicker-acting than the dried yeast, must be kept in a cool place or it will spoil. The liquids used in bread-making are water, milk, or sometimes, potato water. Sweetening is usually added to bread. This can be either sugar or honey. Many people use vegetable shortenings or lards when making breads, but if you wish good flavor and texture you should use only butter. Temperature for rising and oven temperature are exceedingly important. It is truly a laboratory process to make bread correctly. The finished product should be an even-sized, medium-brown loaf with a good crust and a fine grain, not lumpy.

Basic White Bread

1 cake compressed yeast	1 tablespoon salt
2 cups milk, which has been scalded and allowed to become lukewarm	6 cups sifted all-purpose flour
2 tablespoons honey	4 tablespoons butter

Break the yeast into small bits in a mixing bowl. Add the milk, honey, and salt. Stir well until the yeast is completely dissolved.

Add half the flour by cupfuls and beat well with a wooden spoon until dough is smooth. Add the melted butter. Now add the remaining 3 cups of flour and work it well with your hands until thoroughly mixed.

Turn the dough onto a floured board, cover with a large bowl, and let it rest for approximately 10 to 12 minutes. Uncover and knead with the hands until exceedingly smooth and puffy. Place in a large bowl, cover, and allow to rise in a warm place for 2 hours or until double in bulk.

Uncover and deflate the dough with several hard punches. Cover and let rise again until double in bulk.

Turn out onto floured board and divide

into 2 parts. Flatten each part with the hands and form into a smooth, well-shaped loaf. Place in baking pans which have been buttered, cover with a cloth, and allow the loaves to rise in a warm place until they have doubled in bulk. Brush well with melted butter and bake in a moderately hot oven (375°) until done. This should take 40 to 55 minutes.

(Makes 2 loaves.)

VARIATIONS

Nut Bread: Add 1½ cups coarsely chopped nuts.

Raisin Bread: Add 2 cups seedless raisins.

Cinnamon Bread: Before shaping bread into loaves, roll out dough, spread with softened butter, sprinkle well with sugar and cinnamon, and roll and shape into a loaf. Place in loaf pan and allow to rise until double in bulk.

Rolls

The above basic bread recipe may be used for all types of rolls.

For rolls, instead of forming the dough into loaves, form it into rolls of any desired shape, place on a greased pan, brush well with melted butter, and let rolls rise in a warm place until they have doubled in bulk. Rolls should be baked in a hot oven (425°) for approximately 15 to 18 minutes.

Parker House Rolls: Roll dough to ½-inch thickness, cut with a 3-inch cutter, brush with melted butter, and fold over so that the edges just meet. Brush top with melted butter, place rolls on a greased baking pan, and proceed as above.

Twist Roll: Roll dough ½ inch thick, cut in 1-inch strips, and roll into long rolls 8 or 9 inches long. Twist 2 strips together from opposite directions and even them at the ends. Brush with melted butter.

Crescents: Roll dough ¼ inch thick, cut it into large squares and then into triangles. Roll from the broad end to the point. Press down and bend the ends to form a crescent. Brush with melted butter.

Cloverleaf Rolls: Form small pieces of dough into balls, dip them in melted butter, and place 3 in each section of a buttered muffin tin.

Butter Rolls: Roll dough to ¼-inch thickness, cut in small squares, dip each square into melted butter, and place in muffin tins, using about 6 to 8 squares to each roll.

Cinnamon Rolls: Roll dough to ½-inch thickness and spread with softened butter, brown sugar, and cinnamon. Add ½ to 1 cup of Sultana raisins and roll. Cut in 1-inch slices, place very close together in a greased pan, and brush with melted butter. Or proceed as above and place in muffin tins in which you have placed ½ cup brown sugar creamed with ½ cup butter. Place slices of roll on this mixture and brush with melted butter.

Note: You may add pecan halves to the creamed sugar-and-butter mixture.

MISCELLANEOUS

BREAD RECIPES

Garlic Bread

Rub a French or Italian loaf with a large clove of garlic so that the clove thoroughly disintegrates into the crust. Heat in a moderate oven (350°) until bread is heated through and crisp.

Buttered Garlic Bread

Melt ¼ pound butter in a pan which you have rubbed well with a clove of garlic. Grate another clove of garlic and allow it to stand in a warm place for a few minutes, then add to melted butter.

Slice not quite through a loaf of French bread, leaving a portion of the crust intact so slices may be broken off after heating. Spread slices apart and pour garlic butter in between slices. Heat in a moderate oven (350°) until crisp and heated through.

Toast

Making toast in a broiler is something that should not baffle as many people as it does. Bread that is at least a day old makes better toast than fresh bread. Cut it in ¼- to ½-inch slices, depending upon how moist or crisp you like your toast. If you want it moist, brown the slices very quickly under a brisk flame. If you prefer dry, crisp toast, place thin slices well below a medium flame and toast quite slowly on both sides. Spread toast with softened butter and return to the oven for a minute; or brush with melted butter and serve immediately; or serve dry, in a toast rack.

VARIATIONS

Grilled Cinnamon Toast: Mix ½ teaspoon cinnamon with ¼ cup brown sugar. Toast bread on one side only. Spread untoasted side with softened butter and sugar-and-cinnamon mixture. Place under broiler flame until the sugar bubbles.

Plain Cinnamon Toast: Toast bread on both sides until delicately browned. Butter and sprinkle with sugar and cinnamon.

Marmalade Toast: Toast bread lightly on both sides, butter, and spread with orange marmalade. Run under broiler long enough to heat marmalade through.

Melba Toast: Cut stale bread in very thin slices. Place in a cold oven on a baking sheet. Light oven and let it come to slow heat (300°). Leave the toast in the oven until evenly browned and crisp, turning it several times.

Milk Toast: Place slices of hot buttered toast in a soup plate. Sprinkle with salt and pepper and pour over it hot milk or cream.

French Toast: Beat 2 eggs lightly and combine with 1 cup rich milk. Dip slices of stale bread into the mixture and sauté in 3 tablespoons butter in a skillet, turning with a spatula or pancake turner, until both sides are lightly browned. Serve with sugar and lemon or with maple syrup. Or fry in deep fat, heated to 380°, 1 or 2 minutes or until nicely browned.

Croutons: Cut stale bread into cubes of any desired size and bake in a slow oven (300°) until crisp and well browned. Sauté cubes in 4 tablespoons butter. Serve with soup or, on occasion, with noodles.

OUTDOOR COOKERY

There should be simple food of excellent quality, careful cooking, plenty of everything, and well-organized but informal service. Outdoor cooking is primarily man's work, and man-sized portions and simple menus should be the rule.

OUTDOOR COOKERY

Our ancestors, after a day's hunting in the forest or sloshing through marshes and soggy fields, were most enthusiastic outdoor eaters. They would tear a leg off an animal carcass, sear it over a roaring fire, and cram it down with a little wild garlic, perhaps some bananas, and a few leaves from some long-since-forgotten tree. Though such procedure lacked refinement, it might well be borne in mind by the outdoor cook of today. Outdoor cooking is primarily man's work, and man-sized portions and simple menus should be the rule. What fun is a picnic or a barbecue if guest and host are hampered by formality or fuss? Whether you have a small electric grill on the stamp-sized terrace of a New York apartment house or an outdoor fireplace-stove combination in the heart of Wyoming, the guiding principles are the same. For satisfaction all around, there should be simple food of excellent quality, careful cooking, good liquor or wines, plenty of everything, and well-organized but informal service.

No matter how well schooled you may be in buying meat for the family, meat cooked on the outdoor grill presents different problems from that cooked on the kitchen stove. Listed below are the various cuts I find most successful, and the approximate cooking time per pound for spitted meats. Cooking times necessarily vary with the type of grill used.

For some reason, the imagination of certain outdoor cooks never seems to get beyond the broiled-steak, chop, or chicken stage. Without speaking slightly of a good chop, I suggest that it may be well to investigate some other kinds of meats before you get the chop habit.

If you do choose chops for outdoor cooking, never buy thin ones. In fact, I can think of no reason for ever having a thin chop. With an outdoor grill and outdoor appetites, there is even less reason for them.

Note: Always let meat or chicken stand at room temperature at least 2 hours before cooking.

BEEF

Meat to be cooked outdoors *must* be of the best quality. Meat is likely to be the main part of the meal, and open-fire cooking brings out the flavor as no kitchen range can; hence the meat must be good enough to justify the pains taken to cook it by this method. Buy well-marbled beef with flaky, creamy white fat and a deep, cherry red color where it has been cut. Be sure it is well aged.

Steaks

Sirloin, porterhouse, and tenderloin cuts are best. Allow 1 pound beef per person. If there are exceptionally good appetites to be catered to—and they should be encouraged— a pound is not too much.

Choose a thick steak cut from good-quality beef. Have your fire well-fed and full of life. Sear the meat well on both sides with a high heat and then bank your fire slightly, turning the meat frequently for cooking.

Pan-broiling is sometimes an effective way of cooking steak. You must have your pan or griddle spitting hot and just barely smeared with fat—the trimmings of the steak will do nicely. Turn frequently and pour off grease as it accumulates so that the steak does not fry.

Marinated Steak

⅔ cup olive oil
½ teaspoon fresh-ground pepper
Dash of salt
Juice of 1 lemon
1 clove garlic

One of the most delicious steaks I have ever eaten was marinated in olive oil and condiments for 12 hours before it was broiled. Try it this way:

Mix olive oil with pepper, salt, and lemon juice. If you like the flavor of garlic with steak, rub the meat lightly with a clove of garlic before placing it in the oil. Let the steak stand in this marinade in a warm place 12 or 15 hours, or even 24 hours. Turn it several times. When ready to broil, remove the steak from the oil and grill as usual.

Be economical—use some of the same oil to grill onions to be served with the steak.

Steak Sandwiches

For steak sandwiches use tenderloin, shell or club, rump or top sirloin. Steak for sandwiches, unlike steak to be served in the ordi-nary way, should be cut from ½ to 1 inch thick and grilled very quickly.

If you have a large, hungry crowd which loves good steak and yet requires simple, quick service, try this:

Buy a whole tenderloin from your butcher and have him trim it for you. Tell him you want to broil it whole. Oil it well with olive oil or butter, place it on a grill over hot coals, and watch it very carefully. Turn it often and add oil or butter to it from time to time; frequent basting is the rule for this lean cut. Salt and pepper well.

When done to taste (about 30 minutes average cooking time), remove to a plank which has been heated. Slice the steak very thin and place the slices between pieces of lightly toasted and buttered French bread.

A tray of condiments for the sandwiches is in order. It might include raw onion, relishes of several different varieties, sliced tomatoes, and a bowl of potato chips or shoe-string potatoes. Repeats on the sandwiches are usually appreciated; so plan for them.

An easier way of making the same sandwiches is to split a loaf of French bread the long way, toast it lightly, and butter it well. Arrange slices of the steak on one half, cover with the other, and slice through the loaf in large sections.

Hamburger

The most important thing about hamburger is the quality. Don't buy ready-ground hamburger if you value the true beef flavor. Buy a good piece of the round without fat or a piece of the rump or the top sirloin and have it ground to your individual order. For outdoor appetites allow at least ¾ pound per person, and have some extra in reserve. Leftover hamburger, if there should be any, is not hard to use up.

Take the hamburger out of the refrigerator at least 2 hours before grilling. Hamburger must be cooked quickly and served at once, so be sure to have everything, including your guests, in readiness before you begin.

Just in case you've never cooked hamburger on a grill, here is the step-by-step procedure for truly delicious ground beef:

Choose a good piece of top sirloin or boneless rump and have your butcher grind it for you. Buy not less than 3 or 4 pounds. Have it in one large lump and be very careful not to squeeze it or press it down. Mold it very tenderly with your hands into a round steak about 1½ inches thick. Pat, do not press.

If you are broiling it, have your coals just at the peak of glowing heat and slip your steak on a wire grill over the coals. Let it sear on one side, turn, and sear quickly on the other side. Sprinkle heavily with salt and pepper—freshly ground pepper and coarse salt are best—and turn again. Salt the other side and pepper it. By that time the hamburger should be crusted on the outside, tender and rare on the inside.

Slice and serve with slices of onion or with succotash and French bread. Red wine is an old friend of this dish.

Hamburger can be cooked on a dry griddle or in a dry skillet. Salt the skillet or griddle well before putting the meat in, and have it hot as can be. Dress with barbecue sauce if you like.

VEAL

A boned and rolled leg of veal makes a fine roast for the barbecue, lending itself particularly well to a highly flavored barbecue sauce for basting. Veal has a bland flavor that is improved by pungent seasoning. Salt pork tied round the outside of the veal is a good lubricant and will prevent burning. You may buy only the cushion—the fleshy part of the leg—or the whole leg prepared for roasting. Allow 30 to 35 minutes per pound, for veal must be well done.

Veal shoulder may be boned and roasted in the same way as the leg.

I do not advise using the loin or the ribs for roasting outdoors.

Veal Chops

Use kidney chops 1 to 1½ inches thick for outdoor cooking. Broil thoroughly over a medium-hot bed of coals. Serve with a good barbecue sauce.

Veal Steaks

Veal steaks are cut from the leg. They should be about an inch thick to be really delicious. Panbroil or sauté them. Butter and slow cooking improve veal. Veal steaks are good also broiled with a slice of salt pork.

PORK

This delicious meat should be thoroughly cooked through, for safety's sake if for no other reason. Underdone pork is no treat.

Many people think they should never eat pork in the summer, but it is a delicate summer dish, especially suited to cooking outdoors.

Roast Pork

Fresh ham or leg of pork is probably the best cut to roast on the fire. If possible, get a leg with the skin still intact. Score it and let your mouth water for the cracklings which will result from the browning. Although it is not necessary to have the leg boned and rolled for the spit, boning facilitates even cooking and makes carving much easier. Give the pork a rather low fire and roast 35 minutes for each pound. Frequent basting greatly helps the ham. Thyme rubbed into the flesh before roasting gives pork added flavor.

Loin: A whole loin of pork, spitted and roasted slowly—35 minutes per pound—will be delicious. Or you may have it boned and rolled for the spit.

Shoulder: Pork shoulder may be prepared and roasted the same way as fresh ham.

Suckling Pig: This is, of course, one of the choicest of meats for roasting. Stuff it or not, as you please. Then secure it to the spit and give it a good 35 minutes per pound. Baste it frequently during cooking, and brush it well with fat toward the last. Just before removing from the spit, brush it with heavy cream and turn on all sides in front of the coals.

Pork Steaks

Pork steaks are usually cut from the fresh ham or leg. They should be ¾ to 1 inch thick and should be pan-broiled or sautéed till well done. If grilled, they very often become hard and stringy.

Pork Chops

Pork needs thorough cooking; I suggest that you sauté pork chops rather than grill them. However, if you get a good, thick loin chop with the tenderloin in it, it may be broiled for a real treat.

Select thick loin or rib chops, brown them very quickly, cover with barbecue sauce and simmer until tender. Be sure to flavor your sauce with basil or thyme when cooking pork.

Pork chops, loin or rib, may be browned in a pan, covered with sauerkraut, and simmered 1 to 1½ hours, or until done. Beer is in order with this.

Ham Steak

Nothing in the world is better than a good, thick slice of well-cured ham grilled over the coals and a couple of fresh eggs fried in butter to go with it.

Choose a good smoked ham (I don't care what state it comes from) and have slices cut about ¾ to 1 inch thick. Slow cooking brings out the flavor as nothing else does. The ham should have a touch of brown crispness on the outside and a soft pink deliciousness on the inside, with plenty of juices oozing on the plate.

Ham steak may also be pan-broiled and is delicious that way. Take a little of the ham fat and melt it in the pan to give the ham some lubricant and prevent its sticking to the metal.

If you like thin slices of ham, sizzle them very quickly on the grill or in the pan—the quicker, the better.

Ham Steak Supreme

Ham steak, cut 2 inches thick
1 bottle red wine
2 cloves garlic
Sprig of fresh thyme

Place the ham in an earthenware casserole or an iron frying pan and let it stand in half the wine 6 to 12 hours.

Just before cooking, add garlic cloves and thyme and place the pan over a rather brisk fire. When it begins to cook fiercely, cover, move to a less fiery spot on the open grill, and let the meat cook in the wine till tender —about 1 or 1½ hours. If the wine cooks away too rapidly, add more from time to time, taking care not to reduce the temperature of the dish too much.

This, served with a barbecue sauce, baked sweet potatoes, and corn on the cob, is something to remember and something to praise.

LAMB OR MUTTON

Leg of Lamb: Have the leg boned and rolled. Roast it 25 minutes per pound if it is young lamb, 35 if it is mutton. If you care for the flavor of mint with lamb, have the butcher roll some fresh mint into the roast.

Shoulder or Forequarter of Lamb: This may be rolled and boned and cooked the same way. Barbecue sauce for basting is in order.

Lamb Steaks

Select steaks from leg of spring lamb or yearling mutton. Have them cut about an inch thick and broil as you would beef steak. Barbecue sauce is a particularly good complement to lamb steaks.

Lamb and Mutton Chops

If you are wise, you won't bother about trying to cook any kind of chop outdoors but good-sized loin lamb chops or English mutton chops. The delicate little rib and French chops, beloved of ladies at luncheons, are unsuited to the barbecue or the outdoor grill.

Good loin chops of spring lamb should be cut 2 to 3 inches thick for broiling over a charcoal grill. English mutton chops are cut 2 to 3 inches thick and are prepared with the kidney and skewered, or wrapped with bacon and tied.

Broil the chops to the degree of doneness preferred by you and your guests. Broiled lamb and mutton are delicious as is, and require practically no dressing up.

Always serve lamb or mutton on hot plates. Nothing is so distressing as congealed mutton fat on a cold plate.

CHICKENS

Chickens roasted on the spit in front of the fire are a treat. Select either the small squab size, allowing one to a person, or the larger roasting chickens or lordly capons. Stuff them, if you wish, and truss and spit them, cooking fairly quickly and basting often. Small ones should not be stuffed (to my taste), though a few sprigs of parsley inside the body cavities improves them. A small chicken should cook in 25 to 30 minutes; allow about 20 minutes per pound for larger ones. Frequent basting is necessary.

Broiled Chicken (I)

Cream 4 tablespoons butter with teaspoon of paprika and a sprinkling of black pepper. Spread well over the surface of the chicken and place chicken on broiling rack with the bone side—the inside—exposed to the flame. This gives the bones a chance to get really hot so that they hold the heat while the outside is cooking and browning. The juices will run to the breast, and the browning process will not dry out the bird. Brush well with the butter mixture before turning the skin side to the flame, and turn and baste frequently while the chicken browns. Be careful of overcooking chicken—your instinct will have to tell you the exact moment of withdrawal. A final bit of salting and another spooning over of the butter mixture, and your bird is ready for the table.

Broiled Chicken (II)

Split the cleaned birds. About 3 hours before cooking, cover with a marinade made with 2 parts olive oil to 1 part wine vinegar. Chop an onion and a clove of garlic, and add to this a generous pinch of tarragon and one of thyme and chopped parsley. Let your chicken marinate in this in a fairly warm place till the moment arrives for the preparation of dinner. Broil birds as above, basting frequently with the sauce.

Fried Chicken (I)

Cut chicken in convenient pieces for frying. Dredge well with flour.

Put 5 or 6 rashers of bacon in a pan and let it fry out rather quickly. Be careful not to burn the grease. Push bacon to one side of pan and put in chicken. Brown very quickly on both sides, cover, and reduce heat. (An asbestos mat under the pan will do outdoors.) Simmer 20 to 25 minutes, or until tender.

Remove chicken and bacon from the pan. Pour out all but 3 tablespoons of the fat. Then brown 3 tablespoons flour in the pan. Add a pint of milk and stir vigorously until it thickens. Season well with salt and pepper.

Mashed potatoes or tiny new potatoes, hot biscuits and honey, and a green salad are good accompaniments.

Fried Chicken (II)

Disjoint a fryer and let it stand 2 hours in a dish in which you have beaten up 2 eggs with a cup of milk.

Melt ¼ pound butter in a frying pan to the bubbly stage, being very careful not to burn it. Dip the chicken sections in toasted bread crumbs and place very gently in the pan of butter. Brown the chicken on both sides, cover, and let simmer till tender—about 30 minutes. Salt and pepper well and serve.

New potatoes and green peas cooked with little young onions are superb with this. So is watermelon pickle.

Casserole of Chicken

2 large roasting chickens or capons	Several sprigs fresh tarragon, or a small pinch of thyme—fresh, if possible
Flour	
12 small white onions, peeled	½ pound butter
12 small carrots or 24 cubes of carrot	Chopped parsley
½ cup diced celery	1 quart rich milk
	Salt and pepper

This is a perfect dish for anyone who has an oven attached to an outdoor fireplace. Or it may be cooked indoors and heated outdoors. Select 2 large roasting chickens or capons for a good-sized party. Disjoint the chickens or capons and dredge the pieces well with flour. Have ready one or two large casseroles, and in each one place half the onions, carrots, celery, and tarragon or thyme, and a generous sprinkling of parsley.

Fry the pieces of chicken or capon in 2 iron skillets into each of which you have put ¼ pound butter. Brown the pieces thoroughly, season to taste, and, as they become a golden color, place them in the casseroles.

Make an ample quantity of cream gravy by sprinkling 2 or more tablespoons flour in each pan and allowing it to brown slightly. Add 1 pint rich milk to each pan, let it thicken, and add salt and pepper to taste. Pour the milk mixture over the chickens, cover the casseroles, and bake in medium oven 1 to 1¼ hours. I suggest tiny new potatoes with this and perhaps green beans.

TURKEY

Turkey is a favorite with many outdoor cooks. If you have a good-sized grill, it is easy to put on style and give the great American bird a chance at the same time.

The most delicious turkeys are those of tender age and small size, averaging 4 to 6 pounds. A broiling turkey of 4 or 5 pounds is ample for 5 or 6 persons.

Broiled Turkey (I)

Turkey for broiling	Few drops lemon juice
½ pound butter	Pinch of tarragon
1 teaspoon paprika	Salt and pepper
1 teaspoon black pepper	

Have the turkey split and cleaned, saving the giblets for the sauce. Cream 1 cup butter with paprika, black pepper, lemon juice, and tarragon. Spread this well over the surface of the turkey and place the bird bone side down over the fire, which should not be too hot. Let it cook this way about 15 minutes and then turn the skin side to the fire. Baste, and let it cook on that side about 10 minutes before turning and buttering again. Keep turning at intervals of about 5 minutes till the bird is cooked through—but not dry. Baste with butter each time, being very careful not to puncture the skin so that the juices do not escape. Salt and pepper to taste.

The following sauce is pleasant with this:

3 shallots	Chopped giblets
½ cup olive oil	2 tablespoons parsley
2 tablespoons chopped ham	1 cup cream
	2 egg yolks
½ cup chopped mushrooms	

Sauté shallots in olive oil. Add chopped ham, mushrooms, and giblets, and let them cook together. Add parsley and stir in cream mixed with the egg yolks. Stir till it thickens and season to taste.

Broiled Turkey (II)

5- or 6-pound broiling turkey	Several sprigs of parsley
	Sprig of tarragon
Piece of bacon rind or salt pork	Little bacon fat or butter
	Salt and pepper

If you are fortunate enough to have a spit with your outdoor stove, it may be used to cook whole young broiling turkeys with delicious results.

Have the 5- or 6-pound broiling turkey drawn but not split. Have your butcher tie a piece of bacon rind or a long, thin slice of salt pork around the bird. Stuff parsley and tarragon inside the bird and spit it. Place it before the fire, giving it plenty of heat to begin with, and turn often until the turkey is three-quarters cooked. Remove the bacon rind or salt pork, and brown the bird, basting it occasionally with a little bacon fat or butter. Salt and pepper to taste and serve with boiled, riced chestnuts or yams roasted in the ashes or tender sweet corn, roasted in the ashes with husks on.

SAUCES

Good barbecue sauces add a great deal to outdoor cookery. Three recipes are listed below.

Barbecue Sauce (I)

1 cup tomato juice	Cloves
1 cup consommé	2 tablespoons wine
1 tablespoon Escoffier	vinegar
Sauce Diable	2 tablespoons onion juice
Tarragon	1 tablespoon brown sugar
1 tablespoon salt	1 clove garlic, grated
Thyme	½ cup sherry
1 tablespoon freshly	Parsley
ground pepper	

Heat tomato juice and consommé with a sprig of tarragon, a sprig of thyme, and 2 or 3 whole cloves. Just before it gets to the boiling point, add the other seasonings, the salt and sugar having been previously mixed

with the vinegar. Just before removing from the fire, add sherry and allow it to heat for a minute or two longer before it is served.

This sauce is excellent for most types of meat roasted on the spit. It may also be used to baste a roast. Always be sure to have a pan to catch the drippings. You may want to thicken this sauce, which may be done by adding a little flour blended with a little of the fat from the roast.

Barbecue Sauce (II)

2 cloves garlic	2 tablespoons Escoffier
½ cup olive oil	Sauce Diable
2 tablespoons anchovy	Salt
paste or Patum	¼ teaspoon cayenne pepper
Peperium	1 tablespoon minute tapioca
2 cups consommé	

Sauté the garlic cloves in the olive oil and add the anchovy paste. Mix thoroughly, add the consommé, the sauce Diable, and the other seasonings. Simmer about 5 minutes and then add the tapioca for thickening. Allow the mixture to boil up, and when it begins to thicken, remove from fire.

This is delicious with steak and also makes a good sauce for spaghetti. Pass grated cheese with the spaghetti.

Barbecue Sauce (III)

½ pound bacon, diced	Ground cloves
¼ cup chopped onion	2 pounds fresh tomatoes,
2 garlic cloves, chopped	quartered
¼ cup chopped celery	2 cups consommé
Tarragon	1 tablespoon fresh-ground
Rosemary	pepper
Thyme	1 tablespoon sugar
1 tablespoon salt	1 green pepper, chopped
Cayenne	Parsley

Sauté bacon in a large skillet. Add onion, garlic, celery, a sprig of tarragon, a pinch of rosemary, and a pinch of thyme. Add salt and pepper, a generous dash of cayenne, and a pinch of ground cloves. Let these ingredients cook together 4 or 5 minutes; then add tomatoes, consommé, and sugar. Allow to simmer about 40 minutes or until smooth and velvety. Add finely chopped green pepper and about 3 tablespoons chopped parsley. Cook about 5 minutes longer. You may like a hotter sauce; if so, add more cayenne pepper.

The sauce is delicious with barbecue sandwiches, roasts, noodles, or spaghetti. Cold meats may be reheated in it, or it may be poured over pork chops after they have been sautéed.

FROZEN FOODS
AND PICK-UP MEALS

Modern living is coming increasingly to mean informal living; but informality in cooking and entertaining should not by any means signify thrown-together meals. On the contrary, in the modern scheme, in which the unexpected guest fares as royally as the guest invited a week ahead, and the family fares every bit as well as both, it means planning. The kind of informality which is really the result of planning ahead requires food from which the tedious, time-consuming chores of preparation have been eliminated without sacrifice of goodness or variety. With the advent of the marvel of quick freezing, this idea has at last been happily realized.

I take issue on just one count with the companies which pack frozen foods. The number of servings is not accurately estimated. If the members of your family have hearty appetites, you will certainly be misled by the number of servings stated on the package.

Following are a few facts about commercial quick-frozen foods which you should know.

COOKING FROZEN VEGETABLES

Quick-frozen vegetables are washed, trimmed, and fully prepared for cooking. They are choice vegetables picked at the peak of their growth and cleaned, prepared, and quick-frozen within a few hours after leaving the vines. They are economical, saving not only time but the waste of pods and trimmings.

For best results, quick-frozen vegetables need accurate timing and faithful adherence to the directions on the package. The contents of a package need not be thawed before cooking; in fact it is better to plunge the frozen block into the required amount of boiling water and let the vegetables thaw in that way. When the water starts to boil again after the vegetables have thawed, that is the time to

begin counting your cooking period. You will have better results if you do not allow the vegetables to boil vigorously—a gentle bubbling is much to be preferred.

Do not overcook vegetables. Quick-frozen vegetables cook in one half to two thirds of the time that fresh vegetables do, and the same warning against overcooking applies. Overcooking kills the flavor and the crisp freshness of the vegetable.

When cooking two or more vegetables that are to be combined—such as corn and lima beans for succotash, or green peas and string beans for mixed vegetables or for salads—it is much wiser to cook each vegetable separately according to directions and to combine them afterward. One vegetable may require much less cooking than the other and be over-cooked by the time the first one achieves doneness.

If you are experienced in cooking frozen foods, you may like to experiment with certain vegetables. For instance, I prefer to melt a piece of butter in the pan when cooking green peas and add the frozen block of peas without additional water. I place the peas in the butter in a copper-bottomed pan, cover the pan, and cook over a very low flame until the peas are just tender. Spinach may also be cooked covered without additional water if you wish.

For the most part, however, it is safer to be faithful to the directions.

If you are cooking vegetables for salads, allow them to become just tender, with a little of the crispness left in.

Because of the accuracy of time required, quick-frozen vegetables are much better cooked in an open pan, according to the directions, than in a pressure cooker. Pressure-cooking any frozen food is apt to overcook it and make it mushy, while at the same time, in the case of certain foods, the center of the frozen block does not always get thawed.

QUICK-FROZEN FRUITS

Quick-frozen fruits are a year-round blessing, for they give you the full flavor of the tree-ripened fruit in seasons when the fresh would be unavailable or prohibitively expensive. For the best results, they should be thawed according to the directions on the package. If, however, you are in a hurry and need to use the fruits in the shortest possible time, open the package and thaw the fruit. With the addition of a little liqueur to flavor them, fruits such as peaches will not discolor any more than fresh ones treated in the same way.

Quick-frozen fruits may also be used with ice cream or for shortcakes or for tarts just as you would use fresh fruits. It has been my experience that the quick-frozen fruits (some of which, such as peaches and pineapple, are frozen in syrup) require much less sugar than the fresh varieties. It is wise to taste for sweetness before adding additional sugar.

Combining Frozen Fruits

Peaches with Raspberries: Add 2 ounces kirsch to a package of frozen peaches and top with a package of quick-frozen raspberries. Allow the raspberries to thaw over the peaches.

Pineapple with Raspberries: One package frozen pineapple cubes and 1 package raspberries thawed together make an excellent combination. Add kirsch or Triple Sec to taste, if you wish.

Strawberries and Pineapple: Flavor 1 package of quick-frozen pineapple with 2 ounces kirsch. Allow it to thaw until just cold. Add 1 package quick-frozen strawberries and blend well. Add additional kirsch if desired.

Brandied Peaches: Add cognac to taste to 2 packages of quick-frozen peaches which have been half thawed. Let them continue thawing in the brandy.

Minted Pineapple: Add 2 ounces green crème de menthe to a package of quick-frozen pineapple and allow the fruit to thaw in the mint and its own syrup. Turn the cubes several times during the process.

QUICK-FROZEN SHELLFISH

Shellfish—oysters, crabmeat, lobster, scallops, and shrimp—may be purchased in containers.

Oysters

Oysters come raw and may be served as a cocktail, or they may be cooked in any way that fresh oysters are used. Quick-frozen oysters are perhaps the safest for people in the inland states to use, for their freshness is absolutely assured. If thawed in the refrigerator, oysters take 8 hours, but if removed from the carton and thawed at room temperature they may be ready for the table in 2 hours.

Crabmeat

Crabmeat comes cooked and removed from the shell. Thawing in the refrigerator will require about 6 hours. If you are rushed, remove the crabmeat from the carton and let it stand at room temperature, where it will thaw in 1½ hours. It should be thoroughly thawed for the best flavor.

Shrimp

Shrimp come raw and also cooked in the shell. The former may be cooked without thawing for 10 to 15 minutes, drained, and shelled at once. If they are to be recooked, cook them for only 8 or 9 minutes before removing the shells. If you are to chill them and use them for salads or for first-course service, cook them approximately 12 minutes.

Scallops

For thawing, scallops need about 10 hours in the refrigerator or 2½ hours removed from the carton and thawed at room temperature. They may be prepared like fresh scallops.

Lobster

Lobster comes cooked and removed from the shell. It is also possible to buy frozen lobster tails which require cooking. Lobster ordinarily requires 1½ to 2 hours' thawing at room temperature or 6 hours in the refrigerator.

QUICK-FROZEN FISH

Quick-frozen fish may be cooked either frozen or thawed, so it is immensely useful as an "emergency" food. Most of the fish packed in this manner is filleted, though a certain amount is sold in "steaks."

It is wise to follow directions carefully in cooking quick-frozen fish and, as in the case of fresh fish, great care should be taken not to overcook. Cooking is desirable only to the point where the fish loses its translucent quality—that's all. Overcooked fish is dry, tasteless, and thoroughly uninteresting.

QUICK-FROZEN POULTRY

Quick-frozen poultry of the best brands is among the finest procurable anywhere, perfectly cleaned and ready for cooking. The only fault I have to find is that the chickens are cut up rather than disjointed, but that is a minor fault and one that does not affect the quality of the product.

Quick-frozen birds are drawn and cleaned and sold by net weight, which means that when buying this type of poultry you can subtract 1 to 1¾ pounds from the equivalent in fresh poultry, in which it is the undrawn weight that is paid for.

A turkey will take about 6 hours to thaw, and a large roasting chicken about 5 hours. Do not be upset by the rather flattened look of some of the frozen poultry, for, in thawing, the bird returns to its natural shape.

Prepare quick-frozen poultry in any way that you would the fresh.

MEATS

The great advantage of having a stock of quick-frozen meats in your freezer for emergencies is that they may be used without thawing. Any of the frozen meats may be taken from the freezer and placed in the broiler or the roasting or frying pan and cooked at once.

You will find many different types of roasts, chops, steaks, and economy cuts in the various lines. Prepare them in the way that you do fresh meat. If they are cooked unthawed, a lower temperature for cooking may be used for part of the cooking time. And you must add additional cooking time for unthawed meats, according to the packer's directions.

Here again you are paying for net weight, not the weight before trimming, as is the case in buying from a butcher. Also, you are assured, if you buy a reputable brand, of getting well-seasoned meat with a minimum of waste.

PREPARED DISHES

I am obliged to withhold my enthusiasm for the great majority of the prepared dishes which are offered for distribution and sale at the time of writing. Certain ones, such as the French fried potatoes, are excellent. (If directions are followed closely, you will achieve exceedingly good potatoes in 20 minutes without the struggle of peeling, slicing, and frying the potatoes.) I have tasted certain quick-frozen made dishes which were good, but on the whole I feel that there is much to be done in this field if packaged made dishes are to offer the consumer quality and value comparable to that of the uncooked products.

Those which you prepare for yourself are a different matter. If you have the storage room and the proper facilities, you can achieve wonderful results with roasts, cold meats, poultry, cakes, pies, stews, and many other foods. Before freezing, the foods must be packed well in cellophane, foil, or parchment, and sealed. Some experimentation by the novice will perfect his technique and determine which foods may be frozen most satisfactorily.

MISCELLANEOUS FROZEN FOODS

There are a few products on the market which are worth noting and recommending for your frozen-food chest.

Concentrated orange juice is often better than freshly squeezed juice. It is a definite time- and labor-saver as well.

Very acceptable pie crust may be found under several different labels. It is easy to use, well prepared, and a labor-saver as well. It is especially useful for those who have difficulty preparing a good crust.

Rolls and Danish pastries which may be baked at home are excellent and save a great deal of labor for the person who likes to have freshly baked breads at table.

Though it is sometimes difficult to find, the frozen grated coconut is a delight, for it is fresh coconut with the milk and is ideal for preparation of curries and desserts in which the milk forms a definite part of the recipe.

Quick-frozen apple sauce is a boon to those who enjoy this dish for a dessert or as an accompaniment to roast pork or pork chops.

Quick-frozen hors d'oeuvres are an aid to those who are likely to have a number of people dropping in from time to time for cocktails. They are not as good as they might be, but are better than those one gets from a great many commercial houses and catering establishments.

QUICK MEALS FROM THE EMERGENCY SHELF AND THE FREEZER

QUICK COMPANY DINNER

Tenderloin Steaks
French Fried Potatoes   Asparagus Hollandaise
Corn Muffins (made from Muffin Mix)
Brandied Peaches

This meal can be prepared in half an hour or 40 minutes.

Remove the peaches from the package, add cognac to taste, and let peaches thaw at room temperature. Place potatoes on a baking sheet and sprinkle with salt and pepper. Prepare muffin batter from muffin mix and fill muffin pans.

Cook asparagus according to directions. Use Hollandaise from a jar or make your own (page 232). Grill steaks and heat potatoes. Bake muffins.

If you have greens for a salad, mix them and prepare the dressing.

Sit down and finish your cocktail; dinner will be ready to serve within half an hour.

QUICK SUNDAY NIGHT SUPPER

Chicken Shortcake   Artichokes Vinaigrette
Melba Toast
Three-fruit Compote

Open 2 packages of quick-frozen chicken à la king and 1 3-ounce can broiled-in-butter mushroom slices. Combine in double boiler or saucepan, according to recipe on the package.

Make a double batch of biscuit-mix short-cakes, using cream instead of milk for the mixing.

Use canned artichoke hearts and prepare a vinaigrette sauce for them.

Bake biscuit-mix shortcakes.

Add 3 tablespoons sherry or Madeira to chicken-and-mushroom mixture.

Remove shortcakes from oven and arrange on individual plates or on a large service platter. Pour the chicken mixture over them. Serve at once with the artichokes or serve the artichokes later. If you have greens in your refrigerator, you may serve a green salad or a tomato salad instead. *(Serves 6.)*

Three-Fruit Compote

1 box quick-frozen sliced strawberries, thawed
1 box quick-frozen grape-fruit, thawed
1 box quick-frozen sliced peaches, thawed
2 tablespoons lemon juice
Mint sprigs

Combine strawberries and peaches. Drain juice from grapefruit sections and add juice to strawberry mixture. Add lemon juice. Put mixture in glass bowl; top with grapefruit sections and nuts if desired. Garnish with mint sprigs.

To Dress up a Leftover Dinner When an Extra Person Arrives

	Clear Soup with Parmesan Cheese	
	Green Bean and Ham Hash	
Pickles	Toasted Rolls or	Tossed Salad
Cheese	French Bread	Coffee

Use canned consommé and sprinkle with a little grated Parmesan cheese just before serving.

Serve an assortment of pickles with the hash.

Serve cheese with the salad and either toasted rolls or French bread.

Green Bean and Ham Hash

1 box quick-frozen green beans	2 small tomatoes, diced
1 cup water	1 tablespoon chopped parsley
½ cup chopped onion	4 large potatoes, boiled and diced
¾ cup chopped green pepper	
2 tablespoons cooking oil	1 clove garlic, finely chopped
1¼ cups diced cooked ham	½ teaspoon salt
	⅛ teaspoon pepper

Drop frozen beans into briskly boiling salted water. Bring again to a boil, and boil only 8 minutes. Drain.

Sauté onion and green pepper in cooking oil in skillet until tender. Add ham and tomatoes and cook slowly until tomatoes are tender. Then add beans, parsley, potatoes, garlic, and seasonings. Heat thoroughly.

(Serves 4.)

A Quick Buffet Supper for the Holiday Season

	Cold Sliced Turkey or Goose	
Squash with Oranges		Parsley Biscuits
Crabmeat Salad		Dill Pickles
	Ice Cream with Blueberry Sauce	

Thaw crabmeat and cook squash.

Prepare squash dish (see recipe below).

Prepare salad (see recipe below).

Slice turkey or goose, arrange on platter, and garnish with thin pickle slices and tomatoes if available.

Prepare biscuit mix, adding ¼ cup finely chopped parsley to each batch. You will probably need 2 batches.

Prepare blueberry sauce (see recipe below).

(Serves 6.)

Frozen Crabmeat Salad

Thaw 2 packages quick-frozen crabmeat according to directions on the box. When partially thawed, add ½ cup French dressing to crabmeat and allow it to continue thawing. When it is thoroughly thawed, combine with 1 finely chopped medium onion, 2 tablespoons finely chopped parsley, and 1 tablespoon capers. Arrange on a bed of finely shredded greens or a bed of watercress, top with mayonnaise, and garnish with quartered hard-cooked eggs.

Squash with Oranges

2 boxes quick-frozen squash, thawed	1 teaspoon salt
	Dash of pepper
6 tablespoons butter	6 teaspoons grated orange rind
6 tablespoons brown sugar	
4 tablespoons orange juice	

Combine ingredients in top of double boiler. Heat over boiling water until hot.

Blueberry Sauce

1 box quick-frozen blueberries, thawed	¼ teaspoon salt
	Dash of clove
1 cup water	2 teaspoons butter
4 teaspoons flour	2 tablespoons lemon juice
¾ cup sugar	

Bring 1 cup of the berries and water to a boil and simmer 3 minutes. Combine flour, sugar, salt, and cloves, and add to the hot fruit. Add remaining berries, bring to a boil, and cook 3 minutes. Remove from heat. Add butter and lemon juice. Serve warm. (Makes 2½ cups sauce.)

A Quick Meal for Children
When They Bring Home Unexpected Guests

Vegetable Plate

Corn on the Cob	String Beans
Grilled Tomatoes	Spinach with Mushrooms

Toasted Cream Cheese Sandwiches
Sugared Vanilla Crème

Prepare pudding (see recipe below).

Wash and cut tops off tomatoes, allowing 1 to a person. Sprinkle with salt, pepper, and crumbs, and dot with butter.

Make sandwiches with butter and cream cheese, and place them on a rack ready to be placed in the oven.

Cook beans and spinach. If you do not have the chopped type of quick-frozen spinach, cut the frozen block into small cubes with a sharp knife before cooking.

Heat a small can of broiled-in-butter mushrooms.

Prepare water for boiling corn according to directions. Allow 1 ear to each child.

Place tomatoes under the broiler.

Drain spinach when cooked and combine with butter and mushrooms.

Butter beans, adding a little chopped parsley.

Place sandwiches under broiler or in oven.

Arrange plates and serve. Pass the sandwiches.

While this course is being eaten, place desserts under the broiler.

Sugared Vanilla Crème

1 package prepared vanilla pudding	4 tablespoons dark brown sugar
	About 2½ cups milk

Place pudding powder in saucepan. Add milk gradually, stirring constantly. Cook and stir over medium heat until mixture comes to a boil and is thickened. Turn into greased baking dish or individual custard cups. Let cool slightly. Sprinkle sugar over top of pudding and place under broiler until sugar is melted (10 or 15 minutes). Serve warm or cold. *(Serves 5 to 7.)*

DINNER FOR A GLOOMY DAY WHEN ALL THE LEFTOVERS ARE GONE

	Asparagus and Shrimp Parmesan
Popovers	Tossed Salad
	Jellied Strawberry Pie

Asparagus and Shrimp Parmesan

1 box quick-frozen shrimp
1 box quick-frozen asparagus spears
4 tablespoons butter
3 tablespoons flour
1½ cups milk
⅓ cup grated Parmesan (or Swiss) cheese
1 egg yolk, slightly beaten
½ cup cream
1 teaspoon salt
Dash of pepper, cayenne, and nutmeg
Paprika

Cook, shell, and clean shrimp as directed on package. Cook asparagus spears as directed on package.

Melt butter in saucepan, add flour, and stir until smooth. Add milk gradually, stirring constantly. Cook and stir until thickened. Add cheese. Combine cream with egg yolk and add gradually, stirring constantly. Add salt, pepper, cayenne, and nutmeg. Cook and stir over low heat 2 or 3 minutes. Add shrimp.

Arrange asparagus spears in shallow baking dish. Pour shrimp sauce over asparagus and sprinkle with paprika. Place under broiler a few minutes to brown slightly.

(Serves 4 to 6.)

Note: If desired, 1 cup diced cooked chicken or lobster may be substituted for the shrimp.

VARIATION

Asparagus and Shrimp Platter: Use recipe for Asparagus and Shrimp Parmesan, reducing flour to 2 tablespoons. Place 4 to 6 toast points on a hot platter. Arrange cooked asparagus on toast and pour hot shrimp sauce over asparagus. Serve immediately.

Jellied Strawberry Pie

1 box quick-frozen sliced strawberries, thawed
2 cups strawberry juice and water
1 envelope speed-up gelatin
⅓ cup sugar
Dash of salt
1 9-inch pie shell, baked, or crumb crust

Drain strawberries, measure juice, and add water to make 2 cups. Combine gelatin, sugar, and salt in saucepan. Add fruit juice and water, and place over medium heat. Stir constantly until gelatin is dissolved—2 or 3 minutes. Cool and add berries. Chill until slightly thickened. Turn into pie shell and chill until firm. Serve plain or garnished with whipped cream.

VARIATION

Jellied Cherry Pie: Substitute 1 box quick-frozen red sour pitted cherries for sliced strawberries. Use ¼ teaspoon salt.

THE FROZEN FOOD RESERVE

If you have a home freezer or sufficient space in your refrigerator freezing compartment, you will want to keep a well-rounded stock of frozen foods on hand, particularly for pick-up meals. For those who have a cottage in the country or at the shore, a frozen-food backlog is especially desirable.

Meats: Keep a fairly good selection of meats if you are far from good butchers and are likely to need a quick meal at odd hours or for unexpected guests. Either have part of a good beef cut up for you and quick-freeze it yourself, or lay in a stock of individual items.

Vegetables: A good variety of vegetables is essential. About a quarter of your freezing space should be devoted to them. If, however, you freeze your own vegetables, you will probably use a higher percentage of the space. In my experience, the best vegetables for freezing have been asparagus, Frenched green beans, and baby lima beans. But the commercially frozen vegetables are, for the most part, much more successful than home-frozen ones.

Fruits: If you have much freezing space, you may wish to freeze a good deal of fruit for home use. You can freeze your own fruits very successfully if you do it properly. At home, freezing the fruit in jars is generally most successful.

Poultry and Game: Poultry and game are likely to be available more economically at some seasons than at others. If you have ample freezing space, you can take good advantage of these opportunities. For instance, if you have a chance to buy several turkeys at an attractive price, you may freeze several for future use. Turkeys may be cut in half before freezing, so that at any time you can take out half a bird to roast for a small group,

without worrying about the leftovers from a whole bird. Game birds should be frozen in feather and plucked after thawing.

Prepared Foods: There is not space in this book for extended recommendations on what to freeze and what not to freeze. But it should be repeated that experimentation is necessary in regard to the freezing of cooked foods. Magazine articles and advertisements recommend freezing anything from soup to angel food cake. You will have to make up your own mind as to which frozen cooked foods you prefer before you fill up that precious freezing space.

Caution: Consult the best handbooks on quick-freezing before undertaking the process yourself. Until you become experienced in freezing foods at home, stick mainly to the commercial products, which are definitely perfected before being placed on the market.

JUNE

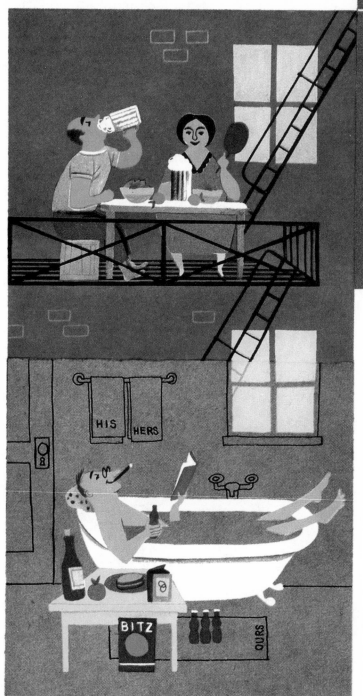

JULY

AUGUST

SEPTEMBER

COOLER

FOR WARM AND COLD WEATHER MEALS

As the tourist may need a guide to plan the perfect trip, so the cook may find a printed menu helpful in planning the perfect meal. Here you will find suitable menus for warm and cold weather—for everyday meals and for parties—including a group of typical menus from various countries. Naturally, you may wish to make changes here and there and to use the national menus combined into a more or less international mélange. That is your privilege.

Those recipes which are not included elsewhere in the book will be found on the pages with the menus.

WARM WEATHER MEALS

Raw Vegetables   Dunking Bowl
Chopped Lamb Kebabs
Kasha (Steamed Cracked Wheat)
Summer Squash with Sour Cream
Fresh Cherry Pie
Coffee

Eggs and Vegetables in Aspic
Veal Chops Parmigiana
Corn Bread
Strawberries with Kirsch
Coffee

Melon
Eggs California
Popovers
Cabbage Salad, Sweet and Sour Dressing
Chocolate Roll
Iced Coffee

Shrimp Rémoulade
Broiled Baby Turkey
Polenta
Zucchini Sauté
Blueberries in Maple Syrup and Cream

Jellied Madrilene
Glazed Broilers
Potatoes Anna   Corn on the Cob
Green Salad with Raw Mushrooms
Melon

Steak Tartare with Raw Egg, Capers, Mustard, and Onions
Tomato, Cucumber, Romaine Salad, Tarragon Dressing
Muffins
Ice Cream with Fresh Peaches and Kirsch

Onions à la Grecque
Chicken Amandine
Asparagus Vinaigrette
Popovers
Baked Bananas

Anchovy Salad Niçoise
Cheese Soufflé
Crisp Bacon
Grilled Tomatoes
Peaches with Raspberries

Consommé with Avocado Slices
Cold Seafood Platter, Rémoulade Sauce
Sliced Tomatoes and Cucumbers
Garlic Bread
Cherry Fritters

Mint Juleps
Shenandoah Fried Chicken
New Potatoes with Parsley
Tossed Salad with Raw Mushrooms
Strawberry Shortcake

Jellied Chicken Broth
Artichoke Stuffed with Crabmeat
Herbed Biscuits
Cheese Platter
Fresh Fruit

Far Eastern Indian Dinner

Vegetable Fritters
Mulligatawny Soup
Vathoo Vindaloo

Chopped Almonds   Coconut

Chutney Rice

Bombay Duck   Pickled Limes
Moghul Pillao
Fresh Fruits
Preserved Kumquats
Rose-flavored Coffee

Mulligatawny Soup:

2 tablespoons butter
¼ cup diced salt pork
1 chopped carrot
3 onions, sliced
Chopped turnip
2 tablespoons curry powder
Cayenne
¼ cup flour
Salt
Chopped parsley
1 clove garlic, chopped
1 stalk rhubarb
2 pints stock
Juice of 1 lime

Melt butter and try out the salt pork in the butter. Add carrot and onions and a bit of turnip. Cook for 2 or 3 minutes with the salt pork and add curry powder and cayenne. Sprinkle with flour and blend well. Cook several minutes—until onion is transparent. Season to taste with salt. Add a little parsley, garlic and rhubarb. Add broth, bring to a boil, and simmer very slowly for 1 hour. Just before serving, skim soup and add lime juice.

This is usually served with a little boiled rice, passed separately.

Vathoo Vindaloo:

Flour
1 large duck cut into serving pieces
¼ cup clarified butter
1 clove garlic
1 large onion, finely sliced
2 chilies, cut in strips
Salt
2 tablespoons ground coriander
½ teaspoon ground ginger
½ teaspoon ground black pepper
½ teaspoon ground Fenugreek
1½ teaspoons turmeric
½ teaspoon ground cumin
½ teaspoon ground red peppers
Lime juice
1 cup stock
1 teaspoon guava jelly

Flour pieces of duck very lightly and sauté gently in butter until nicely browned on all sides. Add onions, garlic, and chilies when you turn the pieces of duck to brown on the upper side. Salt to taste.

Mix coriander, ginger, pepper, Fenugreek, turmeric, cumin, and red peppers, and blend with lime juice to a smooth paste. Add this, mixed with stock, to the duck. Stir gently and simmer until duck is tender—about 1½ to 2 hours. Remove duck to a serving dish and add guava jelly to the sauce. Serve with Moghul Pillao.

Moghul Pillao: This is steamed rice mixed with saffron, crisply fried onions, bits of salt pork, and chopped almonds. Sprinkle with raisins just before serving.

Rose-flavored Coffee: Make Turkish coffee with a flavoring of rose water or rose extract.

Leeks à la Grecque   Eggs à la Russe
Anchovy Salad Nicoise   Eggplant Salad
Beetroot in Sour Cream   Smoked Trout
Prosciutto, Salami, Cold Smoked Tongue
Cheese   Fruit

Cold Vichyssoise
Quick Curry of Chicken   Steamed Rice
Chutney, Shredded Almonds, Bombay Duck
Fresh Sliced Peaches with Cognac
Tea

Avocado with Fresh Crabmeat, French Dressing
Eggs Florentine
Popovers
Watermelon

Hot Chicken Broth with Rice
Shad Roe with Bacon
Steamed New Potatoes in Butter
Tossed Salad with Beetroot, French Dressing
French Rolls
Cheese Board

Cocktails   Onion Ring Appetizers

Chicken Mayonnaise

Noodles with Spinach   Tomatoes Stuffed with Cottage Cheese

Chutney   Refrigerator Rolls

Melon Mélange

Cocktails   Dunking Bowl

Cold Poached Salmon, Mayonnaise

Cucumber Vinaigrette   Baked Rice with Pine Nuts

Cold Roast Beef, Horseradish Sauce

Garlic French Bread   Cheese Tray

Assorted Fresh Fruits

Hot Buttered Rum   Vegetable Bowl

Cold Roast Turkey   Baked Virginia Ham

Green Noodles with Parmesan

Snap Beans and Artichoke Hearts, French Dressing

Toasted French Bread   Cheese Tray

Cherries Jubilee with Ice Cream

Cocktails   French Fried Shrimp

Cold Stuffed Squab

Prosciutto

Beet and Egg Salad   Sliced Tomatoes

Corn Bread

Fresh Strawberries, Sour Cream

Meringues

AUSTRIAN DINNER

Mushroom Soup
Brook Trout with Small Potato Balls
Niernbraten (Roast of Veal)
Risi-Pisi (Rice Combined with Green Peas)
Puree of Spinach
Cucumber Salad
Linzer Torte
Coffee

Cucumber Salad: Peel cucumbers, slice very thinly, and soak for an hour in salted ice water. Press water out before serving and serve with a tart French dressing.

Brook Trout: Fresh-caught live trout are served "au bleu," which means they are cooked very quickly in a vinegar-and-water court-bouillon. If you cannot get live trout, you can sauté trout with good results.

Linzer Torte:

1 cup butter	½ teaspoon cinnamon
2 cups sifted flour	¼ teaspoon allspice
¼ teaspoon salt	1 teaspoon cocoa
1 generous cup powdered sugar	½ lemon
1 cup ground almonds	3 egg yolks

Knead together butter, flour, salt, powdered sugar, almonds, cinnamon, allspice, cocoa, the juice and grated rind of ½ lemon, and egg yolks. When thoroughly blended, chill. Then roll ⅔ of the dough ¼ inch thick and line a spring form, giving it a good edge. Spread the dough generously with raspberry jam. Roll remaining dough into strips ¼ inch wide and place criss-cross over jam.

Then place one wide strip around cake edge. Paint dough with egg white, slightly beaten. Bake in a moderate oven (350°) 45 to 55 minutes. When cool, fill squares formed by the lattice with more jam and sprinkle with powdered sugar.

Potato Balls: These are cut with a ball cutter and cooked in deep hot fat according to directions for French fried potatoes (see Index).

Risi-Pisi: This is a combination of equal parts of freshly boiled rice and fresh peas, buttered and mixed together.

Swedish Dinner

Consomme with Asparagus Tips
Boiled Salmon   Hollandaise Sauce
Dilled New Potatoes
Roast Leg of Lamb   Browned Potatoes
Cauliflower   String Beans
Caramel Pudding
Coffee

AQUAVIT

Caramel Pudding:

Sugar	1 inch vanilla bean,
3 tablespoons boiling water	crushed
6 eggs, well beaten	3 cups light cream
	A pinch of salt

Roast Leg of Lamb: Roast the leg of lamb in the customary way, adding 3 carrots and onions after the roast has cooked for about 30 minutes. After another ½ hour, add 1 cup coffee with sugar and cream. Baste with the juices and the coffee which have mixed in the pan. Serve with the browned potatoes and the pan juices poured over the roast or served separately.

Dilled New Potatoes: Cook new potatoes in the usual way and dress with butter, chopped parsley, and finely chopped fresh dill. These are also good with fish.

Melt 1 cup sugar in an iron or steel skillet. When browned, add boiling water and stir until it makes a syrup. Coat the inside of a baking dish with this syrup. Mix beaten eggs, 3 tablespoons sugar, and vanilla, and stir in cream mixed with salt. Add this mixture to the baking dish.

Place in a pan of hot water in a moderate oven (325°) and bake until set, but not entirely firm, for it will continue cooking when removed from the oven. Unmold when cool and garnish with candied fruits or blanched almonds if you wish.

COLD WEATHER MEALS

Smoked Salmon with Lemon and Ground Pepper
Thin Pumpernickel Butter Sandwiches
Roast Duck with Orange Sauce
Sautéed Lentils
Green Salad
Cheese Board

Avocado with Crabmeat
Hungarian Pot Roast
Noodles
Sautéed Broccoli
Frozen Peaches and Raspberries

Cream of Chicken Soup
Minute Steaks Brazilian
French Fried Potatoes
Cauliflower Salad with Almonds
Continental Apple Cake

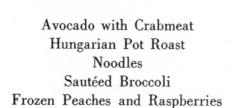

Pungent Eggs
Barbecued Spareribs
Baked Sweet Potatoes   Sautéed Cabbage
Green Salad with Grapefruit
Apple Pie

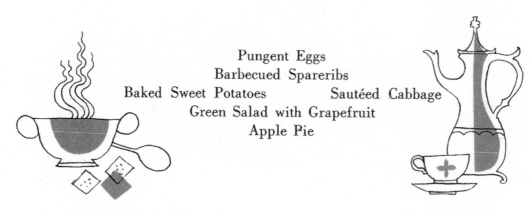

Raw Carrot, Cauliflower, Celery
Risotto (Baked Rice)
Bread Sticks
Cherries with Almonds
Coffee

Mushrooms à la Grecque
Lentil Casserole
Green Salad with Cheese
Baked Pears
Coffee

English Dinner

Scotch Broth

Whitebait   Rissole Potatoes   Sliced Cucumbers

Roast Sirloin of Beef   Yorkshire Pudding

Browned Potatoes   Brussels Sprouts

Freshly Grated Horseradish

Truffles

Demitasse

Nuts   Raisins   Port

Trifle

Scotch Broth:

2 pounds shin of beef	4 onions, sliced
¼ pound pearl barley	6 medium potatoes, cubed
1 large bunch parsley	2 tablespoons salt
4 quarts water	Pepper

Combine beef, barley, parsley, and water. Bring to a boil in a large pot, covered. After 1 hour add pepper to taste and salt, and continue cooking for another hour. Add onions and potatoes and cook for another hour. Remove meat and parsley. Serve with additional chopped parsley.

Rissolé Potatoes: These are potatoes which are sautéed in butter.

Trifle:

Sponge cake	Boiled custard or
Lady fingers or macaroons	dessert cream
Sherry	Vanilla
¼ cup brandy	Cream
Raspberry jam	Candied fruits

Line a mold or glass pudding dish with slices of day-old sponge cake and top with lady fingers or macaroons. Cover with sherry —approximately 1 cup for a trifle for 6 persons. Add brandy for flavoring. Spread the surface with raspberry jam and cover with boiled custard or dessert cream. Chill well and, when ready to serve, cover with vanilla-flavored whipped cream and decorate with candied fruits.

AMERICAN DINNER

Fruit Cup

Celery　　*Radishes*　　*Olives*

Roast Turkey

Chestnut Dressing

Mashed Potatoes　*Giblet Gravy*　*Baked Sweet Potatoes*

Creamed Onions

Cranberry and Almond Relish

Pumpkin Pie

Coffee

Pumpkin Pie:

Pastry for 2 pie shells	½ teaspoon powdered
1 can pumpkin or 3 cups	cloves
cooked mashed pump-	3 teaspoons ginger
kin	3 teaspoons cinnamon
1 cup brown sugar	1 teaspoon mace
1 cup white sugar	4 eggs
2 tablespoons molasses	2 cups cream
1 teaspoon salt	

Line 2 9-inch pie tins with pastry and flute the edges. Place in the refrigerator while you do the following:

Put the pumpkin through a sieve to get it thoroughly fine. Place it in a large mixing bowl and combine with the brown and white sugar, molasses, salt, and the spices. Mix it thoroughly and add the eggs, which have been slightly beaten. Finally add the cream and mix well.

Fill the two shells with the mixture, and place in a preheated hot oven (450°) for 10 minutes, after which reduce the heat to 350° and continue cooking approximately 30 minutes longer or until the custard is just set. Remove from the oven and, when slightly cooled, sprinkle with chopped walnuts or black walnuts. Serve slightly warm, with whipped cream if desired.

Cranberry Almond Relish:

1 pound cranberries	6 teaspoons orange
2 cups granulated sugar	marmalade
1 cup water	Juice of 2 lemons
	⅔ cup almonds

Wash and pick over cranberries. Combine sugar with water and bring to a boil, cooking for 5 minutes. Add the cranberries and cook until they pop and become transparent. Remove from the fire and combine them with orange marmalade and lemon juice. Allow mixture to cool. While it is cooling, blanch and drain almonds. Slip their skins and break them in halves. Chill in the refrigerator and add to the cranberry mixture when it is well chilled.

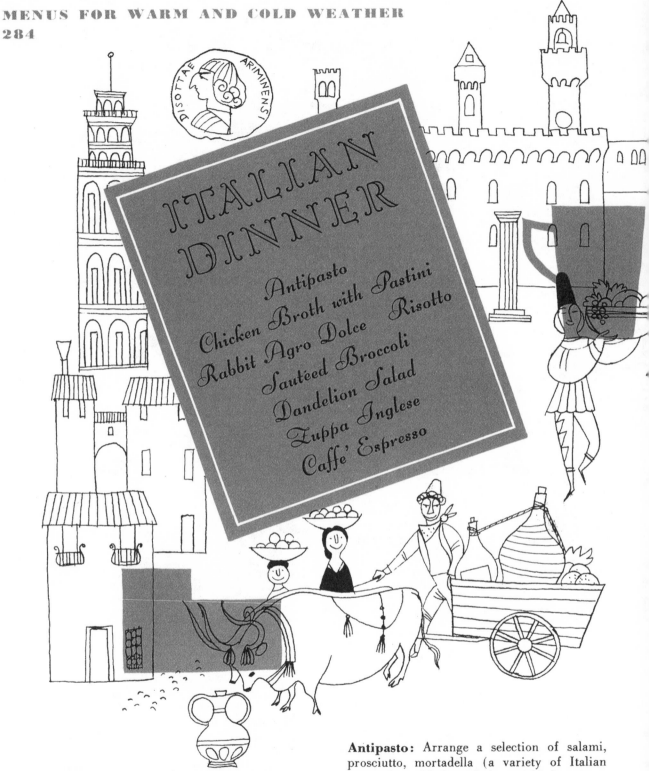

ITALIAN DINNER

Antipasto

Chicken Broth with Pastini

Rabbit Agro Dolce   Risotto

Sautéed Broccoli

Dandelion Salad

Zuppa Inglese

Caffè Espresso

Sautéed Broccoli: Cook broccoli (page 160). Heat 4 tablespoons olive oil with 1 clove garlic in a skillet. Sauté cooked broccoli very quickly in olive oil. Serve with grated cheese.

Antipasto: Arrange a selection of salami, prosciutto, mortadella (a variety of Italian sausage), pickled artichokes, pickled peppers, anchovies, shrimp with mayonnaise, stuffed eggs, fresh radishes, celery hearts, and spring onions on plates. Serve with olive oil and vinegar. Pass the pepper mill.

Rabbit Agro Dolce:

2 ounces salt pork, cubed	1 tablespoon brown sugar
¼ cup olive oil	¼ cup tomato purée
1 clove garlic, crushed	½ cup chicken broth
1 rabbit (3 to 4 pounds)	1 cup dry white wine
6 crushed peppercorns	¼ cup seedless raisins
Juice of 1 lemon	¼ cup shelled pine nuts
Salt and pepper	2 tablespoons chopped parsley

Try out the salt pork for a few minutes and add the olive oil. Add garlic and cook for a few minutes. Brown the pieces of rabbit well on both sides, cooking over a medium flame. Reduce flame and cook for 25 minutes, turning once during cooking process. Add seasonings, brown sugar, tomato paste, chicken broth, and ½ cup wine. Cover and simmer for about 10 minutes.

Add the raisins and nuts and simmer 10 minutes longer. Taste for seasoning. Remove pieces of rabbit to a serving dish and pour the sauce, to which you have added the additional wine, over it. Serve at once with risotto.

Zuppa Inglese:

Sugar	½ teaspoon vanilla
⅓ cup flour	2 layers sponge cake
Salt	Rum
2 cups scalded milk	4 stiffly beaten egg whites
4 slightly beaten egg yolks	

Combine ½ cup sugar, flour, and ¼ teaspoon salt. Gradually stir in scalded milk and beat until smooth. Pour these ingredients over egg yolks, and cook the mixture over boiling water, stirring constantly until thick, taking care not to curdle it. Should there be lumps, strain through a fine sieve. Cool, flavor with vanilla, and set aside.

Soak sponge cake in rum. Make a stiff meringue by beating 4 egg whites until frothy, then add a pinch of salt and continue to beat until stiff but not dry. Fold in ¼ cup sugar. Line the bottom of an ovenproof dish with 1 layer of the rum-soaked cake. Cover with ⅔ of the custard, then place the other cake layer over this. Spread remaining custard over the top, and when thoroughly cold, spread meringue, covering the entire surface, right to the rims of the dish. Sprinkle with a little sugar, and brown lightly in a slow oven (300° to 325°). Chill thoroughly before serving.

Candied orange peel and citron peel may be added to the custard. Apricot jam may be spread on the cake slices, and whipped cream may be used in place of meringue topping.

FRENCH DINNER

Consomme Fines Herbes

Filet de Sole Amandine

Pommes Olives

Pintade Rotie   Cresson

Celeri Braise   Coeur de Romaine

Camembert

Corbeille des Fruits

Demitasse

Pintade Rotie:

2 guinea hens
Salt pork
½ pound chicken livers
¼ pound good sausage
  meat
Butter

6 or 8 pieces bread
2 tablespoons chopped
  parsley
Salt and pepper
½ cup dry white wine

Have the butcher lard the breasts of the guinea hens with small pieces of salt pork. Have him wrap the breasts with large pieces of the salt pork and tie them securely.

Grind chicken livers along with the giblets from the guinea hens. Combine these with sausage meat.

Place guinea hens in a baking dish or pan and dot with butter. Place in a hot oven (400°) and roast, basting occasionally, for 40 minutes. Remove from oven and remove the large pieces of pork from the breasts.

Spread bread slices, trimmed of all crusts, with butter. Toast in oven until delicately browned. Combine chopped giblets and sausage with chopped parsley and salt and pepper to taste. Spread on toast. Place toast with guinea hens and return to oven for 10 minutes.

Remove guineas and the canapés and keep them warm. Skim the fat off the juices in the pan and reserve. Add white wine to the juices in the pan and heat gently over a medium flame. Strain and pour into a sauceboat.

Glaze guineas with the reserved fat from the pan and arrange on a platter surrounded by the canapés with the liver and giblets. Serve the sauce separately.

Serve the hearts of romaine with the guineas, and the celery as a separate course. **Pommes Olives:** These are potatoes, pared and cut into the shape of olives, fried in deep hot fat. See French fried potatoes (page 182).

Smoked Trout
Thin Slices of Buttered Rye Bread
Sauté of Quail with White Grapes
Wild Rice   Sautéed Mushrooms
Endive Salad
Pear Hélène

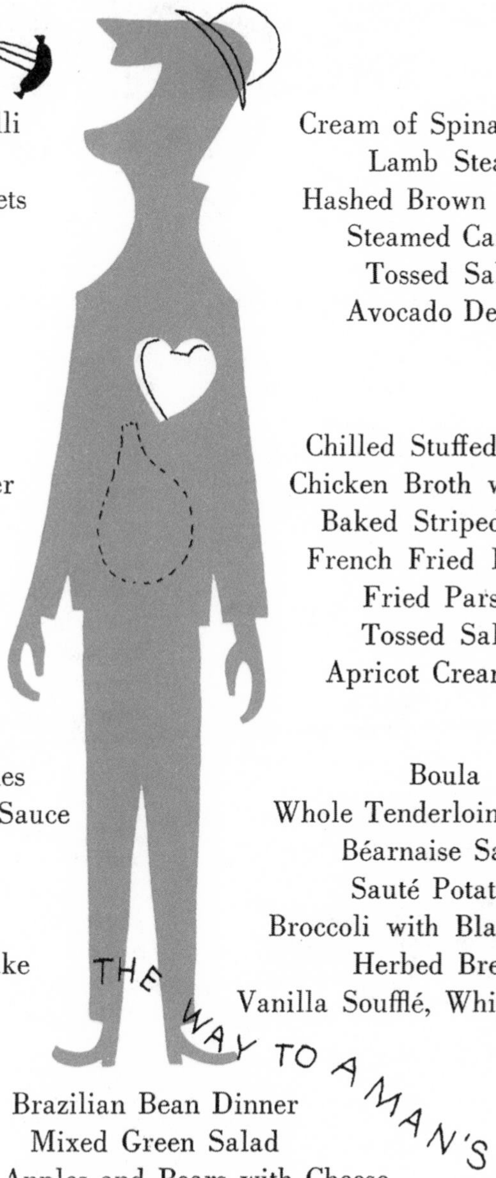

Pot au Feu with Bouilli
Garlic Bread
Green Salad with Beets
Cheese Board
Fresh Fruits
Coffee

Cream of Spinach Soup
Lamb Steaks
Hashed Brown Potatoes
Steamed Carrots
Tossed Salad
Avocado Dessert

Chicken Broth
Baked Stuffed Lobster
Soufflé Potatoes
Pea Pie
Pineapple Delight
Coffee

Chilled Stuffed Celery
Chicken Broth with Rice
Baked Striped Bass
French Fried Potatoes
Fried Parsley
Tossed Salad
Apricot Cream Pie

Consommé with Noodles
Grilled Pig's Feet, Devil Sauce
Toasted Rye Bread
Mashed Potatoes
Spinach Purée
Martha's Chocolate Cake
Coffee

Boula
Whole Tenderloin of Beef,
Béarnaise Sauce
Sauté Potatoes
Broccoli with Black Butter
Herbed Bread
Vanilla Soufflé, Whipped Cream

THE WAY TO A MAN'S

Brazilian Bean Dinner
Mixed Green Salad
Fresh Apples and Pears with Cheese

WINES

FACTS AND SUPERSTITIONS ABOUT WINES

Knowing and testing wines can become a delightful pastime. Wine can add much pleasure to dining and entertaining, yet it need not be more complicated to use than tea or coffee. All too many people deny their friends and themselves the added pleasure that good wine can give to a dinner simply because they believe, erroneously, that serving wine is a ritual and involves a complicated procedure.

The basic rules to observe in the use of wines are:

1. Drink the wine that you like; be it red or white, sweet or dry.
2. Try your wine at the temperature recommended for its type—room temperature for red wines, chilled for white. Most people enjoy a particular wine most at its recommended temperature. Of course, if your own taste differs, by all means drink the wine at the temperature you prefer.
3. It is not necessary to buy the most expensive wine. Many honest wines can be purchased below $2.00.
4. The fact that a wine is imported does not necessarily make it superior. There are many excellent wines produced within our borders.
5. You need not have a whole closetful of glassware to serve wine. One simple all-purpose glass will serve effectively for champagne, red wine, or white wine. (A tulip-shaped glass seems to work out better than others.)

It is no accident that wine drinking and the use of wine in cooking flourish most in countries that have the highest culinary reputations —France, Italy, and Spain. A perfect dinner demands good wine, but drinking good wine is relatively pointless unless it goes with good food.

You need not religiously obey every rule laid down by wine experts. But do not make the error of ignoring the experience of past centuries in the use of wine. To do so is to lose much of the pleasure wine can afford. Become acquainted with the main points of "wine wisdom" and give them a fair trial in your use of wine, then make your own rules.

We have all seen elaborate tables describing just what wine goes with which food. Such tables do not prove that there is a large body of knowledge, akin to geometry, which you must conquer before you can enjoy wine. These tables are merely a product of common sense and experience. There is no need to memorize them. After six months of intelligent wine experimenting, you could probably create your own table, which would be as valid as those in magazines and most so-called learned books on wine. Simplicity and honesty in food and wine are the secret of the true gourmet.

Your own experience tells you not to serve anything sweet before a meal and thus cloy the appetite. You would therefore serve as an apéritif relatively unsweet beverages such as champagne, a very dry sherry, a dry vermouth, the drier cocktails such as a martini or an old fashioned (certainly not the syrupy Alexander or sidecar).

If the food served is relatively robust in flavor and texture, such as steak, roast beef, game, or dishes highly flavored with herbs, garlic, or spices, the accompanying wine should also be robust. The red wines, which are the most full-flavored ones, provide congenial company for these heavier, heartier dishes. The more delicate foods, such as fish, chicken, or shellfish, find happier company in white wines, which do not possess the full flavor of the reds.

However, if you do prefer white wine with steak, by all means drink it. The above generalizations, based on the experience of most wine drinkers, are not laws for those whose individual tastes differ. The important thing is to enjoy the wine and the meal.

Just as it is fun to recognize music when you hear it played and to know a few of the major works of the great composers, so you will find it fun to be familiar with some of the great wines produced in the various parts of the globe. You will want to know the French wines and the various districts from which they come; the Rhine wines and the Moselle, the Chilean wines and our native American wines.

SERVING WINES

Glasses

There are many different types of wine glasses on the market. Many are of no use whatever for the proper service of wine. A small glass is never desirable, for one cannot get the proper bouquet from it.

Several firms have made what they term an all-purpose wine glass, and to my mind it is the ideal choice. It is a tulip-shaped glass with a large bowl, which is good for any type of wine, even champagne. I strongly advise against colored glasses for wine.

Service

Remember—wine must always be handled with great care. Never jiggle a bottle or turn it upside down or handle it roughly. When serving at table, pour a little in the host's glass first so that he may try it and see if it is a good bottle. Then fill the other glasses approximately half full. Never fill a wine glass.

If you are serving several wines at a meal, never serve the finest wine before a less remarkable one. Your best wine should be a climax. Do not serve a white wine after a red wine, except when you wish to have a sweet white wine with the dessert.

If you do not have enough glasses for a double service of wine, see that the glasses are washed between services. Do not add one wine to another.

What Wine with What Foods?

Serve a rosé wine with hors d'oeuvres, or a white wine or a champagne.

With clear soup you may serve a good Madeira or a dry sherry.

Most fish require a dry white wine, well chilled. Certain dishes, notably some salmon dishes, are more delicious with a red wine of light body, a light claret, a Beaujolais or a Fleurie.

White meats and chicken are more delicious with a white wine or a rosé.

Red meats require a claret, burgundy, or Rhone Valley wine.

Game birds and venison seem better if served with one of the fuller-bodied red wines.

Cheese and red wine have natural affinities for each other.

Dessert wines should be the sauternes, some of the Vouvray wines, or champagne.

Champagne may be served throughout a meal, for it is complementary to any dish. To a lesser degree, the same is true of rosé wines. There are few dishes that may not be served with a pleasantly chilled rosé.

Gauging Amounts of Wine

One bottle of wine will provide about six glasses. If you are serving only one wine with a meal, allow at least two or three glasses for each person. A magnum will serve just twice the number of persons. For large parties it is wiser to buy magnums.

If you chill wine for a party, do not return it to your storage room and chill it again. Try to plan not to have more white or sparkling wines chilled than you will need.

Carte des Vins

BOURGOGNE ROUGES

	Bouteille	½ Bouteille
Chambertin (1947)	1.000.	
Pommard Epenots (1945)	750.	
La Tache (1940)	1.400.	375.

BOURGOGNE BLANCS

Meursault (1947)	550.	
Montrachet (1947)	1.100.	
Corton-Charlemagne (1946)	600.	225.

BORDEAUX ROUGES

Château Latour (1943) (Pauillac)	950.	
Château Margaux (1940) (Margaux)	700.	
Château Haut-Brion (1938) (Graves de Pessac)	850.	

BORDEAUX BLANCS

Barsac (1945)	500.	
Château d'Yquem (1943) (Sauternes)	1.200.	250.

COTES DU RHONE

Châteauneuf-du-Pape (1947) (Domaine de Mont-Redon)	400.	200.

VINS D'ALSACE

Riesling (1947)	500.	
Gewurztraminer (1947)	750.	

TEMPERATURES FOR SERVING WINES

All white wines, sparkling wines, and rosé wines should be served chilled. Not all persons will agree on the exact temperature. For my taste, the great white wines and the sparkling wines do have to be well chilled. Chilling in the electric refrigerator is a slower process than chilling by placing the bottle in a wine cooler well packed with ice.

Champagne bottles take longer to chill than the ordinary white wine bottles. It is often wise to chill a bottle in the refrigerator and transfer it to a cooler when serving at table.

When serving a chilled wine, be sure to chill the glasses well before serving. This may be done by placing a cube or two of ice in each glass for 15 minutes before serving.

The ideal temperature for white wines is 42 to 45°. Several hours in a refrigerator and approximately 25 to 30 minutes in a wine cooler will bring the wine to this temperature. If you are chilling a bottle in a cooler, turn the bottle in the ice from time to time.

If you are serving magnums or jereboams, the chilling time will naturally be greater.

Serve red wines at room temperature—68 to 75°. If your wine has been stored in a cellar where the temperature is 55 to 60°, it should stand in the room where it is to be served for several hours before serving. Open the bottle about an hour before serving to give the wine a chance to "breathe." Do not use any artificial means of warming the wine, for in so doing you would ruin it.

Dry sherries and dry Madeiras are much more palatable if served slightly chilled. Some liqueurs, notably eau de vie de Framboise and crème de menthe are much better chilled. Vodka and aquavit also should be chilled.

HANDLING AND OPENING WINE

Wine should be handled very carefully, especially if it is of an older vintage. Shaking and twirling a bottle will do great harm to any wine, especially the reds.

Red wines are frequently served in baskets or cradles so that they may be handled more carefully and so that the sediment, if any, will not get mixed with the wine.

Use a lever-type corkscrew for opening wine bottles. Cut the metal or plastic capsule which covers the cork and remove it carefully. Wipe off with a cloth any dirt or mold that you find. Force the corkscrew in gently as far as it will go and then turn the lever with a gentle, steady motion. Do not try to pull the cork with jerky motions which will disturb the contents of the bottle.

When the cork is removed, wipe the mouth of the bottle both inside and out with a cloth.

Removing the cork from a champagne bottle is often a feat which requires dexterity and strength. Wrap a towel around the bottle if it is wet from being in the cooler. Remove the foil from the cork and, with the bottle at an angle, remove the wiring very carefully. Grasp the cork in your hand and give it a slight turn to the right and push, being careful that it does not fly into someone's face. Hold the bottle at an angle for a minute after opening so that the pressure does not force a great deal of wine out of the bottle in one great surge.

THE CARE OF WINES

Wines, unlike spirits, do not stop their process of development after bottling, but continue to change within their glass confines. Since nature has provided them with a living thing's ability to adjust to confinement, only a few common-sense rules need be followed in storing wines in your home or apartment.

If the temperature gradually changes between 40 to 75 degrees, no irreparable damage will be done. But sudden change might injure the proper development of the wine. And if the temperature goes below freezing or rises close to 100 degrees, then a great deal of damage may ensue. Fortunately, in the average apartment or house a storage space can be found where such extremes do not ordinarily occur. A frost-free cellar is, of course, the ideal spot.

All unfortified wines such as table wine and champagne are imprisoned in their bottles by a sturdy cork which keeps out the air. If any of these wines are stood up for any length of time, the cork will dry up sufficiently to allow air to enter and start a fermentation process which will turn the living wine sour. Hence wines of this type must be laid on their sides, so that the cork will be kept moist. Unlike table wine and champagne, spirits and fortified wines such as sherry, port, and Madeira should stay upright. Since the alcoholic content of these wines has reached a point which prevents further fermentation, there is no danger of souring due to contact with air.

Most wines are better if, before serving, they are kept quiet for at least a week or two after delivery. Very old wines need much longer rest.

You may find it helpful to keep a small "cellar book" with entries of your purchases with the dates and costs, and with comments —yours and your guests'—on the wines when tasted. Data in your book may be of interest and help to you and to other wine drinkers.

THE ENJOYMENT OF WINES

Buy wine as you buy records or antiques or books: with a spirit of adventure and exploration. Browse in wine shops. Since there is no book that can tell you which wines you personally will enjoy, you should—and there will be much pleasure in the process—try various wines until you hit upon those that become your favorites. The following bits of advice may prove helpful in your wine adventuring:

1. Seek out a wine merchant who has an adequate display of and a sympathy for wines. Find one whom you can trust, the way you search out a friendly butcher who will help you in the selection of cuts of meat.

2. Ignore any disapproving looks you may receive when you take wine and seltzer or use wine in other unusual ways. In other words, avoid ritual and "chi-chi." Once you have given wines a fair trial according to their recommended uses, it is your privilege to stand by your preferences—and your duty not to force these preferences upon others.

3. The wines with the highest reputations are, naturally, expensive. But the most expensive wines are not necessarily the best, nor are they necessarily the ones which you will like the most.

4. Do not insist on drinking only imported wine. Do not be a chauvinist who insists that only American wines are really good. Let each wine, regardless of origin, stand on its own feet. If you want to have twenty or fifty dollars' worth of fun that will last through a number of dinners, buy mixed cases of good wine from the world's great vineyards. The investment will give you great pleasure as well as a practical course in wine drinking and wine appreciation.

5. To find out whether you like wine in cooking, experiment with one or more of the dishes in this book which call for wine. Then try the dishes again without the additional flavoring that wine brings, and note the difference.

6. The important thing is to know wine for the living thing that it is, and to enjoy it.

FRENCH WHITE WINES

RHONE VALLEY

CLOS DE CHANTE ALOUETTE: Charming. Nice with veal.

WHITE BURGUNDY

MEURSAULT: Delightful with scallops or lobster.

POUILLY: An excellent wine. Perfect with fish.

CHABLIS: Dry, flinty wine.

MONTRACHET: One of the great wines.

GRAND MONTRACHET

CORTON CHARLEMAGNE: Scarce and expensive but worth it.

BORDEAUX

CHATEAU D'YQUEM

CHATEAU LATOUR BLANCHE

SAUTERNES: Sweet, good with desserts.

BARSAC: Very sweet.

GRAVES: Can be medium dry or dry.

CHATEAU OLIVIER: Dryish.

CHATEAU HAUT BRION BLANC: Good with fish or light meats.

ALSACE

RIESLING: Good with soda as a summer drink.

GEWURZTRAMINER: Flowery, charming wine. Good with seafood.

SYLVANER

ANJOU

ANJOU

JURA

CHATEAU CHALON

SPARKLING WINES

CHAMPAGNE

For gay, festive occasions.

POMMERY AND GRENO
DOM PERIGNON
LOUIS ROEDERER
VEUVE CLICQUOT
POLL ROGER
TAITTINGER
BOLLINGER
MUMM
KRUG

SPARKLING VOUVRAY

MONMOUSSEAU
BLANC DE BLANC

SPARKLING SAUMUR

SCHURMAN AND LAWRENCE

Demi Sec: Sweet
Sec: Medium Dry
Extra dry: Not the driest, in spite of the name.
Brut and English Market: Really Dry.

SPARKLING BURGUNDIES

Forget these.

FRENCH RED WINES

CLARETS

*Greatly esteemed.
Superior with beef
or game.*

**CHATEAU HAUT BRION
CHATEAU MARGAUX**

RHONE

With game, squab.

COTE ROTIE: Small pro-
duction, excellent flavor.
CHATEAU NEUF-DU-PAPE:
With turkey it is perfect.
HERMITAGE

BURGUNDY

The great aristocrat.

LA TACHE: Good with beef.
ROMANEE CONTI: Probably the greatest
wine in the world.
POMMARD: Wonderful with game.
GRAND ECHEZEAUX: Try this with duck.
NUITS SAINT GEORGES: Sound and mellow.

RICHEBOURG  **CHAMBERTIN
CORTON** **FLEURIE**

ROSE

(Pink wine)

TAVEL: Perfection when chilled.
Most accommodating.
ANJOU ROSE: Delicate.
ARBOIS ROSE: Heartier; distinc-
tive bouquet and taste.

Bordeaux

The Bordeaux district, an area approximately the size of Rhode Island in the southwest part of France, is the most important wine-growing district in the world. Here the classic red clarets and the distinguished natural sweet wines are produced. This district is divided into several well-known sub-districts, among them the Médoc, Graves, St. Emilion, Sauternes, St. Estèphe, and Pomerol.

The Médoc district is the most illustrious for red wines, the Sauternes for its magnificent white wines, and the Graves for its relatively dry white wines and a few great red wines. Just as a Médoc is superior to a wine bearing only the general name "Château Rouge," so would a wine named after a specific parish in the Médoc, such as "Margaux" or "St. Julien," be superior to a Médoc.

The wines most specifically identified as to origin are the "chateau-bottled" wines. The phrase "chateau-bottled" is an automatic guarantee of authenticity in origin, but not necessarily of quality. The phrase simply means that the owner of the chateau grew the grapes on his property, did not mix them with grapes or wine from any other source, and did not permit the wine to leave the property until it was bottled and labeled (usually, about three years after the year grapes were picked, or the vintage year). A "chateau-bottled" wine of a great vintage year is one of the greatest contributions to the pleasure of those who enjoy good wine. However, a regional claret of a great year may be superior to a "chateau-bottled" wine of a poor year.

Burgundy

The Burgundy district produces far less wine than the district of Bordeaux. The district is merely a chain of hills about thirty miles long and never more than a mile wide, running south from Dijon. These hills are known as the Côte d'Or, or the Golden Slope. In this very small area originate some of the greatest red and white wines in the world. Since the area is small and the production limited, prices for authentic burgundies are never low.

Burgundies are the most imitated of wines. Practically every wine-producing country has tried to produce a similar wine and attached the term "burgundy" to it.

The labeling of burgundies differs from labeling practices elsewhere. The vineyards in the district are exceedingly small, the largest, the Clos de Vougeot, being but 127 acres, and the smallest, La Romanée, about two acres. With few exceptions, these small tracts are held by as many as forty owners, each one having the title to a very small portion of the vineyard. Naturally, where there are groups of people each gathering grapes from their own vines, pressing them, and making them into wine, there will be variations in the resulting product. There is in the Burgundy district no direct counterpart of chateau-bottling. However, certain great wines from great vineyards are marked "estate-bottled." Labels on burgundy usually carry the name of the most famous district. If the wine is from a world-famous vineyard, it will carry that name. If the parish is more famous than the vineyard, it will carry the parish name. If neither is well known, the wine will go forth with the district name. Finally, if the wine is a blend of wines from several parishes or districts, or does not come within the rules governing production, which are strictly set by French law, it will be labeled simply *Bourgogne Blanc* or *Bourgogne Rouge* (red burgundy or white burgundy).

Some of the great names you will find in red burgundy are Romanée-Conti (which is the most famous name and the most expensive of the red burgundies), Chambertin, Chambolle-Musigny, Pommard and Volnay. In the white burgundies you will find the names Meursault, Montrachet, and Chablis, with many additional parish names.

Rhone Valley

One of the oldest wine-producing districts in France—and, in America, one of the lesser known—is the Rhone Valley. This historic district was probably first planted by the Romans many centuries ago when they conquered Gaul. Today the great vineyards of the region lie along the river below Lyons.

Probably the most famous of the Rhone wines is the Châteauneuf-du-Pape, which in great years is one of the most splendid red wines. Near Tain, which is situated on the left

bank of the Rhone between Lyons and Avignon, lie the picturesque vineyards of Hermitage. These are planted on three sides of the hill which rises sharply from the town.

Closer to Lyons lie the smaller vineyards which produce the excellent red wine known as Côte-Rotie. These can be particularly interesting and mellow wines.

One of the most delightful white wines of France is produced in this valley—Clos de Chante Alouette. It is not widely known in America but will prove a favorite of yours once you try it.

The tavel rosé wines come from the lower part of the Rhone Valley. Any wine carrying the name "tavel" must be produced within certain boundaries of that district. There are several other rosé wines in the Rhone Valley but they do not carry that name.

Alsace

From the lower slopes of the Vosges Mountains, along the banks of the Rhine, come the dry white wines of Alsace. These wines, some of which are delicious for summer wine bowls and the best of which are superior for drinking with fish and other delicate foods, are easily distinguished by their characteristic long-necked bottles.

Most of the Alsatian wines take their names from the grape from which they are made. Some of the more notable of these are the light, sometimes too lightly flavored Sylvaner; the Riesling; the Traminer; and the Gewurztraminer. The latter are fuller and far more distinguished wines. They all make for delightful drinking, especially in warm weather.

Champagne

Champagne has become a word synonymous with gaiety and celebration. No other wine has been so widely accepted as the symbol of festive occasions.

In France champagne is produced under most stringent supervision. If producers do not adhere to the government rules, the wine cannot be sold as "champagne."

Champagne making is a highly specialized process. The pressings of the grapes ferment in casks or barrels just as other wines do. But instead of being allowed to remain quiet, the wine is removed from the barrels, blended with other wines, given a small addition of sugar syrup and a little yeast, and placed in bottles, securely sealed for a second period of fermentation. Carbonic acid gas now begins to form in the bottles.

During this second fermentation, a good deal of sediment appears. If the bottle were opened under normal conditions, the gas would escape and the wine would be ruined. Yet the sediment must be removed. The champagne is therefore placed in racks with the bottle necks down. The bottles, constantly watched, are turned frequently, and the sediment collects in the necks. After a time, the bottles are submerged in a chilled brine solution, which freezes the sediment. The corks, which have been held in by wooden clamps, are then released, and the gas in the bottles ejects the sediment.

The bottle is then given the "dosage"—a quick filler of sweetened aged wine—and a new cork with a wire holder around it. The "dosage" determines the type of champagne that you buy. "Brut" is the driest, and the type usually preferred by connoisseurs. Then, in order of sweetness, come Extra Dry, Dry, and Demi-Sec. The latter has a great market in some European countries and in parts of South America.

Following the "dosage," the champagne bottles are placed on their sides for a number of weeks to permit the added wine to blend with the original. Then the bottles are labeled, packed, and prepared for shipping.

Champagne comes in more sizes of bottles than any other wine. The largest usually sent to this country is the Methuselah—equal to eight ordinary bottles. The largest of all is the Nebuchadnezzar—equal to 20 bottles. The giant bottles are used for especially festive occasions.

Rhine and Moselle

The Rhine and Moselle districts of Germany produce some of the most famous of the white wines. These are greatly prized by a certain group of wine fanciers and have a good market all over the world.

Rhine wines are generally more full-bodied and longer-lived than the Moselles, which should be drunk while quite young. Moselles, sometimes magnificently fragrant and delicate, afford a great deal of palate pleasure.

AMERICAN WINES

*The best ones are known by the names
of the grapes from which they are made*

red

PINOT NOIR
MOURESTEL
CABERNET
GAMAY
ZINFANDEL

white

PINOT BLANC
SYLVANER
SEMILLON
TRAMINER
RIESLING
CATAWBA
DELAWARE
SAUVIGNON BLANC

OTHER AMERICAN WINES

BEAUMONT
MOUNTAIN RED

BEAUCLAIR
MOUNTAIN WHITE
OHIO WHITE

ITALIAN WINES

The best known; good with highly seasoned dishes.

CHIANTI : Red and white
BARBERA : Red
ORVIETO : White
EST! EST!! EST!!! : White

MOSELLE

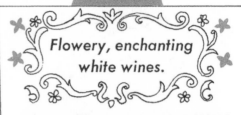

Flowery, enchanting white wines.

PIESPORTER GOLDTROPFCHEN
BERNKASTELER
PIESPORTER LAYCHEN SPATLESE
UERSIGER WURSGARTEN

FORTIFIED WINES

MADEIRA

As an apéritif or after dinner.

RAINWATER:
should be slightly chilled
SERCIAL

Dry, chilled as an apéritif
Sweet, for afternoon or with desserts.

SHERRY

MANZANILLA:
very dry
CREAM:
rich and heady
MILK:
semi-sweet
OLOROSO:
sweet
AMONTILLADO:
pleasantly dry

PORT

TAWNY
RUBY:
a blend of Tawny and young wine
WHITE
VINTAGE

The distinguishing thing about the Rhine wines is the system of harvesting the grapes. None but the ripest are gathered; the rest of the bunches are left to ripen and be gathered another day or another week. In some cases only parts of bunches are gathered—the grapes which are ripest of all. The wine made from these grapes is not blended, but made into separate batches of wine and reserved for the trade under various type names such as "Auslese," which means that the wine was made from fully ripe, perfect bunches of grapes; "Spatlese," which means that the grapes were gathered late; and "Beerenauslese," which means that the grapes were picked at their very ripest point and picked individually.

Naturally, these methods make for great differences in the wines from the same vineyard and make it difficult to tell which wines are of the early and which of the late pickings.

They are considered by some to be among the finest wines of the world, but my personal feeling is that they are not nearly the equal of fine French white wines. In fact I am not fond of the Rhine wines at all and find only a passing interest in Moselles.

Rhine wines are as a rule comparatively expensive because they are cherished by many people and the supply nowhere equals the demand.

Italian Wines

Second only to France in production of wines is Italy. However, Italian wines are less known throughout the world, because there is a larger consumption of the native product in Italy and less wine is available for export. However, three or four rather well-known types of Italian wines are familiar to many people in America.

Chianti is probably the best-known foreign red wine in America. The finest of the Chiantis comes from a district known as Chianti Ferrese near Siena. Although most people associate the word with a red wine, there are some quite good white Chiantis.

Barolo is another well-known Italian wine from the north—the piedmont area, to be exact. Less well known Italian wines are Orvieto, Est! Est!! Est!!!, Lacrima Christi, and the sparkling wines—Asti Spumante.

American Wines

The Spanish friars who entered California long ago to establish the Church are generally credited with establishing the "vine" also. Since those early days wine has been made in many parts of the United States. Today California leads in wine production, with her Napa and Sonoma Valleys foremost. New York State, with its Finger Lake region, is second, and Ohio third. Other states produce lesser quantities and varieties.

Many of the grape varieties that flourish in France are raised in California with great success. One finds excellent California wines which should be judged on their own merits and never compared with imported wines. They have become fine wines in their own right. This statement applies to the great vineyards such as Beaulieu, Wente Bors, and Louis Martini. Such producers are constantly striving for the finest possible products.

Most fine California wines are known by the names of grape varieties, not by names of districts copied from the wines of France and Italy. Thus you will find "Cabernet," "Dry Semillon," "Riesling," "Pinot Noir," or "Pinot Blanc" on the label. Some vineyards have coined names of their own, such as Beaumont, Beauclair, and California Mountain Red and White.

Certain lesser California wines, produced in great quantities, bear the same names as European wines, but can hardly be classed with the great wines of the state. Acquaint yourself with the great producers who specialize in truly fine wines, and buy accordingly.

New York and Ohio produce some excellent wines, the whites being more interesting to my taste than the reds. Some of the native grapes in these states produce exceedingly interesting wines. Among these are the Delaware, the Elvira, and the Catawba. If you have not already tried some of these wines, it is part of your development as a wine taster to do so.

Consult your wine dealer and some of the excellent books on American wines. Use them as guides for your excursions among the pleasures of wine drinking.

LIQUORS

The liquor cabinet is as important in some ways as the wine cellar. But liquors do not demand the caution in handling that wines demand. The main thing is to keep on hand a fair stock of liquors so that you do not have to make repeated calls to the nearest liquor store.

If you are not well acquainted with brands of bourbon, Scotch, rye, gin, and rum, do not try out new brands on your friends unless you have tried them yourself. It is wise to sample several of the brands of reputable houses and find one which satisfies your taste and your pocketbook. But compare several brands. This is especially true with gin, which in quality varies tremendously according to the distiller.

There are many types of whiskies on the market.

Bonded bourbons and ryes are those which have mellowed under government seal. They are usually sold at 100 proof, which means they are 50 per cent alcohol. Naturally the older whiskies are much more in demand and are scarce. They are the finest whiskies produced in this country.

The term "straight bourbon" or "straight rye" usually means that the whiskey has been cut to 86 proof and is not bonded whiskey. It is excellent nonetheless.

Blends of straight whiskies are blended whiskies of various ages. They are thoroughly dependable if they show a reputable mark.

Blended whiskies are very popular in this country. They are blends of straight whiskies and grain neutral spirits. Naturally you will not find the fine flavor in blended whiskey that you will find in straight, but many people find them adequate for all types of drinks. For myself, I prefer a straight whiskey.

Scotch whiskey is usually a blend of highland and lowland whiskies. Aged Scotches are in great demand, but they are exceedingly scarce at this time. There is a limited quantity of a pure highland malt Scotch that has a heavy smoky flavor which is most pleasing to one who loves Scotch.

There are great differences of flavor between various types of rum. For the average cocktail, unless it specifies a heavier rum, the light Cuban or Puerto Rican rum is used. For long drinks or for old fashioneds you will find the heavier Jamaica, Barbados, or Martinique rums are much more satisfactory.

For your supplementary liquors, try the various brands on the market before you settle on one, because there is a great variance among them.

Vermouths can make or break a cocktail, especially a martini. You may have to try three or four different ones before you find one which is perfect for your palate.

You will find that a simple syrup, or Falernum, will be of greater value to you than plain sugar. Because it blends with the liquors so much more quickly, it makes for a better drink.

Be certain that your fruit juices are freshly squeezed. Remember that good ingredients are necessary to a good drink.

COCKTAILS

(Recipes are for one serving)

Abbey Cocktail

2 ounces gin
¾ ounce orange juice
Dash of sweet vermouth
2 dashes angostura bitters

Shake with cracked ice and serve with maraschino cherry.

Alexander Cocktail

1 jigger gin
¾ ounce crème de cacao
¾ ounce cream

Shake with cracked ice.

Applejack Cocktail

2 ounces applejack
½ ounce simple syrup
Juice of ½ lemon

Shake with ice.

Bacardi Cocktail

Juice of ½ lime
½ teaspoon fine granulated sugar
1 jigger Bacardi rum

Place in mixing glass and stir thoroughly. Then add fine cracked ice and shake vigorously. Strain into cocktail glass.

Bijou Cocktail

¾ ounce dry gin
¾ ounce Chartreuse
¾ ounce sweet vermouth
1 dash orange bitters

Stir with cracked ice and strain into cocktail glass. Serve with a twist of lemon peel and a cherry.

Black Velvet

½ chilled champagne
½ chilled stout

Pour together simultaneously and slowly into Collins glass.

Bobby Burns Cocktail

1 jigger Scotch
1 ounce sweet vermouth
1 teaspoon benedictine

Stir with cracked ice and serve with a twist of lemon peel.

Brandy Cocktail

2 ounces brandy
½ teaspoon simple syrup
½ ounce curaçao
1 dash angostura bitters

Shake with cracked ice, strain into cocktail glass, and serve with a twist of lemon peel.

Brandy Smash

4 leaves mint
1 teaspoon fine granulated sugar
Splash of soda
1 jigger brandy

Muddle the mint and sugar in an old fashioned glass. Add the splash of soda and fill glass with cracked ice. Pour over the brandy and garnish with a sprig of mint.

Bronx Cocktail

1 ounce dry gin
¾ ounce sweet vermouth
¾ ounce dry vermouth
½ ounce orange juice

Shake with cracked ice and strain into cocktail glass.

Clover Club Cocktail

½ teaspoon fine sugar
1 jigger gin
4 dashes grenadine
Juice ½ lemon
White of 1 egg

Shake with ice and strain into cocktail glass.

Daiquiri

1 jigger West Indies white rum
Juice of ½ lime
1 teaspoon powdered sugar

Shake with finely shaved ice and strain into cocktail glass.

Dubonnet Cocktail

½ dry gin
½ Dubonnet, chilled

Stir in a chilled cocktail glass.

French '75

Juice of 1 lemon
1 teaspoon fine granulated sugar
2 ounces dry gin
Champagne

Shake with cracked ice and pour into highball glass. Fill glass with champagne.

Frozen Daiquiri

1 jigger white rum
Juice of ½ lime
1 teaspoon fine granulated sugar

Shake vigorously with shaved ice, or use electric blender, and serve unstrained in champagne glasses.

Gibson Cocktail

2 ounces gin
¾ ounce dry vermouth

Stir with cracked ice and strain into cocktail glass. Serve with small pearl onion.

Jack Rose Cocktail

1 jigger applejack
Juice of ½ lemon
½ ounce grenadine

Shake with cracked ice and strain into cocktail glass.

Manhattan Cocktail

2 ounces rye
¾ ounce sweet vermouth
2 dashes angostura bitters

Stir with cracked ice and strain into cocktail glass. Serve with a cherry.

Martini Cocktail (dry)

2 ounces dry gin
½ ounce dry vermouth

Stir with cracked ice, strain into cocktail glass, and serve with a twist of lemon peel.

Martini Cocktail (sweet)

2 ounces gin
¾ ounce sweet vermouth

Stir with cracked ice, strain into cocktail glass, and serve with a cherry.

Old Fashioned Cocktail

1 lump sugar (or 1 teaspoon simple syrup)

2 dashes angostura bitters

Splash of soda water

1 or 2 cubes ice

1 jigger (or more) rye, Scotch, or bourbon

Put the sugar into an old fashioned glass and saturate with the bitters. Add the soda and muddle. Add ice, a twist of lemon peel, and a cherry. Pour in the liquor, stir, and serve with a stirring rod. Garnish with lemon slice, ½ orange slice, and stick of pineapple, if desired.

Pink Lady Cocktail

1 jigger gin

½ ounce applejack

½ ounce grenadine

Juice of ½ lemon

1 white of egg

Shake with cracked ice and strain into cocktail glass.

Rob Roy Cocktail

2 ounces Scotch

¾ ounce sweet vermouth

1 dash angostura bitters

Stir with cracked ice and strain into cocktail glass. Serve with a cherry.

Sidecar Cocktail

2 ounces brandy

¾ ounce Cointreau

Juice of ½ lemon

Shake with ice and strain into cocktail glass.

Stinger Cocktail

1 jigger brandy

1 jigger white crème de menthe

Shake with cracked ice and strain into cocktail glass.

Vodka Cocktail

1 jigger vodka

¾ ounce cherry brandy

Juice of ½ lemon

Shake with cracked ice and strain into cocktail glass.

Zombie

1 ounce tropical heavy-bodied rum

2 ounces Gold Label rum

1 ounce White Label rum

2 teaspoons apricot brandy

¾ ounce pineapple juice

¾ ounce papaya juice

1 teaspoon fine granulated sugar

Shake well with cracked ice and pour into a 14-ounce glass. Float a splash of tropical heavy-bodied rum on top. Decorate with 1 green cherry, a pineapple stick, 1 red cherry, and a sprig of mint. Sprinkle powdered sugar on top and serve.

LONG DRINKS

(Recipes are for one serving unless otherwise indicated)

Blue Blazer

3 ounces Scotch

3 ounces boiling water

1 teaspoon fine granulated sugar

Lemon peel

Use 2 large mugs. Into 1 mug put Scotch, and into the other the boiling water. Ignite the whiskey, and while blazing mix both ingredients by pouring them from one mug to the other. Sweeten with fine granulated sugar and serve in a tumbler with a piece of lemon peel.

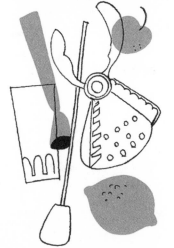

Champagne Punch (for 20)

2 boxes fresh strawberries

1 cup fine granulated sugar

1 bottle Moselle

2 bottles champagne

½ bottle claret

Place hulled berries in large glass bowl set in cracked ice. Sprinkle with the sugar and pour over the Moselle. Let stand 2 to 6 hours. When ready to serve, add chilled champagne and the claret for color. Serve with a berry in each glass.

Cobblers

Fill a goblet with finely shaved ice. Over this pour 3 ounces claret, sauterne, sherry, port wine, Rhine wine, rum, or whiskey. Add 1 teaspoon fine granulated sugar if desired, and stir. Decorate with fruit and a sprig of mint.

Collins

1 teaspoon fine granulated sugar
Juice of ½ lemon
3 ounces gin, applejack, bourbon, brandy, Irish whiskey, rum, rye, or Scotch
Soda water

Place 2 or 3 ice cubes in a collins glass. Dissolve the sugar in the lemon juice and pour over the ice. Add the liquor and fill glass with soda water. Garnish according to taste with a cherry, a slice of orange, or a sprig of mint. Stir and serve.

Daisy

Juice of ½ lemon
4 dashes grenadine
Soda water
2 ounces brandy, gin, rum, applejack, or whiskey

Serve in goblet filled with finely chopped ice. Garnish with fruit and top with a squirt of soda water.

Eggnog

1 fresh egg
1 teaspoon fine granulated sugar
2 ounces brandy, port, rum, sherry, bourbon, or rye
8 ounces rich milk
Nutmeg

Shake ingredients together and strain into tall glass. Garnish with a sprinkle of nutmeg on top.

Fizz

Juice of 1 lemon
1 teaspoon fine granulated sugar
1 jigger gin, sloe gin, or brandy
Soda water

Shake well with cracked ice and strain into 10-ounce highball glass. Add 1 ice cube and fill with soda water. Decorate with sprig of mint.

Flips

2 ounces brandy, port, sherry or rum
1 teaspoon fine granulated sugar
1 egg

Shake and strain into a wineglass. Serve with a sprinkle of nutmeg on top.

Golden Fizz

Juice of 1 lemon
1 teaspoon fine granulated sugar
1 jigger gin
1 yolk of egg
Soda water

Shake well with ice and strain into highball glass. Add 1 ice cube and fill with soda water.

Highballs

1 or 2 ice cubes
1 to 3 ounces liquor
Soda water

Place ice cubes in highball glass. Pour liquor over it. Fill glass with soda water—or ginger ale if preferred.

Hot Buttered Rum

3 ounces Jamaica Rum
Lemon peel
Stick of cinnamon
Clove
Boiling cider
1 pat butter

Place rum, lemon peel, clove, and stick of cinnamon in a pewter tankard or heavy mug. Fill with boiling cider and float a pat of butter in the hot liquid. Stir well. More or less rum may be used according to taste.

Mint Julep

Mint
1 teaspoon fine granulated sugar
3 ounces bourbon
Soda water

Fill a collins glass with finely cracked ice and place aside. Strip leaves from 2 sprigs of mint and muddle with the sugar. Add a splash of soda water and the bourbon. Stir and strain into the prepared glass over the ice. Work a long-handled spoon up and down in the mixture until the outside of the glass begins to frost. Top with a splash of rum and decorate with a sprig of mint and a cherry.

Rickeys

Juice of ½ lime
2 ounces brandy, rum, rye, bourbon, Scotch, gin, or sloe gin
Soda water

Squeeze juice of lime into small highball glass, leaving the lime in the glass. Add the liquor and 2 ice cubes. Fill glass with soda water, stir, and serve.

Silver Fizz

Juice of ½ lemon
1 teaspoon fine granulated sugar
1 jigger gin
1 white of egg
Soda water

Shake and strain into highball glass. Add 1 cube ice and fill with soda water.

Singapore Sling

2 ounces gin
¾ ounce cherry brandy
Dash of benedictine
Juice of ½ lemon
Soda water

Serve in highball glass with 2 ice cubes. Decorate with slice of orange and sprig of mint. Top with soda water.

Slings

Serve 1 jigger gin, brandy, Scotch, bourbon, or rye in highball glass with cracked ice. Fill with soda water and garnish with a twist of lemon peel. Stir.

Smashers

1 lump sugar
3 sprigs mint
2 ounces brandy, gin, or whiskey
Soda water

In the bottom of an old fashioned glass muddle the sugar with the mint sprigs. Add 1 ice cube, decorate with fruit, and pour in the liquor. Top with soda water and serve.

Sours

2 ounces rye, bourbon, Scotch, applejack, brandy, gin, or rum
Juice of ½ lemon
1 teaspoon sugar
Soda water

Shake with cracked ice and strain into Delmonico glass. Decorate with fruit and add a dash of soda water.

Swizzles

2 ounces gin, rum, or whiskey
2 dashes angostura bitters
¾ ounce lime juice
1 teaspoon fine granulated sugar

Pour ingredients into cocktail shaker. Add a quantity of shaved ice and shake vigorously until the shaker begins to frost, then strain into cocktail glass.

Toddies

2 ounces applejack, brandy, rum, or whiskey
1 teaspoon sugar
2 cloves
Slice of lemon
1 inch cinnamon stick

Place ingredients in old fashioned glass along with a silver spoon (or use a china mug). Fill glass with boiling water and stir.

Tom and Jerry (for 12)

12 eggs
1 pound sugar
4 ounces Jamaica rum
Whiskey
Boiling water
Nutmeg

Beat the eggs (without separating) until very light. Gradually beat in the sugar and continue beating until you have a thick batter. You may need additional sugar. Flavor with Jamaica rum and set aside to ripen, for 2 or 3 hours.

To serve, add a heaping tablespoon of the batter to a mug or cup and add whiskey or rum to taste—approximately 2 ounces. Fill the mug with boiling water and sprinkle with nutmeg. Stir well.

Whiskey Cooler

1 teaspoon fine granulated sugar
1 teaspoon lemon juice
3 ounces whiskey
Ginger ale

Put sugar and lemon juice into highball glass. Add ice, then pour in whiskey. Fill glass with ginger ale, stir, and serve with stirring rod.

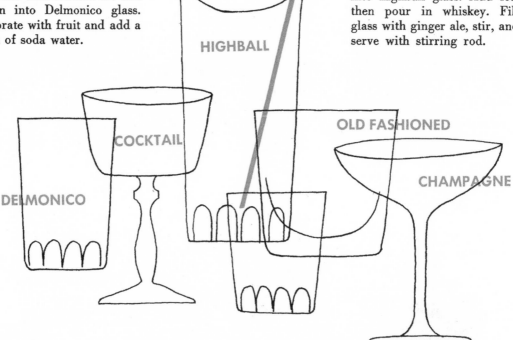

HIGHBALL

COCKTAIL

OLD FASHIONED

CHAMPAGNE

DELMONICO

INDEX

THE 1949 EDITION OF THIS BOOK WAS DESIGNED AND PRODUCED

BY THE SANDPIPER PRESS AND ARTISTS AND WRITERS GUILD, INC.,

WHO PAY SPECIAL TRIBUTE

TO GUITON CHABANCE AND ALICE AND MARTIN PROVENSEN.

THE TYPE WAS SET BY JEFFREY COMPOSITION CO., NEW YORK CITY,

IN LINOTYPE BODONI BOOK, BODONI BOLD, POSTER BODONI,

AND SPARTAN, AND IN BAUER'S BERNHARD CURSIVE.

THE LITHOGRAPHIC PLATES, AS WELL AS THE PRINTING AND BINDING,

WERE DONE BY WESTERN PRINTING AND LITHOGRAPHING COMPANY

IN POUGHKEEPSIE, NEW YORK.

THE PAPER WAS MADE

BY CHAMPION PAPER COMPANY IN HAMILTON, OHIO,

AND THE CLOTH WAS MADE

BY BANCROFT MILLS IN WILMINGTON, DELAWARE.

Photo by Dan Wynn © Elisabeth Wynn,
courtesy of the James Beard Foundation

ABOUT THE AUTHOR

JAMES BEARD had a national reputation as an authority on every phase of food. Consultant to a wine and spirits establishment, he wrote seventy-six other books and numerous articles for national magazines on widely varied phases of cooking. Mr. Beard, who knew the cooking of every corner of our country, cooked in nearly every language. He lived abroad, traveled throughout Europe a number of times, saw most of the Western Hemisphere, and visited Hawaii and North Africa. His familiarity with exotic foreign foods spiced his extensive knowledge of American cooking at its best.

Mr. Beard was adviser to several large food companies, was food editor of *Argosy* magazine, and made many appearances on radio and television. His first three books are *Hors d'Oeuvres and Canapes*, *Cook It Outdoors*, and *Fowl and Game Cookery*. Equally at home in the kitchen of his own New York apartment and that of a hotel, James Beard brought the same sure touch to a half-hour supper and to the most elaborate buffet. He died in 1985.